HISTORY A
OF
CHARLESTON ORPHAN HOUSE
1790-1860

Abstracted and Transcribed
by
Susan L. King

Southern Historical Press, Inc.
Greenville, South Carolina

Please direct all correspondence and orders to:

www.southernhistoricalpress.com
or
SOUTHERN HISTORICAL PRESS, Inc.
PO BOX 1267
375 West Broad Street
Greenville, SC   29601
southernhistoricalpress@gmail.com

ISBN #0-89308-292-9

Printed in the United States of America

PREFACE

The sources cited in this book were cited in two ways. Footnotes were notated in the general history and in the charts. The source immediately follows the information contained in the genealogical section of children.
The following abbreviations were used:

```
ARC, date....................ANNUAL REPORT OF THE COMMISSIONERS
ARP, date....................ANNUAL REPORT OF THE PHYSICIAN
A to A.......................APPLICATION TO ADMIT
By-Laws......................BY-LAWS OF THE CHARLESTON ORPHAN HOUSE
BO...........................BINDING-OUT APPLICATION
BO, rejected.................BINDING-OUT APPLICATION, rejected
CP...........................CENTENNIAL PROCEEDINGS
DR...........................DOCTOR'S RECORD
ROB, 1856....................REGISTER OF BOYS, 1856-1949
ROC, 1821....................REGISTER OF CHILDREN, 1821
ROG, 1856....................REGISTER OF GIRLS, 1856-1949
ROSP, date...................REGISTER OF STEWARD AND PHYSICIAN
ROSSC........................REGISTER OF STAFF, SERVANTS, AND CHILDREN
letter, number (ex. A-14)....INDENTURE BOOKS
```

The following manuscript sources were used:

APPLICATION TO ADMIT

BINDING-OUT APPLICATION

BINDING-OUT APPLICATION, REFECTED

CHARLESTON ORPHAN HOUSE DONATIONS FILES

CHARLESTON ORPHAN HOUSE GENERAL FILES-RECORDS PROGRAM

CHARLESTON ORPHAN HOUSE INMATES'FILES

CHARLESTON ORPHAN HOUSE OFFICERS' FILES-PORTER/GARDENER

CHARLESTON ORPHAN HOUSE OFFICERS'FILES-STEWARD AND MATRON

CHARLESTON ORPHAN HOUSE OFFICERS' FILES-WASHERS

CHARLESTON ORPHAN HOUSE WILLS AND LEGACIES FILES

COMMISSIONERS' CORRESPONDENCE

MEDICAL MATTERS-ILLNESSES AND TREATMENTS

The following bound sources were used:

ANNUAL REPORT OF THE COMMISSIONERS

BY-LAWS OF THE CHARLESTON ORPHAN HOUSE. CHARLESTON: EVANS & COGSWELL, 1861.

CENTENNIAL PROCEEDINGS OF THE CHARLESTON ORPHAN HOUSE. CHARLESTON: WALKER, EVANS AND COGSWELL, 1891.

DIGEST OF THE ORDINANCES OF THE CITY COUNCIL OF CHARLESTON. CHARLESTON: ARCHIBALD E. MILLER, 1818.

DOCTORS'RECORDS

INDENTURE BOOKS. A-T

MINUTES OF THE COMMISSIONERS OF THE CHARLESTON ORPHAN HOUSE.

REGISTER OF BOYS, 1856-1949.

REGISTER OF CHILDREN, 1821.

REGISTER OF GIRLS, 1856-1949.

REGISTER OF STEWARD AND PHYSICIAN.

REGISTER OF STAFF, SERVANTS AND CHILDREN, 1791-1835.

STATUTES OF THE STATE OF SOUTH CAROLINA. VOL. 5. 1789-1814.
    Thomas Cooper, editor. Columbia, South Carolina: A.S. Johnston,
    1839.

INTRODUCTION

The Charleston Orphan House, the oldest municipal orphanage in the United States, was founded October 18, 1790, at the instigation of John Robertson, a philanthropic citizen and a member of City Council. (Minutes, October 18, 1790) The ordinance to establish the Institution stated it was for the "purpose of supporting and educating poor and orphan children and those of poor and disabled parents who are unable to support and maintain them." (Ibid.) During the 1800's the Orphan House was a well-known child care institution. Letters were received by the Commissioners from many other states for information on the management of the Orphan House. (COH Commissioners' Correspondence Files) Charlestonians were also proud of the Institution. The Reverend Doctor Charles Vedder declared "Strangers are regarded as having missed what is best with us, if they have not visited the Orphan House." (CP, p. 22) The Institution was a completely self-sufficient entity. The children were fed by home-grown food, dressed in home-spun clothing, and educated in the building by former students trained by the Principal of the School This method of management was established in order to reduce the cost of maintaining the children. (CP, p. 35)

The Orphan House was governed by a Board of Commissioners annually elected by City Council. This Board met weekly, with each member alternating his services as a Visiting Commissioner. The Visiting Commissioner primarily investigated applicants for admission or indenture; however, he also conducted religious services on Sunday afternoon and inspected the house, grounds and staff. Nine standing committees of at least three members were appointed by the Commissioners to oversee the operation of the Institution: Committee on Improvement and Discipline, Committee on Retrenchment, Committee on Schools, Committee on Accounts, Committee on Binding Out, Committee on Repairs, Committee on Purveyance and Supervision, Committee on Chapel and Anniversary and Committee on the Library. (By-Laws, pp. 13-18)

COMMISSIONERS OF THE CHARLESTON ORPHAN HOUSE, 1790-1860

COMMISSIONER	ELECTED	RESIGNED
Aiken, William	November 29, 1850	December 16, 1856
Alexander, Alexander	August 24, 1796	February 21, 1800
Alston, Charles	May 8, 1845	July 31, 1851
Axson, Jacob	November 4, 1841	October 27, 1842
Bacot, Thomas	October 27, 1817	November 6, 1828
Ball, John	October 25, 1832	November 6, 1834
Bee, William C.	October 7, 1853	February 15, 1881
Bell, William	November 4, 1841	October 13, 1853
Beckman, Samuel	October 25, 1790	August 18, 1796
Bennett, Thomas	October 26, 1818	April 1, 1824
Bennett, Thomas, Jr.	March 6, 1811	October 27, 1814
Bennett, W.J.	November 1, 1849	October 31, 1850
Bennett, W.J.	February 6, 1851	December 5, 1865
Blackwood, Thomas	November 6, 1828	October 29, 1829
Brisbane, William	August 22, 1821	February 21, 1822
Brownlee, John	October 23, 1809	October 24, 1816
Bryan, John	November 6, 1834	November 2, 1837
Buist, George	October 29, 1850	January 6, 1863
Bulow, John J.	February 21, 1822	October 31, 1822
Caldwell, James M.	August 14, 1851	December 16, 1856
Campbell, Dr. J.M.	November 5, 1835	November 2, 1837
Capers, Thos. Farr	July 27, 1848	March 20, 1851
Capers, Reverend William	November 2, 1837	October 25, 1838
Champneys, John	December 13, 1792	August 18, 1796
Cheves, Langdon	October 23, 1809	October 24, 1810
Cheves, Langdon	October 25, 1816	October 27, 1817
Coffin, George M.	May 29, 1855	January 6, 1863
Cogdell, John S.	October 23, 1820	May 10, 1826
Cogdell, John S.	November 2, 1837	November 4, 1841
Cohen, Mordecai	October 25, 1838	May 30, 1844
Colcock, Charles J.	October 27, 1831	November 3, 1836
Cole, Richard	October 25, 1790	July 5, 1792
Corbett, Thomas	October 25, 1790	August 18, 1796
Crafts, William	August 24, 1796	October 16, 1797
Cuthbert, James	May 29, 1828	July 28, 1831
Dawson, John, Jr.	June 26, 1807	November 4, 1823
Deas, Henry	October 27, 1814	October 25, 1838
Deas, William	October 18, 1803	October 20, 1806
DeSaussure, Henry W.	April 4, 1800	April 16, 1812
DeSaussure, Henry A.	June 19, 1827	December __, 1865
Dickson, Dr. S.H.	December 16, 1856	November 12, 1857
Dukes, W.C.	December 19, 1850	August 14, 1851
Edwards, Edward H.	May 3, 1832	April 25, 1843

2

COMMISSIONER	ELECTED	RESIGNED
Edwards, John	July 29, 1797	February 1, 1799
Elliott, Benjamin	November 6, 1834	November 3, 1836
Elliott, Stephen	April 9, 1821	October 29, 1829
Elliott, Stephen	October 27, 1831	February 16, 1832
Faber, John C.	October 24, 1810	October 24, 1811
Ford, Timothy	October 25, 1790	November 1, 1792
Frampton, Dr. L.A.	December 19, 1850	December 22, 1857
Frost, Edward	November 7, 1839	May 8, 1845
Gadsden, John	October 21, 1826	October 25, 1827
Gadsden, Philip	August 24, 1796	October 27, 1814
Gadsden, Thomas	November 6, 1834	November 5, 1835
Geddes, John	October 24, 1810	October 19, 1812
Gilchrist, Robert B.	November 2, 1837	November 4, 1841
Gilliland, William H.	July 7, 1854	March 15, 1868
Greene, C.R.	October 25, 1816	October 27, 1817
Grimke, Thomas	October 25, 1827	October 29, 1829
Hall, Daniel	October 16, 1797	October 20, 1800
Hall, Daniel	February 1, 1805	October 23, 1809
Hall, Thomas	October 30, 1794	August 18, 1796
Hamilton, James, Jr.	November 7, 1833	November 6, 1834
Hanscombe, Thomas	March 22, 1821	March 11, 1823
Harris, Tucker	November 1, 1792	November 27, 1794
Hayne, Arthur P.	November 3, 1836	November 2, 1837
Heyward, Nathaniel	October 27, 1817	October 26, 1818
Holmes, Isaac	October 25, 1831	October 25, 1832
Holmes, John Bee	August 24, 1796	October 28, 1808
Honour, John H.	December 22, 1857	December 29, 1868
Horry, Elias	October 27, 1814	November 6, 1834
Houston, William H.	December 16, 1856	July 9, 1869
Huger, Dr. Benjamin	November 6, 1851	December 5, 1865
Huger, Daniel	October 29, 1814	October 25, 1816
Huger, Daniel	October 29, 1829	October 27, 1831
Huger, John	November 1, 1792	August 18, 1796
Huger, John	October 25, 1838	July 27, 1848
Hunter, John	November 4, 1841	January 28, 1847
Jenkins, Reverend Mr.	August 24, 1796	October 16, 1797
Jervey, James	March 22, 1821	May 31, 1838
Jervey, J.P.	November 1, 1849	October 31, 1850
Johnson, William, Jr.	October 16, 1797	October 17, 1803
Johnson, William, Jr.	November 1, 1804	June 26, 1807
Johnson, William, Jr.	October 24, 1811	October 25, 1816
Jones, Thomas	October 25, 1790	November 1, 1792
Kennedy, Lionel H.	June 5, 1828	November 2, 1837
Ker, John C.	October 25, 1838	November 4, 1841
Ladson, James H.	November 4, 1841	November 1, 1849

3

COMMISSIONER	ELECTED	RESIGNED
Lance, Francis	October 25, 1838	November 4, 1841
Lee, Stephen	November 1, 1792	August 18, 1796
Lee, Thomas	October 19, 1812	June 19, 1827
Legare, James	October 25, 1838	November 12, 1840
Lesesne, Henry D.	May 30, 1844	July 13, 1854
Lining, Charles	October 25, 1790	August 18, 1796
Lowndes, Charles D.	November 4, 1841	November 6, 1851
Lowndes, Rawlins	August 24, 1796	July 29, 1797
Lowndes, Thomas	June 20, 1814	October 22, 1821
McCalla, Dr. T.H.	October 23, 1809	March 6, 1811
Magrath, John	November 2, 1837	October 25, 1838
Manigault, Edward	October 29, 1850	December 19, 1850
Manigault, Joseph	October 24, 1810	October 23, 1820
Marshall, William	October 25, 1790	November 1, 1792
Memminger, C.G.	March 20, 1851	December 5, 1865
Mendenhall, M.T.	May 30, 1844	October 29, 1846
Middleton, N.R.	November 12, 1840	November 7, 1844
Mitchell, John	October 25, 1790	November 27, 1794
Moultrie, Dr. James	July 29, 1851	December 29, 1868
North, Dr. Edward	June 28, 1847	October 31, 1850
Parker, John	July 24, 1796	June 20, 1814
Parker, John, Jr.	November 6, 1828	November 3, 1836
Patrick, Casimir	November 7, 1839	November 4, 1841
Patrick, Casimir	October 26, 1843	November 4, 1847
Peronneau, Henry W.	October 29, 1829	May 3, 1832
Petigru, James L.	May 10, 1826	November 6, 1828
Pinckney, Charles	July 31, 1818	October 26, 1818
Pinckney, Charles C.	October 29, 1829	May 26, 1831
Pinckney, H.L.	October 25, 1832	November 6, 1834
Pringle, W.B.	November 4, 1841	February 6, 1851
Prioleau, Samuel	October 31, 1822	October 31, 1826
Ravenel, Daniel	July 28, 1831	October 27, 1831
Revenel, Daniel	November 3, 1836	November 7, 1839
Read, John J.	April 1, 1824	October 27, 1831
Ripley, Samuel	April 25, 1843	October 26, 1843
Ripley, S.P.	November 4, 1847	November 2, 1848
Robertson, John	October 25, 1790	December 13, 1792
Roper, Thomas	October 30, 1794	August 18, 1796
Roper, Thomas	November 4, 1823	October 25, 1827
Russell, Nathaniel	February 1, 1797	October 23, 1809
Rutledge, John, Jr.	September 1, 1796	October 16, 1797
Sebring, Edward	October 29, 1846	June 7, 1855
Simons, Keating	October 24, 1808	October 23, 1809
Simons, Thomas	October 16, 1797	February 1, 1805
Simons, Dr. Thomas Y.	February 16, 1832	November 2, 1832

COMMISSIONERS	ELECTED	RESIGNED
Smith, William M.	June 2, 1831	October 27, 1831
Somarsall, Alexander	August 24, 1796	October 24, 1810
Steedman, Charles J.	April 16, 1812	October 27, 1814
Stevens, Daniel	February 2, 1848	June 5, 1828
Tidyman, Dr. P.	November 2, 1848	November 1, 1849
Toomer, Joshua W.	October 25, 1827	October 25, 1838
Tupper, James	December 22, 1857	January 6, 1863
Turnbull, R.J.	October 27, 1831	October 25, 1832
Vanderhorst, Arnoldus	October 25, 1790	August 18, 1796
Wainwright, Richard	August 24, 1796	October 16, 1797
Washington, William	March 11, 1823	November 6, 1828
Webb, Daniel C.	November 3, 1836	November 4, 1841
Webb, Daniel C.	October 27, 1842	December 19, 1850
Wilson, Dr. Samuel	November 2, 1837	October 25, 1838
Wyatt, Peter	July 31, 1818	October 26, 1818*

CHAIRMEN OF THE COMMISSIONERS

CHAIRMAN	ELECTED	RESIGNED
Arnoldus Vanderhorst	October 1790	October 1792
John Huger	October 1792	December 1792
Charles Lining	December 1792	August 1796
Rawlins Lowndes	August 1796	July 1797
John Bee Holmes	August 1797	October 1808
Henry William DeSaussure	October 1808	April 1812
Daniel Stevens	May 1812	January 1819
John Dawson	January 1819	May 1823
Thomas Lee	June 1823	December 1825
Thomas Roper	December 1825	February 1826
James Jervey	May 1826	May 1838
Henry Alexander DeSaussure	June 1838	December 1865**

In order to "superintend the West Wing" (Minutes, August 12, 1800) the Board of Commissioners appointed a group of ladies to assist them. The first Lady Commissioners Mrs. Edwards, Mrs. Russell, Mrs. Ferguson, Mrs. Lowndes, Jr., and Mrs. Vanderhorst, were appointed in 1800. These ladies investigates situations for female inmates, requested necessary items such as mattresses, sheets, and tableclothes, and supervised the sewing, spinning, and cooking departments. (Ibid.) Apparently, these ladies had little authority or influence because there is scarcely any mention of their activities, appointments, etc, in the Minutes.

* Taken from a chronological list of Commissioners in the Centennial Proceedings of the Charleston Orphan House. Charleston, S.C.: Waler, Evans & Cogswell Co., 1891. p. 55-59.
** Ibid., p. 55.

The Charleston Orphan House stood at the corner of Calhoun and
St. Philip Streets. Built on the site of Revolutionary War Barracks
(CP, p. 27), the Institution was officially occupied October 18, 1794.
(Minutes, October 18, 1794). Until it was completed, the children were
housed in "a commodious building...(provided by) Mrs. Elizabeth Pinckney,
in Ellery, now Market Street, on or near the site of the..."Sailor's
Home." (CP. p. 28) Designed by Thomas Bennett (Minutes, April 12,
1792), the building was described as having a "center 40 x 40, the wings
65 by 30 feet each. The foundation to the first floor, to the top of
floor 2½ feet high, 3 Bricks thick. The first story 10 feet high,
2½ bricks. The second Story 15 feet high 2½ bricks. Third story 13
feet, 2 brick. And the Fourth Story 10 feet high 2 brick." (Minutes,
May 12, 1792) The Commissioners directed that "the South Front should
be 250 feet from Boundary Street (now Calhoun Street), 24 feet North-
ward of the House to be Inclosed as a yard, and the remainder a kitchen
garden, the South front to be laid out in walkes to be determined by
the Commissioners." (Minutes, November 4, 1792) Anthony Toomer performed
the brickwork duties and the firm of Cannon and Bennett did the carpentry work. (Ibid.)

Money was raised for the completion of the building in many ways.
Thomas Middleton donated $48.00 "as his pay as a member of the Legis-
lature for the year 1789." (Minutes, December 15, 1791) Ralph Izard
"presented...16 Turkies and 16 Geese." (Minutes, August 9, 1792).
The Carpenters Society donated twenty-five poinds. (Minutes,December
6, 1792). John Blake gave his $45.00 legislative salary.
(Minutes, October 23, 1794). The majority of the funds; however, came
from Charity Sermons preached by local ministers.

MINISTER-DONATION	CHURCH	DATE
Rev. Dr. Purcell 45 pounds, 16 shillings, 9 pence[1]	St. Michaels	July 10, 1791
Rev. Mr. Hollingshead 49 pounds, 2 shillings, 4 pence[2]	Independent Church on Meeting Street	July 24, 1791
Rev. Mr. Furman 19 pounds[3]	Baptist Church	July 31, 1791
Rev. Mr. Faber 62 pounds, 25 shillings, 2 pence[4]	St. Johns Lutheran	August 17, 1791
Rev. Mr. Coaste 18 pounds, 15 shillings, 2 pence[5]	French Church	August 14, 1791
Joseph Meyers 58 pounds, 15 shillings,[6]	Hebrew Synagogue	August 21, 1791
Rev. Dr. Keating 30 pounds, 3 shillings, 9 pence[7]	Catholic Church	August 28, 1791
Rev. Mr. Wm. Hammet 60 pounds, 13 shillings, 11 pence[8]	Methodist Episcopal	September 4, 1791

Rev. Mr. Isaac Keith	Independent New Church Archdale Street [9]	September 11, 1791
86 pounds, 3 shillings, 8 pence		
Rev. Dr. Robert Smith	St. Philips [10]	September 18, 1791
200 pounds, 1 shilling, 10 pence		
Rev. Mr. Wilson	Presbyterian Church	December 4, 1791
206 pounds, 14 shillings, 9 pence [11]		

In 1853, the building was renovated. Plans submitted by Jones and Lee on January 27, 1852 were accepted. (Minutes, January 27, 1853). The architects described the completed building as being constructed in "the Italian style being 236 feet long by 76 feet wide. The main building is five stories high, including the attic. The front is divided into three sections, the central portion being surmounted by a pediment and with an Italian portico projecting in front. This portico consists of Corinthian pillars, between which are arches supporting a Corinthian balustrade. On each side of this central section are wings rising the whole height of the building, perforated on the several stories by windows with characteristic embellishments. The building is surmounted by a Mansard roof, the attic windows projecting from the first slope of the roof, with moulded pediments. Above the roof of the central section of the front rises the belfry, constructed for the city alarm bell. This belfry is supported by an octagonal stage, in the centre of which arises the main cupola, being two stories high; on the first story there are four porticos of Corinthian columns with rustic blocks, surmounted by entableture and pediment. The second story is perforated on the four sides, in which is suspended the alarm bell. This stage is surmounted by a square dome, which supports a figure of Charity." (CP, p. 78). Others who worked on the renovation were Luis Rebb, Contractor and Carpenter; G.W. Busby, Bricklayer; W.H. Gruver, Plasterer; W.T. White, Stonecutter; W.S. Henerey, Cast Iron Work; Horton & Parks, Tinner and Plumber; T. Newel, Gas Fitter; J.U. Boesch, Coppersmith; Wm. Arnot, Painter; James Cook, Steam Fitter; J.M. Eason & Bro., Engine Maker; R. Wing, Bell Hanger; and J.M. Mulvany, Slater. (CP, p. 80).

A chapel was constructed on the Orphan House grounds in 1802 in order that the children would no longer be forced to attend area churches in rotation. Nondenominational, the chapel was staffed by ministers of various faiths. (Minutes, July 9, 1801). No public money was used for the building. "It was erected by voluntary benevolence of the citizens (of Charleston)" (CP, p. 30). The cornerstone was laid August 6, 1801 (Minutes, August 6, 1801) and the building was officially opened September 19, 1802. (Minutes, September 19, 1802). The architect of the Orphan House Chapel is not known. Gabriel Manigault is usually credited with the design; however, there is no mention of an architect in any of the Orphan House records. A small cemetary surrounded the Chapel and was used for inmates and officers of the institution.* See bottom page 8 for footnote.

Religion played an important role in the life of the Institution. Prayers were said morning and evening and Masters were expected to continue this religious training during an inmate's apprenticeship. Although the Commissioners placed great emphasis on religion, it was a particular form of religion. For example, in 1857 Rabbi Mayer of the Hazel Street Synagogue requested that two Jewish children be allowed to worship on Saturday or to be instructed in the Hebrew faith. (Minutes, June 18, 1857). The Commissioners refused because "the regulation of the House would be so materially interferred with." (Ibid.) . Perhaps the most vehement protests came from John, Bishop of Charleston, who objected to Roman Catholic children being "taught the Catechism of a Society which protests the religion of their parents as erroneous." (Minutes, June 23, 1825). After he was informed that Catholic priests would be allowed to conduct services in the Chapel in rotation with other ministers, Bishop England stated "that poverty shall not deprive its victim of religious rights." (Ibid.)

Financial support for the Orphan House came from both public and private sources. City Council made annual appropriations and state law permitted the Orphan House to share in funds collected from escheated property. (Statutes of the State of South Carolina, Vol. 5, p. 366). Philanthropic citizens often made liberal donations and bequests. A Private Fund, established in September 1808 (CP, p. 31), was used for "donations given directly to the Board of Commissioners for the personal comfort and private benefit of the children." (Digest of the Ordinances of the City Council of Charleston. Archibald E. Miller, Printer. 1818. p. 199-200). The money was invested in stocks and bonds and the interest used. The money was spent in various ways including dowries for the girls when they married, expenses accrued by boys away at school, and to pay teachers and buy supplies for the schoolroom. Other gifts were food, fuel, land or clothing. Another source of revenue was the return of apprentices. Masters were required to pay the Commissioners a sum of money for the forfeiture of the indentures.

The Orphan House was proud of its history. In the 1850's the Commissioners directed the Steward to organize the manuscript records of the Institution. Applications to Admit, requests for apprentices, financial matters, officer's papers and the records of the Commissioners were to be arranged in order that the history of the Orphan House would be preserved. (COH General Files - Records Program). Each year on October 18 (or as close to that date as possible) the Anniversary of the Institution was celebrated with speeches, recitations, premiums for schoolwork and a special dinner among the activities. In order to honor the memory of benefactors to the Orphan House, memorial tablets stating the name, date, and amount of the donation, hung in

* The Cemetary continued to be used until 1855 when the Commissioners purchased six lots at Magnolia Cemetary. (Minutes, September 6, 1855)

the entrance hall of the building.

The staff, or officers, as they were called, consisted of a steward, a matron, the nurses, the sewing mistress, and teachers. Most of the officers lived either in the Orphan House building or inside the enclosure in small cottages. Each officer was allowed rations for himself and his family. In 1826, the daily rations for the officers consisted of:[1]

STEWARD: 1 quart rice, 1 pound bread, 2 pounds beef, and ½ pint milk.

MATRON: 1 quart rice, 1 pound bread, 1 pound beef, and ½ pint milk.

SEWING
MISTRESS: 1 quart rice, 1 pound bread, 2 pounds beef, ½ pint milk.

NURSE: 1 pint rice, 1 pound bread, ½ pint milk.

In 1840 the weekly rations consisted of:

STEWARD: 7 quarts rice, 2½ pounds sugar, 1½ pounds coffee, 1 quart molasses, 1½ pounds soap, 2 pounds butter, 1 pound candles, 2 pounds bread, 1 pound beef, 3½ pints milk, 4 oz. tea

MATRON: 7 quarts rice, 2 pounds sugar, 1 pound coffee, 1 quart molasses, 1½ pounds soap, 1½ pounds butter, 1 pound candles, 2 pounds bread, 2 pounds beef, 3½ pints milk, 4 oz tea

SEWING
MISTRESS: 7 quarts rice, 2 pounds sugar, 1½ pounds butter, 1 pound candles, 1 pound bread, 2 pounds beef, 3½ pints milk, 4 oz. tea

SCHOOL-
MASTER: 7 quarts rice, 1 pounds sugar, 1 pound coffee, 1 pound bread, 2 pounds beef, 3½ pints milk, 4 oz. tea

NURSE: 3½ quarts rice, 1 pound sugar, ½ pound coffee, 1 quart molasses, ½ pound soap, 1 pound butter, 3/4 pound candles, 1 pound bread, 3½ pints milk

YEARLY SALARIES FOR OFFICERS IN 1818[3]

MATRON: $300.00

SCHOOL MISTRESS: $250.00

NURSE: $90.00

SCHOOLMASTER: $800.00 plus $500.00 for living expenses.

STEWARD: $500.00

The steward of the Orphan House was responsible for the overall operation of the Institution. These duties included the ordering and distribution of supplies, supervision of the inmates and staff, recording the Commissioners' Minutes, and directing the daily religious services. (By-Laws, p. 19-21). The office of Steward was abolished in 1869 and the entire operation of the Institution came under the control of Miss Agnes K. Irving, the Principal of the School. (Minutes, January 18, 1869). The combining of the offices ended years of disputes between the Steward and the Principal. (COH Problems File)

STEWARD	ELECTED	RESIGNED:
John Wedderspoon	November 18, 1790[1]	Died November 5, 1798[2]
John Neal	November 16, 1798[3]	Unknown
Benjamin Cudworth	February 20, 1803	November 20, 1810[4]
Eliab Kingman	November 21, 1810[5]	February __, 1835[6]
Robert Wright	July 17, 1835[7]	Died October 18, 1841[8]
John Dewes	November 25, 1841	August 20, 1850[9]
Archibald Campbell	August 8, 1850[10]	January 4, 1856[11]
Robert Small	January 17, 1856[12]	December 14, 1865[13]

9

The office of matron coincided with that of the steward. The Matron was in charge of the day-to-day affairs of the Orphan House; such as the preparation of food, supervision of the sewing room, cleaning of clothes, instruction of moral and religious values and the direction of the nurses. (By-Laws, p. 21-23). After 1840, the Commissioners preferred to employ a married couple as steward and matron. (COH Steward and Matron Files). In 1869 the office of matron was downgraded because of the appointment of Miss Agnes K. Irving as Superintendent. (Minutes, January 28, 1869). The nurses' duties were expanded to include those tasks formerly performed by the matron that were not taken over by the Superintendent. After 1870, nurses were referred to as assistant matrons. (COH Matrons' Files)

MATRON	ELECTED	RESIGNED
Sarah Bricken	October 28, 1790[1]	November 1, 1791[2]
Sarah Hatfield	November 1, 1791[3]	March 14, 1793[4]
Susannah Wells	March 28, 1793[5]	September 14, 1795[6]
Ann Robinson	November 5, 1795[7]	_____, 1796[8]
Martha Bolton	November 10, 1796[9]	Unknown
Mrs. _____ Gourley	Unknown	April 30, 1801[10]
Margaret Holmes	January 11, 1802	June 21, 1819[11]
Elizabeth Kerrison	July 8, 1819[12]	September 27, 1827[13]
Mary E. Phelps	October 25, 1827[14]	February 9, 1843[15]
Sarah LeQueux Dewes	March 16, 1843[16]	August 20, 1850[17]
Ann Campbell	August 8, 1850[18]	January 4, 1856[19]
Ann Small	January 17, 1856[20]	Died August 2, 1862[21]

The nurses performed the day-to-day supervision of the children. Each nurse was assigned a dormitory of either males or females of uniform ages. Living either in the room with the children or in an adjoining area, the nurse was responsible for the children's cleanliness, clothes, church attendance and general health. (By-Laws, p. 24-25). Although an up-to-date record of COH officers was supposed to be kept by the steward, there is not a complete record of the women employed as nurses.

NURSE	ELECTED	RESIGNED	FORMER INMATE	CHILDREN IN COH
Eleanor Allen	March 8, 1810[1]	Died August 1817[2]	C-74	
Agnes Beahan	August 2, 1860[3]	July 15, 1869[4]		Agnes ( ) & Thomas ( )
Ann Brooks	February 21, 1811[5]	Died October 17, 1828[6]	D-82	
Mary Brooks	October 28, 1790[7]	November 18, 1790[8]		Ann Elizabeth (D-82)
Ann Brower	October 4, 1819[9]	Unknown		
Jane Brown	January 5, 1809[10]			
Jane Buchanan	February 17, 1825[11]			
Emmeline Cantley	January 9, 1840[13]	May 13, 1852[14]	H-14	William (N-59) & James (N-60)
Charlotte Chanson	November 12, 1811[15]	Elected Sewing Mistress[16]		Catherine (F-95, Mary (F-94 & Henrietta (F-93)
Maryann Conlon	November 15, 1855[17]	December 3, 1857[18]		
Mary Darrell	September 9, 1817[19]	January 30, 1823[20]		
Susan Dawson	December ___, 1853[21]	Died ___ 1855[22]		William (Q-38)
Mary (Polly) Edwards	February 29, 1816[23]	December 12, 1822[24]		
Elizabeth Ellis	January 5, 1854[25]	Unknown		Josephine Ann (R-81)
Ann Evans	August 20, 1840[26]	Unknown		Joseph (P-66) & Mary Ann (O-59)
Ann Farley	November 5, 1801[27]	Elected Spinner[28]		
Rebecca Fields	May 2, 1802[29]	June 10, 1804[30]		
Harriot Figures	February 28, 1822[31]	August 20, 1823[32]		
Elizabeth Findley	November 5, 1798[33]	March 29, 1799[34]		
Maria Fisher	January 29, 1807[35]	February 26, 1807[36]		
Elizabeth Furchess	July 7, 1822[37]	October 20, 1853[38]		
Jane Gory	January 31, 1856[39]	Unknown		
Loveridge Gray (Grey)	September 29, 1836[40]	December 19, 1839[41]	G-87	
Emily Eliza Green	June 24, 1852[42]	May 27, 1858[43]		
Elizabeth Griffin	July 18, 1796[43]	Unknown		
Elizabeth Griffith	October 28, 1790[45]	October 13, 1791[46]		
Elizabeth Griffith	January 5, 1854[47]	Unknown		

Name				
Ann Guyon	June 23, 1814[48]	April 23, 1829[49]		Loveridge (G-87) & Ann (G-88)
Hannah Hayes	January 25, 1855[50]	October 12, 1864[51]		
Isabel Henderson	June 30, 1859[52]	October 13, 1881[53]		David R. (W-213)
Rosanna Higgins	December 17, 1856[54]	Died March 21, 1861[55]	R-25	
Elizabeth How	November 17, 1791[56]	May 17, 1792[57]		
Ann Husen	May 8, 1801[58]	March 18, 1802[59]		
C. Kortman	December 23, 1857[60]	July 21, 1859[61]		Zachariah (D-21) & Richard (D-20)
Catherine Lambers	November 26, 1840[62]	June 23, 1859[63]		
Eleanor Lambert	October 7, 1824[64]	February 3, 1825[65]		Minutes, 1834-1841, p. 465 states she was a former inmate, no name given
E. Lucas	December 24, 1835[66]	Elected School Mistress[67]		
Mary M. McCants	June 30, 1853[68]	April 12, 1855[69]		
Mary McClelland	July 23, 1799[70]	June 6, 1822[71]		
Jane McIndoo	June 24, 1858[72]	July 15, 1858[73]		
" " (Reelected)	July 28, 1859[74]	June 24, 1864[75]		
Frances McKean	March 27, 1806[76]	March 31, 1817[77]		
Janet McLarty	August 19, 1858[78]	September 5, 1861[79]		
Susan McPherson	June 17, 1824[80]	June 10, 1852[81]		
Ann Mackay (McKay)	June 17, 1824[82]	February 17, 1825[83]		
Nelly Manning	August 25, 1791[84]	November 15, 1791[85]		
Mary Manno	April 30, 1829[86]	Elected Sewing Mistress	F-43	
Ann Maromet	August 12, 1797[88]	October 7, 1797[89]	C-21	Eliza (L-41), others not in COH: Martha, Mary, Sarah, John Hugh (K-97), John (K-46) Robert (K-47)
Margaret Marshall	August 6, 1802[90]	July 25, 1803[91]		Mary (R-101) & William (S-79) LeQueux, grandchildren
Mary A. Michel	May __, 1855[92]	July 19, 1860[93]		
Susannah Moore	July 6, 1811[94]	May 27, 1824[95]		Virginia (V-131) Susannah Miesenbery (F-83)
Lydia Muir	November 15, 1855[96]	Unknown		
Jane Mulryne	November 5, 1814[97]	February 2, 1816[98]		Ann Selina (G-44) & Thomas Hill (G-43) 5 others not in COH

Name	Date	Elected Sewing Mistress	Children / Relatives
Elizabeth Murphy	March 6, 1817[99]	March 27, 1806[102]	
Martha Nelson	January 20, 1804[101]	Died March 28, 1798[104]	Thomas (C-52) & Philip (C-53)
Mrs. _____ O'Keefe	January 27, 1798[103]	October 12, 1864[106]	Rosa (V-67)
Elizabeth Owens	June 12, 1856[105]	December 30, 1869[108]	
Catherine Pardue	May 30, 1857[107]	December 20, 1832[110]	
Elizabeth Payne	June 17, 1824[109]	August 29, 1839[112]	
Susannah Pennington	April 3, 1834[111]	May 20, 1811[114]	
Jane Peters	January 1, 1808	August 1, 1800[116]	
Mrs. _____ Rambert	November 8, 1799[115]	Died December 21, 1853[118]	
Margaret Ransford	May 13, 1852[117]	September 17, 1824[120]	
Ann M. Reid	February 27, 1823[119]	Died June ___, 1843[122] C-91	David (N-10) & William (N-11)
Eliza Rivers	January 10, 1833[121]	October 28, 1869[124]	
Mary Roberts	November 22, 1855[123]	Elected Cook[126]	
Mary Ann Robertson	September 12, 1800[125]	August 6, 1802[128]	
Margaret Ryan	June 1, 1801[127]	Elected School Mistress[130] 1834[132]	
Ann Serjeant	August 21, 1823[129]	March 6, 1817[134]	
Smith, Esther (Hester)	February 17, 1825[131]		Harriet (E-40), Sarah (E-42) & Susannah (E-41)
Mary Spinter	July 2, 1804[133]		Lydia (L-27)
Mary Taylor	December 12, 1822[135]	September 22, 1836[136]	
Elizabeth Thomson	January 20, 1798[137]	May 22, 1798[138]	Mary Ann (C-50) & Susannah (C-51)
Mary Tschudy	April 11, 1822[139]	June 3, 1824	Oliver (K-26), Elizabeth (L-15)
Biddy Turnbill	August 12, 1803[141]	January 29, 1807[142]	Paul (K-27) Hazard
Susan (Sarah) Wienges	June 21, 1855[143]	May 30, 1861[144]	

The Sewing Mistress supervised the operation of the Sewing Department. (By-Laws), p. 25). The female inmates of the Orphan House made most of the clothing worn and liners used by the Institution. For example, from November 1817 to November 1818, 1640 garments were made, and from April 1821 to October 1821, 55 frocks (striped homespun), 155 pairs of summer pantaloons, 296 linen garmets, 55 winter frocks, and 50 cambric tippits were made. (Minutes, October 4, 1821). The woman responsible for the continued smooth operation of the Sewing Department was a former inmate, Mary Manno,* who trained the girls of the Orphan House for over fifty years.

SEWING MISTRESS	ELECTED	RESIGNED
Margaret Coleman	January 17, 1805	November 4, 1814[1]
Charlotte Chanson	November 5, 1814	March 20, 1822[2]
Elizabeth Murphy	April 4, 1822[3]	Unknown
Mary E. Phelps	January 16, 1823	November 1, 1827[4]
Elizabeth Gilliard	November 1, 1827[5]	December 12, 1835[6]
Mary Manno	December 24, 1835[7]	January 31, 1889[8]

Children were given an education during their stay in the Orphan House. At first, these lessons consisted primarily of simple reading and arithmetic. Later, however, a complete range of subjects was taught with quarterly examinations by the Commissioners. Children were segregated by sex and placed in classes according to their abilities. (By-Laws, p. 29). The Commissioners directed that the "School shall have two sessions daily, throughout the year, excepting Saturdays and Sundays; fourth of July, two weeks in August, eighteenth day of October, thanksgiving and fast days, Christmas and the days following to the first regular school day after the first of January." (Ibid). Until the reorganization of the school in 1854, boys were taught by a schoolmaster and girls by a schoolmistress.

SCHOOLMASTER	ELECTED	RESIGNED
Samuel Abbot	February 18, 1807[1]	February 26, 1807[2]
Abiel Bolles (Bowles)	October 19, 1812[3]	November 20, 1817[4]
Amos Brewster	December 1, 1798[5]	Unknown
Rev. William T. Capers	June 9, 1853[6]	Unknown
Frederick Daser	January 22, 1795[7]	_____, 1796[8]
John Fisher	October 10, 1805[9]	Died February 12, 1807[10]
John H. Harris	June 23, 1796[11]	August 4, 1798[12]
John Kingman	November 21, 1817[13]	November 16, 1837[14]
Thomas P. Lockwood	November 23, 1837[15]	October 9, 1856[16]
John Neal	August 20, 1798[17]	Elected Steward[18]
George Peters	March 5, 1807[19]	October 25, 1812[20]
Amos Pilsbury	September 20, 1799[21]	November 1, 1800[22]
" " (Reelected)	July 21, 1802[23]	March 31, 1803[24]
Moses Sanford	June 2, 1803[25]	October 10, 1805[26]
Mr. _____ Wrainch	_____, 1801[27]	August 28, 1802[28]
W.H. Wright	February 21, 1856[29]	Unknown

* Admitted as Mary Claybrook February 8, 1810 (F-43)

SCHOOL MISTRESS (FEMALE TEACHERS)	ELECTED	RESIGNED
Ann Bowles	February 26, 1799[1]	April 10, 1814[2]
Hannah Browning	January 5, 1832[3]	January 18, 1838[4]
Agnes K. Irving	December 12, 1854[5]	Elected Superintendent[6]
Mary L. Lequeux	June 24, 1858[7]	Elected Superintendent[8]
Ellen Lucas	February 15, 1838[9]	April 6, 1854[10]
Mary Phelps Mills	March 31, 1814[11]	May 1, 1828[12]
Ann Serjeant	June 5, 1828[13]	January 5, 1832[14]
Laura E. Wilbur (Later Mrs. Campbell)	December 28, 1854[15]	January 10, 1856[16]

No event affected the Orphan House more than the appointment of Miss Agnes K. Irving as Principal Teacher in 1854. Recruited in New York by Commissioners W.J. Bennett and C.G. Memminger, Miss Irving completely reorganized the Institution's schoolroom. (CP, P. 37). The most important innovation brought by Miss Irving was assistant teachers. Promising female students were chosen to instruct the younger children and to assist in the older classes. Many of these students continued until the children began to attend public schools in 1928. (ARC, 1928)

ASSISTANT TEACHER	ELECTED	RESIGNED	FORMER INMATE
A.C. Bernheim	_____, 1857[1]	June 17, 1860[2]	
Mary Crogan	June 24, 1858[3]	In COH Aug. 1869[4]	R-56
Mary J. Green	January 31, 1856	March 12, 1857[6]	
Louisa Icard	July 19, 1860[7]	March 12, 1863[8]	R-30
Ellen King	June 24, 1858	Died Feb. 5, 1917[10]	O-101
Harriet E. Patterson	February 19, 1857[11]	August 2, 1860[12]	
Alice G. Rians (Later Mrs. W.H. Wright)	January 31, 1856[13]	February 19, 1857[14]	R-6
Mary Ryburn	May 4, 1850[15]	May 27, 1869[16]	O-30
Susan Tarrant	_____, 1857[17]	April 3, 1884[18]	
Amelia Yates (Later Mrs. Wm. W. Reilly)	December 4, 1856[19]	Married Jan. 2, 1866[20]	O-107

As Principal, Miss Irving controlled the Educational Department; however, she also felt some changes were necessary in other areas of the Orphan House. Numerous letters were sent to the Commissioners from Miss Irving and the steward or matron complaining of mismanagement or interference by the other part. Miss Irving was a domineering woman who always referred to herself in the third person in her letters. While extolling her virtues and bemoaning her tribulations, Miss Irving criticized the management of the Orphan House by the steward and matron. Her complaints usually centered around discipline or interference in school matters. The steward and matron stated that Miss Irving was overstepping her authority and was causing dissension within the Institution. (COH Problems Files). Finally, in 1869 the Commissioners abolished the offices of steward, matron, and Principal. Miss Irving was appointed Superintendent of the Institution with complete control over both the Education Department and the management of the Orphan House itself. (Minutes, January 28, 1869)

Other minor positions in the Orphan House were cook, porter/gardener, spinner/weaver, and washer. These jobs were often vacant or not considered important enough to mention frequently in the Minutes or other official records.

COOK	ELECTED	RESIGNED	CHILDREN IN COH
Ann Evans	Unknown	January 15, 1846[1]	Catherine (0-100)
E. McClosky Webster	Unknown	July 16, 1811[4]	

PORTER/GARDENER	ELECTED	RESIGNED
David Fitz-Gibbon	January 17, 1850[1]	May 22, 1869[2]
John Heinburger	May 29, 1834[3]	November 4, 1834[4]
John Hood	August 3, 1840[5]	Unknown
John Hovell	July 30, 1840[6]	May 27, 1841[7]
John Kasey	January 20, 1835[8]	Unknown
Thomas Miller	July 17, 1835[9]	Died December 16, 1836[10]
John A. Smyth	June 17, 1841[11]	Unknown
Laurent Voegelin	March 4, 1833	May 20, 1833[12]
John Webster	November 23, 1837[13]	May 21, 1840[14]

SPINNERS/WEAVERS	ELECTED	RESIGNED
Jane Brown	January 5, 1809[1]	November 6, 1813[2]
Ann Clark	June 2, 1801	June 22, 1804[3]
Ann Farley	April 19, 1804[4]	Unknown
Mary Ford	November 4, 1813[5]	June 9, 1814[6]
Ruth Lloyd	October 20, 1808	November 6, 1813[7]
William Morecraft	January 11, 1801[8]	Unknown
Mary Robertson	November 28, 1801	Died October 22, 1808[9]
John Steel	November 19, 1802	Died November 20, 1809[10]
Chloe Wotton	March 10, 1814[11]	July 20, 1817[12]

WASHER	ELECTED	RESIGNED
Jane Andrews	February 1, 1855[1]	December 15, 1859[2]
" " (Reelected)	July 12, 1866[3]	July 28, 1870[4]
Julia Ellard	July 17, 1832[5]	December 14, 1837[6]
Elizabeth Ingham	December 22, 1859[7]	Elected Assistant Matron[8]
Christina Voegelin	March 4, 1833	May 20, 1833[9]

Children, or inmates as they were known, were admitted to the Orphan House by a church or city warden, parent or guardian. After a short investigation by the Visiting Commissioner, full orphans, fatherless or motherless children, and even children with two living parents were admitted. The child was then indentured to the Orphan House, which retained the right to bind the child out at a later date. This apprenticeship was a legal and binding document whereby the parent or

16

guardian lost all control of the child. Boys at the age of fourteen and girls at the age of twelve were placed on a "Binding Out List" and were presented to prospective masters by an officer of the Institution. (Rules and Regulations for the Government of the Orphan House in the City of Charleston, quoted in Minutes, July 28, 1791). A master agreed to train, house, clothe, and oversee the moral and religious development of the apprentices. Boys were apprenticed until age twenty-one and girls until age eighteen. (COH Indenture Books). The Commissioners were very strict about the masters and occupations of the inmates. Occupations for boys included mariners, shoemakers, clerks, farmers, sailmakers, ship chandlers, and metal workers. Girls were apprenticed as domestics, mantuamakers, or seamstresses. On very rare occasions, children were adopted. Special arrangements were made for some of the children. For example, in the 1840's several groups of boys were sent to the Naval School of the United States. (COH Inmates' Files). Funds were provided for deserving male students to attend the High School of Charleston, the College of Charleston, (By-Laws, p. 32), South Carolina College (Acts of the General Assembly, December 21, 1811 quoted in By-Laws, p. 32), and the Military Schools of the State. (Acts of the General Assembly, December 21, 1854 quoted in By-Laws, p. 32)

Several former inmates of the Orphan House were well-known for their accomplishments in business or other fields. Two who were especially successful were C.G. Memminger and Andrew Buist Murray. C.G. Memminger (E-90) was a founding father of the Charleston Public School System, an Orphan House Commissioner and the Secretary of the Confederate Treasury. (CP, p. 59). Andrew Buist Murray, (S-97), became a wealthy businessman, an Orphan House Commissioner, and a member of City Council. During his lifetime, Murray made many liberal donations including an annonymous gift in 1895 of $5,000.00 in City Bonds. (COH Donations Files). In his will Murray left $100,000.00 to his early home. (COH Wills and Legacies Files). Lit. Thomas R. Gedney (F-54) discovered a new channel from New York to the Atlantic Ocean. For this accomplishment, Gedney received a valuable silver service and later a Coast Guard Vessel was named for him. (COH Inmates' Files).

An alphabetical list of inmates arranged by decades follows. Most of the information comes from COH Indenture Books. These volumes contained the legal document signed by a parent or guardian to admit a child. Two copies were completed. One remained in the book and the second was given to the master when a child was apprenticed. Surnames of masters and apprentices were often spelled several different ways on a single page. The spelling most frequently written was used for this list. As mentioned earlier, the indenture expired when the apprentice was twenty-one if a male and eighteen if a female. If the child's birthdate was known, this date was used. If it was not known, the date of admission was used. Occasionally, the date of expiration of the indenture did not coincide with the given age. Information, such as parents' deaths, etc. is not duplicated on siblings' notations.

ADAM, LEWIS. Admitted November 7, 1793 by ELIZABETH MILLICENT HERIOTT, mother. Born January 23, 1785. Delivered to his mother October 30, 1794. Indentures expired January 23, 1806. (B-34). His father was "ANTOINE ADAM, native of Doll in the province of Conti." (Minutes, November 7, 1793)

AGAR, ELIZABETH. Admitted June 19, 1795 by JAMES AGAR, father. (C-1). Died September 9, 1796. (Minutes, September 22, 1796)

AGAR, GEORGE. Admitted June 18, 1795 by JAMES AGAR, father. Indentured to JOHN HOWARD as a bricklayer June 23, 1803. Indentures expired March 1, 1810. (B-72). His mother, Sarah, from Ireland. (ROSSC)

AGAR, ROBERT. Admitted June 18, 1795 by JAMES AGAR, father. Indentured to JOSEPH MILLIGAN as a merchant July 8, 1802. Indentures expired March 1, 1810. (B-73)

ALDERJOE, JAMES. Admitted November 1, 1790 aged four years. An orphan. Indentured to ROBERT BRODIE as a house carpenter July 1, 1802. Indentures expired November 1, 1806. (A-102)

ALLEN, ELEANOR. Admitted March 9, 1799 by Church Warden of St. Philip's Church. Indentured to JANE HUNTER as a domestic March 5, 1801. Indentures expired September 9, 1804. (C-74)

ALLEN, JANE. Admitted May 18, 1797 by MARTHA ALLEN, mother. Born May ___, 1795. (C-30). Born in Ireland. (Minutes, May 18, 1797) No further information.

ALLEN, MATILDA. Admitted October 12, 1798 by Church Wardens of St. Philip's Church. Indentured to JAMES PENNALL as a domestic May 31, 1810. Transferred to JOHN LINN as a domestic November 15, 1810. Indentures expired October 10, 1814. (D-81).

ANDERSON, ANN. Admitted May 18, 1797 by MARIA ANDERSON, mother. Born March 14, 1791. Indentured to JANE MUIR, wife of WILLIAM MUIR, as a domestic November 15, 1804. Indentures expired March 14, 1809. (C-27). Father was JOHN ANDERSON, MA. (A to A)

ANDERSON, CHARLOTTE. Admitted May 18, 1797 by MARIA ANDERSON, mother. Indentured to SARAH HOUSE as a domestic August 24, 1798. Indentures expired January 3, 1804. (C-24).

ANDERSON, JONATHAN. Admitted May 18, 1797 aged eight years by MARIA ANDERSON, mother. Born April 1, 1789. Indentured to DANIEL STEVENS, JR., SAMUEL E. ASH, and GEORGE NORTON REYNOLDS as a coachmaker and trimmer November 25, 1803. Indentures expired April 1, 1810. (C-26)

ANDERSON, MARGARET. Admitted May 18, 1797 aged eight years by MARIA ANDERSON, mother. Born August 6, 1787. Indentured to CAROLINE SMITH as a domestic November 6, 1799. Indentures expired August 6, 1805. (C-25)

ANDERSON, ROBERT. Admitted May 18, 1797 aged three years by MARIA ANDERSON, mother. Born April 5, 1794. Indentured to DANIEL HENDERSON as a blacksmith April 20, 1809. Indentures expired April 5, 1815. (C-28)

ANDREWS, JAMES. Admitted October 13, 1794 by JOHN ANDREWS, father. (C-54). No further information.

ARMSTRONG, ANN. Admitted November 20, 1790 aged five years. An orphan. (A-68). No further information.

ARMSTRONG, WILLIAM. Admitted January 1, 1791 aged nine years. An orphan. Indentured to GEORGE NORRIS as a saddler, November 18, 1794. Indentures expired January 1, 1805. (A-16)

ATTINGER, ANNA. Admitted April 7, 1791 aged five years by SARAH RITFIELD, mother. Delivered to her mother March 9, 1801. Indentures expired April 17, 1805. (A-36)

ATTINGER, CHARLES. Admitted April 16, 1791 aged eight years by SARAH RITFIELD, mother. Died August 2, 1794. Indentures expired April 17, 1805. (A-36)

ATTINGER, MARY. Admitted November 20, 1790 aged ten years by SARAH RITFIELD, mother. Indentured to WILLIAM PURSE as a mantuamaker December 11, 1794. Indentures expired November 20, 1798. (A-58)

BAKER, SUSANNAH. Admitted September 28, 1797 aged eight years by SUSANNAH SAWYER, mother. Indentured to JOHN ARMOUR (of Winnsborough) as a domestic March 24, 1803. Transferred to THOMAS BEARD (of Columbia), occupation unknown, June 6, 1804. Indentures expired July 31, 1805. (C-48)

BARGES, LEWIS. Admitted April 15, 1796. A son of DAVID and MARIE BARGES of old France. Indentured to WILLIAM SOMARSALL and SON as a navigator July 5, 1798. Indentures expired April 14, 1805. (C-9). Born in Philadelphia. (Minutes, April 14, 1796)

BARKER, LYDIA. Admitted November 5, 1795 by ROBERT BARKER, father. No further information. (C-5)

BARRY, HENRY REYNOLD. Admitted September 15, 1797 aged seven years by JAMES BARRY, father. Indentures expired January 17, 1811. (C-42). Born January 17, 1790. (Minutes, September 15, 1797). His mother was "a Lunatick in the Poor House." (Ibid.) Sent to the Poor House September 9, 1803 because of his frequent fits. (Minutes, September 9, 1803)

BARRY, JAMES. Admitted September 15, 1797 by JAMES BARRY, father. Delivered to his father to learn the carpentry trade December 23, 1802. Indentures expired July 23, 1809. (C-41). Born January 26, 1788. (Minutes, September 15, 1797).

BARRY, MARGARET. Admitted September 16, 1797 aged five years by JAMES BARRY, father. Indentured to AMELIA PERRAULT, wife of P.H. PERRAULT, as a domestic August 2, 1804. Transferred to MARGARET COCHRAN as a mantuamaker January 16, 1806. Indentures expired April 11, 1810. (C-43). Born April 11, 1794. (Minutes, September 15, 1797)

BARTON, WILLIAM. Admitted February 29, 1795. An orphan. Indentured to TIMOTHY and MASON as a printer June 25, 1795. Indentures expired February 29, 1802. (B-66). Born in Baltimore. (Minutes, February 26, 1795)

BATES, JOHN. Admitted August 8, 1793. Indentured to JOHN PAUL SNYDER as a ship carpenter August 8, 1793. Indentures expired August 8, 1795. (B-12)

BAZON, JOHN. Admitted February 7, 1793 aged seven years. Indentured to NORBERT VINORE as a baker October 24, 1798. Transferred to JOHN WISSINGER as a baker May 4, 1802. Indentures expired February 7, 1807. (B-5). Born November 30, 1786 in Abbeville County. Parents were RACHEL and NICHOLAS. (Minutes, February 7, 1793)

BLACKALLER, JOHN. Admitted May 31, 1797 aged nine years by MARTHA MOORE, mother. Indentured to JOHN ELLISON as a merchant and accountant July 8, 1802. Indentures expired May 31, 1809. (C-33)

BLACKALLER, LOUISA. Admitted May 31, 1797 aged five years by MARTHA MOORE, mother. Indentured to SUSANNAH D. THOMAS, wife of JOHN JAMES THOMAS, as a seamstress and housekeeper July 26, 1804. Indentures expired May 31, 1810. (C-34). Indentures transferred to MARY ANN LONG, her sister, due to the death of Mrs. THOMAS, September 23, 1807. (Minutes, September 23, 1807)

BLACKALLER, MARY ANN. Admitted August 8, 1798 by MARTHA MOORE, mother. Indentured to ELIZABETH STEEDMAN, widow of JAMES STEEDMAN, as a seamtress and housekeeper, 1800. Indentures expired March 19, 1804. (C-67)

BOUYSSOU, JACQUES. Admitted October 24, 1793 by PIERRE BOUYSSOU, father. Absconded, nd. Indentures expired June 15, 1804. (A-8). Born June 15, 1783. (Minutes, October 24, 1793)

BOWDEN, MARY. Admitted November 20, 1790 aged eight years. An orphan. Indentured to JOHN WATSON as an upholsterer June 10, 1796. Transferred to BENJAMIN STILES as a domestic November 13, 1798. Indentures expired November 20, 1800. (A-61). Married to BENJAMIN GABRIEL December 19, 1799 by Rev. Mr. FURMAN. (Minutes, December 19, 1799)

BOWEN, GEORGE. Admitted July 1, 1790 aged nine years and seven months by GEORGE and MARY BOWEN, parents. Indentured to JAMES MUIRHEAD as a bookbinder May 22, 1795. Indentures expired July 1, 1801. (A-8)

BOWLES, MARY. Admitted August 11, 1797 aged five years by ANN BOWLES, mother. Born March 13, 1792. Deliver to her mother October 22, 1801. Indentures expired March 13, 1810. (C-40)

BOWLES, THOMAS. Admitted August 11, 1797 aged seven years by ANN BOWLES, mother. Born December 6, 1789. Indentured to JOHN McKEE as a bricklayer July 28, 1803. Transferred to JOHN N. MARTIN as a bricklayer May 13, 1808. Indentures expired December 6, 1810. (C-39)

BOWLES, WILLIAM. Admitted September 6, 1798 aged four years by ANN BOWLES, mother. Delivered to his mother September 1, 1803. Indentures expired September 6, 1815. (C-69)

BOZMAN, JOHN. Admitted May 1, 1794 by RACHEL BOZMAN, mother. Indentured to LEMUEL BOZMAN as a shoemaker January 5, 1797. Indentures expired August 3, 1804. (B-45). Born in St. Marks Parish August 10, 1783. (Minutes, May 1, 1794)

BRINEWOOD, THOMAS. Admitted August 7, 1792 aged twelve years. Born in Pourthmouth, old England. Indentured to JAMES THEUS, of the ship Sisters of New York, as a mariner March 26, 1795. Indentures expired August 7, 1801. (A-41). JACOB MILLIGAN, step-father. (Minutes, October 25, 1792)

BRINKS, JOHN. Admitted January 2, 1790 aged seven years and six months. Indentured to BENJAMIN CASEY as a coachmaker May 18, 1797. Indentures expired January 2, 1804. (A-35)

BROOKMAN, ANN. Admitted July 18, 1793 aged eight years by NANCY NEDDER-MAN, mother. Indentured to MRS. A. LOCKWOOD as a mantuamaker and house keeper October 2, 1798. Indentures expired July 18, 1803. (A-95) Born in Amsterdam. Father, CONRAD BROOKMAN. (Minutes, July 18, 1793)

BROOKMAN, ELIZABETH REBECCA. Admitted July 18, 1793 aged six years by NANCY NEDDERMAN, mother. Delivered to ANN SMITH, mother, October 11, 1801. Indentures expired July 18, 1805. (A-96). Born at sea on board the Cap Bass. Father, CONRAD BROOKMAN. (Minutes, July 18, 1793)

BROWER, JOHN. Admitted May 18, 1797 by MARY BROWER, mother. Born September 30, 1794. Died, nd. (C-29)

BRUCE, MARY. Admitted January 13, 1794 by ANN SMITH, mother. Indentured to WILLIAM McWRIGHT as a weaver, seamtress and housekeeper May 8, 1801. Indentures expired January 13, 1804. (B-41)

BULIT, PETER (PIERRE). Admitted June 23, 1796 by CATHERINE BULIT, mother and widow of Bordeaux. Delivered to his mother July 21, 1796. Indentures expired October 12, 1807. (C-15)

BURCH, ELIZABETH. Admitted October 4, 1792 aged twelve years by ANN WOODMANCE (WOODMAN), mother. Indentured to BENJAMIN MERRALL as a seamtress August 29, 1793. Indentures expired October 4, 1800. (A-89) Born March 22, 1783. Father, THOMAS BURCH. (Minutes, October 4, 1792)

BURN, JOHN ALEXANDER. Admitted May 7, 1792 aged eight years and two months by ELIZABETH WHITE, sister. Born March 7, 1784. Indentured to JAMES GIBSON as a coachmaker October 28, 1796. Indentures expired March 7, 1805. (A-30). Parents, HUGH and SARAH BURN. (Minutes, May 7, 1792)

BURROW, ISAAC. Admitted October 30, 1790 by MARY BURROW, mother. Indentured to WILLIAM SMITH, step-father, as a house carpenter July 2, 1801. Indentures expired October 26, 1809. (B-56). Born October 26, 1788. (Minutes, October 30, 1794)

BURROW, ISAAC. Admitted October 13, 1794 by MARY BURROW, mother. Indentured to WILLIAM SMITH as a house carpenter July 2, 1801. Indentures expired October 29, 1809. (B-74)

BURROW, MARGARET. Admitted October 30, 1794 by MARY BURROW, mother. Delivered to her mother, MARY SMITH, September 10, 1799. Indentures expired May 9, 1804. (B-55). Born May 9, 1786. (Minutes, October 30, 1794)

BYRD, ORAN D. Admitted June 14, 1791 aged nine years and three months by SAMUEL BYRD, father. Indentured to ENOS REEVES as a goldsmith and tinmaker February 29, 1795. Indentures expired June 14, 1803. (A-7)

BYRNS, ANN. Admitted April 18, 1799 by BRIDGET BYRNS, mother. Indentured to CHARLOTTE MAURAY (wife of EVERESTE MAURAY) as a milliner and seamtress April 3, 1809. Indentures expired April 18, 1811. (C-77)

CAMERON, MARY. Admitted November 20, 1790 aged seven years by ALEXANDER CAMERON, father. Indentured to SARAH THORNE as a mantuamaker November 21, 1796. Indentures expired November 20, 1801. (A-64)

CANAND, JOHN PETER PAUL. Admitted April 4, 1793 aged nine years by FRANCES CANAND, mother. Absconded, nd. (A-53). Born June 12, 1784. (Minutes, April 4, 1793)

CAPRY, HENRY. Admitted October 12, 1793 by STEPHEN JOSEPH CAPRY, father, from Cape Francis. Delivered to his parents September 7, 1794. Indentures expired November 20, 1806. (E-19)

CAPRY, JAMES. Admitted October 12, 1793 by STEPHEN JOSEPH CAPRY, father, from Cape Francis. Delivered to his parents September 7, 1794. Indentures expired November 20, 1809. (B-20). Born September 12, 1787. (Minutes, October 10, 1793)

CAPRY, MARY JOVERT. Admitted October 12, 1793 by STEPHEN JOSEPH CAPRY, father, from Cape Francois. Delivered to her parents September 7, 1794. Indentures expired October 10, 1802. (B-18)

CAREW, BRIDGET. Admitted January 27, 1791 aged nine years. Indentured to THOMAS BRADFORD as an upholsterer December 5, 1794. Indentures expired January 27, 1800. (A-75)

CAREW, JOSEPH. Admitted February 26, 1795 by CATHARINE CAREW, mother. Indentures expired July 23, 1813. (B-67). Died week of August 19, 1802 of measles. (Minutes, August 19, 1802)

CAREW, SARAH. Admitted November 7, 1793 by ANN CAREW, sister. An orphan. Indentured to NAOMI BURCH as a domestic September 28, 1797. Indentures expired October 7, 1803. (B-33). Born March 1, 1784 at sea. JOHN and MARY CAREW, parents from Tipparrary in Ireland. (Minutes, October 31, 1793)

CATISTAL, JEAN BATISTA MICHAEL. Admitted October 19, 1793 by FRANCOIS CATISTAL, mother. Delivered to his parents, nd. Indentures expired January 29, 1803. (B-23)

CLARK, MARGARET. Admitted December 18, 1794 aged four years by EDWARD CLARK, father. Indentured to MARY CLARK as a domestic May 9, 1803. Transferred to MARY ANN ARTHUR, occupation unknown, August 4, 1803.

CLARK, MARGARET, cont'd. Indentures expired December 18, 1808. (B-70). Born in Salem County. Mother, ANN. (ROSSC)

CONNOLLY, THOMAS. Admitted February 15, 1791 aged eight years and six months by MARY CONNOLLY, mother. Indentured to ALEXANDER CALDER as a cabinetmaker January 31, 1797. Transferred to JACOB STROUP as a carpenter September 30, 1799. Indentures expired February 15, 1803. (A-24)

CONNOR, JOHN. Admitted September 18, 1794 by LETITIA PEARSE, mother. Indentured to PETER FRENEAU and DAVID R. WILLIAMS as a printer April 28, 1803. Indentures expired October 15, 1810. (B-50). JOHN CONNOR, father. (ROSSC)

COOPER, PETER. Admitted May 30, 1792 aged ten years by MARY COOPER, mother. Indentured to ALEXANDER CALDER as a cabinetmaker March 22, 1798. Indentures expired May 30, 1803. (A-42). Born May 30, 1783. (Minutes, November 22, 1792)

COURNAND, PIERRE. Admitted February 20, 1794 by URSULA CONSTANCE CHADRIAC, mother. Born on Martinique. Indentures expired May 25, 1806. (B-42). Absconded aboard a privateer April 28, 1796. (Minutes, April 28, 1796). Father, PIERRE COURNAND. (Minutes, February 28, 1796)

COWDEN, (COWDY) ELIZABETH. Admitted May 29, 1798 aged six years by JANE FOUNTAINE, friend. Indentured to GEORGE ROBERTSON (of Fairfield County), as a domestic June 22, 1805. Indentures expired May 29, 1810. (C-59)

COX, JOSEPH. Admitted January 26, 1792 aged eight years by JANE COX, mother. Delivered to his sister, MARY COX, April 28, 1796. Indentures expired January 26, 1805. (A-108). Father, JOHN COX, was a tavern keeper. (Minutes, January 26, 1792)

COX, MARIA. Admitted May 17, 1792 aged thirteen years. Indentured to ANNE A. HENRY as a milliner August 9, 1793. Indentures expired May 17, 1797. (A-85). Born near Wassamsan, S.C. Parents, THOMAS and ANN COX. (Minutes, May 17, 1792)

CROW, EDWARD. Admitted September 10, 1799 aged seven years by ELIZABETH CROW, mother. Indentured to PETER TIMOTHY MARCHANT, A.S. WILLINGTON, H. CARPENTER and FREDERICK DALCHO as a printer January 23, 1806. Indentures expired March 13, 1813. (C-84)

CROW, ELIZABETH. Admitted September 10, 1799 aged four years by ELIZABETH MAHAN, mother. Indentured to FRANCIS CORAM as a domestic March 13, 1807. Indentures expired May 10, 1813. (C-85)

DEAN, JAMES. Admitted December 10, 1790 aged nine years and seven months by JOSEPH and DOROTHY DEAN, parents. Indentured to ABRAHAM GORY (JORY) as a house carpenter and ship joiner November 20, 1794. Indentures expired December 10, 1802. (A-18)

DEAN, JOSEPH. Admitted August 5, 1792 aged ten years by JOSEPH and DOROTHY DEAN, parents. Indentured to ENOS REEVES as a goldsmith August 10, 1795. Indentures expired August 5, 1802. (A-19)

DISHER, LEWIS. Admitted April 25, 1793 aged seven years. Indentured to JAMES DUDELL as a cabinetmaker March 28, 1800. (B-6). Parents, MARY and LEWIS DISHER. Born July 22, 1786. (Minutes, April 25, 1793)

DISHER, MARY. Admitted November 20, 1790 aged five years by MARY DISHER, mother. Indentured to MARY HICKS (HEXTS) as a domestic September 15, 1797. Indentures expired November 20, 1803. (A-69)

DISHER, STEPHEN. Admitted March 26, 1791 aged nine years by MARY DISHER, mother. Indentured to ULRICK FRIEND as a baker March 28, 1794. Indentures expired March 26, 1803. (A-22)

DOGARTHY, JAMES. Admitted November 1, 1790 aged ten years. An orphan. Indentured to DAVID BURGER as a gunsmith October 23, 1794. Indentures expired November 1, 1801. (A-45)

DORUM, MARY. Admitted November 10, 1794. An orphan, the daughter of DEMPSEY and MARY DORUM. Indentured to JOHN JACKSON as a domestic June 26, 1795. Indentures expired November 6, 1800. (B-59)

DOWNEY, WILLIAM. Admitted February 3, 1791 aged four years by MARGARET DEMPSEY, mother. Indentured to THOMAS RAMSAY as a baker August 1, 1800. Indentures expired February 3, 1808. (A-103)

EDWARDS, MARY. Admitted November 7, 1799 aged five years by ELIZABETH EDWARDS, mother. Allowed to live with her mother in the Poor House because of her weak eyes March 27, 1806. Indentures expired November 7, 1812. (C-88)

EINSITTER, CHARLES. Admitted June 29, 1794 by DOROTHEA SILLER, mother. Absconded, nd. (B-47). No further information.

ELLIOTT, GEORGE. Admitted June 17, 1799 by Church Wardens of St. Philip's Church. Delivered to his father, THOMAS ELLIOTT, to become a mariner July 16, 1801. Indentures expired June 17, 1810. (C-80)

FAIR, GEORGE. Admitted October 1, 1792 aged twelve years by MARY BOYER, mother. Indentured to JACOB SASS as a cabinetmaker October 2, 1794. Indentures expired October 1, 1801. (A-14)

FAIR, JOHN. Admitted November 1, 1790 aged seven years by MARY BOYER, mother. Indentured to TIMOTHY and MASON as a printer June 25, 1795. (A-46). Born in Baltimore. (Minutes, November 1, 1790)

FARMER, ROBERT. Admitted March 20, 1797 by ROBERT FARMER, father. Born September 21, 1784. Indentured to WILLIAM SOMARSALL and SON as a naviagtor December 16, 1799. Indentures expired September 21, 1805. (C-23)

FAYOLLE, (FAYOLE), L. ADELAIDE. Admitted October 31, 1793 by MARIANNE FAYOLLE, mother. Delivered to her mother September 7, 1794. Indentures expired February 10, 1806. (B-29). Born February 4, 1788. (Minutes, October 31, 1793)

FAYOLLE (FAYOLE), MARIE JEANNE. Admitted October 31, 1793 by MARIANNE FAYOLLE, mother. Delivered to her mother September 7, 1794. (B-28) Born January 24, 1782. (Minutes, October 31, 1793)

FIELDS, ANDREW. Admitted November 24, 1799 aged five years by JOHN FIELDS, father. Indentured to THOMAS LEE as a cabinetmaker April 10, 1809. Indentures expired November 24, 1815. (C-92)

FIELDS, ELIZABETH. Admitted November 24, 1799 aged seven years by JOHN FIELDS, father. Indentured to MARY ANN CALDWELL as a mantuamaker April 4, 1805. Transferred to CATHERINE SMITH as a domestic March 7, 1806. Transferred to GEORGE PETERS, occupation unknown, January 1, 1808. Indentures expired August 31, 1810. (C-91)

FIGURES, MARY. Admitted June 9, 1796 by BARTHOLOMEW FIGURES, father and a sailmaker. (C-12). Died March __, 1802 of consumption. (Minutes, March 25, 1802)

FIGURES, PETER. Admitted June 9, 1796 aged four years by BARTHOLOMEW FIGURES, father and sailmaker. Indentured to FOSTER BURNET as a house and carriage painter August 14, 1806. Indentures expired February 6, 1813. (C-13). Born February 6, 1792. (Minutes, June 9, 1796). Born in Georgetown. (ROSSC)

FIGURES, RICHARD BARTHOLOMEW. Admitted June 9, 1796 by BARTHOLOMEW FIGURES, father and sailmaker. Indentured to JAMES DRUMMOND as a shoemaker December 16, 1799. Indentures expired June 4, 1808. (C-11) Born in Virginia June 4, 1787. (Minutes, June 7, 1796)

FINDLAY, ANN MARIA. Admitted May 14, 1798 by MARY FINDLAY, mother. (C-58) Died October 8, 1801 of yellow fever. (Medical Matters, Illnesses and Treatments Files, 1801)

FLEMING, JANE. Admitted November 20, 1790 aged nine years. An orphan. Indentured to SARAH and JOHN SPEISSEGER as a seamtress August 21, 1794. Transferred to JOSEPH DICKINSON as a seamtress December 3, 1795. Indentures expired November 20, 1799. (A-60)

FORD (FORT), ANN. Admitted June 27, 1793 aged six years by WINNIFRED RAND, mother. Indentured to FRANCES A.R. PEARSON, wife of CAPTAIN PEARSON, as a domestic November 8, 1802. Transferred to WILLIAM HEMMINGWAY November 15, 1803 as a domestic. Indentures expired June 27, 1805. (A-94). Born on Beach Island, Georgia October __, 1787. (Minutes, June 27, 1793)

FORDHAM, BENJAMIN. Admitted September 3, 1791 aged nine years by MARY FORDHAM, mother. Indentures to THOMAS BAAS as a pump and blockmaker August 3, 1795. Indentures expired September 3, 1803. (A-6)

FRANKS, WILLIAM. Admitted October 28, 1790 aged nine years by MARY FRANKS, mother. Indentured to JOHN CONNOLLY as a mariner December 17, 1794. Indentures expired October 28, 1802. (A-90). Absconded to New York "in a Brig called the Sukey, Captain Sundas', nd. (COH Inmates Files). Returned December 16, 1794 by ISIAH SWAIN of the Brig Eliza. (Ibid)

FULLUM, ANN. Admitted February 21, 1793 aged ten years. Indentures expired February 21, 1801. (A-90). Died March 1798. (Minutes, May 26, 1798)

GLEN, CHARLES. Admitted August 13, 1790 aged nine years and ten months. Indentured to JOSEPH HAZELWOOD as a painter or glazier September 4, 1794. Indentures expired August 13, 1802. (A-28). On August 30, 1794 his age was corrected to be fourteen years. (Minutes, August 30, 1794)

GLEN, JAMES. Admitted November 1, 1791 aged seven years and five months. Indentured to FRENEAU and PAINE as a printer October 25, 1796. Indentures expired November 1, 1805. (A-29)

GLUE, ELIZABETH. Admitted July 28, 1791 aged thirteen years. Indentured to JULIUS SMITH as a seamtress August 9, 1793. Indentures expired July 28, 1796. (A-80). Parents, ANN and RICHARD GLUE. Born in Mt. Holly, New Jersey. (Minutes, July 28, 1791)

GRAY, MARGARET. Admitted November 20, 1790 aged eight years by MARTHA GRAY, mother. Indentured to ANN and ELIZABETH BUFORD, occupation unknown, July 14, 1796. Indentures expired November 20, 1800. (A-63)

GRAY, ELIZABETH. Admitted December 3, 1798 by SARAH EASON, aunt. Indentured to SARAH FRANCIS as a mantuamaker and seamtress April 16, 1789. Indentures expired October 31, 1807. (C-72). Born October 31, 1789. (Minutes, December 3, 1798)

GROATH (GROSS), JOHN. Admitted November 29, 1790 aged nine years by CATHARINE GROATH, mother. Indentured to JACOB SASS as a cabinetmaker November 29, 1794. Indentures expired November 29, 1802. (A-4)

HARRAGAN, TERESIA. Admitted January 9, 1794 by ELEANOR HARRAGAN, mother. Delivered to PETER BOUNETHEAU by his request and with the consent of his mother. Later readmitted, nd. Indentures expired December 23, 1803. (B-38). Born December 23, 1785. (Minutes, January 2, 1794). No further information.

HARRIS, MARY. Admitted November 20, 1790 aged five years. An orphan Indentured to MARIA MORRISON as a mantuamaker and domestic August 31, 1797. Indentures expired November 20, 1803. (A-67)

HARRISON, ELIZABETH. Admitted December 11, 1794 by ANN HARRISON, mother. Born in Cavan Inneskeen, Ireland. Delivered to her mother, ANN GAILBRAITH, August 8, 1798. Indentures expired January 16, 1805. (B-62)

HARRISON, JAMES. Admitted December 11, 1794 by ANN HARRISON, mother. Delivered to his step-father, ROBERT GAILBRAITH, to be taught the house carpentry trade February 16, 1801. Indentures expired February 13, 1811. (B-63)

HARRISON, JOSEPH. Admitted July 3, 1795 aged three years by ANN HARRISON, mother. Delivered to his step-father, ROBERT GAILBRAITH, to be taught the house carpentry trade October 20, 1803. Indentures expired June 12, 1813. (C-2). Born June 12, 1792. (Minutes, July 2, 1795. Father, JOHN, born in Ireland. (ROSSC)

HAYS, JANE. Admitted November 20, 1790 aged six years by DOROTHY GILCHRIST, mother. Delivered to her mother June 9, 1798. Indentures expired November 20, 1802. (A-66). Born in New York. (Minutes, November 20, 1798)

HEINSINGER, ISAAC. Admitted June 21, 1798 by Church Wardens of St. Philip's Church. Indentures expired June 21, 1814. (C-63). No further information.

HEINSINGER, JACOB. Admitted June 21, 1798 by Church Wardens of St. Philip's Church. Indentures expired December 21, 1815. (C-64). No further information.

HEYNEMAN, WILLIAM. Admitted July 17, 1794. Absconded, nd. Indentures expired September 1, 1808. (B-48). The son of VALENTINE HEYNEMAN, born September 1, 1787. (Minutes, July 3, 1794)

HOFF, CHARLES. Admitted September 12, 1793 by MARY BROOKS, mother. Indentured to FRENAU and PAINE as a printer March 24, 1797. Indentures expired January 30, 1805. (B-14). Father, EVERHART HOFF. Born January 30, 1784. (Minutes, October 12, 1793)

HOFF, MICHAEL. Admitted June 9, 1796 by MARY BROOKS, mother. Indentured to CHARLES FRISH (FRISK) as a grocer September 9, 1799. Indentures expired August 1, 1809. (C-14)

HOLLIDAY, MARGARET MARY. Admitted April 28, 1796. (C-10). Died July 10, 1797 of consumption. (Minutes, July 10, 1797)

HOW, MARIA. Admitted November 10, 1797 aged four years by MARY ANN BLAIR, mother. Indentured to MARY LONG as a domestic July ___, 1800. Transferred to ROSINA GYLESS as a milliner and seamstress June 1, 1801. (A-81)

HOW, MICHAEL. Admitted ____, 1791 by MARY ANN BLAIR, mother. Indentured to THOMAS WALKER as a stonecutter August 6, 1795. (A-44). No further information.

HOWELL, JOHN. Admitted November 1, 1790 aged seven years. An orphan. Indentured to FRENAU and PAINE as a printer October 25, 1796. (A-49) No further information.

HUGHES, EDWARD H. Admitted June 21, 1798 by Church Wardens of St. Philip's Church. Indentured to JAMES MAULL as a taylor February 18, 1803. Indentures expired June 27, 1810. (C-62)

HUGHES, ELIZABETH. Admitted January 27, 1791 aged seven years by ELEANOR STONE, mother. Indentured to ANN LEWIS as a domestic May 29, 1798. Indentures expired January 27, 1802. (A-73)

HUGHES, JOHN JAMES. Admitted June 27, 1793 aged four years. (B-7) ELEANOR STONE, mother. Born in Savannah. (Minutes, June 27, 1793)

HUGHES, MARY. Admitted January 27, 1791 aged five years by ELEANOR STONE, mother. Indentured to ELIZABETH QUINBY as a domestic August 20, 1798. Indentures expired January 27, 1804. (A-72)

JOHNSON, JAMES. Admitted March 8, 1792 aged eight years and four months by RACHEL WINSTON, mother-in-law. An orphan. Indentured to ARCHIBALD DUNCAN as a blacksmith February 28, 1797. Indentures expired March 8, 1805. (A-37)

JOHNSON, (JOHNSTON), JAMES. Admitted December 24, 1792 aged ten years and five months. An orphan. Indentured to BENJAMIN CASEY as a coachmaker May 18, 1797. Indentures expired December 24, 1803. (A-43) Born December 24, 1782 in Abbeville County. Mother, RACHEL BAZON and father, JAMES JOHNSON. (Minutes, February 7, 1793)

JOHNSTON (JOHNSON), ELIZABETH. Admitted March 7, 1793 aged thirteen years. Died September 12, 1794. (A-91). Born March 9, 1780. Mother RACHEL BAZON and father, JAMES JOHNSTON. (Minutes, March 7, 1793)

JOHNSTON, THOMAS. Admitted August 25, 1791 aged six years. An orphan. Indentured to JAMES DRUMMOND as a shoemaker November 17, 1798. Indentures expired August 25, 1806. (A-106)

JONES, ABRAHAM. Admitted October 22, 1791 aged nine years and seven months by MARY HOWARD, mother. Indentured to JOHN DOUGLAS as a cabinetmaker August 21, 1795. Indentures expired October 22, 1803. (A-25)

JUGGS, BENJAMIN. Admitted November 1, 1790 aged four years. Indentured to NEAL McLARTY as a boatbuilder July 29, 1799. Transferred to JACOB BUNCE, occupation unknown, September 15, 1703. Indentures expired November 1, 1807. (A-101)

KELLY, MARGARET. Admitted November 20, 1790 aged fourteen years by ANN KEILY, mother. Indentured to WILLIAM HOLMES as a seamtress August 9, 1791. Indentures expired November 20, 1795. (A-71)

KELLER, JOHN ANDREW. Admitted May 9, 1790 aged nine years and two months by HENRY KELLER, father. Indentured to JAMES COURTENAY as a taylor January 31, 1797. Indentures expired May 9, 1804. (A-38)

KIMMONS, JOHN. Admitted _____, 1795 by MARY CARTER, mother. Indentured to PHILIP CRASK as a painter and glazier July 25, 1805. Indentures expired December 1, 1812. (B-86). Father, ROBERT KIMMONS. (ROSSC)

KINGDON, ABRAHAM. Admitted August 18, 1796 aged two years. An orphan. Parents, THOMAS and SARAH KINGDON, from London. Indentured to OWEN PHILIP ROBERTS as an architect and house carpenter June 30, 1808. Transferred to JOHN EVANS as a boot and shoemaker March 14, 1811. Indentures expired August 18, 1815. (C-19)

KINGDON, HENRY. Admitted August 18, 1796 aged seven years. An orphan. Parents THOMAS and SARAH KINGDON from London. Indentured to WILLIAM GREEN, brother-in-law, to train as a wheelwright November 29, 1804. Transferred to OWEN P. ROBERTS as an architect and carpenter June 9, 1808. Indentures expired August 18, 1810. (C-18)

KINGDON, THOMAS. Admitted August 18, 1796. An orphan. Parents, THOMAS and SARAH KINGDON, from London. Indentured to HENRY INGLESBY as a taylor November 13, 1798. Indentures expired November 13, 1806. (C-17)

KRUGER, CHARLES. Admitted July 28, 1796 by MATTA KRUGER, mother. Indentures expired September 17, 1812. (C-16). No further information.

LAMBERT, LOUISE ELIZABETH. Admitted October 24, 1793 by JEAN JACQUES LAMBERT, father. From Grand Riverre. Delivered to her father June 8, 1796. Indentures expired June 29, 1805. (B-25). Born June 29, 17871 Mother, LOUISE FELICITE LETETTIER LAMBERT. (Minutes, October 24, 1793)

LAMBERT, MARIE CATHERINE. Admitted October 24, 1793 by JEAN JACQUES LAMBERT, father. Of Grand Riverre. Delivered to her father June 8, 1796. Indentures expired October 17, 1808. (B-27). Born October 17, 1790. (Minutes, October 24, 1793)

LAMBERT, MICHAEL. Admitted October 24, 1793 by JEAN JACQUES LAMBERT, father. Of Grand Riverre. Delivered to his father June 8, 1796. Indentures expired March 21, 1810. (B-26)

LAUNDERSHEIM (LANDERSHINE), MARY. Admitted July 7, 1791 aged seven years by MARY LONG, mother. Indentured to CHRISTINA and ELIZABETH MARTIN as a seamtress June 3, 1796. Transferred to her mother March 7, 1797. Indentures expired July 7, 1802. (A-79)

LAUNDERSHEIM, CHRISTIAN. Admitted November 10, 1794 by MARY LONG, mother. Indentured to JAMES DRUMMOND as a shoemaker May 4, 1799. Indentures expired January 10, 1808. (B-57)

LETELLIER, JOSEPH. Admitted March 10, 1794 by JEAN JACQUES LAMBERT, cousin. A son of JACQUES LETELLIER of Cape Francois. Absconded, nd. Indentures expired March 10, 1805. (B-43)

LEWIS, BENJAMIN. Admitted December 14, 1792 aged seven years and seven months. An orphan. Indentures to ARCHIBALD BREBNER as a taylor May 4, 1799. Transferred to CHARLES LOWRY as a taylor February 10, 1802. Indentures expired December 14, 1807. (A-50)

LEWIS, JOHN. Admitted December 13, 1792 aged four years and four months by CHRISTIANA LEWIS, mother. Indentures expired December 13, 1809. (B-4). Born August 9, 1788. (Minutes, December 13, 1792) Died September 16, 1796. (Minutes, September 22, 1796)

LINDERSHINE, CHRISTIAN. Admitted January 10, 1792 aged six years and six months by MARY LINDERSHINE, mother. Indentured to SAMUEL GRUBER as a house carpenter June 17, 1799. Transferred to JACOB STROUB as a house carpenter November 24, 1799. Indentures expired January 10, 1806. (A-9). Born January 10, 1787. (Minutes, November 11, 1792)

LOGAN, GEORGE ROBERT. Admitted April 19, 1792 aged six years by ANN LOGAN, mother. Indentured to HENRY BAILEY as an attorney March 22, 1800. (B-1). No further information.

LOGAN, JOHN. Admitted April 19, 1792 aged eight years. Indentured to WILLIAM and JAMES THAYER as a sailor July 21, 1794. Indentures expired April 19, 1803. (A-48). ANN ROWLY, mother. (Minutes, April 19, 1792)

LOWRY, ANDREW. Admitted October 16, 1798 aged eight years by JOHN LOWRY, brother. Indentured to EDWARD LYNCH as a planter February 27, 1806. Indentures expired October 16, 1811. (C-71)

LOWRY, MICHAEL. Admitted October 16, 1798 aged ten years by JOHN LOWRY, brother. Indentured to SAMUEL CORRIE as a wheelwright July 14, 1803. Indentures expired October 16, 1809. (C-70)

LOWRY, ROBERT. Admitted October 4, 1792 aged six years by JOHN LOWRY, father. Indentured to JACOB STOLL as a tinplate worker November 26, 1796. Indentures expired October 4, 1807. (B-2)

LYNCH, JAMES. Admitted August 20, 1795 by MARGARET LYNCH, mother and widow of BERNARD LYNCH. Died October 18, 1795. Indentures expired _____, 1806. (C-4)

LYNCH, PATRICK. Admitted August 20, 1795 by MARGARET LYNCH, mother and widow of BERNARD LYNCH. Indentures expired May 3, 1812. (C-3) No further information.

McAVOY, THOMAS. Admitted April 1, 1791 aged ten years by THOMAS McAVOY, father. Of County Kerry, Ireland. Indentured to JOHN PRATT as a mariner January 24, 1794. Indentures expired April ___, 1802. (A-23)

McCARTEY, JOHN. Admitted May 31, 1797 aged five years by JAMES GORDON, friend. Indentured to PETER TIMOTHY MARCHANT, A.S. WILLINGTON, A.C. CARPENTER, and FREDERICK DALCHO as a printer January 23, 1806. Indentures expired May 31, 1811. (C-35)

McCOUN (McCOWN), PETER. Admitted December 14, 1791 aged nine years. An orphan, son of PETER and ELIZABETH McCOUN. Indentured to JOHN DOUGLAS as a cabinetmaker October 13, 1795. Transferred to DAVID BLAIN, occupation unknown, August 2, 1796. (A-27)

McGUIRE, ELIZABETH. Admitted August 2, 1792 aged nine years. Indentured to ANN HALL as a domestic October 23, 1797. Indentures expired August 2, 1801. (A-87). Father, BARNEY McGUIRE. (Minutes, August 2, 1792)

McKENZIE, MARGARET. Admitted April 14, 1791 aged four years by SARAH McKENZIE, mother. Delivered to her mother May 19, 1796. Indentures expired April 14, 1805. (A-77)

McKIMMEY, (McKINNEY), WILLIAM. Admitted May 8, 1794 by JOHN McKIMMEY, father and a bricklayer. Born April 27, 1787. Indentured to GEORGE GIBBES as a baker August ___, 1800. Indentures expired April 27, 1808. (B-46)

McLEAN, SARAH. Admitted November 20, 1790 aged thirteen years by ELIZABETH McLEAN, mother. Indentured to S. DAVID HAMILTON, occupation unknown, August 9, 1793. Indentures expired November 20, 1795. (A-54)

McMULLIN, JOHN. Admitted November 1, 1790 aged eight years. Indentured to JOHN PRATT as a mariner June 25, 1795. Indentures expired November 1, 1703. (A-47)

McPHERSON, ALEXANDER. Admitted March 1, 1790 aged ten years. Indentured to EILLIAM WILLIAMS as a tinplate worker May 22, 1795. Transferred to ROBERT BEARD, occupation unknown, January 27, 1796. Indentures expired March 25, 1802. (A-13)

McQUEEN, JEAN. Admitted November 20, 1790 aged eleven years. Died April 27, 1794. (A-55)

MAGRATH, EDWARD. Admitted January 23, 1791 aged eleven years and four months by HANNAH MAGRATH, mother. Indentured to JOHN CHAMPNEYS as a wharfinger October 12, 1793. Indentures expired January 23, 1801. (A-26)

MAHONEY, MARY. Admitted October 10, 1793 by JOHN and MARY MAHONEY, parents. Indentured to JENNET and CHRISTOPHER FULLER as a seamstress and housekeeper November 8, 1802. Indentures expired December 29, 1804. (B-22)

MAILLIART, ANDREW. Admitted September 26, 1793 by FRANCOIS MAILLAIRT, parent. Delivered to his parents June 24, 1795. (B-17). Father, born in Nanby, France, was a carpenter. Born June 16, 1790 in Cape Francois. (Minutes, September 26, 1793)

MAILLART, JOHN BAPTISTE. Admitted September 26, 1793 by FRANCOIS MAILLART, parent. Delivered to his parents June 24, 1795. (B-16). Born March 15, 1784 at Cape Francois. (Minutes, September 26, 1793)

MAIRS, RICHARD. Admitted May 29, 1793 by Church Wardens of St. Philip's Church. Indentures expired May 29, 1809. (C-60) Sent to the Poor House in January 1799 because of his idiocy. (Minutes, January 7, 1799)

MAROMET, ANN. Admitted December 16, 1796. Indentured to MARTHA BOLTON as a domestic December 14, 1797. Indentures expired December 16, 1802. (C-21). Elected teacher August 12, 1797. (Minutes, August 12, 1797)

MARSH, CATHERINE. Admitted November 10, 1791 aged ten years by ELEANOR HILL, mother. Indentured to ROGER PARKER SAUNDERS, occupation unknown, March 24, 1795. Transferred

MARSH, JAMES. Admitted October 25, 1792 aged six years. Indentures expired October 25, 1807. (B-3). No further information.

MARSH, WILLIAM. Admitted November 1, 1790 aged five years by ELEANOR
(ELINOR) HILL, mother. Indentured to THOMAS SCOTT as a mariner
October 4, 1797. Indentures expired November 1, 1806. (A-99)

MARSHALL, MARGARET. Admitted January 7, 1796 by ALICE MARSHALL, mother
and a widow. Indentures expired December 24, 1803. (C-7). Born
December 24, 1785. (Minutes, January 7, 1796). No further information.

MARSHALL, SARAH. Admitted January 11, 1796 by ALICE MARSHALL, mother
and a widow. Delivered to her mother May 23, 1799. Indentures expired
May 20, 1806. (C-8). Born May 20, 1788. (Minutes, January 7, 1796)

MEARS, JOHN. Admitted June 27, 1793 aged five years by JOHN MEARS,
father. Died May 9, 1794. (B-8). Born January 1, 1788. Mother, MARY.
(Minutes, June 27, 1793)

MEARS, WILLIAM. Admitted June 27, 1793 aged four years by JOHN MEARS,
father. Indentures expired June 27, 1810. (B-9). Died September 21,
1796. (Minutes, September 22, 1796). Born April 21, 1789. (Minutes,
June 27, 1793)

MELLAIN, JEAN BAPTISTE JOSEPH BENJAMIN. Admitted January 2, 1794 by
JOHN BAPTISTE ANTOINE MELLAIN, father. Born November 2, 1783 at Cape
Francois. Indentures expired November 2, 1804. (B-37). No further
information.

MERLIN, HENRY. Admitted January 16, 1794 by MARIE LOUISE DROUET,
mother. Died, nd. Indentures expired May 29, 1807. (B-40). Born
April 14, 1783. (Minutes, January 16, 1794)

MERLIN, SIMON FRANCOIS. Admitted January 16, 1794 by MARIE LOUISE
DROUET, mother. Absconded, nd. Indentures expired April 14, 1804.
(B-39). Born May 29, 1786. (Minutes, January 16, 1794)

MILLER, JOHN. Admitted June 23, 1791 aged seven years by MARY MILLER,
mother. Delivered to his mother, nd. Indentures expired June 23,
1805. (A-40)

MILLIGAN, WILLIAM. Admitted December 9, 1790 aged nine years by
ELIZABETH MILLIGAN, mother. Indentured to WILLIAM PRITCHARD as a
ship carpenter March 2, 1795. Indentures expired December 9, 1802.
(A-3)

MITCHELL, JOHN. Admitted July 1, 1799 aged seven years by SARAH MITCHELL,
mother. Indentured to JOSEPH MILLIGAN as a merchant and accountant
July 17, 1806. Transferred to THOMAS FLEMMING as a merchant July 1,
_____. Indentures expired February 28, 1813. (C-81)

MITCHELL, MARY. Admitted July 1, 1799 aged seven years by SARAH
MITCHELL, mother. Indentured to ELIZA FRANCES CARRERE as a domestic
December 12, 1805. Indentures expired February 28, 1810. (C-81)

MORIARTY, JEAN BAPTISTE. Admitted December 20, 1795 by MARIA MERCIER,
aunt. An orphan. Delivered to his aunt June 4, 1798 to sail to
St. Domingo. (C-6)

NAUMAN, CATHERINE. Admitted January 22, 1795. Indentured to MARGARET
HORLBECK as a domestic May 29, 1798. Indentures expired November 19,
1804. (B-65). Born November 19, 1786. Parents, MARGARET and JOHN
NAUMAN. (Minutes, January 8, 1795)

NEDDERMAN, MARIA WILHELMINA. Admitted December 21, 1796 aged four years
by ANN NEDDERMAN, mother. Indentured to SARAH BREMER NORTON as a
domestic June 4, 1807. Indentures expired March 15, 1810. (C-22)

NEILSON, CHARLES. Admitted September 1, 1795 by ANDREW NEILSON, father
and a tinsmith of Lisbourne, Ireland. Born June 1, 1794. Died nd.
Indentures expired June 1, 1815. (C-20)

NELSON, JANE. Admitted October 16, 1790 by JANE NELSON, grandmother. (C986). Died December 17, 1799 of croup. (Minutes, December 17, 1799)

NORRIS, STEPHEN. Admitted July 1, 1790 aged ten years. An orphan. Mother, MARY NORO. Indentured to CHARLES MORGAN as a shipwright May 22, 1795. Indentures expired July 1, 1801. (A-20)

O'KEEFE, PHILIP. Admitted January 29, 1798 aged five years and nine months by MARY O'KEEFE, mother. Indentured to SAMUEL E. ASH as a coach & harness maker November 29, 1804. Indentures expired May 7, 1810. (C-53)

O'KEEFE, THOMAS. Admitted January 29, 1798 aged six years and nine months by MARY O'KEEFE, mother. Indentured to DANIEL STEVENS, JR., SAMUEL E. ASH, and GEORGE NORTON REYNOLDS as a coachmaker and trimmer November 24, 1803. Indentures expired May 27, 1811. (C-52)

OLIVER, THOMAS. Admitted December 11, 1794. Absconded June 16, 1796 and returned December 8, 1797. Indentured to JAMES GIBSON as a coach-maker April 6, 1798. Indentures expired July 6, 1805. (B-61)

PHRON, JOHN. Admitted December 27, 1792 aged eleven years and seven months by SUSANNA ALEBITEN (sp?), aunt. Indentured to JACOB STOLL as a tinmaker February 26, 1795. Indentures expired December 27, 1802. (A-11)

POPE, ELIZABETH. Admitted May 31, 1797 by MARY POPE, mother. Born April 16, 1790. Indentured to MARIA WILLARD SOMARSALL as a domestic November 8, 1802. Indentures expired April 16, 1808. (C-36)

POPE, JOHN. Admitted May 31, 1797 aged five years and six months by MARY POPE, mother. Born September 12, 1791. Delivered to his friends who lived in Roxbury, Massachusetts May 9, 1805. Indentures expired September 12, 1812. (C-37). Born in Boston. (Minutes, May 31, 1797)

QUAN, ROBERT. Admitted August 25, 1791 aged four years by MARTHA QUAN, mother. Indentured to EDWARD NORTH as a merchant January 8, 1798. Indentures expired August 25, 1808. (A-105)

RAMBERT, RACHEL. Admitted September 15, 1797 by MARY RAMBERT, mother. Indentured to CATHERINE CUDWORTH, wife of BENJAMIN CUDWORTH, Steward of the Orphan House, as a domestic July 11, 1800. Indentures expired December 25, 1806. (C-44)

RASDALE, JOHN WILLIAM. Admitted August 8, 1793 by ELIZA MURPHY, mother. Absconded, nd. Indentures expired March 10, 1810. (B-11)

RATCLIFFE, JOHN. Admitted April 6, 1798. Indentured to HENRY INGLESBY as a taylor May 4, 1799. Indentures expired July 6, 1805. (C-57)

REILEY, MOLSEY. Admitted November 24, 1799 by Church Wardens of St. Philip's Church. Died, nd. Indentures expired November 24, 1806. (C-90)

RELEQUIST, JOSEPHINE. Admitted October 30, 1793 by MAGORITE RELEQUIST, mother. Absconded, nd. Indentures expired March 15, 1807. (B-30) Born March 15, 1789. (Minutes, October 30, 1793)

REMLEY, ELIZABETH. Admitted March 22, 1798 aged five years by MARY REMLEY, mother. Indentured to JAMES ROBINSON (of Winnsborough in the County of Fairfield) as a domestic June 22, 1805. Indentures expired February 18, 1811. (C-56)

REMLEY, HENRY. Admitted March 22, 1798 aged seven years by MARY REMLEY, mother. Indentured to WILLIAM CHUCKSHANKS as a shoemaker September 13, 1805. Indentures expired January 26, 1812. (C-55)

REYER, JOHN. Admitted November 7, 1799 aged eleven years by ELIZABETH REYER, mother. Indentured to WILLIAM HOGARTH, JR. as a shoemaker September 6, 1805. Indentures expired November 7, 1809. (C-87)

RICHARDS, CHARLES. Admitted September 25, 1794 aged six years and two months by CASPER and BARBARA RICHARDS, parents. Indentured to WILLIAM BRAND as a bricklayer and mason November 17, 1803. Transferred to JOHN KEARNEY as a bricklayer May 7, 1804. Indentures expired September 25, 1808. (B-51). Born January 31, 1787. (Minutes, September 25, 1794). His daughter, ANN ELIZABETH OWENS, admitted her children, April 10, 1856. (Minutes, April 10, 1856)

RICHARDS, FREDERICK. Admitted September 25, 1794 aged five years by CASPER and BARBARA RICHARDS, parents. Indentured to JOHN HOWARD as a bricklayer June 23, 1803. Indentures expired September 25, 1810. (B-52). Born October 15, 1789. (Minutes, September 25, 1794)

RICHE, JOHN. Admitted October 6, 1791 aged seven years and six months by MARY RICHE, mother. Indentures expired October 6, 1805. (A-107) Born in Jacksonborough and delivered to his step-father, JOHN BROWN, (ROSSC) "Weak in intellect and a cripple". (Ibid)

RITCHIE, MARY. Admitted January 22, 1795 by FRANCES RITFIELD, mother. Died, nd. Indentures expired December 17, 1809. (B-64)

RITIFIELD, HENRY. Admitted March 28, 1799 aged nine years by SARAH RITFIELD, mother. Indentured to THOMAS and JOHN DUGAN as a bricklayer March 20, 1805. Indentures expired March 28, 1812. (D-6)

ROGERS (RODGERS), LEWIS. Admitted August 20, 1798 aged five years by Church Wardens of St. Philip's Church. Indentured to JOHN ZYLK as a wheelwright and chainmaker December 12, 1807. Transferred to WILLIAM VANVELSEY, occupation unknown, October 28, 1813. Indentures expired August 20, 1815. (C-68)

ROSENBOHN, CATHERINE. Admitted September 28, 1797 by CATHERINE ROSENBOHN, mother. Delivered to her mother, CATHERINE GRUBER, June 11, 1800. Transferred to ELIZA FRANCES CARRERE as a domestic August 23, 1804. Indentures expired December 22, 1807. (C-45). Transferred to the wife of CAPTAIN WILLIAM HALL as a domestic May 10, 1805. (ROSSC)

ROSENBOHN, JOHN. Admitted September 28, 1797 by CATHERINE ROSENBOHN, mother. Indentures expired October 2, 1811. (C-46) No further information

ROSEHBOHN, MARY. Admitted September 28, 1797 aged three years by CATHERINE ROSENBOHN, mother. Indentured to ELIZA FRANCES CARRERE as a domestic August 23, 1804. Indentures expired January 22, 1812. (C-47)

ROUIER, JEAN BAPTISTE PIERRE. Admitted October 13, 1793 by MARIE ROUIER, mother. Absconded, nd. Indentures expired December 1, 1804. (B-31)

ROWE, DOROTHY. Admitted November 20, 1790 aged seven years by MARY MAGDALENE ROWE, sister. Indentured to GEORGE PRITCHARD as a seamtress April 5, 1797. Transferred to MARY CARPENTER, occupation unknown, October 25, 1799. Indentures expired November 20, 1801. (A-65)

ROWE, PAUL. Admitted May 11, 1790 aged ten years by MARY MAGDALENE ROWE, sister. Indentured to CHARLES WATTS as a cabinetmaker November 20, 1794. (A-12)

RUTLEDGE, ANDREW. Admitted March 9, 1790 aged ten years by ANDREW and CATHERINE DAVIS, unknown. Indentures expired March 9, 1801. (A-1) Refused to be bound out and was removed from the Institution. (Minutes, October 10, 1793)

SCOTT, WILLIAM. Admitted November 14, 1790 aged ten years. Indentured to JAMES SPEAR as a carpenter October 23, 1794. Indentures expired November 14, 1801. (A-2)

SEALE, NANCY. Admitted August 22, 1793 by CATHERINE SEALE, mother.
Carried away by her parents, nd. Indentures expired November 20, 1805.
(B-13). Born November 20, 1787. Father, JOHN SEALE. (Minutes,
August 22, 1793)

SHAFFER, CHARLES G. Admitted August 8, 1798 aged seven years by
MARGARET SHAFFER, mother. Indentured to PETER FRENAU and DAVID WILLIAMS
as a printer April 28, 1803. Indentures expired January 17, 1811. (C-66)

SHAFFER, FREDERICK. Admitted April 18, 1799 aged three years by MARGARET
SHAFFER, mother. Indentured to GILBERT McCLYMONT and PATRICK McCLURE
as a grocer and accountant April 13, 1809. Indentures expired April
18, 1817. (C-76)

SHAFFER, MICHAEL. Admitted April 18, 1799 aged seven years by MARGARET
SHAFFER, mother. Indentured to JOHNSON and FINCH as a cut nail
manufacturer September 13, 1805. Indentures expired April 18, 1813.
(C-75)

SHEFFER (SHAFER), CATHERINE. Admitted August 8, 1798 by MARGARET
SHEFFER, mother. Indentured to ANNA BENNETT as a domestic October 7,
1802. Indentures expired June 7, 1807. (C-65)

SICKLES, MARGARET. Admitted May 10, 1792 aged seven years by THEOPHILUS
ELSWORTH, unknown. Indentures expired May 10, 1803. (A-84). Sent
to relatives in New York in August 1795. (Minutes, August 6, 1795)

SINGLETARY, STEPHEN G. Admitted March 21, 1795 by MARY SUSANNAH
SINGLETARY, mother. Indentured to BRIAN CANE as an insurance broker
and factor September 15, 1797. Indentures expired October 26, 1806.
(B-69)

SINGLETARY, STEPHEN THOMAS. Admitted May 11, 1799 aged eight years by
MARY SUSANNAH SINGLETARY, mother. Indentured to WILLIAM KEATING as
a merchant and accountant September 3, 1806. Indentures expired
December 28, 1812. (C-79)

SINGLETON, JAMES. Admitted April 22, 1799 by the Poor House. Indentured
to PETER FRENAU as a printer February 14, 1805. Indentures expired
April 22, 1812. (C-78)

SMITH, CATHERINE. Admitted November 7, 1793 by CATHERINE SMITH, mother.
Remained in the House until of age. Indentures expired March 15,
1803. (B-35). Born March 15, 1785. (Minutes, November 7, 1793)

SMITH, JAMES. Admitted July 29, 1799 by Church Wardens of St. Philip's
Church. Indentured to JAMES CLARK as a coachmaker July 31, 1799.
Indentures expired July 19, 1808. (C-83)

SMITH, MARY. Admitted November 20, 1790 aged eight years. An orphan.
Indentures expired November 20, 1800. (A-62). Indentured to MRS.
MARIA FOWLER as a mantuamaker June 2, 1796. (Minutes, June 2, 1796)

SOWERS, ELIZABETH. Admitted November 20, 1790 aged ten years by CATHERINE
LEGG, aunt. Indentured to MARY and BENJAMIN DUPREE as a mantuamaker
September 12, 1793. Indentures expired November 20, 1798. (A-59)
Returned to the Institution September 19, 1793. (Minutes, September
19, 1793). Indentured to ANNE HENRY as a milliner November 21, 1793.
(B-36)

SPENCE, ADAM. Admitted May 18, 1797 by SARAH SPENCE, mother. Born
September 10, 1787. Indentured to ROBERT GIBSON, step-father, as a
blacksmith February 16, 1801. Indentures expired September 10, 1808.
(C-31)

SPENCE, WILLIAM. Admitted May 18, 1797 by SARAH SPENCE, mother. Born
February 14, 1790. Indentured to JOHN CUNNINGHAM and JOHN O'NEALE as
a merchant and bookkeeper September 2, 1802. Indentures expired
February 14, 1811. (C-32)

STANDLAND, MARY. Admitted July 5, 1792 aged eleven years. Absconded nd. Indentures expired July 5, 1799. (A-86)

STECKER, JOHN CHARLES. Admitted November 16, 1797 by Rev. JOHN CHRISTOPHER FABER, friend. (C-49). Died March 1798. (Minutes, May 26, 1798)

STILLWELL, SAMUEL. Admitted May 26, 1791 aged two years and six months by MARY STILLWELL, mother. Indentured to JAMES DRUMMOND as a shoemaker January 11, 1801. Indentures expired May 26, 1809. (A-104)

SUDER, CHARLOTTE. Admitted November 7, 1799 by ELIZABETH SUDER, mother. Indentured to MARY LONG, wife of JOHN LONG, as a domestic November 8, 1802. Indentures expired November 7, 1806. (C-89)

SWORDS, JOHN THOMAS. Admitted August 8, 1793 by MARGARET GRAHAM, mother. Indentured to GEORGE BROWN as a taylor August 31, 1797. Transferred to SIMON ELSTOB as a house painter May 4, 1799. (B-10). Born December 1, 1786. (Minutes, August 8, 1793)

SYKES, MARY ANN. Admitted November 13, 1794 by ANN ASHMAN, mother. Indentures expired January 28, 1802. (B-60). Delivered to her mother January 4, 1796. (Minutes, January 4, 1796)

SYKES, THOMAS ABRAHAM. Admitted November 10, 1795 by ANN ASHMAN, mother. Indentures expired May 20, 1807. (B-58). Delivered to his mother January 4, 1796. (Minutes, January 4, 1796)

TARDIEU, LEWIS. Admitted September 26, 1793 by LOUISA ALEXANDRA GRACE TARDIEU, mother. Absconded aboard a privateer, nd. Indentures expired August 25, 1803. (B-15). Father, MICHEL TARDIEU, a captain and merchant of Cape Francis. Born August 25, 1782. (Minutes, September 26, 1793)

TENNANT, JAMES. Admitted October 12, 1793. Parents, JOHN and ELIZABETH TENNANT. Indentured to JAMES COURTENAY as a taylor January 31, 1797. Indentures expired January 12, 1807. (B-21). Born January 12, 1786. (Minutes, October 10, 1793)

TENNANT, THOMAS. Admitted March 5, 1791 aged ten years and three months. An orphan. Indentured to WILLIAM WILLIAMS as a tinplate worker October 13, 1795. Transferred to JOHN FREW as a tinplate worker January 27, 1796. Transferred to JOHN MARSHALL as a cabinetmaker November 21, 1796. Indentures expired March 5, 1802. (A-32)

THOMASON, JAMES. Admitted November 1, 1790 aged five years. An orphan. Indentured to JOHN PHILLIPS as a painter and glazier July 1, 1799. Indentures expired November 1, 1806. (A-100)

THOMSON, MARY ANN. Admitted January 27, 1798 by ELIZABETH THOMSON, mother. Indentured to JANE THORNEY as a domestic March 19, 1801. Indentures expired December 10, 1805. (C-50)

THOMSON, SUSANNAH. Admitted January 27, 1798 by ELIZABETH THOMSON, mother. Delivered to ELIZABETH KENNEDY, aunt, as a domestic January 20, 1803. Indentures expired June 25, 1809. (C-51)

TURNER, ANN. Admitted March 26, 1795 by CATHERINE TURNER, mother. Indentured to KEZIA NORRIS as a seamstress February 13, 1798. Transferred to ANN WIDDELL, occupation unknown, May 29, 1798. Indentures expired April 7, 1803. (B-71)

TURNIER, HESTER. Admitted November 20, 1790 aged eleven years. Indentured to THOMAS BRADFORD as an upholsterer August 9, 1793. Indentures expired November 20, 1797. (A-57)

TWINING, JOHN. Admitted October 23, 1794 by MARGARET TWINING, mother. Indentured to CAPTAIN THOMAS CHISOLM as a seaman and navigator November 2, 1799. Indentures expired April 12, 1809. (B-53). Father, HENRY TWINING, dead. Born April 12, 1788 at Wilmington, North Carolina. (Minutes, October 6, 1794)

VANDERLINDA, JOHN. Admitted November 18, 1791 aged seven years and four months by his mother, unknown. Indentured to JOHN FREDERICK KERN as a mariner on the ship Harmony August 21, 1795. Indentures expired November 18, 1804. (A-39). Born in the Netherlands. (Minutes, November 18, 1791)

VLIEX (FLIXX), TRACEY (SERESA). Admitted June 8, 1798 by FREDERICK VLIEX, father. Indentured to ELIZABETH MARTIN as a domestic February 26, 1807. Indentures expired December 26, 1811. (C-61)

WALKER, ELIZA. Admitted November 20, 1790 aged four years. Indentured to RACHEL MONK as a mantuamaker December 3, 1798. Transferred to AMARANTHIA SEREVEN as a domestic Axgust 9, 1793. Indentures expired November 20, 1804. (A-70)

WALKER, HARRIET. Admitted October 13, 1790 aged seven years by MARTHA WALKER, mother. Indentured to WILLIAM and SARAH TUNNO as a domestic January 1, 1796. Indentures expired January 20, 1801. (A-72)

WALTER, MARY. Admitted April 19, 1792 aged four years. Delivered to her father, nd. Indentures expired April 19, 1806. (A-83). Parents, CATHERINE and WILLIAM WALTER. (Minutes, April 19, 1792)

WALTER, THOMAS. Admitted February 23, 1792 aged six years by WILLIAM WALTER, unknown. Indentured to DAVID OLIPHANT as a painter, particularly a coach painter October 20, 1796. (A-51)

WALTERS, WILLIAM. Admitted December 27, 1790 aged ten years and six months by WILLIAM WALTERS, father. Indentures expired December 27, 1801. (A-34). Born in Baltimore. (Minutes, February 23, 1792) Absconded aboard a French privateer, April 14, 1796. (Minutes, April 14, 1796)

WARD, SUSANNAH. Admitted September 20, 1792 aged three years. An orphan. Indentured to CORNELIA GLEN as a domestic January 19, 1804. Transferred to MARTHA SMALLWOOD, occupation unknown, July 10, 1806. Indentures expired September 20, 1807. (A-88). Parents, WILLIAM and ELIZA WARD. (ROSSC)

WEAVER, SARAH. Admitted June 23, 1791 aged nine years by CHRISTIANA WEAVER, mother. Indentured to ANN HENRY as a milliner February 27, 1795. Transferred to SUSANNA BRYAN as a seamstress October 6, 1795. Indentures expired June 23, 1800. (A-78). Born March 5, 1782. (Minutes, June 23, 1791)

WELSH, MARGARET. Admitted June 27, 1793 aged seven years. Indentured to THOMAS ROPER as a domestic July 14, 1802. Indentures expired June 27, 1805. (A-92). Mother, MARGARET WELSH. Born in Limerick, Ireland in May 1787. (Minutes, June 27, 1793)

WHEELER, JOHN. Admitted March 1, 1790 aged ten years by SARAH WHEELER, mother. Indentured to GEORGE NORRIS as a saddler October 23, 1794. Indentures expired March 1, 1801. (A-15)

WHEELER, ZACHARIAH. Admitted November 22, 1790 aged seven years and seven months by SARAH WHEELER, mother. Indentured to DAVID OLIPHANT as a coach painter October 28, 1796. Transferred to RAYMOND CLIFFEY occupation unknown, March 3, 1802. Indentures expired November 22, 1804. (A-31)

WHITNEY, THOMAS HENRY, Admitted January 4, 1791 aged ten years by MARYANN WHITNEY, mother. Indentured to WILLIAM GARDNER as a carver and gilder February 29, 1795. Indentures expired January 4, 1802. (A-5)

WILKINSON, SARAH. Admitted November 20, 1790 aged eleven years. An orphan. Indentured to CHARLES BRADFORD as a seamstress September 5, 1793. Transferred to GEORGE WAGNER, occupation unknown, December 3, 1795. Transferred to CHARLES HOWARD SIMONS, occupation unknown, nd. Indentures expired November 20, 1797. (A-56). Became pregnant by Charles H. Simon's son. At first, Sarah claimed Charles H. Simon was

WILKINSON, SARAH, cont'd. the father; however, later she admitted the son had fathered her child. Sarah was sent to a house near Santee to have her baby. (Minutes, July 29, 1797). In November 1797 the Commissioners agreed to send "some Necessaries for Sarah Wilkinson's child, and to allow a Sum not five pounds for the purpose." (Minutes, November 11, 1797)

WOOD, JACOB. Admitted June 6, 1791 aged ten years by MARY WOOD, mother. Absconded, nd. Indentures expired June 26, 1804. (A-17)

WOOLF, ANN. Admitted August 7, 1794 by MARY KNIGHT, grandmother. Indentured to REBECCA PILSBURY as a mantuamaker December 3, 1798. Indentures expired January 15, 1804. (B-49)

YATES, ELEANOR. Admitted March 22, 1798 by WILLIAM YATES, father. Indentures expired December 22, 1804. (C-54). Sent to her father in 1800 because she was "thought to be a detriment to the other girls." (Minutes, March 28, 1800)

ZOELLER, JOHN JACOB. Admitted August 11, 1797 aged six years by PHILIP ZOELLER, father. Died December 14, 1797 of dropsy of the head. (Minutes, January 20, 1798).

1800 - 1810

AGNEW, JAMES. Admitted July 12, 1809 aged three years by MARY AGNEW, mother. Indentured to SAMUEL PEARSE (of Columbia) as a tinplate worker January 26, 1820. Indentures expired July 14, 1827. (F-34) Born in Charleston. (Minutes, July 13, 1809)

AIRS (AYRES), ELIZABETH. Admitted October 6, 1803 aged nine years by MARY McCELLAND, guardian. Indentured to DANIEL McMILLAN (of Chester District) as a domestic December 12, 1807. Indentures expired October 6, 1812. (D-96) Born in Charleston. (ROSSC)

ARNOLD, JOHN B. Admitted June 23, 1803 aged four years by MARY ARNOLD, mother. Indentured to JAMES and JOHN GORDON as a bricklayer November 12, 1812. Transferred to JOHN FERGUSON as a taylor April 7, 1814. Indentures expired September 23, 1820. (D-90) Born in Charleston. (ROSSC)

ARNOLD, THOMAS. Admitted June 23, 1803 aged eleven years by MARY ARNOLD, mother. Died March 3, 1804. (D-77) Born in Charleston. (ROSSC)

ASHLEY, MARY. Admitted January 17, 1805 aged six years by MARGARET GREEN, mother. Indentured to MARGARET COCHRAN as a mantuamaker December 6, 1810. Transferred to SAMUEL THOMB, occupation unknown, November 3, 1812. Indentures expired January 17, 1816. (E-47) "The natural daughter of a sailor." (Minutes, January 10, 1805)

BAYNE, ANN. Admitted March 23, 1800 by the Poor House. Indentures expired March 28, 1809. (D-8) No further information.

BERRY, THOMAS. Admitted November 16, 1809 aged six years by CATHERINE BERRY, mother. Born in New York, now in the Poor House. Indentured to WILLIAM VANVELSEY as a wheelwright February 26, 1818. Indentures expired November 16, 1824. (F-38)

BERRY, WILLIAM. Admitted November 16, 1809 aged eight years by CATHERINE BERRY, mother. Born in Philadelphia, now in the Poor House. Indentured to DAVID COWEN as a farmer May 12, 1814. Indentures expired November 16, 1822. (F-37)

BLADEN, EDWARD. Admitted January 14, 1808 aged nine years by MARY ANN BLADEN, mother. Indentured to JOHN DUNMAINE as a doctor March 21, 1811. Indentures expired January 14, 1820. (F-23) Father, REV. MR. BLADEN. (Minutes, January 14, 1808) Born in Charleston. (ROSSC)

BLADEN, THOMAS. Admitted January 4, 1808 aged twelve years by MARY ANN BLADEN, mother. Indentured to HENRY PURCELL as a mariner March 28 1811. Indentures expired January 14, 1817. (F-2) Born in Charleston. (ROSSC)

BLUME, ELIAS. Admitted June 22, 1809 aged nine years by SAMUEL ULRICK, friend. From Philadelphia. Indentured to DAVID MILLER as a tanner and currier June 8, 1815. Indentures expired June 22, 1821. (F-31)

BONNEAU, MARY. Admitted August 23, 1804 aged eight years and nine months by MARY BONNEAU, mother. Indentured to ANN VANBIBBER, widow (of St. James Parish, Goose Creek) as a domestic March 24, 1808. Indentures expired August 23, 1813. (E-35) Born in Charleston. (ROSSC)

BOSSELL, ELIZABETH SHORE. Admitted December 15, 1803 aged seven years by JAMES BOSSELL, father. Indentured to JOHN and REBECCA LLOYD as a domestic January 12, 1809. Indentures expired December 15, 1814. (E-22) Born in Charleston. Mother, ELEANOR. (ROSSC)

BOSSELL, WILLIAM. Admitted December 15, 1803 aged ten years by JAMES BOSSELL, father. Indentured to ROBERT W. JONES as a cabinetmaker January 1, 1808. Transferred to PHILIP MOORE as a cabinetmaker June 1, 1809. Indentures expired December 15, 1814. (E-21) Born in Virginia. Mother, ELEANOR. (ROSSC)

BOAK, RICHARD. Admitted March 19, 1818 aged eight years by RICHARD BOAK, father. Indentured to HENRY WILLIS as a carpenter September 19, 1822. Indentures expired May 26, 1830. (H-64) Father in gaol for debts. (AtoA)

BOGARIN, WILLIAM. Admitted January 3, 1811 aged seven years by DOROTHY BOGARIN, mother. Indentured to PETER AITMAN as a coachmaker July 9, 1818. Indentures expired January 3, 1825. (F-65)

BOONE, WILLIAM. Admitted December 18, 1817 aged seven years by MARIA BOONE, mother. Born May 10, 1810. Delivered to his mother, MARIA WILLIAMS, March 28, 1822. Indentures expired May 10, 1831. (H-50)

BOUGAUD, ANTOINE. Admitted July 18, 1816 aged ten years by MARGARET CLENET, mother, a native of St. Domingo. (AtoA) Indentured to L. MARTIN as a taylor August 16, 1821. Indentures expired July 4, 1827 (G-126)

BOWERS, WILLIAM. Admitted December 31, 1818 by SARAH BOWERS, mother. Born December 5, 1812. (I-15) Absconded, nd. (ROSP, January 23, 1828)

BOWLING, THOMAS. Admitted January 9, 1817 aged eleven years by ELIZABETH BOWLING, mother. Born January 1, 1806. Died August 20, 1817. (H-13)

BOZEMAN, JAMES. Admitted February 11, 1813, aged six years by HARDY BOZEMAN, father. Delivered to his father March 9, 1815. Indentures expired February 11, 1828. (G-15)

BOZEMAN, WILLIAM. Admitted February 11, 1813 aged eleven years by HARDY BOZEMAN, father. Indentured to SAMUEL JONES (of Columbia) as a drygoods storekeeper April 27, 1815. Indentures expired February 11, 1823. (G-14)

BRADFORD, WILLIAM. Admitted May 20, 1819 aged seven years by City Warden. A derelict. Indentured to JAMES MARSH and SON as a ship carpenter June 1, 1826. Indentures expired May 20, 1833. (I-34) "His mother is ...a woman of ill-fame, who passed by the name of BETHUNE and he an illigetimate child. His mother boarded with a woman who kept a Bawdy House in Archdale Street by the name GOLLETT." (AtoA)

BRINDLEY, FREDERICK. Admitted August 31, 1815 aged five years by Warden of Charleston. Born December 2, 1809. Indentured to WILLIAM KELLY as a planter January 8, 1824. Indentures expired December 2, 1830. (G-93)

BRODERICK, WILLIAM THOMAS. Admitted April 12, 1811 aged nine years by CATHERINE BRODERICK, mother. Indentured to SAMUEL THOMB (of Chester District) as a farmer December 16, 1813. Indentures expired November 12, 1822. (F-74) Thomb was "committed to goal for trading with a Negroe contrary to the Act of the General Assembly." (Minutes, December 24, 1816) Transferred to SAMUEL and ROBERT TODD (of Laurens) as Clerk, nd. (Ibid).

BROOKS, HENRY. Admitted May 21, 1818 aged nine years by ELIZA McINTYRE, mother. Indentured to JAMES SUTCLIFFE as a baker November 9, 1821. Indentures expired November 21, 1829. (H-73)

BOYD, MARGARET. Admitted December 22, 1803 aged three years by Church Wardens of St. Philip's Church. Indentured to SARAH BROWN as a domestic January 9, 1812. Transferred to ELEANOR TOOHY, occupation unknown, July 14, 1815. Indentures expired December 22, 1818. (E-25). Born in Charleston. (ROSSC)

BRIGHT, HANNAH. Admitted February 4, 1808 aged four years by ANN BRIGHT, mother. Delivered to her mother, HANNAH GAMMON, March 23, 1815. Indentures expired February 4, 1822. (F-4). Born in Charleston. (ROSSC)

BROOKS, ANN. Admitted November 7, 1801 aged thirteen years by Church Wardens of St. Philip's Church. Allowed to live and work in the Institution as an Assistant Nurse. Died October 17, 1828. Indentures expired November 7, 1806. (D-82). Born in Charleston. (ROSSC) "Permission was granted to Mrs. MARY DURAND to erect a head and foot stone over the grave (of Ann Brooks)...in the cemetary of this Institution." (Minutes, July 28, 1831)

BROWN, ALEXANDER. Admitted August 11, 1808 aged four years and six months by MARY BROWN, mother-in-law. (E-15). Died December 10, 1815 of worm fever. (ROSP, December 9, 1815). Brother, MITCHELL, aged three years not admitted. (Minutes, August 11, 1808)

BROWN ELEANOR. Admitted July 21, 1802 aged four years by ELIZABETH BROWN, mother. Indentured to GEORGE W. McDILL (of Chester District) as a domestic May 3, 1810. Indentures expired July 21, 1816. (D-41). Born in Charleston. (ROSSC) Twin of JANE BROWN. (ROSP) May 5, 1810)

BROWN, ELIZABETH. Admitted July 21, 1802 aged six years by ELIZABETH BROWN, mother. Indentured to MRS. ELIZABETH STONEY (D-39) of Hilton Head (ROSP, April 7, 1810) as a domestic April 6, 1810. Indentures expired July 21, 1814. (D-39). Born in Charleston. (ROSSC)

BROWN, JANE. Admitted July 21, 1802 aged four years by ELIZABETH BROWN, mother. Indentured to DAVID MOFFITT (of Chester District) as a domestic May 3, 1810. Indentures expired July 21, 1816. (D-40). Born in Charleston. (ROSSC) Twin of ELEANOR BROWN. (ROSP, May 5, 1810)

BROWN, JOHN. Admitted June 6, 1800 aged eight years by THOMAS BROWN, father and a wheelwright. Indentured to THOMAS DUGGAN as a bricklayer, plasterer and stucco worker June ___, 1803. (D-12). Born in Charleston. (ROSSC)

BROWN, JOHN. Admitted August 20, 1802 aged one year and six months by Church Wardens of St. Philip's Church. (D-86). Died August 15, 1804. Father, THOMAS BROWN. Born in Charleston. (ROSSC)

BROWN, WILLIAM. Admitted February 8, 1806 aged three years and six months by CATHERINE L. BROWN, mother. Indentured to JOHN CORDES PRIOLEAU as a factor and commission merchant August 24, 1815. Transferred to SAMUEL YATES occupation unknown, October 29, 1818. Indentures expired July 23, 1823. (E-74). Born in Charleston. (Minutes, February 6, 1806)

BUCHANAN, JAMES. Admitted October 13, 1803 aged ten years by JOHN BUCHANAN, father. Indentured to JOHN LITTLE as a turner in wood and gin making July 14, 1808. Indentures expired October 13, 1814. (E-6) Born in Charleston. (ROSSC)

BUCHANAN, MARGARET. Admitted October 13, 1803 aged eight years by JOHN BUCHANAN, father. Child not actually admitted until August 30, 1804. Indentured to JOHN WEIR as a domestic March 22, 1810. Indentures expired October 13, 1813. (E-7). Born in Charleston. (ROSSC)

BUTCHER, MARY. Admitted November 26, 1807 aged three years by MARY BUTCHER mother. Died September 10, 1813. (E-106). Born in Charleston. (ROSSC) Mother, a former inmate, name unknown. (Minutes, November 26, 1807) Buried in the Methodist Burial Ground. (ROSP, September 11, 1813)

BYERS (BEYERS), MARGARET. Admitted July 14, 1803 aged twelve years by ELIZABETH BYERS, mother. Indentured to JAMES STEWART (of Winnsboro District) as a domestic May 23, 1805. Indentures expired July 14, 1806. (D-79). Admitted from the Poor House. (AtoA). Sent to her mother in Philadelphia September 1, 1808. (Minutes, September 1, 1808)

CALVERT, JAMES. Admitted April 10, 1801 aged one year and three months by JUDITH CALVERT, mother. Indentured to ALEXANDER DUNCAN as a black-smith October 29, 1814. Indentures expired April 10, 1819. (D-60). Accused of fowl snatching July 5, 1811. (Minutes, July 5, 1811)

CALVERT, WILLIAM. Admitted March __, 1800 aged five years by JUDITH CALVERT, mother. Indentures expired March __, 1816. (C-95). No further information.

CARMINADE, HENRY. Admitted May 12, 1808 aged ten years by VERONIQUE CARMINADE, mother. Delivered to his mother January 31, 1812. Inden-tures expired May 12, 1819. (H-56)

CARTER, LOISA. Admitted December 23, 1808 aged five years and six months by SARAH CARTER, mother. Delivered to mother, SARAH KNURST (KNUFF), April 25, 1816. Indentures expired July 1, 1821. (F-20). Born in Charleston. (ROSSC)

CARTER, WILLIAM. Admitted December 23, 1808 aged eight years by SARAH CARTER, mother. Indentured to THOMAS OGIER as a merchant August 19, 1813. Indentures expired August 20, 1821. (F-19)

CHRISTIAN, JOHN. Admitted October 24, 1807 aged ten years by REBECCAH CHRISTIAN, mother. Indentured to PAUL PRITCHARD, SR. as a shipwright January 31, 1811. Transferred to JAMES GEORGE, occupation unknown, April 22, 1814. Indentures expired September 1, 1818. (E-103)

CLARK, CHARLES. Admitted June 27, 1800 by SARAH CLARK, mother. Inden-tured to PETER M. EHNEY as a taylor September 27, 1804. Indentures expired June 27, 1812. (D-10

CLARK, CHARLOTTE CATHERINE. Admitted June 27, 1800 by SARAH CLARK, mother. Indentured to REBECCA BYRNES, wife of JOSEPH BYRNES, as a domestic March 1, 1804. Indentures expired June 27, 1806. (D-9). Born in Charleston. (ROSSC) Father, JOHN, dead. (Minutes, June 27, 1800)

CLARK, EDWARD. Admitted April 29, 1808 aged six years and six months by MARY CLARK, mother. Born in New York. Indentured to LATHAM HULL as a storekeeper March 3, 1814. Indentures expired April 29, 1823. (F-8)

CLARK, ELIZABETH. Admitted January 7, 1803 aged six years by SARAH CLARK, mother. Indentured to WILLIAM C. FABER, for his wife CATHERINE, as a domestic June 15, 1809. Indentures expired January 7, 1815. (D-7) Born in Charleston. (ROSSC)

CLARK, HANNAH MARIA. Admitted June 27, 1800 by SARAH CLARK, mother. Indentured to DOROTHY SHRENER (SHRIENER) as a domestic October 23, 1806. Indentures expired June 27, 1811. (D-11). Born in Charleston (ROSSC)

CLARK, ZACHARIAH. Admitted February 23, 1809 aged eleven years by SUSANNAH CLARK, guardian. Indentured to JOSEPH SIMONS as a grocer December 6, 1810. Indentures expired February 23, 1819. (F-26). Born in Charleston, (ROSSC) Died March 13, 1812 and sent to relatives to the country for burial. (ROSP, March 13, 1812)

CLAYTON, ANDREW. Admitted November 3, 1803 aged nine years by JANE CLAYTON, mother. (E-10). Indentured to his brother-in-law, ISHAM CLAYTON (of Statesboro in the County of Claremont) as a house carpenter December 29, 1806. (Minutes, December 4, 1806) Indentures expired November 3, 1815. (E-10). Born in Charleston. (ROSSC) Mother had seven children, including two sets of twins. Father, unknown, died February 6, 1803. (AtoA)

COMMAULT, ANN. Admitted June 22, 1809 aged four years by MARY SMITH, friend. Indentured to ELIZABETH NAGEL as a seamstress June 4, 1818. Indentures expired April 16, 1823. (F-32). Born in Charleston. (ROSSC)

CONNOR, HANNAH. Admitted July 2, 1801 aged nine years by Church Wardens of St. Philip's Church. Indentured to SARAH JAMES, wife of Judge JAMES, (of Statesboro in the County of Claremont) as a domestic January 19, 1805. Indentures expired July 2, 1810. (D-27). Born in Ireland. (ROSSC) Step-father, JAMES McKAIN. (Minutes, July 2, 1801)

COOMBS, GEORGE P. Admitted August 13, 1801 aged seven years by Church Wardens of St. Philip's Church. (D-33). Indentured to WILLIAM McCULLOCH (of Fairfield District) as a storekeeper and farmer March 31, 1808. Indentures expired August 13, 1814. (D-33)

DAVIS, JOHN. Admitted January 1, 1808 aged nine years and six months by ADAM VARANCE, friend, and Church Wardens of St. Philip's Church. Indentured to WILLIAM TURPIN, JR., as a merchant and farmer February 8, 1810. Indentures expired June 1, 1819. (F-1). Born in Charleston and an orphan. (Minutes, December 31, 1807)

DISHER, WILLIAM. Admitted September 5, 1800 aged nine years by MARY DISHER, mother. Indentured to BENJAMIN BOYD as a shopkeeper and trader December 20, 1805. Indentures expired September 5, 1812. (D-15) Born in Charleston. (ROSSC)

DUFF, MATTHEW. Admitted September 2, 1802 aged four years by Church Wardens of St. Philip's Church. (D-38). Indentured to CHRISTIAN JERGAINS (of Pendleton) as a farmer July 1, 1813. (ROSP, July 3, 1813) Indentures expired September 2, 1819. (D-38). Born in Charleston. (ROSSC)

DUNLAP, ALEXANDER. Admitted May 20, 1808 aged seven years and eight months by CATHERINE DUNLAP, mother. Indentured to WILLIAM McNELLAGE as a coachmaker May 18, 1815. Indentures expired September 20, 1821. (F-11). Master left the state and abandoned his apprentice. Indentures transferred to JOHN M. FRAZER as a ship-joiner December 5, 1816. (BO)

EFFLER, JOHN. Admitted September 20, 1805 aged seven years by Church Wardens of St. Philip's Church. Indentured to EVARISTE MAURY as a shopkeeper and merchant April 26, 1810. Indentures expired September 20, 1819. (E-62). Born in Charleston. Mother was dead and father was unable to care for him. (Minutes, September 19, 1805)

ELLIOTT, MARIA. Admitted July 13, 1809 aged four years and six months by JOHN ELLIOTT, father. Indentured to WILLIAM CURRY and wife (of Chester District) as a domestic March 7, 1811. Indentures expired January 1, 1822. (F-35). Born in Philadelphia. (ROSSC)

ESTILLE, WILLIAM. Admitted May 15, 1806 aged six years by SARAH ESTILLE (EARLETE), mother. (E-81). Delivered to his mother, MRS. SARAH CURTIS October 27, 1814. (ROSP, October 29, 1814). Indentures expired May 15, 1821. (E-81). Born in Charleston. (ROSSC)

FARLEY, JOHN. Admitted October 5, 1801 aged nine years by ANN FARLEY, mother. Sent to college, unknown, nd. (COH Inmates' Files). Indentures expired October 5, 1816. (D-63). Born in Ireland. (ROSSC)

FARLEY, MARGARET. Admitted October 5, 1801 aged one year and six months by ANNE FARLEY, mother. Indentured to E. ANNE DENT as a domestic March 10, 1814. Indentures expired October 5, 1816. (D-63). Born in Philadelphia. (ROSSC)

FARLEY, THOMAS. Admitted October 5, 1801 aged three years by ANNE FARLEY, mother. Indentured to MADAME MANSUET as a baker July 29, 1811. Indentures expired October 5, 1817. (D-62). Farley left his mistress to enter the army. Later, he requested the Commissioners to secure his release. (Minutes, August 31, 1815). The Commissioners certified he was a bound apprentice and only eighteen years old. (COH Inmates' Files)

FIELDS, NATHANIEL. Admitted June 6, 1805 aged eight years and six months by ANN M. FIELDS, mother. Indentured to CHARLES CLEAPOR as a sailmaker November 1, 1810. Indentures expired December 6, 1815. (E-54). Born in Charleston. (ROSSC) Father, WILLIAM BROWN FIELDS, dead. (Minutes, May 30, 1805)

FIELDS, SARAH. Admitted June 6, 1805 aged five years by ANN M. FIELDS, mother. Indentured to MARGARET MOLES as a shopkeeper, milliner and seamtress March 24, 1814. Transferred to MRS. ANN W. CLEAPOR, occupation unknown. June 4, 1814. Indentures expired June y, 1818. (E-55) Born in Charleston. (ROSSC)

FORRESTER, HESTER, (ESTHER). Admitted November 16, 1809 aged five years by JANE FORRESTER, mother. Born in New York and now in the Poor House. Indentured to JOHN BLACK as a seamtress April 23, 1818. Indentures expired November 16, 1822. (F-39)

FRAZIER, JOHN. Admitted October 6, 1803 aged eight years by ELIZABETH MINOR, mother. Delivered to his mother October 6, 1806. Indentures expired October 6, 1816. Born in Charleston. (ROSSC)

GALAWAY (GALLOWAY), MARGARET. Admitted November 24, 1803 aged eleven years by Church Wardens of St. Philip's Church. Indentured to DAVID CHESTNUT, for his wife JANE (of Fairfield County) as a domestic March 13, 1806. Indentures expired November 24, 1810. Admitted from the Poor House. Mother dead. (Minutes, November 24, 1803)

GANN, JANE. Admitted June 1, 1809 aged six years by Church Wardens of St. Philip's Church. Indentured to ELIZABETH ANN YATES as a seamtress July 9, 1818. Indentures expired June 1, 1821. (F-29). Born in Charleston. (ROSSC)

GARRISON, WILLIAM. Admitted April 7, 1803 aged six years by ANN GARRISON, mother. Indentured to FRANCIS COBIA as a house carpenter December 29, 1809. Indentures expired April 7, 1818. (D-56). Born in Philadelphia. (ROSSC)

GRADO, LOUISE. Admitted September 28, 1805 aged eight years and six months by MARIAN GRADO, unknown. Indentured to MARGARET McLEAN as a domestic June 8, 1809. Transferred to WILLIAM GRAFTON, occupation unknown, June 11, 1812. Indentures expired April 1, 1815. (E-63) Born in Charleston. (ROSSC)

GRANBY, GEORGE. Admitted August 10, 1802 aged twelve years by Church Wardens of St. Philip's Church. Indentured to DAVID SHWING (SHEVING) as a boatbuilder March 14, 1805. Indentures expired August 10, 1809. (D-73). Born in Charleston. (ROSSC)

GREEN, JAMES. Admitted July 3, 1806 aged nine years by Church Wardens of St. Philip's Church. Indentured to HENRY BARTLESS as a blacksmith January 24, 1811. Indentures expired July 3, 1818. (E-84). Born in Charleston. (ROSSC) Admitted from the Poor House. (Minutes, June 26, 1806)

GUY, ELIZA. Admitted November 28, 1805 aged seven years by MARY GUY, mother. Delivered to her mother February 4, 1808. Indentures expired November 28, 1816. (E-69). Born in Charleston. (ROSSC)

HAMBLETON, ALEXANDER. Admitted December 10, 1801 aged three years by Church Wardens of St. Philip's Church. Indentured to MORDECAI COHEN and MICHAEL LAZARUS as a saddler and harnessmaker July 14, 1814. Indentures expired December 15, 1819. (D-65). Born in Charleston. (ROSSC)

HAMBLETON, ELEANOR. Admitted December 10, 1801 aged one year and six months by Church Wardens of St. Philip's Church. Indentured to MARTHA MOWBRAY as a baker April 16, 1812. Transferred to SARAH MILLER as a mantuamaker May 11, 1815. Indentures expired December 10, 1818. (D-64) Born in Charleston. (ROSSC)

HAMILTON, CATHARINE. Admitted June 6, 1805 aged three years by Church
Wardens of St. Philip's Church. Indentured to ELIZABETH BRAILSFORD,
occupation unknown, May 19, 1814. Indentures expired June 6, 1820.
(E-53). Born in Charleston. Father, THOMAS HAMILTON. (ROSSC)

HAMILTON, ISABELLA. Admitted June 6, 1805 aged five years by Church
Wardens of St. Philip's Church. Indentured to HANNAH BOLLES as a
domestic April 28, 1814. Indentures expired June 6, 1818. (E-52).
Born in Charleston. (ROSSC) Became pregnant and swore the father was
Mr. _____ KURAC. (Minutes, August 14, 1817). Sent to the family of
DR. MAYNARD and gave birth to a child, nd. (Minutes, November 6, 1817)
No further information.

HAMPTON, MARY ANN. Admitted November 1, 1800 aged ten years by GRACE
INGRAHAM, mother. Indentured to ANNA PATTERSON, wife of ROBERT
PATTERSON a carpenter, as a domestic August 16, 1804. Transferred to
MARY G. RIVERS, occupation unknown, September 25, 1806. Indentures
expired November 1, 1808. (D-19). Born in Charleston. (ROSSC)
Absconded January 13, 1803. (Minutes, January 13, 1803)

HELTE, ELIZA. Admitted January 17, 1805 aged nine years by Church
Wardens of St. Philip's Church. Indentured to JOHN CART, for his wife
SUSANNAH, as a domestic June 4, 1807. Indentures expired January 17,
1813. Allowed $35.00 as a dowry. (Minutes, April 8, 1813). Married
name was WELSH. (Minutes, December 14, 1815)

HOLLAND, SARAH. Admitted June 29, 1805 aged eleven years and six months
by ELIZABETH COVENEY, aunt. Indentured to MARY DeBOW as a domestic
June 4, 1807. Transferred to MARY SEEBERT as a domestic February 2,
1809. Indentures expired January 1, 1812. Born in Charleston (ROSSC)

HORTON, ANN. Admitted February 1, 1806 aged six years by ANN MINSEY,
aunt. Indentured to DAVID COWEN as a domestic May 12, 1814. Indentures
expired February 1, 1818. (E-73). Born in Charleston. (ROSSC)
Transferred to her brother, GILLESIE, October 23, 1815. (Minutes,
October 23, 1815)

HUNTER, JOHN. Admitted September 15, 1803 aged two years by JANE HUNTER,
mother. Indentured to WILLIAM McNELLAGE as a coachmaker April 27, 1815.
Transferred to his mother May 12, 1815. Indentures expired September
15, 1822. (E-5). Born in Charleston. (ROSSC)

HUNTER, MARGARET CRAWFORD. Admitted September 15, 1803 aged four years
by JANE HUNTER, mother. Delivered to her mother March 8, 1810. Indentures expired September 15, 1817. (E-4). Born in Charleston. (ROSSC)

HUSEN, RICHARD. Admitted December 18, 1800 by Poor House. Indentures
expired December 18, 1811. (D-20). Mother in the Poor House. (Minutes,
December 11, 1800). Delivered to his mother, ANN HUSEN, a COH nurse,
March 18, 1802. (Minutes, March 18, 1802)

HUSEN, ZACHARIAH. Admitted December 18, 1800 aged three years by Poor
House. Indentures expired December 18, 1818. (D-21). Mother in the
Poor House. (Minutes, December 11, 1800). Delivered to his mother,
ANN HUSEN, a COH nurse, March 18, 1802. (Minutes, March 18, 1802)

HUTTON, FANNY. Admitted January 7, 1802 aged seven years by Church
Wardens of St. Philip's Church. (D-66). Died March 20, 1811 of a
chest complaint and buried in the Public Burial Ground. (ROSP, March
23, 1811)

INGRAHAM, JANE. Admitted November 3, 1803 aged eight years by GRACE
GRET (GUY), mother. Delivered to her sister, ANN GUYON, July 26, 1810.
Indentures expired November 3, 1813. (E-11). Born in Charleston.
(ROSSC)

IRELAND, WILLIAM. Admitted August 7, 1806 aged nine years and ten months
by Church Wardens of St. Philip's Church. Indentured to WILLIAM GRAFTON
as a farmer April 19, 1810. Indentures expired October 7, 1817. (E-85)
Born in Charleston. (ROSSC) Father, EDWARD IRELAND, dead, worked for
KEATING SIMONS. (AtoA)

JACOBS, JAMES BISHOP. Admitted June 18, 1807 aged nine years by ELIZABETH WEBBER, mother. Indentured to NATHANIEL INGRAHAM as a merchant December 20, 1811. Transferred to JAMES SHARP, occupation unknown, November 10, 1814. Indentures expired April 18, 1819. (E-99). Born in Charleston. (ROSSC)

JAMES, CHARLES. Admitted December 15, 1803 aged six years by SAMUEL JAMES, father. (E-23). Died March 6, 1812 of a lumbar abcess. (ROSP, November 9, 1811) and buried in the Public Burial Ground. (ROSP, March 7, 1812)

HERBERT,(HARBIRD), SAMUEL. Admitted November 15, 1804 aged nine years by Church Wardens of St. Philip's Church. Indentured to JOHN ROGERS (of Union District) as a storekeeper November 24, 1808. Transferred to FRANCIS ALLEN (of Newberry District), occupation unknown, April ___, 1809 and served his time with Mr. _____ INGLESBY in Charleston. Indentures expired November 15, 1815. (E-39). Born in Charleston. (ROSSC)

HILL, WILLIAM. Admitted July 21, 1802 aged nine years by Church Wardens of St. Philip's Church. Indentured to GEORGE GIBBES as a baker March 13, 1807. Indentures expired July 21, 1813. (D-89)

HOAR, MARY ANN. Admitted September 18, 1806 aged four years by MARY HOAR, mother. Indentured to SAMUEL TODD (of Laurens District) as a spinner December 14, 1815. Indentures expired September 18, 1820. (E-87). Born in Charleston. (ROSSC)

HOAR, THOMAS. Admitted February 27, 1806 aged six years by MARY HOAR, mother. Indentured to DAVID LEWIS as a cabinetmaker November 24, 1814. Indentures expired February 27, 1820. (E-77). Born in Charleston. (ROSSC). Father, unknown, worked for WILLIAM CLARKSON and deserted his family, nd. Mother lived in Champney Street. (AtoA)

HOLDRUPE (HOLDROPE), GEORGE. Admitted November 24, 1803 aged six years by Church Wardens of St. Philip's Church. Indentured to PIERRE EIMARRET as a cabinetmaker January 17, 1811. Indentures expired November 24, 1818. (E-19). Born in Charleston. (ROSSC) Admitted from the Poor House. (AtoA)

HOLDRUPE, JAMES. Admitted October 21, 1805 aged five years by Church Wardens of St. Philip's Church. Indentured to DANIEL McMILLAN (of Chester District) as a farmer May 12, 1814. Indentures expired October 21, 1821. (E-66). Admitted from the Poor House. (ROSSC)

HOLDRUPE, THOMAS. Admitted November 24, 1803 aged eight years by Church Wardens of St. Philip's Church. Placed aboard the U.S. Brig Hornet as a midshipman, nd. (E-18). Admitted from the Poor House. (AtoA) Served with Commodore Perry at the Battle of Lake Erie. (Minutes, October 19, 1813) and as Commodore of the Naval Station at Washington, D.C. (Minutes, January 28, 1841). His son, FREDERICK STEVENS, asked the Commissioners for a reccommendation as a purser in Charleston in 1841. (Minutes, March 18, 1841)

HOLLAND, BARNABUS. Admitted July 16, 1805 aged seven years and six months by BRIDGET HOLLAND, mother and widow of PATRICK HOLLAND, a bricklayer. Indentured to JOHN DITMOR as a house carpenter April 6, 1810. Transferred to THOMAS LESESNE, occupation unknown, July 30, 1813. Indentures expired December 17, 1818. (E-60). Born in Charleston. (ROSSC)

HOLLAND, PETER. Admitted July 26, 1805 aged three years and three months by BRIDGET HOLLAND, mother and widow of PATRICK HOLLAND, a bricklayer. Indentured to SAMUEL LOPEZ as a tinplate worker July 13, 1815. Indentures expired April 7, 1823. (E-61). Born in Charleston. (ROSSC)

JAMES, HARRIOTT. Admitted December 15, 1803 aged two years by SAMUEL JAMES, father. Delivered to her father, a carpenter, January 3, 1811. Indentures expired December 15, 1819. (E-24). Born in Charleston. (ROSSC)

_____, JOHN. Admitted August ___, 1800 by Church Wardens of St. Philip's Church. Found in the streets without parents. Died, nd. Indentures expired August 1820. (D-16)

JOHNSON, JACOB. Admitted January 10, 1807 aged seven years and five months by BARBARA JOHNSON, mother. Indentured to RICHARD HOWARD as a cooper December 1, 1814. Indentures expired August 17, 1820. (E-89)

JOHNSON (JOHNSTON), JOHN. Admitted May 25, 1801 aged nine years by MRS. _____ JOHNSON, mother and widow of JACOB JOHNSON, house carpenter. Indentured to ROBERT WILSON as a physician and apothecary December 20, 1805. Indentures expired May 25, 1812. (D-26)

JONES, EDWARD. Admitted December 2, 1802 aged eleven years by Church Wardens of St. Philip's Church. Indentured to JAMES NOLEN as a house carpenter December 4, 1806. Indentures expired December 2, 1812. (D-50)

JONES, JOHN. Admitted December 2, 1802 aged nine years by Church Wardens of St. Philip's Church. Indentures expired December 2, 1814. (D-51). Father, HENRY, dead. (Minutes, December 2, 1802). On November 10, 1813 was sent to Columbia College. (ROSSC)

JONES, JOSEPH. Admitted December 2, 1802 aged seven years by Church Wardens of St. Philip's Church. Indentured to WILLIAM SCOTT as an accountant and merchant September 15, 1808. Transferred to JACOB SASS and SON as a cabinetmaker May 4, 1810. Indentures expired December 2, 1816. (D-52). Father, HENRY, dead. (Minutes, December 2, 1802)

JONES, MARIA. Admitted January 26, 1809 aged eleven years by ELIZA CHILDS, friend and foster mother. Indentured to THOMAS McCALLA (of Chester District) as a domestic December 2, 1809. Indentures expired January 26, 1816. (F-25). Born in Philadelphia. (ROSSC) An orphan. (Minutes, January 26, 1809)

JORDAN, SAMUEL. Admitted April 7, 1803 aged six years by Church Wardens of St. Philip's Church. Indentured to KEATING SIMONS as a merchant and factor June 7, 1810. Indentures expired April 7, 1818. (D-57) Born in Charleston. (ROSSC)

KAIN, ANN. Admitted March 2, 1809 aged six years by CATHERINE KAIN, mother. Indentured to ELLEN MOLES as a milliner August 17, 1815. Indentures expired March 2, 1821. (F-27). Born in Charleston. (ROSSC)

KENNEDY, ELEANOR. Admitted January 5, 1809 aged four years by Church Wardens of St. Philip's Church. Born in New York. Indentured to M.L. HORLBECK (HURLBECK) as a seamtress September 19, 1816. Transferred to JANE WISH as a mantuamaker May 21, 1818. Indentures expired January 5, 1823. (F-22). Admitted from Poor House. (Minutes, January 5, 1809)

KENNEDY, MORRIS. Admitted January 5, 1809 aged eight years by Church Wardens of St. Philip's Church. Born in New York. Indentured to JAMES MORK as a mariner in the U.S. Navy January 26, 1815. Indentures expired January 5, 1822. (F-21). Admitted from the Poor House. (Minutes, January 5, 1809)

KING, JAMES. Admitted January 13, 1802 aged seven years by Church Wardens of St. Philip's Church. Indentured to JAMES DRUMMOND as a boot and shoemaker November 17, 1808. Indentures expired August 13, 1816. (D-85). Born in Charleston. (ROSSC)

KOHLER, CHRISTOPHER FREDERICK. Admitted December 5, 1805 aged twelve years by MAGDALENA KOHLER, mother. Indentured to FREDERICK KOHLER as a tanner and currier January 29, 1807. Indentures expired December 5, 1814. (E-70). Born in Germany. (ROSSC)

KOHLER, MARIA CATHARINE. Admitted December 5, 1805 aged nine years by MAGDALENA KOHLER, mother. Delivered to her mother January 11, 1810. Indentures expired December 5, 1814. (E-71). Born in Germany. (ROSSC)

LANG, SARAH. Admitted October 21, 1805 aged five years by Church Wardens of St. Philip's Church. Indentured to JAMES STRONG (of Chester District) as a domestic December 2, 1813. Indentures expired April 7, 1818. (E-67)

LANG, THOMAS. Admitted October 21, 1805 aged four years by Church Wardens of St. Philip's Church. Indentured to DR. JOSEPH JOHNSON as an apothecary and druggist July 7, 1814. Indentures expired October 21, 1822. (E-68). Admitted from Poor House. (Minutes, July 11, 1805)

LANSDEL, WILLIAM. Admitted March 8, 1804 aged eight years by SARAH ANN GROOMS, mother. Indentured to ARTHUR HINTON and WILLIAM HALL as a hatter April 4, 1811. Transferred to RENHARD and JACOB FREY, occupation unknown, February 11, 1813. Indentures expired March 8, 1817. (E-27) Born in Charleston. (ROSSC) His father, WILLIAM LANSDEL, was a soldier in the Contennental Army. (AtoA)

LARUE (LeROUE), JOHN. Admitted July 2, 1801 by THOMAS KARVOY, Executor of his father's estate. Indentured to ISAAC DODGE PARSONS as a grocer and accountant March 24, 1808. Transferred to JOSEPH COLE as a boot and shoemaker October 13, 1808. Indentures expired July 2, 1812. (D-28) Born in Charleston. (ROSSC)

LEONARD, RICHARD. Admitted September 29, 1808 aged six years by Church Wardens of St. Philip's Church. Indentured to WILLIAM TIMMONS as a merchant October 31, 1816. Indentures expired September 29, 1823. (F-16). Born in Charleston. (ROSSC) Found derelict in the streets. (Minutes, September 29, 1808)

LEWIS, WILLIAM. Admitted September 21, 1809 aged seven years by ANN LEWIS, mother. Indentured to HENRY B. TOOMER as a commission merchant July 20, 1820. Indentures expired September 21, 1823. (F-36) Born in Charleston. (ROSSC)

LLOYD, WILLIAM. Admitted June 29, 1807 aged four years by Church Wardens of St. Philip's Church. Delivered to his father, WILLIAM LLOYD, April 6, 1810. Indentures expired July 1, 1824. (E-101) Admitted from the Poor House. (Minutes, June 25, 1807)

LONERGAN, THOMAS. Admitted June 21, 1804 aged five years by Church Warden of St. Philip's Church. Indentured to ROBERT WALLACE as a brass founder March 18, 1813. Indentures expired June 21, 1820. (E-34) Born in Philadelphia. (ROSSC) Admitted from the Poor House. (Minutes, June 14, 1804)

LONG, ANN. Admitted October 9, 1800 aged five years by Church Wardens of St. Philip's Church. Indentured to JOHN McNINCH (of Chester District) as a domestic February 26, 1807. Indentures expired October 9, 1813. (D-18). Born in Charleston. (ROSSC)

LONG, GEORGE. Admitted October 9, 1800 by Church Wardens of St. Philip's Church. Indentured to PETER FRENEAU as a printer March 22, 1804. Indentures expired October 9, 1809. (D-17). Absconded; was "enticed away, by one JOHN KIELE, a waggoner and carried to Mecklinburgh County in North Carolina." (Minutes, November 12, 1801) Returned March 1, 1804. (Minutes, March 1, 1804)

LOPER, MARY R. Admitted September 5, 1800 by ANN LOPER, mother. (D-14) Died July 1, 1802. (Minutes, July 1, 1802)

LOVE, CATHERINE. Admitted November 20, 1803 aged seven years by ELIZABETH LOVE, mother. Indentured to SYLVANUS KEITH as a domestic June 1, 1809. Transferred to ANN BOWLES, occupation unknown, June 3, 1813. (E-13). Born in Charleston. (ROSSC)

LOVE, EDWARD APPLEFORD. Admitted November 20, 1803 aged six years by ELIZABETH LOVE, mother. Indentures expired November 20, 1818. (E-14) Born in Charleston. (ROSSC) Sent to South Carolina College where he became insane. The Commissioners felt it was because he had lost money in a card game to JOHN JONES, another inmate. (COH Inmates' Files)

LOWRY, WILLIAM. Admitted January 1, 1808 aged thirteen years and six months by Church Wardens of St. Philip's Church. Indentured to JOHN MOFFETT (of Chester District) as a farmer November 21, 1811. Indentures expired May 21, 1815. (E-107) Born in Charleston: an orphan. (Minutes, December 31, 1807)

McCARTNEY, SUSAN. Admitted March 7, 1805 aged six years by Church Wardens of St. Philp's Church. Taken away by a friend March 14, 1805. Indentures expired March 7, 1817. (E-49)

McCLEARY, JOHN. Admitted June 25, 1804 aged seven years by Church Wardens of St. Philip's Church. Indentured to ROBERT EASON as a shipwright February 21, 1811. Indentures expired June 21, 1818. (E-30) Born in Charleston. (ROSSC)

McCRACKEN, RUTH. Admitted July 28, 1803 aged three years and six months by ANN McCRACKEN, mother. Died Sunday morning June 9, 1805. (E-12) Born in Charleston. (ROSSC)

McGUIRE, RODERICK. Admitted July 14, 1803 aged four years and six months by Church Wardens of St. Philip's Church. Indentured to THOMAS JOHNSTON as a storekeeper February 11, 1813. Indentures expired January 14, 1820. (D-78) Mother, MARY McGUIRE. (ROSSC)

McKEE, JAMES. Admitted December 1, 1808 aged twelve years by Church Wardens of St. Philip's Church. Indentured to JOHN HESLY as a taylor July 6, 1810. Indentures expired December 1, 1817. (F-17)

McNEAL, ANN. Admitted August 26, 1802 aged five years by Church Wardens of St. Philip's Church. Indentured to MARY KREITSBURGH as a domestic June 1, 1809. Transferred to JOHN MOFFET as a seamstress December 2, 1809. Indentures expired August 27, 1815. (D-44). Born in Charleston. (ROSSC)

McNEAL, ARCHIBALD. Admitted January 21, 1802 aged nine years by Church Wardens of St. Philip's Church. Indentured to JOHN CUNNINGHAM as a merchant May 25, 1809. Indentures expired January 21, 1814. (D-37) An orphan. (Minutes, January 14, 1802)

McNEAL, (McNEIL), HARRIOT. Admitted August 26, 1802 aged eleven years by Church Wardens of St. Philip's Church. Indentured to AMELIA PERRAULT as a domestic January 16, 1806. Transferred to ANN STEWART as a seamstress March 27, 1807. Transferred to PATRICK and JANE GLADNEY (of Fairfield District) as a seamstress May 7, 1808. Indentures expired August 26, 1809. *D-43). Born in Charleston. (ROSSC). Placed in the Poor House August 19, 1813. (Minutes, August 19, 1813).

McNEAL (McNEIL), HENRY. Admitted August 26, 1802 aged seven years by Church Wardens of St. Philip's Church. (D-45). Indentured to ANDREW YOUNG (of Chester District) as a farmer and husbandman December 23, 1808. (Minutes, November 24, 1808). Indentures expired August 26, 1816. (D-45).

McNEIL (McNEAL), MARIA. Admitted August 26, 1802 aged seven years by Church Wardens of St. Philip's Church. Indentured to FRANCES PEARSON as a domestic April 2, 1807. Transferred to WILLIAM GRAFTON for his wife, ESTHER, as a seamstress December 9, 1811. Indentures expired August 26, 1813. (D-80). Born in Charleston. (ROSSC)

MACKEY (McKIE), JAMES. Admitted September 2, 1802 aged nine years by Church Wardens of St. Philip's Church. Indentured to THOMAS HINSON as a house carpenter December 1, 1808. Transferred to JOHN OGIER as a silversmith and jeweller March 30, 1809. Transferred to SAMUEL STINE as a taylor June 2, 1809. Transferred to CALVINE MINNES (of Chester District) as a planter August 9, 1810. Indentures expired September 2, 1814. (D-42)

MASON, SAMUEL. Admitted January 20, 1803 aged eight years by MARY MASON, mother. Indentured to JULIUS PETSCH as a bookbinder November 3, 1808. Indentures expired January 20, 1815. (D-55). Born in Charleston. (ROSSC)

MAXEY, ANN. Admitted October 13, 1802 aged nine years by Church Wardens of St. Philip's Church. Indentured to CHARLOTTE DURAND as a mantuamaker April 23, 1807. Transferred to ANN and W.P. CATONNET, occupation unknown, January 5, 1809. Transferred to HUGH SIMPSON, occupation unknown, December 14, 1810. Indentures expired October 13, 1811. (D-49). Born in Charleston. (ROSSC) Admitted from the Poor House. (AtoA)

MAXEY, ELIZABETH. Admitted October 13, 1802 aged eleven years by Church Wardens of St. Philip's Church. Indentured to JOHN HARVEY (of Fairfield County) for his wife, ELIZABETH, as a domestic March 13, 1806. Indentures expired October 13, 1809. (D-48). Born in Charleston. (ROSSC)

MEMMINGER, CHRISTOPHER GUSTAVUS. Admitted January 28, 1807 aged four years and six months by MAGDALENA KOHLER, mother. Indentures expired January 9, 1824. (E-90). The Commissioners described him as "possessing a great native genius, particularly in Mathematics." (Minutes, January 9, 1812). Delivered to THOMAS BENNETT, JR., ESQ., occupation unknown, 1814. (Minutes, February 5, 1814)

MERCIER, SAMUEL. Admitted March 16, 1809 aged ten years by Church Wardens of St. Philip's Church. Indentured to CAPTAIN EDWARD P. KENNEDY as a mariner in the U.S. Navy July 8, 1813. Indentures expired March 16, 1820. (F-28). Born in Baltimore. SARAH STEWART guardian. (ROSSC)

MERRATT (MERRITT), ANN. Admitted March 12, 1801 aged four years by CATHERINE MERRATT, mother. Indentured to JOSEPH and MARTHA GLADNEY (of Fairfield County on the Black River) as a domestic February 1, 1810. Indentures expired March 12, 1814. (D-24). Born in Charleston. (ROSSC)

MERRATT, CATHARINE. Admitted October 9, 1800 aged five years by CATHARINE MERRATT, mother. Indentured to MARY SEWERS, wife of THOMAS SEWERS, (of Columbia), as a domestic March 24, 1808. Indentures expired October 9, 1813. (D-59). Born in Charleston. (ROSSC)

MERRATT, GEORGE. Admitted March 12, 1801 aged two years by CATHARINE MERRATT, mother. Died May 18, 1801. Indentures expired March 12, 1819. (D-25)

MINER, (MINOR), HENRY PEREGRINE. Admitted October 6, 1803 aged four years by ELIZABETH MINER, mother. Delivered to his mother October 6, 1806. Indentures expired October 6, 1820. (D-3). Born in Charleston. (ROSSC)

MILLER, JAMES. Admitted September 10, 1807 aged four years by MARY MILLER, mother. Indentured to JACOB MILLER as a ropemaker July 2, 1818. Indentures expired November 20, 1824. (E-102)

MORRIS, DORCAS. Admitted April 10, 1802 aged seven years by Church Warden of St. Philip's Church. Indentured to MATTHEW HARDISON (of Chester District), as a domestic March 15, 1810. Indentures expired April 10, 1813. (D-83). Born in Charleston. (ROSSC)

MURRAY, JAMES. Admitted January 29, 1807 aged six years by ANN ELIZABETH MURRAY, mother. Delivered to his mother January 18, 1810. Indentures expired January 29, 1821. (E-91). Born in Charleston. (ROSSC)

MURRAY, WILLIAM. Admitted January 29, 1807 aged four years by ANN ELIZABETH MURRAY, mother. Delivered to his mother January 18, 1810. Indentures expired January 29, 1823. (E-92). Born in Charleston. (ROSSC)

NEUFFER, CATHERINE. Admitted February 8, 1806 aged nine years by MARY NEUFFER, mother. Indentured to JOHN and ELIZA VINYARD as a domestic August 3, 1809. Indentures expired February 8, 1815. (E-75). Born in Charleston. (Minutes, January 30, 1806)

NEUFFER, JOHN A. Admitted February 8, 1806 aged six years and six months by MARY NEUFFER, mother. Indentured to WILLIAM THOMPSON as a ship chandler March 19, 1812. Indentures expired July 1, 1820. (E-76). Born in Charleston. (Minutes, January 30, 1806)

NUNES, (UNICE), LUCY. Admitted June 4, 1807 aged seven years by ELIZABETH NUNES, mother. Indentured to MARGARET MOLES as a domestic July 16, 1812. Indentures expired June 4, 1818. (E-97). Born in Charleston. (ROSSC)

NUNES (UNICE), SELINA. Admitted June 4, 1807 aged six years by ELIZABETH NUNES, mother. Indentured to JOHN McCLURE (of Chester District) as a spinner and weaver December 1, 1814. Indentures expired June 4, 1819. (E-97). Born in Charleston. (ROSSC)

PAGE, JOHN. Admitted July 25, 1802 aged seven years by Church Wardens of St. Philip's Church. Indentured to JOHN JOHNSON as a blacksmith October 21, 1811. Transferred to JOHN DUPONT as a boot and shoemaker February 21, 1811. Transferred to JOHN FREY, occupation unknown, December 2, 1813. Indentures expired July 25, 1816. (D-87). Born in Charleston. (ROSSC)

PAGE, SAMUEL. Admitted March 12, 1801 aged three years and six months by Church Wardens of St. Philip's Church. (D-91). Died ____, 1809 of dropsy and was buried in the Strangers' Burial Ground. (ROSP, November 4, 1809)

PALMER, JOHN. Admitted March 28, 1800 aged four years by ANN YOUNG, friend. Indentured to THOMAS McCALLA as a planter December 2, 1809. Indentures expired March 28, 1817. (C-94)

PEASTER, ELIZA. Admitted October 22, 1801 aged two years by SARAH PEASTER, mother. (D-36). Died July __, 1802 of measles. (Minutes, July 14, 1802)

PEASTER, MARIA. Admitted October 22, 1801 aged six years by SARAH PEASTER, mother. Indentured to HUGH SIMPSON (of Chester District) for his mother, AGNES SIMPSON, as a domestic February 1, 1806. Indentures expired October 22, 1813. (D-35). Born in Charleston. (ROSSC)

PEASTER (PEISTER), SARAH. Admitted October 22, 1801 aged seven years and ten months by SARAH PEASTER, mother. Indentured to SUSANNAH HARRISON, wife of THOMAS HARRISON, as a domestic June 26, 1806. Indentures expired October 22, 1811. (D-34). Born in Charleston. (ROSSC)

PRICE, DAVID. Admitted November 29, 1804 aged ten years by SARAH FINDLEY, mother. Indentured to JAMES McDOWELL as a merchant and accountant October 29, 1807. Indentures expired November 19, 1815. (E-43) Born in Jamaica. (ROSSC)

QUARTERMAN, MARY. Admitted March 29, 1804 aged thirteen years by Church Wardens of St. Philip's Church. Indentured to WILLIAM BLACK, for his wife, SARAH, (of St. Luke's Parish), as a domestic February 1, 1806. Indentures expired March 29, 1809. (E-28). Born in Charleston. (ROSSC)

QUACKENBUSH, ALEXANDER. Admitted March 24, 1808 aged six years by MARY QUACKENBUSH, mother. Delivered to his mother, MRS. FAUST, May 27, 1814. Indentures expired March 24, 1823. (F-5). Born in Charleston. (ROSSC)

RAND (WRAND), HESTER. Admitted September 8, 1802 aged seven years by WINIFRED RAND, mother. Indentured to MARGARET FREAN as a domestic February 1810. Transferred to NATHANIEL BLACK, for his wife ELIZABETH, as a domestic September 27, 1810. Indentures expired September 8, 1813. (D-69). Born in Charleston. (ROSSC)

RAND, MARY. Admitted September 8, 1802 aged five years by WINIFRED RAND, mother. Indentured to ELIZABETH M. LIVINGSTON as a mantuamaker February 14, 1811. Transferred to MARIAN HYAMS, occupation unknown, July 16, 1812. Indentures expired September 8, 1813. (D-68). Born in Charleston. (ROSSC)

REDMON, ANN. Admitted June 18, 1805 aged four years and six months by SARAH REDMON, mother. Indentured to ELIZABETH JOHNSTON as a domestic June 13, 1816. Indentures expired December 18, 1818. (E-58). Born in Charleston. (ROSSC)

REDMON, JAMES. Admitted June 18, 1805 aged eight years by SARAH REDMON, mother. Indentured to JOHN STROHECKER as a blacksmith September 2, 1813. Indentures expired June 18, 1820. (E-57). Born in Charleston. (ROSSC)

REYER, CHARLES. Admitted October 21, 1805 aged twelve years by Church Wardens of St. Philip's Church. Indentured to JOHN CALDWELL as a house carpenter November 3, 1808. Indentures expired October 21, 1814. (E-65)

RINTY, JOHN. (ALSO KNOWN AS JOHN HILL). Admitted July 21, 1802 aged nine years by Church Wardens of St. Philip's Church. Indentured to JOHN ZYLK as a wheelwright and chainmaker December 12, 1807. Indentures expired July 21, 1814. (D-88). Born in Charleston. (ROSSC)

RITFIELD, HENRY. Admitted March 28, 1800 aged nine years by SARAH RITFIELD, mother. Indentured to THOMAS DUGGAN and JOHN DUGGAN as a bricklayer, plasterer and stuccoworker March 21, 1805. Indentures expired March 28, 1812. (D-6). Born in Charleston. (ROSSC)

ROBERTSON, JOHN. Admitted March 28, 1800 by Church Wardens of St. Philip's Church. Indentured to JOHN MUNCEY, the elder, as a house carpenter April 8, 1807. Transferred to LEWIS FITZGERALD as a house carpenter Jan. 2, 1807. Indentures expired March 28, 1808. (D-1)

RYCHBOSCH, ELIZA. Admitted February 27, 1806 aged ten years by Church Wardens of St. Philip's Church. Indentured to ANNIS STENT as a domestic February 14, 1811. Indentures expired February 20, 1814. (E-78). Born in Charleston. (ROSSC)

RYCHBOSCH, JOSEPH. Admitted March 20, 1806 aged two years and eight months by Church Wardens of St. Philip's Church. Indentured to TYCKBON (RICHON) as a sailmaker December 4, 1817. Indentures expired March 20, 1824. (E-80). Born in Charleston. (ROSSC) Father, FRANCIS, a broker died September 28, 1800. Mother was insane. (Minutes, February 27, 1806)

RYCHBOSCH, MARY ANN. Admitted February 27, 1806 aged eight years by Church Warden of St. Philip's Church. Indentured to ANNA DRAYTON as a domestic November 16, 1813. Indentures expired February 27, 1816. (E-79). Born in Charleston. (ROSSC)

ROZENBAUM (ROSANBOHM), FRANCIS. Admitted April 15, 1802 aged eight years by Church Wardens of St. Philip's Church. Indentured to JOSEPH TAYLOR as a bricklayer and mason January 5, 1809. Indentures expired April 15, 1813. (D-67). Born in Charleston. JOHN GRUBER father. (ROSSC)

SANFORD, ANN. Admitted October 6, 1803 aged six years by Church Wardens of St. Philip's Church. ANN SANFORD, mother. Indentured to PATRICK PHENNEY and wife as a seamstress March 23, 1810. Indentures expired October 6, 1815. (D-97). Born in Charleston. (ROSSC)

SCHOOLER, THOMAS. Admitted June 29, 1807 aged nine years by Church Wardens of St. Philip's Church. Indentured to JAMES BARKLEY, JR. as a merchant and accountant March 7, 1811. Indentures expired July 1, 1819. (E-100). Born in Charleston. (ROSSC) Admitted from the Poor House. (Minutes, June 25, 1807)

SHAFTON, CATHARINE. Admitted November 10, 1801 aged nine years by Church Wardens of St. Philip's Church. Indentured to ANDREW CRAWFORD for his wife JANE (of Winnsborough), as a domestic March 21, 1805. Indentures expired November 21, 1809. (D-74). Married name MIOT. (Minutes, April 25, 1816)

SHANNON, JOHN. Admitted October 5, 1800 aged four years by ELIZABETH SHANNON, mother. Indentured to FRANCIS COBIA as a house carpenter December 1, 1810. Indentures expired September 14, 1817. (F-63)

SHELBACK, CATHERINE. Admitted November 3, 1803 aged two years by SARAH SHELBACK, mother. Indentured to STEPHEN BRITTON (of Savannah, Georgia) as a domestic July 11, 1816. Indentures expired November 3, 1819. (E-9) Born in Charleston. (ROSSC) Father CHARLES, a baker, dead. (AtoA)

SHELBACK, ELIZA. Admitted November 3, 1803 aged five years by SARAH SHELBACK, mother. Indentured to J. ALLEN SMITH as a domestic February 14, 1811. Indentures expired November 3, 1816. (E-8). Born in Charleston. (ROSSC)

SHILLING, GEORGE. Admitted June 21, 1804 aged nine years by Church Warden of St. Philip's Church. Indentured to FRANCIS ROBERTS as a saddler and harnessmaker November 2, 1809. Indentures expired June 21, 1816. (E-31) Born in Charleston. (ROSSC) Admitted from the Poor House. (Minutes, June 14, 1804)

SHILLING, ROBERT. Admitted June 21, 1804 aged seven years by Church Wardens of St. Philip's Church. Indentured to ANTHONY MENICKEN (of Orangeburgh District) as a storekeeper December 13, 1810. Indentures expired June 21, 1818. (E-32) Born in Charleston. (ROSSC) Admitted from the Poor House. (Minutes, June 14, 1804)

SHILLING, SAMUEL. Admitted June 21, 1804 aged three years by Church Wardens of St. Philip's Church. (E-33) Born in Charleston. (ROSSC) April 14, 1806. (ROSSC) Admitted from the Poor House. (Minutes, June 14, 1804)

SHUAN (SHUHAN), JOHN. Admitted March 12, 1801 aged twelve years by Church Wardens of St. Philip's Church. Indentured to JOHN JOHNSON and JOSEPH FINCH (of Johnson and Finch) as a cut nail manufacturer August 24, 1805. Indentures expired March 12, 1811. (D-23). Born in Charleston. (ROSSC)

SMITH, ANN MARGARET. Admitted October 11, 1804 aged twenty months by SARAH SMITH, mother. Delivered to her mother SARAH VAN HAGEN May 18, 1814. Indentures expired August 11, 1820. (E-38)

SMITH, CHARLES. Admitted April 4, 1805 aged four years and six months by CATHERINE WELSH, mother. Indentured to JACOB MILLER as a ropemaker November 25, 1813. Indentures expired September 4, 1821. (E-51) Born in Charleston. (ROSSC) "A few months ago was convicted before the Commissioners, of pilfering some money out of the shop of Mr. Woods (and) has again been guilty of a like offence..." (Minutes, August 1, 1812)

SMITH, ELIZABETH. Admitted October 11, 1805 aged ten years by Church Wardens of St. Philip's Church. Indentured to MARY CAMERON as a domestic April 6, 1809. Indentures expired October 11, 1813. (E-64) Born in Charleston. (ROSSC)

SMITH (SCHOUP), JOHN HENRY. Admitted October 11, 1804 aged four years and three months by SARAH SMITH, mother. Indentured to CHARLES COQUEREAU as a cabinetmaker May 19, 1814. (E-37) Coquereau left the state and indentures transferred to JAMES MAIN as a cabinetmaker May 7, 1817. (BO) Born in Charleston. (ROSSC) Indentures expired January 11, 1821. (E-37)

SMITH, SARAH. Admitted April 4, 1805 aged seven years and six months by CATHARINE WELSH, mother. Indentured to JOHN AIKEN (of Fairfield District) as a domestic May 11, 1810. Indentures expired September 4, 1815. (E-50) Born in Charleston. (ROSSC)

SPENCER, JAMES. Admitted May 13, 1808 aged three years and three months by MARGARET SPENCER, mother. Indentured to THOMAS WEST as a painter June 26, 1817. Transferred to HENRY WILLIS as a house carpenter January 14, 1819. Indentures expired January 25, 1826. (F-10) Born in Charles-

SPENCER, JAMES, cont'd. ton. Admitted from the Poor House. Father deserted the family. (Minutes, May 12, 1808)

SPINTER, HARRIET. Admitted November 15, 1804 aged eight years by JACOB and MARY SPINTER, parents. Delivered to her mother, a COH Nurse, March 15, 1810. Indentures expired August 15, 1814. (E-40) Born in Charleston. (ROSSC)

SPINTER, SARAH. Admitted November 15, 1804 aged four years by JACOB and MARY SPINTER, parents. Indentured to ELIZA SHIRER as a mantuamaker September 16, 1813. Indentures expired August 15, 1818. (E-42). Born in Charleston. (ROSSC)

SPINTER, SUSANNAH. Admitted November 15, 1804 aged six years by JACOB and MARY SPINTER, parents. Died October 9, 1811. (E-41) Born in Charleston. (ROSSC)

STEWART, AGNES SINCLAIR. Admitted September 7, 1803 aged seven years by Church Warden of St. Philip's Church. Indentured to JOSEPH FERSNER (D-94) of Orangeburg District (ROSP, April 6, 1811) as a domestic April 4, 1811. Indentures expired September 7, 1814. (D-94) Mother, JANE YOUNG. (Minutes, September 8, 1803)

STEWART, JANET. Admitted September 7, 1803 aged twelve years by Church Wardens of St. Philip's Church. Indentured to ANNA BENNETT, wife of THOMAS BENNETT, as a domestic April 17, 1807. Indentures expired September 7, 1809. (D-93) Born in Charleston. (ROSSC)

STEWART, JOHN WARD. Admitted September 7, 1803 aged five years by Church Wardens of St. Philip's Church. Indentured to REINHARD and JACOB FREY as a tanner February 11, 1813. Indentures expired September 7, 1819. (D-95). Born in Charleston. (ROSSC)

STILES, ELIZABETH. Admitted November 16, 1809 aged four years by Church Wardens of St. Philip's Church. Born in New York, now in the Poor House. Indentured to MARY BLANK, wife of CAPTAIN BLANK, as a domestic November 7, 1811. Indentures expired November 16, 1823. (F-40)

STODDARD, WILLIAM. Admitted April 29, 1808 aged three years by Church Wardens of St. Philip's Church. Delivered to his brother, LUTHER STODDARD, as a mariner February 5, 1818. Indentures expired April 26, 1826. (F-9). Born in Charleston. (ROSSC) Mother was insane. (Minutes, April 28, 1808)

SYMONDS (SIMONS), CHARLES. Admitted December 23, 1802 aged three years by Church Wardens of St. Philip's Church. Indentured to SAMUEL ROBERTSON as a merchant June 3, 1813. Indentures expired December 23, 1820. (D-53) Born in Charleston. (ROSSC) Father was dead and the mother eloped to St. Domingo. (AtoA) "CHARLES SIMONS (formerly an Orphan of this Institution)...requested to have the use of the Orphan House Yard to exhibit a display of Fire Works on the 4th July next." (Minutes, April 25, 1822)

TOOL, CHRISTOPHER. Admitted September 3, 1801 aged six years by HENRY JONES, grandfather. An old family record corrected his birthdate to May 21, 1793. Indentured to JOHN WHITING as a turner in all its various branches September 3, 1807. (D032). Born in Charleston. (ROSSC)

TOOL, HENRY JONES. Admitted September 3, 1801 aged five years by HENRY JONES, grandfather. Died July ___, 1802. (D-31)

TORRANS, HUGH HUNTER. Admitted January 3, 1805 aged ten years and eight months by WILLIAM HUNTER TORRANS, father. Indentured to ROBERT EASON as a shipwright May 4, 1809. Indentures expired January 3, 1814. (E-45) Born in Charleston. (ROSSC)

TORRANS, JAMES. Admitted June 23, 1808 aged four years by MARY TORRANS, mother. Born August 24, 1804. Indentured to JOHN ROBERT TORRANS (of Orangeburgh District) as a carpenter April 13, 1818. Indentures expired June 23, 1825. (F-14). Born in Charleston. (ROSSC)

TORRANS, THOMAS GORDON. Admitted January 3, 1805 aged four years and eight months by WILLIAM HUNTER TORRANS, father. Indentured to GRAY and CODY (WILLIAM GRAY and JOHN CODY) as a blacksmith March 23, 1815. Indentures expired January 3, 1820. (E-46) Born in Charleston. (ROSSC)

TORRANS, WILLIAM HAMMETT S. Admitted January 3, 1805 aged twelve years by WILLIAM HUNTER TORRANS, father. Indentured to JOSEPH RIGHTON as a cooper November 26, 1807. Indentures expired January 3, 1813. (E-44) Born in Charleston. (ROSSC)

TUCKER, WILLIAM. Admitted January 5, 1809 aged four years by Church Wardens of St. Philip's Church. Indentured to ALEXANDER CABEEN as a tanner and currier November 28, 1816. Indentures expired January 5, 1826. (F-23) Born in Charleston. (ROSSC) Admitted from the Poor House. (Minutes, January 5, 1809)

TURNER, MARYANN. Admitted December 16, 1808 aged five years by UNITY TURNER, mother, now in the Poor House. Indentured to AMELIA MIMS as a seamstress, spinner and weaver November 10, 1814. Transferred to LUCRETIA SMITH as a mantuamaker July 16, 1818. Indentures expired January 1, 1822. (F018) Born in Charleston. (ROSSC)

UHTORMEHL, FANNY. Admitted June 8, 1809 aged eight years and six months by LEWIS UHTORMEHL, father. Indentured to LEWIS UHTERMOHL (of James Island) as a seamstress January 17, 1811. Indentures expired June 8, 1818. (F-30) Born in Charleston. (ROSSC)

VAILLANT, PETER (PIER). Admitted June 15, 1805 aged six years and six months by CLEMENT VAILLANT, father. Delivered to his aunt, ROZE TALVANDE, September 6, 1810. Indentures expired December 1, 1819. (E-56) Born in St. Domingo. (ROSSC) Father from St. Domingo. (Minutes, May 9, 1805)

VAN NORDON, ELIZA. Admitted September 11, 1806 aged six years and nine months by ABRAHAM VAN NORDON, father. Indentured to ANN BOWLES as a domestic March 31, 1814. Transferred to JOSIAH S. LOVELL, occupation unknown, March 7, 1816. Indentures expired September 11, 1817. (E-86)

VAN NORDON, PETER. Admitted January 29, 1802 aged eleven years by Church Wardens of St. Philip's Church. Indentured to COIT and FRASER as a merchant February 2, 1809. Indentures expired January 29, 1817. (E-93) Born in Charleston. (Minutes, January 19, 1807)

VERONEY, (VERONEE), ELIZABETH. Admitted May 22, 1807 aged ten years by ELIZABETH VERONEY, mother. Indentured to JAMES H. MILLARD (of Orangeburg District) as a domestic January 24, 1811. Indentures expired May 22, 1815. (E-95) Born in Charleston. (ROSSC)

VERONEY (VERONEE), FRANCES. Admitted June 9, 1808 aged five years by ELIZABETH VERONEY, mother. Indentured to WILLIAM PORTER (of Chester District) as a seamstress and weaver November 17, 1814. Due to misusage and ill-treatment, by the master, apprentice returned to the Orphan House, June 25, 1818. Indentures expired June 9, 1821. (F-12) Born in Charleston. (ROSSC) No further information.

VERONEY (VERONEE), SAMUEL. Admitted June 9, 1808 aged three years by ELIZABETH VERONEY, mother. Indentured to JOHN LeCOMPTE as an apothecary November 11, 1819. Transferred to GRIEG CALDER as a baker March 15, 1821. Indentures expired June 9, 1826. (F-13) Born in Charleston. (ROSSC)

VERONEY (VERONEE), WILLIAM JOHN. Admitted May 22, 1807 aged seven years by ELIZABETH VERONEY, mother. Indentured to JACOB HENRY as a cabinetmaker December 9, 1816. Indentures expired May 22, 1820. (E-96) Born in Charleston. (ROSSC)

VINRO, CHARLES ANTHONY. Admitted April 7, 1808 aged eight years by SARAH VINRO, mother. Indentured to JAMES LEVINE as a mariner March 9, 1815. Indentures expired April 7, 1821. (F-21) Born in Charleston. (ROSSC)

VINRO, JOHN WARREN. Admitted April 7, 1808 aged eleven years and six months by SARAH VINRO, mother. Indentured to KIRKPATRICK and DOUGLAS as a merchant and factor September 20, 1810. Indentures expired April 7, 1817. (F-6) Born in Charleston. (ROSSC)

WALTERS, ANN. Admitted June 23, 1803 aged eleven years by ELIZABETH WILLIS, mother. Indentured to ELIZABETH FRAZIER (Indenture signed by ANN FERGUSON) as a domestic May 11, 1807. Indentures expired June 23, 1810. (D-75) Born in South Carolina. (ROSSC) Father, JOHN WALTER, dead. (AtoA)

WALTERS, JANE. Admitted June 23, 1803 aged eight years by ELIZABETH WILLIS, mother. Indentured to MARGARET COCHRAN as a domestic August 10, 1810. Transferred to DAVID RUMPH (of Orangeburg District), occupation unknown, November 28, 1810. Indentures expired June 23, 1813. (D-76) Born in South Carolina. (ROSSC)

WEATHERS, JANE. Admitted January 20, 1803 aged six years by JEMIMA WEATHERS, mother. Indentured to HENRY H. MOORE as a domestic February 15, 1810. Transferred to JOSEPH MOSES, occupation unknown, July 13, 1810. Transferred to MARY WOOD, occupation unknown, February 28, 1811. Indentures expired January 20, 1915. (D-71) Born in Charleston. (ROSSC)

WEATHERS, THOMAS GEORGE. Admitted January 20, 1803 aged nine years by JEMIMA WEATHERS, mother. Indentured to RICHARD WELLS as a boatbuilder October 30, 1806. Indentures expired January 20, 1814. (D-72) Born in Charleston. (ROSSC)

WILKINS, WILLIAM. Admitted November 24, 1803 aged four years by Church Wardens of St. Philip's Church. Indentured to JOHN SIMONTON (of Fairfield District) as a farmer October 29, 1812. Indentures expired November 24, 1820. (E-17)

WILLIAMS, JAMES. Admitted January 20, 1803 by Church Wardens of St. Philip's Church. (D-54) Father, unknown, was a drayman. (AtoA) No further information.

WILLIS, JACOB. Admitted July 21, 1802 aged seven years by Church Wardens of St. Philip's Church. Indentured to DR. JOHN NOBLE as a doctor of medicine April 13, 1809. Transferred to JOHN WIGHTMAN as a turner March 21, 1811. Transferred to DR. STANISLAS HUARD as a doctor of medicine April 25, 1811. Indentures expired July 24, 1816. (D-84) Born in Charleston. (ROSSC)

WILLIS, WILLIAM. Admitted July 21, 1802 aged nine years by Church Wardens of St. Philip's Church. Indentured to GEORGE GIBBES as a baker March 16, 1807. Indentures expired July 21, 1814. (D-89) Born in Charleston. (ROSSC) In 1831 Willis [of Farmville, Prince Edward County, Virginia] (Minutes, October 11, 1831) offered to furnish books for the Sunday School Library. (Minutes, August 11, 1831)

WILSON, ARCHIBALD. Admitted November 19, 1807 aged twelve years by MARY WILSON, mother. Indentured to THOMAS McCULLOUGH (of Fairfield District) as a farmer April 6, 1810. Indentures expired November 19, 1816. (E-104) Born in Charleston. (ROSSC) Father, JOHN WILSON, dead and was a cabinet-maker. (Minutes, November 19, 1807)

WILSON, JAMES. Admitted November 19, 1807 aged nine years by MARY MILLER, mother. Indentured to WILLIAM WALKER as a saddler and harnessmaker February 11, 1813. Indentures expired November 19, 1819. (E-105) Born in Charleston. (ROSSC)

WISH, JOHN. Admitted June 26, 1806 aged nine years by WILLIAM WISH, uncle. Placed aboard the U.S. Frigate John Adams (CAPTAIN DENT) as a midshipman February 23, 1811. Indentures expired June 26, 1818. (E-82) Born in Charleston. (ROSSC)

WISH, WILLIAM. Admitted June 26, 1806 aged six years by WILLIAM WISH, uncle. Indentured to LAWRENCE KEARNEY as a mariner July 7, 1814. Indentures expired June 26, 1821. (E-83) Born in Charleston. (ROSSC)

WOLFE, JOHN. Admitted March 28, 1800 by the Poor House. Taken away by his aunt and carried to the north ward, nd. Indentures expired March 28, 1810. (D-7)

WOOLCOCK, JOHN. Admitted May 10, 1804 aged seven years by JANE WOOLCOCK, mother. Indentured to PETER GAUTH as a bricklayer August 2, 1811. Indentures expired May 10, 1818. (E-29) Born in Charleston. (ROSSC)

WRIGHT, MARGARET. Admitted July 13, 1809 aged nine years by MARY AGNEW, mother. Indentured to MARY S. GADSDEN as a seamstress March 9, 1815. Indentures expired July 14, 1818. (F-33) Born in Charleston. (ROSSC)

YOUNG, AGNES STEWART. Admitted September 8, 1803 aged four years by JANE YOUNG, mother. (D-92) Died of an ulcer of the hip in 1813 and buried in the First Presbyterian Burial Ground. (ROSP, March 20, 1813)

ZACHMAN, CHRISTINA ELIZABETH. Admitted January 12, 1809 aged five years by ANN ZACHMAN, mother. Delivered to her mother, MARGARET BALLUND, April 6, 1815. (F-24) Born December 30, 1803 (Minutes, January 12, 1809). Sister, MARGARET, born October 9, 1806 not admitted. (Minutes, January 12, 1809)

ABRAMS, SAMUEL. Admitted June 16, 1814 aged four years by ANN ABRAMS, mother. Delivered to his father, LEVY ABRAMS, July 1, 1814. Indentures expired June 16, 1831. (G-64)

ADAMS, CATHARINE. Admitted July 13, 1815 aged seven years by Warden of Charleston. Indentured to EDWARD BRAILSFORD, physician, as a domestic August 13, 1818. Indentures expired May 21, 1825. (G-91)

ADAMS, SARAH. Admitted February 3, 1814 aged nine years by Warden of Charleston. Delivered to her brother-in-law, FRANCIS KRIEF, January 7, 1819. Indentures expired February 3, 1823. (G-45)

AIKEN, ELIZABETH. Admitted June 24, 1819 aged eight years by CATHERINE AIKEN, mother. Born July 2, 1810. Delivered to her mother December 7, 1820. Indentures expired July 2, 1828. (I-36)

AIKEN, MARY. Admitted June 24, 1819 aged seven years by CATHERINE AIKEN, mother. Delivered to her mother December 7, 1820. Indentures expired March 22, 1830. (I-37)

ANDERSON, ELIZABETH. Admitted January 13, 1814 aged ten years by Warden of Charleston. Indentured to JOHN REILY (of Chester District) as a spinner and weaver November 9, 1815. Indentures expired January 13, 1822. (G-38)

BETERSON, ELIZABETH. Admitted July 18, 1816 aged four years by FRANCES BETERSON, mother. Delivered to her mother June 16, 1825. (G-128)

BETERSON, HARRIET. Admitted July 18, 1816 aged five years by FRANCES BETERSON, mother. Died September 4, 1817. (G-127)

BEVIN, JOHN KING. Admitted July 15, 1819 aged three years by Warden of Charleston. Indentured to JOSEPH RIGHTON as a cooper February 3, 1831. (I-39) Grandfather, FRANCIS BEVIN. (AtoA)

BLAKELEY, ELIAS. Admitted March 21, 1811 aged ten years by SETH BLAKELEY, father. Indentured to JOSEPH McCULLOUGH (of Greenville District) as a farmer May 12, 1814. Indentures expired March 21, 1822. (F-71)

BLAKELEY, WILLIAM. Admitted March 21, 1811 aged twelve years by SETH BLAKELEY, father. Indentured to WILLIAM VANVELSEY as a wheelwright October 27, 1814. Indentures expired March 21, 1820. (F-70)

BOAK, BENJAMIN. Admitted November 20, 1817 aged nine years by RICHARD BOAK, father. Indentured to ELIZA TURNER as a storekeeper March 14, 1822. Indentures expired March 26, 1829. (H-45)

BOAK, EDWARD. Admitted November 20, 1817 aged five years and three months by RICHARD BOAK, father. (H-47) Indentured to T.W. CARDOZO, editor of the Southern Patriot, as a printer June 29, 1826. (ROSP, July 5, 1826) Indentures expired August 28, 1833. (H-47)

BOAK, HENRY. Admitted November 20, 1817 aged eight years and six months by RICHARD BOAK, father. Indentured to WILLIAM PARKS (of Laurens District) as a farmer December 9, 1824. Indentures expired April 26, 1830. (H-46)

BROSS, BENJAMIN. Admitted August 31, 1815 aged four years by Warden of Charleston. Born May 1, 1811. Indentured to JOHN BROSS (of Abbeville District) as a taylor June 12, 1823. Transferred to CHARLES H. CHURCH as a copperplate printer September 18, 1826. Transferred to WILLIAM W. PURSE as a cabinetmaker September 27, 1827. Indentures expired May 1, 1832. (G-94)

BROSS, ELIZA. Admitted November 4, 1813 aged eight years by MARY BROSS, mother. Indentured to M.F. HARVES as a domestic June 18, 1818. Indentures expired November 4, 1823. (G-25) From Sullivan's Island. (AtoA)

BROSS, FRANCIS. Admitted November 4, 1813 aged ten years by MARY BROSS, mother. Indentured to DAVID R. WILLIAMS of the firm of DAVID R. WILLIAMS & CO. of the Cheraw Union Factory (of Darlington District) as a machinist and manufacturer of paper January 15, 1816. Indentures expired November 4, 1824. (G-24) From Sullivan's Island. (AtoA)

BROSS, JOHN. Admitted November 4, 1813 aged twelve years by MARY BROSS, mother. Indentured to CHARLES COQUEREAU as a cabinet maker September 21, 1815. Transferred to ETHAN PARROTT, occupation unknown. March 27, 1817. Indentures expired November 4, 1822. (G-23) From Sullivan's Island. (AtoA)

BROWN, COLLIN. Admitted June 2, 1814 aged three years and six months by the Warden of Charleston. Indentured to THOMAS FULTON, SR. (of Laurens District) as a farmer July 29, 1824. Indentures expired December 2, 1831. (G-57) An orphan. (AtoA) "Absconded during the Holy Days." (ROSP, April 14, 1824) Returned the week of July 25, 1824. (ROSP, July 25, 1824)

BROWN, JAMES. Admitted May 24, 1810 aged seven years and six months by ELIZABETH SHEKE, mother. Indentured to DAVID R. WILLIAMS & CO., DAVID MATTHEWS and DAVID R. WILLIAMS (of Cheraw District) as a mechanist and manufacturer of paper January 15, 1816. Indentures expired May 24, 1823. (F-49)

BROWN, MICHAEL. Admitted July 13, 1815 aged nine years by Warden of Charleston. Indentured to MICHAEL ELLARD as a carpenter January 27, 1820. Transferred to ELIAS GREGG (of Society Hill, Darlington District) as a storekeeper February 22, 1821. Indentures expired August 11, 1826. (G-92)

BROWN, WILLIAM. Admitted January 13, 1814 aged seven years by REBECCA BROWN, mother. Died September 23, 1818. (G-37) Admitted from the Poor House. (ROSP, January 15, 1814)

BUCHANAN, CATHERINE CAROLINE. Admitted October 10, 1813 aged ten years by JOHN BUCHANAN, father. Indentured to M.A. CHATELIN as a milliner March 12, 1818. Transferred to JOHN LACKS, occupation unknown, September 24, 1818. Indentures expired October 7, 1821. (G-22)

BUNCH, HEZEKIAH. Admitted March 20, 1817 aged six years by ELIZABETH BUNCH, mother. (H-19) Absconded, nd. (ROSP, January 23, 1828)

BUNCH, TIMOTHY. Admitted March 20, 1817 aged two years by ELIZABETH BUNCH, mother. (H-20) Absconded, nd. (ROSP, January 23, 1828)

BURROWS, JAMES. Admitted March 27, 1817 aged eleven years by MARY BURROWS, mother. Indentured to FRAZER and SON as a ship joiner November 25, 1819. Transferred to his mother June 7, 1821. Indentures expired November 13, 1826. (H-21) Born November 13, 1805. Father, unknown, was a branch pilot who had drowned, nd. (AtoA)

BURROWS, SAMUEL. Admitted March 27, 1817 aged nine years by MARY BURROWS, mother. Indentured to OCTAVIUS CRIPPS as a merchant May 4, 1820. Due to the death of the master, indentures transferred to DAVIS and DUFFUS as a bookkeeper April 5, 1821. Indentures expired March 14, 1829. (H-22)

BUTLER, DANIEL. Admitted June 6, 1811 aged five years by MARTHA BUTLER, mother. (F-79) Died December __, 1813 of worm fever and was buried in the Roman Church Burial Ground. (ROSP, December 25, 1813)

BUTLER, EDWARD WILLIAM. Admitted November 10, 1814 aged seven years by MARIA BUTLER, mother. Born March 29, 1807. Indentured to JOSHUA NEVILLE and SON as a cabinetmaker. (G-74) Father, JOSEPH BUTLER, dead. Grandfather, EDWARD TASH, a gunsmith. (AtoA)

BUTLER, JOHN. Admitted January 13, 1814 aged five years by MARTHA BUTLER, mother. Indentured to HENRY BARTLESS as a blacksmith September 19, 1822. Transferred to JOHN McKEEGAN as a blacksmith August 26, 1824. Transferred to JAMES ROSS (ROSE), occupation unknown, April 5, 1827. Indentures expired January 13, 1830. (G-35) Admitted from the Poor House. (ROSP, January 15, 1814)

BUTLER, JOSEPH PIERCE. Admitted November 10, 1814 aged five years by MARIA BUTLER, mother. Born February 20, 1809. Delivered to his mother May 18, 1820. Indentures expired February 20, 1830. (G-75)

BUTLER, MARY. Admitted June 6, 1811 aged eight years by MARTHA BUTLER, mother. Indentured to MARY HUNTER as a milliner and mantuamaker November 23, 1815. Indentures expired June 6, 1821. (F-77) In 1821, S. STANTON declared that "he (DANIEL BUTLER, father) told me he placed Money in the Bank for the Benefit of his children, also two Negroes, likely and young, to be sold to the best advantage. As far as I can recollect it is about thirteen years ago. He made choice of Mr. SIMON MAGWOOD as Guardian for his Children - THOMAS FLIN, Grocer drew the will. He is since dead." (Minutes, August 9, 1821)

BUTLER, THOMAS JAMES. Admitted November 10, 1814 aged three years by MARIA BUTLER, mother. Born December 23, 1811. Indentured to WILLIAM BURCHALL & CO. (of Fairfield) as a merchant November 20, 1824. Indentures expired December 23, 1832. (G-76)

CAMPBELL, JOHN. Admitted June 11, 1812 aged nine years and ten months by Warden of Charleston. Indentures expired August 11, 1823. (F-109) Sent to college. (COH Inmates' Files) "An offer being made to JOHN CAMPBELL by Mr. EPPS of Virginia, by letter and thro' his son now at Columbia College, to reside in his family as a private tutor...there to be boarded, and to receive besides a salary of $150.00 per annum and also that during the time he will study Law with a view to practice the profession with Mr. EPPS' son." (Minutes, July 12, 1821) Later became a District Attorney of the United States. (CP, p. 74)

CAMPBELL, JOSEPH. Admitted May 14, 1818, aged eleven years by Warden of Charleston. Indentured to PETER DREGE as a storekeeper September 27, 1821. Indentures expired November 20, 1828. (H-72)

CARMINADE, JOHN Admitted January 22, 1818 aged eight years by VERONIQUE CARMINADE, mother. Born November 27, 1810. Delivered to his mother January 31, 1822. Indentures expired November 27, 1831. (H-57)

CARMINADE, PETER. Admitted January 22, 1818 aged six years by VERONIQUE CARMINADE, mother. Born September 28, 1812. Delivered to his mother January 31, 1822. Indentures expired September 28, 1833. (H-58)

CARROLL, ELIZABETH. Admitted January 2, 1818 aged seven years by MARY ANN CARROLL, mother. Born August 27, 1810. Delivered to her mother, MARY ANN EVANS, December 6, 1821. Indentures expired August 27, 1828. (H-53)

CARROLL, MARY ANN. Admitted January 2, 1818 aged two years by MARY ANN CARROLL, mother. Born April 3, 1815. Delivered to her mother, MARY ANN EVANS, December 6, 1821. Indentures expired April 3, 1833. (H-54)

CHANSON, CATHERINE. Admitted November 7, 1811 aged five years by CHARLOTTE CHANSON, mother. Delivered to her mother, a COH Nurse, October 23, 1817. Indentures expired January 9, 1823. (F-95)

CHANSON, HENRIETTA. Admitted November 7, 1811 aged seven years by CHARLOTTE CHANSON, mother. (F-94) Died January 1816 of pneumonia. (ROSP, January 13, 1816)

CHANSON, MARY. Admitted November 7, 1811 aged nine years by CHARLOTTE CHANSON, mother. Delivered to her mother, a COH Nurse May 29, 1817. Indentures expired November 7, 1823. (F-93)

CHATBURN, MARY. Admitted August 7, 1817 by FRANCES ANN CHATBURN, mother. Born March 26, 1809. Delivered to her mother November 12, 1819. Indentures expired March 26, 1830. (H-31)

CHURCH, CHARLES. Admitted May 21, 1812 aged ten years by MARGARET CHURCH, mother. Indentured to ROBERT STEVENS, JR. as a merchant November 30, 1815. Transferred to WILLIAM THOMPSON as a merchant and ship chandler April 29, 1816. Indentures expired May 21, 1823. (F-104)

CLARKE, CORNELIUS VANDERBUILT HENRY. Admitted February 19, 1818 aged six years by ELIZABETH CLARKE, mother. (H-59) Indentured to JOEL THORP of the Line Ship Commodore Perry as a mariner October 11, 1825. (ROSP, October 19, 1825)

CLAYBROOK, MARY. Admitted February 8, 1810 aged seven years by Church Wardens of St. Philip's Church. Delivered to her uncle, JOHN D. KIRK, June 18, 1818. Indentures expired February 8, 1821. (F-43) Later MARY MANNO, COH Nurse and Sewing Mistress. In 1829, she had been a widow for two years and had one child aged three years. REV. H. CHRIETZBERG - grandson. (COH Officers' Files - Nurse and Sewing Mistress)

CLAYTON, MARY. Admitted June 28, 1811 aged eleven years by Warden of Charleston. Indentured to MRS. JULIET ELLIOTT as a domestic December 15, 1813. Indentures expired March 1, 1818. (F-80)

COGHLAN, BENJAMIN FRANKLIN. Admitted February 15, 13 16 aged four years by ELLEN COGHLAN, mother. Born April 11, ____. Indentured to THOMAS FULTON (of Laurens District) as a planter July 29, 1824. Indentures expired April 11, 1832. (G-106)

COGHLAN, JACKSON. Admitted September 23, 1818 aged five years by ELESNOR COGHLAN, mother. Indentured to JOHN DUFF as a shoemaker June 14, 1827. Indentures expired September 24, 1834. (I-6) Admitted from the Poor House. (AtoA) Absconded April 14, 1824 and returned July 25, 1824. (ROSP, July 25, 1824)

COLLINS, JOHN. Admitted March 9, 1815 aged ten years by CATHERINE COLLINS, mother. Born December 10, 1804. Indentured to HENRY BONDO as a jeweller and goldsmith June 6, 1816. Transferred to HENRY VOGLER, occupation unknown, March 13, 1817. Indentures expired December 10, 1825. (G-85)

CONNOLY, EDWARD. Admitted April 22, 1813 aged ten years by ELIZA CONNOLY, mother. Indentured to JOSEPH YATES as a cooper July 11, 1816. Indentures expired September 27, 1824. (G-18)

CONNOLY, FREDERICK. Admitted April 22, 1813 aged seven years by ELIZA CONNOLY, mother. Born January 4, 1806. (G-19) Died November __, 1813, of a dropsical affection and diseased lungs. (ROSP, November 13, 1813) Mother's parents, THOMAS and SARAH HAM. Mother was married three times. Father, CAPTAIN THOMAS CONNOLY, died in New Orleans in September 1812. (AtoA)

CONNOLY, MARIA. Admitted April 22, 1813 aged twelve years by ELIZA CONNOLY, mother. Indentured to ANN R. ROYAS (of Georgetown) as a seamtress and housekeeper October 21, 1813. Indentures expired August 17, 1819. (G-17)

COURTMAN, JOHN FREDERIC. Admitted May 16, 1816 aged seven years by MARY McGEE, mother. Sent to the Poor House June 29, 1826. (G-116)

CREAMER (CAMERON), AMELIA. Admitted December 14, 1815 aged four years by MARY CREAMER, mother. (G-100) Delivered to her mother returning to Scotland August 22, 1822. (Minutes, August 22, 1822) Indentures expired December 14, 1829. (G-100)

CREAMER (CAMERON), GEORGE. Admitted June 25, 1814 by MARY CREAMER, mother. Born July 7, 1807. (G-56) Delivered to his mother returning to Scotland August 22, 1822. (Minutes, August 22, 1822) Indentures expired July 7, 1828. (G-56)

CREAMER (CAMERON), HANNAH. Admitted May 27, 1814 aged four years and six months by MARY CREAMER, mother. Indentured to JANE WHITE as a domestic June 1, 1820. Indentures expired November 27, 1827. (G-52)

CREAMER, (CAMERON), JANET. Admitted May 27, 1814 aged nine years by MARY CREAMER, mother. Indentured to ANN CATHERINE DAVIS as a mantua-maker May 21, 1818. Indentures expired May 27, 1823. (G-51)

CROOK, AMELIA (EMMA). Admitted April 27, 1815 aged seven years and six months by Warden of Charleston. Delivered to her aunt, JANE ENGLAND, March 12, 1818. Indentures expired October 15, 1825. (G-86)

CUTTER, ANNA. Admitted October 20, 1814 aged thirteen years by Warden of Charleston. (G-71) Indentured to MARTIN BLANK (BLANCH) of Edgefield as a spinner and weaver December 1, 1814. (ROSP, December 3, 1814) Indentures expired October 20, 1819. (G-71)

CUTTER, ROBERT. Admitted August 2, 1811 aged four years and six months by Warden of Charleston. Born December __, 1807. Indentured to GIBSON and MARINER as a sailmaker September 20, 1821. Indentures expired December 10, 1828. (F-88)

DANIEL, LEWIS. Admitted October 16, 1817 aged six years by ELIZA LOVE, mother. Born September 15, 1811. Indentured to COL. WILLIAM KINCAID (of Fairfield District) as a merchant December 4, 1824. Indentures expired September 15, 1832. (H-43)

DARNES, JULIANA. Admitted October 14, 1819 aged ten years by NANCY DARNES, mother. Born January 1, 1809. Indentured to JOSEPH YATES as a domestic June 28, 1821. Indentures expired January 1, 1827. (I-40) Grandfather, MR. DARNES, lived in Virginia. (Minutes, April 27, 1820)

DAVIDSON, JOHN. Admitted October 20, 1814 aged nine years by Warden of Charleston. Indentured to SAMUEL BERBANT as a taylor July 14, 1820. Indentures expired October 20, 1826. (G-72)

DAVIS, JOHN. Admitted January 9, 1812 aged ten years by Warden of Charleston. Indentured to WILLIAM MATTHEWS and DAVID R. WILLIAMS of DAVID R. WILLIAMS & CO. of the Cheraw Union Factory (of Darlington District) as a merchant January 15, 1816. Indentures expired January 9, 1823. (F-96)

DAVIS, MARY ANN. Admitted December 18, 1817 aged twelve years by Warden of Charleston. Born December 25, 1805. Indentured to ABIGAIL PHILLIPS as a domestic December 7, 1820. Indentures expired December 25, 1823. (H-51)

DAVIS, ROBERT. Admitted January 9, 1812 aged seven years by Warden of Charleston. (F-97) Indentured to JAMES R. ERVIN (of Marion District) as a merchant May 2, 1816. (ROSP, May 5, 1816) Indentures expired January 9, 1824. (ROSSC)

DAWSON, MARGARET. Admitted November 13, 1817 aged seven years by ELIZABETH MURPHY, mother. Born October 28, 1810. Indentures expired October 28, 1828. (H-44) No further information.

DEAN, ANN. Admitted December 31, 1818 aged ten years by GLADUS DEAN, mother. Born March 1, 1808. Died April 8, 1820. (I-16)

DEAN, JAMES. Admitted December 31, 1818 aged five years by GLADUS DEAN, mother. Born January 17, 1812. (I-18) "This unhappy little object is deformed - both in his hands and feet and there is enough to apprehend a malconformation of brain - he is in some degree Idiotic. This porpoensity to indulge in mischevous Tricks is remarkable... which increases with his growth - His are frequent and violent." (Medical Matters - Illnesses and Treatments, 1825) No further information.

DEAN, ROBERT. Admitted December 31, 1818 aged nine years by GLADUS
DEAN, mother. Born May 5, 1809. (I-17) Absconded nd. (ROSP,
January 23, 1828)

DELANY, DANIEL SHARP. Admitted July 16, 1818 aged six years by ANN
DELANY, mother. Indentured to HENRY BOISDON as a baker April 27, 1826.
(H-78) Transferred to his brother-in-law, JOHN BLANCHARD, as a shoe-
maker April 30, 1829. (BO)

DILLON, HENRY. Admitted August 5, 1819 aged ten years by JOHN DILLON,
father. Indentured to ROBERT W. WILL as a bricklayer September 4, 1823.
Transferred to PAUL REMLEY as a bricklayer December 2, 1825. Indentures
expired December 9, 1829. (I-40)

DISHER, MARY. Admitted March 10, 1819 aged four years by E. DISHER,
mother. Died June 11, 1822. (I-27)

DOITY, JANE. Admitted January 2, 1818 aged two years by Warden of
Charleston. Born July 1, 1815. Died November 13, 1819. (H-55)

DONOHOE, ANN. Admitted November 25, 1819 aged five years by ANN DONOHOE,
mother. Born November 7, 1815. (I-51) Delivered to her mother
returning to Ireland. July 14, 1820. (BO) Indentures expired November
7, 1833. (I-51)

DONOHOE, MARGARET. Admitted November 25, 1819 aged seven years by ANN
DONOHOE, mother. (I-50) Delivered to her mother, returning to Ireland.
July 14, 1820. (BO)

DOSON, LEVY. Admitted October 13, 1814 aged nine years by ANN DOSON,
mother. Born May __, 1805. Indentured to JOHN LING as a grocer and
storekeeper October 30, 1817. Indentures expired May 10, 1826.
(G-70) Alias FERNANDO PRINCE. (ROSP, October 15, 1814)

DOWNIE (DOWNEY), ANN. Admitted October 3, 1816 aged eight years by
PETER DOWNIE, father. Born August 13, 1808. Indentured to WILLIAM
SMITH as a domestic November 25, 1819. Transferred to RACHEL BROOKS.
Occupation unknown, June 13, 1822. Indentures expired August 13,
1826. (H-7) Born in Ireland. (AtoA)

DOWNEY, JOHN. Admitted October 17, 1816 aged six years by PETER DOWNEY,
father. Indentured to JAMES HAIG, owner of the Charleston Gazette,
as a printer February 16, 1826. Indentures expired September 5, 1831.
(H-10) Born September 5, 1810 in Lancaster. (AtoA)

DOYLE, ANN. Admitted July 18, 1819 aged two years by Warden of Charleston. Born June 8, 1817. Indentured to REV. JOHN JACOB TSCHUDY as
a domestic May 28, 1830. Indentures expired June 8, 1835. (I-38)
An orphan. (AtoA)

DUKE, WILLIAM. Admitted October 1, 1812 aged three years and six
months by JOHN C. DUKE, father. Indentured to NATHANIEL BOSWORTH
as an organ and pianomaker May 2, 1822. Transferred to JAMES HAIG,
owner of the City Gazette, as a printer June 9, 1825. Indentures
expired April 1, 1830. (G-4) "Died about three years ago, at the
house of MR. CHARLES MILLHOUSE, in Barnwell District, eleven miles
from the Court House, on the road to Orangeburgh." (Minutes, November
5, 1829)

DUNCAN, CATHERINE. Admitted July 16, 1818 aged eleven years by ANN
C. DUNCAN, mother. Indentured to EDWARD BLAKE as a domestic January
27, 1820. (H-79) Father died October 18, 1817. WILLIAM DISHER,
uncle. (AtoA)

DUNCAN, MARY. Admitted November 26, 1818 aged six years by ANN C.
DUNCAN, mother. Indentured to REV. EDWARD RUTLEDGE as a domestic
May 22, 1823. Transferred to ANN R. FASH as a taylor February 26, 1824.
Indentures expired November 6, 1830. (I-12) Each master returned
her for stealing. (BO)

DUNMIRE (DUNMYRE), PHILIP. Admitted July 23, 1818 aged six years by
GRACEY DUNMIRE, mother. Indentured to WILLIAM ABRAHAMS (of Laurens
District) as a farmer December 14, 1826. (H-82)

EAGAN, WILLIAM THOMAS. Admitted October 2, 1817 aged nine years by
Warden of Charleston. A derelict. Indentures expired October 2, 1829.
(H-38) No further information.

ELLIOTT, MARY ANN. Admitted January 29, 1819 aged four years by MRS.
_____ ELLIOTT, mother. Born April 8, 1814. Indentured to THOMAS Y.
SIMONS as a domestic January 27, 1825. Transferred to J.M. CHISOLM,
occupation unknown, May 18, 1826. Indentures expired April 8, 1832.
(I-21)

ELLIOTT, THOMAS. Admitted February 25, 1819 aged three years by CHARLOTTE
ELLIOTT, mother. Born April 16, 1816. Died August 11, 1827 of "a
bilious (fever) aggravated by worms." (ROSP, August 15, 1827)

ELLIOTT, WILLIAM. Admitted January 29, 1819 aged six years by MRS.
_____ ELLIOTT, mother. Born November 5, ____. Indentured to JAMES
MARSH and SON as a ship carpenter June 1, 1826. Indentures expired
November 5, 1833. (I-20) Absconded June 29, 1831 and was thought
to be in North Carolina. (BO)

ERHARD, DANIEL. Admitted October 16, 1817 aged twelve years by Warden
of Charleston. Born January 1, 1805. Indentured to JOHN A. BENNET as
a black and white smith February 18, 1819. Indentures expired January
1, 1826. (H-39)

ERHARD, ELIZA. Admitted October 16, 1817 aged two years by Warden of
Charleston. Born February 4, 1815. Indentures expired February 4,
1833. (H-42) Adopted by THOMAS CHRISTBURG October 15, 1825. (BO)

ERHARD, MARGARET. Admitted October 16, 1817 aged seven years by Warden
of Charleston. Born December 18, 1809. Indentured to C.E. CHANNER as
a taylor February 26, 1824. Indentures expired December 18, 1827. (H-41)

ERHARD, MARY. Admitted October 16, 1817 aged seven years by Warden of
Charleston. Born December 18, 1809. Indentured to THOMAS HART (of
Lancaster District) as a spinner and weaver December 9, 1819. Inden-
tures expired December 18, 1827. (H-40)

EVANS (EVEANS), JOHN. Admitted January 13, 1814 aged five years by
ELIZABETH EVANS, mother. Indentured to GEORGE CHRETZBERG as a baker
February 12, 1824. Indentures expired January 13, 1830. (G-34) Admitted
from the Poor House. (ROSP, January 15, 1814)

EVANS, (EVEANS), WILLIAM. Admitted September 2, 1815 aged three years
by ELIZABETH EVANS, mother. Indentured to WILLIAM H. FULTON (of Laurens
District) as a farmer February 1, 1827. Indentures expired September
2, 1832. (G-82) Born October 25, ____ (AtoA)

FAIRCHILD, LEWIS JOHNSON BLAKELEY. Admitted December 28, 1815 aged two
years by MARY BISHOP, mother. Delivered to his mother April 4, 1816.
Indentures expired December 28, 1834. (G-101)

FERNEAU, FRANCIS HENRY. Admitted January 11, 1810 aged three years
and nine months by ANN FERNEAU, mother. Delivered to his mother, SARAH
LOWREY, October 15, 1818. Indentures expired April 1, 1827. (F-41)

FINDLAY (FINLAY), MARGARET. Admitted March 26, 1812 aged five years by
Warden of Charleston. Indentured to MARY ANN WHITE as a mantuamaker
January 29, 1819. Transferred to SUSAN D. MAYER, occupation unknown,
February 25, 1820. Indentures expired March 26, 1825. (F-103)

FORDHAM, BENJAMIN. Admitted February 20, 1817 aged eight years by ELIZA
(ELEANOR) FORDHAM, mother. Delivered to his mother May 27, 1819.
Indentures expired February 15, 1830. (H-16)

FORDHAM, JOHN. Admitted February 20, 1817 aged six years by ELIZA
(ELEANOR) FORDHAM, mother. Born December 12, ____. Delivered to his
mother May 27, 1819. Indentures expired December 12, 1833. (H-17)

FORRESTER, JANE. Admitted January 13, 1814 aged eight years by JANE
FORRESTER, mother. Indentured to ARATHUSA BELTON as a mantuamaker
August 13, 1818. Indentures expired January 13, 1824. (G-33) Admitted
from the Poor House. (ROSP, January 15, 1814)

FRASER, JACOB. Admitted April 9, 1818 aged five years by WILLIAM SCOTT,
friend. (H-69) Indentured to JONATHAN EMERY, captain of the Schooner
Harvest, as a mariner October 7, 1825. (ROSP, October 12, 1825)
Indentures expired April 9, 1834. (H-69)

FURCHESS, JOHN. Admitted March 26, 1818 aged six years by ELIZABETH
FURCHESS, mother. (H-65) "Drowned in Bennett's Mill Pond on Monday
last...deposited in the Burial Ground of the Methodist Episcopal Church."
(ROSP, May 2, 1825)

GAINER, THOMAS. Admitted May 21, 1812 aged six years by Warden of
Charleston. Indentured to H. DENISON as a storekeeper November 25,
1819. Indentures expired May 21, 1827. (F-105)

GAPPIN, ELIZA HILL. Admitted December 1, 1814 aged nine years by
WILLIAM GAPPIN, father. Born January 15, 1805. Indentured to SILAS
HARDIN (of Fairfield District) as a spinner and weaver April 4, 1816.
Indentures expired January 15, 1823. (G-77) Father a private in the
18th Regiment, U.S. Army. (AtoA)

GAPPIN, JOHN. Admitted June 4, 1812 aged two years by WILLIAM GAPPIN,
father. Indentured to THOMAS S. LEAK (of Laurens District) as a farmer
January 27, 1825. Indentures expired June 4, 1831. (F-108)

GAPPIN, WILLIAM. Admitted June 4, 1812 aged four years by WILLIAM GAPPIN,
father. Indentured to THOMAS CHERRYTREE (of Newberry District) as a
farmer September 3, 1821. Indentures expired June 4, 1829. (F-107)

GARDNER, LOUISA. Admitted January 23, 1812 aged ten years by Warden of
Charleston. Indentured to AMELIA MIMS (of Four Holes) as a seamtress,
spinner, and weaver November 10, 1814. Transferred to ANNE PORTER as
a seamstress July 9, 1818. Indentures expired January 23, 1820. (F-98)
As LOUISA A. SWAIN of Richmond, Indiana, she requested aid from the
Commissioners in 1845, which was refused. (Minutes, September 4, 1845)

GEDNEY, JOHN SIMPSON. Admitted May 31, 1810 aged eight years by JANE
GEDNEY, mother. Indentured to CHARLES D. TORRE as a merchant September
14, 1815. Transferred to JOHN M. SCHIERLE as a carpenter November 19,
1819. Indentures expired May 31, 1823. (F-53) LYDIA MAIN - sister.
(Minutes, July 22, 1819)

GEDNEY, JOSEPH HENRY. Admitted August 30, 1810 aged two years by JANE
GEDNEY, mother. (F-56) Died February 22, 1816 of pleurisy complicated
by worms. (ROSP, February 17, 1816)

GEDNEY, THOMAS ROBERT. Admitted June 14, 1810 aged eleven years by
JANE GEDNEY, mother. Indentured to CAPTAIN EDWARD P. KENNEDY as a
mariner in the U.S. Navy July 8, 1813. Indentures expired June 14,
1820. (F-54) For his discovery of a new channel to the Atlantic
Ocean Gedney was awarded "The Gedney Plate" a silver service. Later,
a Coast Guard Cutter was named for him. (COH inmates' Files)

GILBERT, JOHN. Admitted July 7, 1814 aged thirteen years by JOSEPH
GILBERT, father. Born February 7, 1802. Indentured to D.A. RING as
a painter and glazier August 3, 1815. Released from his indentures
by a Magistrate July 9, 1818. Indentures expired February 7, 1823.
(G-65)

GILBERT, WILLIAM. Admitted July 7, 1814 aged ten years by JOSEPH GILBERT, father. Born July __, 1804. Indentured to WILLIAM MATTHEWS of DAVID R. WILLIAMS & CO. of the Cheraw Union Factory (of Darlington District) as a mechanic and manufacturer of paper January 15, 1816. Indentures expired July 7, 1825. (G-66)

GILES, ROBERT FENWICKE. Admitted May 2, 1811 aged nine years by MATILDA GILES, mother. Delivered to his mother, MATILDA WHITE, January 20, 1815. Indentures expired May 2, 1823. (F-75)

GILES, THOMAS WASHINGTON. Admitted September 12, 1811 aged five years by MATILDA GILES, mother. Indentured to FRAZIER and SON as a boat-builder November 18, 1819. Indentures expired September 12, 1827. (F-91)

GLADDING, ANNE. Admitted June 18, 1812 aged six years by MARTHA GLADDING mother. Born May 6, 1806. Indentured to JOHN H. WIENGES as a domestic October 1, 1819. Indentures expired May 6, 1824. (F-110)

GLADDING, CHARLES. Admitted July 17, 1811 aged eight years by MARTHA GLADDING, mother. (F-86) Died July 11, 1815 of worm fever. (ROSP, July 8, 1815)

GLADDING, JOSEPH. Admitted July 17, 1811 aged six years by MARTHA GLADDING, mother. Indentured to JOHN BENNET as a black and white smith February 18, 1819. Transferred to HENRY BARTLESS as a blacksmith March 15, 1821. Indentures expired July 17, 1825. (F-87)

GORDON, GEORGE MARTIN. Admitted August 6, 1812 aged five years by MARY GORDON, mother. Delivered to his mother December 30, 1819. Indentures expired August 6, 1828. (F-113)

GORDON, JOHN. Admitted May 25, 1818 aged six years by Warden of Charleston. Indentured to PETER GALAHER (of Laurens District) as a farmer March 5, 1829. Indentures expired June 25, 1833. (H-75) Mother, unknown, died in the Poor House, nd. (AtoA)

GORDY, NATHAN. Admitted July 18, 1816 aged ten years by NANCY GORDY, mother. Delivered to his father, JOHN GORDY, January 2, 1818. (G-124) Father in the United States Army. (AtoA)

GRAINGER, MARY. Admitted July 16, 1818 aged four years by ANN GRAINGER, mother. Father, unknown, a cripple. (AtoA) Indentured to MARGARET and ROBERT HARRISON as a trimmer and maker of button and artificial flowers December 22, 1825. Transferred to HENRY W. GRAINGER, occupation unknown, June 8, 1827. (H-81)

GRAINGER, WILLIAM JAMES. Admitted July 16, 1818 aged six years by ANN GRAINGER, mother. Father, unknown, a cripple. (AtoA) Indentured to JOSHUA BROWN (of Laurens District) as a farmer January 26, 1826. (H-80)

GRANT, GEORGE. Admitted March 15, 1810 aged six years by FRANCES FRANCIS, mother. Indentured to JOHN REILY (of Chester District) as a farmer November 9, 1815. Indentures expired March 15, 1825. (F-47)

GRANT, SARAH E. Admitted March 15, 1810 aged three years and two months by FRANCES FRANCIS, mother. Delivered to her mother in Baltimore November 14, 1811. Indentures expired March 15, 1825. (F-48)

GREENWOOD, ELIZA. Admitted November 25, 1819 aged four years by MARY GREENWOOD, mother. Indentured to DANIEL JOHNSTON as a domestic May 10, 1827. Indentures expired November 5, 1833. (I-52)

GREGORIE, JOSEPH. Admitted January 4, 1816 aged nineteen months by ELIZABETH GREGORIE, mother. Died June 12, 1816. (G-102)

GUERIN, EMILLE (EMIEL). Admitted August 6, 1818 aged eight years by Warden of Charleston. Indentured to CHARLES TOTURAU as a goldsmith February 4, 1819. (H-85) Delivered to his godfather, JOHN BAPTIST FAURE, (FORD), February 12, 1819. (BO) Mother, JEANNE GUERIN, was dead. (AtoA)

GUERIN, JULIA. Admitted May 6, 1819 aged seven years by Warden of Charleston. Delivered to MISS J. DOTTY (DATTY), occupation unknown, July 15, 1819 (I-31)

GUYON, ANN. Admitted May 18, 1815 aged four years by ANN GUYON, mother. Born March 14, 1811. Delivered to her mother January 29, 1819. Indentures expired March 14, 1829. (G-88)

GUYON, LOVERIDGE DRAKE. Admitted May 18, 1815 aged seven years by ANN GUYON, mother. Delivered to her mother January 29, 1819. Indentures expired July 18, 1808. (G-87) Sent to her godmother MRS. MAYER, to attend her Academy of Needlework and for other education. (BO)

HACKER, GEORGE. Admitted October 29, 1812 aged four years by MARY HACKER, mother. Delivered to his mother February 11, 1817. Indentures expired October 29, 1829. (G-5)

HAMMILL (HAMMELL), JACOB. Admitted September 17, 1818 aged seven years by MARY HAMMILL, mother. (I-4) Indentured to his uncle, JOHN BENNET (of Alabama) as a blacksmith January 20, 1825. Benet was the husband of Hammill's mother's half-sister. Mother died June 7, 1824. (Minutes, June 10, 1824)

HAMMILL, JAMES R. Admitted September 17, 1818 aged eight years by MARY HAMMILL, mother. Indentured to his uncle, JOHN BENNET (of Alabama) as a blacksmith January 20, 1825. (I-3)

HAZZARD, OLIVER. Admitted August 13, 1818 aged six years by MARY HAZZARD, mother. Delivered to his mother December 31, 1818. (H-88)

HAZZARD, RICHARD. Admitted August 13, 1818 aged twelve years by MARY HAZZARD, mother. Indentured to WILLIAM TIMMONS as a merchant November 18, 1819. Transferred to W. MICHAEL KEILY, occupation unknown, July 15, 1823. Indentures expired January 1, 1827. (H-87)

HEADWRIGHT, EVELINA. Admitted August 13, 1812 aged five years by ELIZABETH HEADWRIGHT, mother. Indentured to ELIZA LIVINGSTON as a domestic February 10, 1820. Transferred to her mother, ELIZABETH LOUIS, November 15, 1821. Indentures expired August 13, 1825. (F-115)

HEADWRIGHT, MARY. Admitted August 13, 1812 aged seven years by ELIZABETH HEADWRIGHT, mother. Delivered to her mother, ELIZABETH LOUIS, February 20, 1817. Indentures expired August 13, 1823. (F-114)

HEADWRIGHT, WILLIAM. Admitted June 22, 1815 aged four years by ELIZABETH HEADWRIGHT, mother. Born March 24, 1811. Indentured to THOMAS H. YATES as a carpenter March 25, 1824. Transferred to J.C. STECHER as a blacksmith April 7, 1825. Indentures expired March 24, 1832. (G-90)

HENDERSON, EDWARD. Admitted November 7, 1816 aged nine years by Warden of Charleston. Born March 13, ____. Indentured to RICHARD GOULDSMITH as a cabinetmaker November 29, 1821. Indentures expired March 13, ____. (H-11)

HENNON, JOHN. Admitted November 7, 1812 aged six years by CATHERINE HENNON, mother. Died August 16, 1817. (G-6)

HENNON, REBECCA. Admitted November 7, 1812 aged five years by CATHERINE HENNON, mother. Indentured to ANN C. MARTIN as a mantuamaker September 3, 1818. Indentures expired November 7, 1825. (G-7)

HILDRETH, BENJAMIN. Admitted March 28, 1811 aged eight years by MARY GROSHEN, mother. Indentured to ELIZABETH BRIDE as an umbrellamaker August 10, 1815. Indentures expired March 28, 1824. (F-72)

HOLMSTROM(HOLMSTRONG), THOMAS LAWRENCE. Admitted January 13, 1814 aged seven years by JANE HOLMSTROM, mother. Indentured to GEORGE LYON as a watchmaker January 31, 1822. Transferred to WILLIAM O. WILBUR as a combmaker January 9, 1823. Indentures expired January 13, 1828. (G-41)

HOPKINS, FRANCES. Admitted May 27, 1814 aged two years by EBENEZER
HOPKINS, father. Indentured to ELIZA SHIRER as a domestic October 27,
1820. Returned to the Institution January 2, 1822. Died September 22,
1822. Indentures expired May 27, 1830. (G-55)

HOPKINS, JOHN E. Admitted May 27, 1814 aged eight years by EBENEZER
HOPKINS, father. Indentured to WILLIAM EDWARD DELESSIVE as a ship
carpenter September 23, 1824. Indentures expired May 27, 1827. (G-53)
A cripple. (AtoA)

HOPKINS, MARY L. Admitted May 27, 1814 aged eleven years by EBENEZER
HOPKINS, father. Indentured to MARTHA LAFILLY as a domestic June 23,
1814. Transferred to MARY ANN SERJEANT, occupation unknown, May 29,
1817. Transferred to ARATHUSA BELTON, occupation unknown, October 2,
1818. Indentures expired May 27, 1821. (G-54) A cripple. (AtoA)

HOWARD, SARAH. Admitted January 13, 1814 aged eleven years by Warden
of Charleston. From Washington, D.C. Indentured to T.L. COULLION
as a domestic December 5, 1816. Indentures expired January 13, 1821.
(G-36) Admitted from the Poor House. (ROSP, January 15, 1814)

HUTCHINSON, JOHN WILLIAM. Admitted April 3, 1817 aged seven years and
six months by MARY HUTCHINSON, mother. (H-24) Indentured to JAMES
MITCHELL, of Gillon Street, as a pump and blockmaker May 29, 1823.
(BO) Transferred to JAMES MODEREN as a boatbuilder November 9, 1826.
Indentures expired October 3, 1831. (H-24)

ISAACS, RACHEL. Admitted November 18, 1813 aged eleven years by
ELIZABETH ISAACS, mother. Indentured to MARY B. LECOMPTE as a milliner
April 9, 1818. Indentures expired November 18, 1820. (G-26)

JARMON, JOHN. Admitted November 19, 1818 aged ten years by HARRIET
JARMON, mother. (I-10) Delivered to his mother (of Columbia) June
29, 1820. (BO)

JAUSSET, CATHERINE. Admitted August 13, 1818 by ANN JAUSSET, mother.
Indentured to MARY E. PHELPS as a mantuamaker February 25, 1819. (H-86)
Father was a sea captain who died in the West Indies. (AtoA)

JERMON, AUGUST. Admitted August 11, 1814 aged eleven years by MARY
JERMON, mother. Indentured to JOHN C. PILLANS as a baker July 25,
1822. Transferred to ANTHONY CARIVENE, occupation unknown, December
11, 1823. Indentures expired August 1, 1824. (H-3) Born in Savannah.
(AtoA)

JOCELYN, HENRY GEORGE CARMAN. Admitted July 17, 1817 by Warden of
Charleston. Born December 14, 1804. Indentured to W. WALLER as a
saddler December 23, 1818. Indentures expired December 14, 1825.
(H-30)

JOCELYN, SAMUEL RUSSELL. Admitted July 10, 1817 by Warden of Charleston.
Born July 18, 1809. Indentured to GEORGE MOORE as a harnessmaker
October 31, 1822. (H-28) Transferred to WILLIAM GUY as a saddler
August 28, 1823. (BO) Transferred to WILLIAM WALLER as a saddler
December 15, 1825. Indentures expired July 18, 1830. (H-28)

JOHNSON (JOHNSTON), LOUISA. Admitted May 31, 1810 aged six years by
ELIZABETH JOHNSON, mother. Indentured to SARAH BUTLER as a domestic
June 3, 1813. (F-52) Transferred to ELIZABETH WOTTON, mother, December
1, 1814. (ROSSC) Indentures expired May 31, 1822. (F-52)

JOHNSON, MARGARET. Admitted May 31, 1810 aged seven years by ELIZABETH
JOHNSON, mother. Delivered to ELIZABETH WOTTON, mother, December 1,
1814. Indentures expired May 31, 1821. (H-51)

JOHNSON, MARY. Admitted March 2, 1815 aged five years by JOHN JOHNSON,
father. Born June 27, 1809. Indentured to JANE MURRAY as a seamstress
December 6, 1821. Transferred to MRS. _____ STROUP, occupation unknown,
July 15, 1822. (Indentures not signed) Indentures expired June 27,
1827. (G-80)

JOHNSON, PAUL. Admitted August 26, 1819 aged six years by ANN JOHNSON, mother. Born September 20, 1812. Indentured to JOHN C. WALKER as a bookbinder February 23, 1826. Indentures expired September 20, 1833. (I-46)

JOHNSON, PETER. Admitted May 31, 1810 aged eight years by ELIZABETH JOHNSON, mother. Indentured to ISAAC GILL as a watch and clockmaker March 16, 1815. Indentures expired May 31, 1823. (F-50)

JOHNSON, RUTH. Admitted March 2, 1815 aged four years by JOHN JOHNSON, father. Born September 2, 1810. Indentured to ANN CROSS as a seamtress August 4, 1825. Indentures expired September 2, 1828. (G-81)

JOHNSON, WILLIAM. Admitted November 25, 1819 aged three years by Warden of Charleston. (I-53) Father, unknown, was a soldier at Fort Johnson. (AtoA) No further information.

JONES, JAMES. Admitted March 8, 1810 aged ten years by CHRISTIANA JOHNSON, mother. Delivered to his grandmother, ANN BOWLES, November 11, 1813. Indentures expired March 8, 1821. (F-46)

JUELL (JEWEL), CAROLINE. Admitted May 28, 1818 by ESTHER NEILSON, mother. Indentured to AARON FAIRCHILD as a domestic October 4, 1821. Transferred to ELIZABETH STAFFORD as a taylor July 1, 1824. Indentures expired May 1, 1829. (H-74)

KAIN (KEON), SARAH. Admitted September 7, 1810 aged six years by CATHERINE KAIN, mother. Indentured to JOHN WHITING, turner as a domestic January 8, 1818. Indentures expired September 7, 1822. (F-57)

KEAN, FERDINAND. Admitted November 20, 1817 aged six years by BRIDGET KEAN, mother. Born February 24, 1811. No indenture, but the back of the application stated "In consequence of an application from JOHN GARLINGTON, ESQ., Laurens C.H. dated May 27, 1832 on behalf of FERDINAND KEAN, the indenture between the said Kean and WILLIAM H. FULTON of Laurens District by the Direction of the Commissioners of the O.H. was sent to the said J. GARLINGTON, February 24, 1832." Indentures expired June __, 1832. (H-48)

KEAN, JAMES. Admitted November 20, 1817 aged five years by BRIDGET KEAN, mother. Born July 23, 1812 (age corrected). Indentured to CHISTIAN ORR (of Pendleton District) as a merchant April 26, 1827. Indentures expired July 23, 1833. (H-49)

KEMPTMEYER, DIEDERICK (DEDRICK).Admitted February 26, 1818 aged seven years by CHARLES KEMPTMEYER, father. Born September 6, 1811. Indentured to J.E. WIENGES as a baker October 7, 1824. Indentures expired September 6, 1832. Transferred to JAMES SUTCLIFFE, occupation unknown, March 16, 1824. (BO) Father in the Poor House. (AtoA)

KING, ANN. Admitted November 12, 1812 aged six years by LEONARD KING, father. Delivered to her father April 25, 1816. Indentures expired November 12, 1824. (G-9)

KING, GEORGE HARKNESS. Admitted December 30, 1813 by LEONARD KING, father. Born December 3, 1803. Indentured to JAMES YOUNG (of Laurens District) as a storekeeper January 9, 1817. Transferred to his father October 15, 1818. Indentures expired December 3, 1824. (G-27)

KING, JOHN HENDERSON. Admitted December 30, 1813 aged five years by LEONARD KING, father. Indentured to THOMAS STEENSON as a millwright September 12, 1822. Transferred to his father May 22, 1823. (G-28)

LACY, JOHN. Admitted July 25, 1816 by MARY LACY, mother. Born February 17, 1811. Indentured to F.O. O'SULLIVAN as a coachpainter February 24, 1825. Indentures expired February 17, 1832. (H-2)

LACY, WILLIAM. Admitted July 25, 1816 by MARY LACY, mother. Born October 5, 1808. (H-1) Indentured to JOHN LIPSCOMB (of Abbeville District) as a storekeeper January 23, 1823. (BO) Indentures expired October 5, 1829. (H-1)

LAHIFFE (LEHAFF), MARY. Admitted February 11, 1813 aged six years by MARY LAHIFFE, mother. Indentured to MARY HUNTER as a milliner November 6, 1817. Indentures expired February 11, 1825. (G-12)

LAHIFFE (LEHAFF), SAMUEL. Admitted February 11, 1813 aged three years by MARY LAHIFFE, mother. Indentured to JOSEPH POHL as a merchant December 12, 1822. Indentures expired February 11, 1831. (G-31)

LANE, ESKELLS. Admitted June 25, 1818 aged five years by Warden of Charleston. Delivered to his brother-in-law, JOHN HUMPHREYS, December 18, 1828. Indentures expired June 25, 1834. (H-77) Mother was insane. (AtoA)

LANE, WILLIAM. Admitted June 25, 1818 aged nine years by Warden of Charleston. Indentured to HENRY BARTLESS as a blacksmith September 26, 1822. Transferred to WILLIAM EVANS, occupation unknown, August 26, 1828. Indentures expired June 25, 1830. (H-76)

LAWRENCE, ANN. Admitted September 24, 1818 aged six years by ELIZABETH LAWRENCE, mother. Born December 15, 1812. Indentured to JOHN P. LLOYD as a domestic November 9, 1821. Indentures expired December 15, 1830. (I-7)

LAWRENCE (LAURENS), JAMES. Admitted January 9, 1817 by Warden of Charleston. Born December 20, ____. Indentured to ROBERT STEPHENS (of Laurens District) as a farmer January 3, 1828. Indentures expired December 20, 1825. (H-12)

LAWRENCE (LAURENS), JOHN. Admitted September 24, 1818 aged five years by ELIZABETH LAWRENCE, mother. Born October 24, 1813. Indentured to TIMOTHY W. JOHNSON as a baker September 18, 1828. Indentures expired October 24, 1834. (I-8)

LAZER, ALEXANDER ANTHONY. Admitted September 21, 1810 aged four years by MARGARET LAZER, mother. Born in New York. Indentured to EDWARD MYATT as a boatbuilder July 13, 1820. Indentures expired April 20, 1827. (F-58)

LESPENES, CAROLINE. Admitted August 1, 1816 aged eleven years by Warden of Charleston. Indentured to REV. ALBERT A. MULLER as a domestic February 11, 1819. (H-4) Transferred to her half-sister, MRS. LONG June 9, 1819. (BO) Indentures expired August 1, 1823. (H-4) A derelict. (AtoA)

McBETH, CHARLES. Admitted June 5, 1817 aged five years by SARAH McBETH, mother. Indentured to JOSEPH McCULLOUGH (of Greenville District) as a planter and storekeeper May 10, 1826. Indentures expired June 5, 1832. (H-27) "The sum of $12.25, two gold rings, and an earring, as the property of SARAH McBETH...the mother of CHARLES McBETH...Resolved that the Chairman do deliver the money and articles to MRS. POWERS, wife of JAMES POWERS, a painter in this City, the friend of the late Mrs. McBETH." (Minutes, May 21, 1825)

McCLELLAND, MARY. Admitted June 2, 1814 aged eleven years by HANNAH SMITH, mother. Indentured to PATRICK PHENNY as a spinner and weaver January 23, 1817. (G-60) Delivered to her mother, MRS. ANDERSON, May 9, 1816. (BO) Indentures expired June 2, 1821. (G-60)

McCLELLAND, MOSES. Admitted June 2, 1814 aged eight years by HANNAH SMITH, mother. Indentured to RICHARD BRINGLOE as a boatbuilder December 23, 1819. Indentures expired June 2, 1827 (G-61)

McDOWELL, ROBERT. Admitted March 26, 1818 aged seven years by Warden of Charleston. Delivered to his grandmother, N. HISLOP, February 2, 1826. (H-66) An orphan. (AtoA)

McGOLDRICK, EDWARD M. Admitted October 11, 1811 by CATHERINE EVE McGOLDRICK, mother. Born March 17, 1808. Indentured to DANIEL BURNICE as a blacksmith June 15, 1820. Transferred to PETER AITMAN as a coach-maker November 20, 1821. Indentures expired March 17, 1829. (F-92)

McGRATH, EDWARD. Admitted August 12, 1813 aged six years by MARY McGRATH, mother. Indentured to L. MARTIN as a tailor January 24, 1822. Trans-ferred to EDWARD MYATT, occupation unknown, April 4, 1822. Indentures expired August 12, 1828. (G-21) Father - EDWARD McGRATH. (AtoA) Grandfather - TRENT WILKINS "fell in defense of his Country's rights." (Ibid.)

McIRIEL, JOHN. Admitted August 27, 1818 aged twelve years by JOHN M. McIRIEL, father, a doctor now in gaol for three months. (AtoA) Inden-tured to ZACHARIAH STANDISH as a chairmaker November 9, 1820. Trans-ferred to JACOB RABB as a pump and blockmaker May 24, 1821. (I-2)

McLANE, JAMES. Admitted July 12, 1811 by SUSANNAH McLANE, mother. Born March 20, 1802. Delivered to his mother November 26, 1812. Inden-tures expired March 20, 1823. (F-82)

McLANE, WILLIAM. Admitted July 12, 1811 by SUSANNAH McLANE, mother. Born October 3, 1799. Delivered to his mother November 26, 1812. In-dentures expired October 3, 1820. (F-81)

McMILLAN, JAMES. Admitted October 19, 1815 aged two years by MARY McMILLAN, mother. Indentured to PETER GALAHER (of Laurens District) as a storekeeper and farmer March 21, 1828. (G-95) Father, CHARLES McMILLAN, died August 1, 1815. (AtoA)

MADISON, EUNICE E. Admitted December 2, 1819 aged three years by Warden of Charleston. Indentured to CATHERINE ELIZA CHANNER as a seamstress August 15, 1822. Indentured expired April 15, 1834. (I-57)

MARKEY, JOHN. Admitted August 16, 1811 aged seven years by MARTHA C. THOMAS, mother. Indentured to JEREMIAH CONDY as a merchant and store-keeper October 30, 1817. Indentures expired August 16, 1825. (F-90)

MARMAJEAN, ELIZA. Admitted September 19, 1816 aged five years by ELIZA MARMAJEAN, mother. Born November 7, ____. Delivered to her mother June 8, 1820. Indentures expired November 7, 1828. (H-6)

MARTIN, JOHN VALANTINE. Admitted March 21, 1816 aged three years by ANN MARTIN, mother. Born December 21, ____. Indentured to THOMAS MOORE as a carpenter June 20, 1822. Indentures expired December 21, 1834. (G-108)

MAULL, CHARLES. Admitted May 30, 1818 by MARY E. MAULL, mother. Born July 5, 1808. Delivered to his mother May 25, 1820. Indentures expired July 5, 1829. (G-118)

MAULL, DAVID M. Admitted May 30, 1816 aged five years by MARY E. MAULL, mother. Delivered to his mother May 25, 1820. Indentures expired May 3, 1835. (G-119) Born May 3, 1814. (AtoA)

MAULL, JAMES DAVID. Admitted May 30, 1816 aged thirteen years by MARY E. MAULL, mother. Indentured to JAMES S. GALBRAITH as a black-smith August 5, 1818. Transferred to his mother May 25, 1820. Inden-tures expired April 12, 1826. (G-117) Born April 12, 1805. (AtoA)

MEDERS (MEADOWS), SARAH. Admitted February 4, 1813 by Warden of Charleston. Born September 24, 1803. Delivered to her mother, unknown, November 9, 1815. Indentures expired September 24, 1821. (G-11)

MIESENBERY, SUSANNAH. Admitted July 15, 1811 by SUSANNAH MOORE, mother. Born February 14, 1802. (F-83) Delivered to her mother, a COH nurse, October 20, 1814. (COH Officers' Files)

MILES, MARGARET. Admitted August 9, 1818 by Warden of Charleston. Indentured to WILLIAM ROBINSON as a domestic January 27, 1825. Transferred to JOHN PHILIPS, occupation unknown, July 7, 1825. (I-1)

MILLER, ELIZABETH. Admitted January 13, 1814 aged eight years by SYLVIA MILLER, mother. Indentured to LUCRETIA SMITH as a mantuamaker July 16, 1818. (G-40) Released by Magistrate because of cruel treatment by the master July 30, 1819. (BO) Admitted from the Poor House. (ROSP, January 15, 1814) Indentures expired January 13, 1824. (G-40) No further information.

MIOT, JOHN. Admitted July 5, 1816 aged eleven years by HARRIET MIOT, mother. Born May 20, ____. Indentured to WILLIAM THOMPSON as a merchant December 23, 1819. Indentures expired May 20, 1826. (G-123)

MISCALLY, MARTHA. Admitted May 6, 1819 aged nine years by ELIZA MISCALLY, mother. Indentured to CHARLES ROGERS as a domestic March 7, 1822. Indentures expired February 6, 1828. (I-32)

MISCALLY, MARY. Admitted March 6, 1819 aged four years by ELIZA MISCALLY, mother. Indentured to JOHN and ELIZA BONNER as a milliner and housekeeper November 3, 1825. Indentures expired March 15, 1833. (I-33)

MORDECAI, FANNY. Admitted April 25, 1816 aged twelve years by JANE MORDECAI, mother. Born May 11, 1803. Indentured to E. ABRAMS, storekeeper, occupation unknown, July 20, 1820. Indentures expired May 11, 1821. (G-111) AARON DAVIS, uncle. (Minutes, March 27, 1819) Religion: Jewish. (Minutes, April 25, 1819)

MORTON, JOHN. Admitted December 23, 1818 aged six years by ELIZABETH MORTON, mother. Indentured to THOMAS ADDISON as a grocer September 27, 1827. Indentures expired December 23, 1833. (I-14)

MORTON, WILLIAM. Admitted December 23, 1818 aged eight years by ELIZABETH MORTON, mother. Indentured to JOHN MARKLEY as a painter February 3, 1825. (I-13)

MUCK, JOHN MITCHELL. Admitted October 27, 1818 aged eleven years by Church Wardens of St. Philip's Church. Indentured to DANIEL McMILLAN (Of Chester District) as a farmer May 12, 1814. Indentures expired October 27, 1820. (F-61)

MULLRYNE (MULRYNE), ANN SELINA. Admitted January 27, 1814 aged nine years by JANE MULLRYNE, mother. Born May 14, 1805. Delivered to her mother April 4, 1816. Indentures expired May 31, 1823. (G-44)

MULLRYNE, THOMAS HILL. Admitted January 27, 1814 aged twelve years by JANE MULLRYNE, mother. Delivered to his mother September 29, 1814. Indentures expired May 26, 1823. (G-43)

MURPHY, ELIZABETH. Admitted October 26, 1815 aged four years by ANN MURPHY, mother. Born February 27, 1811. Delivered to her uncle, THOMAS PRICE, May 9, 1816. Indentures expired February 27, 1829. (G-97)

MURPHY, JOHN D. Admitted October 26, 1815 aged seven years by ANN MURPHY, mother. Born November 17, 1807. Delivered to his uncle, THOMAS PRICE, May 9, 1816. Indentures expired November 17, 1828. (G-96)

MURPHY, THOMAS P. Admitted July 10, 1817 by ANN MURPHY, mother. Born January 1, 1815. Died July 31, 1817. Indentures expired January 1, 1836. (H-39)

MURRELL, JOHN ROBERT. Admitted March 10, 1814 aged ten years by MARTHA LeQUEUX MURRELL, mother. Indentured to JOHN TAYLOR as a merchant December 4, 1817. Indentures expired March 10, 1825. (G-46)

MURRELL, PETER LeQUEUX. Admitted March 10, 1814 aged ten years by MARY LeQUEUX MURRELL, mother. Died September 3, 1817. (G-47)

MYERS, DAVID. Admitted January 11, 1816 aged five years by Warden of Charleston. Indentured to ROBERT OAKLEY as a druggist and apothecary June 24, 1824. Indentures expired January 11, 1832. (G-103)

MYERS, MAACHAR. Admitted December 3, 1812 aged nine years by REV. THOMAS MILLS, guardian. Indentures expired December 3, 1821. (G-10) Delivered to her aunt, RACHEL TIMMONS, April 25, 1816. (BO)

NESBETT, SAMUEL. Admitted May 9, 1816 aged five years by ANN MAXCEY, mother. Delivered to his mother April 5, 1821. Indentures expired May 9, 1832. (G-114)

NOPIE, (NOPEE), WILLIAM. Admitted January 13, 1814 aged five years by ESTHER NOPIE, mother. Indentured to HENRY WILLIS as a carpenter September 26, 1822. Transferred to JOHN C. SIGWALD, occupation unknown, July 19, 1827. Indentures expired January 13, 1830. (G-32) Admitted from the Poor House. (ROSP, January 15, 1814)

NOPPEE, JAMES. Admitted March 27, 1817 aged five years by ANN NOPPEE, mother. Indentured to WILLIAM TEMPLETON (of Laurens District) as a farmer March 24, 1825. Indentures expired July 6, 1832. (H-23)

O'BRIEN, CATHERINE. Admitted February 13, 1812 aged eight years by Warden of Charleston. From New York. Indentured to LUCRETIA HORRY, occupation unknown, July 21, 1814. Indentures expired February 13, 1822. (F-99)

O'FERRALL, AGNES. Admitted March 12, 1818 aged five years by ELIZABETH O'FERRALL, mother. Born October 10, 1812. Indentured to JANE CORKRAN as a domestic October 5, 1820. Indentures expired October 10, 1830. (H-63) Father, JAMES, died of a fever in August 1817. (AtoA)

O'FERRALL, PATRICK. Admitted March 12, 1818 aged ten years by ELIZABETH O'FERRALL, mother. Born January 10, 1808. Indentures expired January 10, 1829. (H-61) Father, JAMES, died of a fever August 1817. (AtoA)

O'FERRALL, THOMAS. Admitted March 12, 1818 aged seven years by ELIZABETH O'FERRALL, mother. Born April 15, 1810. Died January 23, 1819. Indentures expired April 15, 1831. (H-62)

OHRING, CATHERINE. Admitted July 23, 1818 aged eight years by CATHERINE OHRING, mother. Indentured to ELIZABETH BRAILSFORD as a domestic April 25, 1822. Indentures expired December 9, 1827. (H-83)

OHRING, MATILDA. Admitted July 23, 1818 aged five years by CATHERINE OHRING, mother. Delivered to her mother, CATHERINE DENNEBY, October 21, 1824. Indentures expired November 24, 1830. (H-84)

OLIVER, JULIET. Admitted August 14, 1817 aged nine years by MARY OLIVER, mother. Delivered to her sister, CHARLOTTE PHILLIPS, August 20, 1818. (H-32)

PAGE, ELIZABETH. Admitted May 14, 1818 aged seven years by JANE PAGE, mother. (H-71) Admitted from the Poor House. (AtoA) Delivered to her mother, 1815. (ROSP, December 30, 1815)

PAGE, JANE ELIZABETH. Admitted January 6, 1814 aged six years by JANE PAGE, mother. Indentured to CATHERINE VOGLER as a domestic June 22, 1820. (G-31) The mother complained that Mrs. Vogler was of "bad fame" and requested a transfer. (BO) Transferred to JANE PAGE who never called for her, December 28, 1815. Transferred to JOHN BLACK, occupation unknown, November 8, 1821. Indentures expired January 6, 1826. (G-31)

PAPILLOT, FELIX. Admitted October 6, 1814 aged eleven years by the Widow PAPILLOT, mother. Indentured to MARTIN LUCO as a tinplate worker March 13, 1817. Transferred to WILLIAM FORBES as a tinplate worker July 10, 1817. Indentures expired October 6, 1824. (G-69) from St. Domingo. (AtoA)

PARKER, FRANCES CAROLINE. Admitted July 17, 1811 aged eight years by Warden of Charleston. Indentured to JAMES HARPER as a domestic November 7, 1812. Indentures expired July 17, 1821. (F-85) Father, PHINEAS PARKER, was a dryer. (Minutes, July 18, 1811)

PARKER, PHINEAS WARREN. Admitted July 17, 1811 aged ten years and six months by Warden of Charleston. Born April 1, 1800 (corrected) Indentured bo JAMES BULKLEY as a ship chandler February 16, 1815. (F-84)

PATTON, JANE (ANN). Admitted July 23, 1812 aged six years by ANNE PATTON, mother. Delivered to her mother, ANN FAIRWITHER, April 22, 1813. Indentures expired July 23, 1824. (F-112)

PAYNE, CHARLES. Admitted November 2, 1815 aged five years by WILLIAM R. PAYNE, father. Indentured to RICHARD STEEL as a stonecutter May 19, 1825. Indentures expired November 2, 1831. (G-99)

PAYNE, HARRIET. Admitted November 2, 1815 aged twelve years by WILLIAM R. PAYNE, father. Delivered to her father July 25, 1916. Indentures expired November 2, 1821. (G-98) Father was a stonecutter. (AtoA)

PELCAS, AMELIA. Admitted June 2, 1813 aged eleven years by Warden of Charleston. Indentured to JAMES WELDON (of Jackson Creek, Fairfield County), occupation unknown, nd. Indentures expired April 10, 1820. (ROSSC)

PETIT, CHARLES. Admitted December 9, 1819 aged eleven years by MAXIM PETIT, father. Born December 28, 1808. Delivered to his father March 23, 1820. Indentures expired December 28, 1829. (I-58)

PETIT, WILLIAM. Admitted December 9, 1819 aged nine years by MAXIM PETIT, father. Born March 18, 1810. Delivered to his father March 23, 1820. Indentures expired March 18, 1831. (I-59)

PLAYER, WILLIAM. Admitted Janurary 21, 1819 aged eleven years by Warden of Charleston. (I-19) Father, unknown, died in the War of 1812 at Dorchester. (AtoA) No further information.

POLAND, CATHERINE. Admitted January 29, 1819 aged seven years by MOURNING POLAND, mother. Born March 6, 1812. Delivered to her mother, MOURNING CARTER, December 20, 1821. Indentures expired March 6, 1830. (I-23)

POLAND, DAVID. Admitted January 29, 1819 aged ten years by MOURNING POLAND, mother. Born March 24, ____. Died September 28, 1819. (I-22)

POLAND, HESTER ANN RISHER. Admitted March 25, 1819 aged four years by MOURNING POLAND, mother. Delivered to her mother, MOURNING CARTER, December 20, 1821. (I-28)

PORTER, ROBERT. Admitted September 24, 1812 aged four years by JANE PORTER, mother. (G-1) Delivered to his mother, MRS. JOSEPH EVE, February 29, 1816. (BO) Indentures expired September 24, 1829. (G-1)

POSTELL, MARY. Admitted June 25, 1812 aged ten years by Warden of Charleston. Indentured to BEALENTOE CALWELL (CETOWELL) as a domestic January 26, 1815. Indentured expired June 25, 1820. (F-111)

POULSON, PETER. Admitted October 1, 1818 by JUDITH POULSON, mother. Indentured to MARY WHITNEY for "liberally educating" October 22, 1818. (I-9) Mother was insane. (AtoA)

PREGNALE, HENRY. Admitted February 25, 1819 aged nine years by Warden of Charleston. Indentured to WILLIAM MICHELL as a practitioner of medicine March 11, 1824. Transferred to WILLIAM BULL as a house carpenter February 7, 1825. (I-25)

REDMON, CHARLOTTE. Admitted February 7, 1811 aged six years by SARAH REDMON, mother. Delivered to her mother November 26, 1818. Indentures expired February 7, 1823. (F-66)

RHODES, CATHERINE F. Admitted December 2, 1819 aged four years by MARY RHODES, mother. Born March 5, 1815. Delivered to her mother November 27, 1823. Indentures expired March 5, 1833. (I-56)

RHODES, ELIZA. Admitted January 23, 1817 aged twelve years by Warden of Charleston. Indentured to ARATHUSA BELTON as a mantuamaker August 13, 1818. Transferred to her sister, REBECCA KINGDON, December 23, 1820. Transferred to ELIZA MURDEN, occupation unknown, February 17, 1820. Indentures expired December 15, 1824. (H-24)

RHODES, MARY. Admitted December 2, 1819 aged eight years by MARY RHODES, mother. Born October 25, 1811. Delivered to her mother November 27, 1823. Indentures expired October 25, 1829. (I-55)

RHODES, THOMAS. Admitted December 2, 1819 aged nine years by MARY RHODES, mother. Born January 26, 1809. Indentures expired January 26, 1831. (I-34) Delivered to his mother in a "a dropsical condition, nd. (BO)

RHONEY (ROANEY, ROAN), MARY JANE. Admitted September 4, 1817 aged seven years by Warden of Charleston. Indentured to MRS. SARAH GIBBES as a domestic November 30, 1820. Transferred to ELIZA BONNER, occupation unknown, May 5, 1825. Transferred to JANE DAVIS, occupation unknown, August 5, 1825. Indentures expired September 4, 1828. (H-37) Father, THOMAS, was born in Ireland and mother, unknown, was born in Halifax. On a voyage from New York to New Orleans, her parents were shipwrecked at Nassau, nd. They arrived in Charleston on the British Schooner Conch, and died of a fever in August 1811. (AtoA)

RHULMAN, ADAM. Admitted October 5, 1810 aged seven years by CHRISTIANA RHULMAN, mother. Of Goose Creek in St. James Parish. Indentured to JAMES MEAD (MEADS) as a storekeeper August 18, 1814. (F-59) Transferred to A. MAJOR CARRUTH (of Greenville District) as a gunsmith June 8, 1815. (Minutes, June 10, 1815) Indentures expired October 5, 1824. (F-59)

RHULMAN, MARY ANN. Admitted October 5, 1810 aged four years and eight months by CHRISTIANA RHULMAN, mother. Indentured to ELIZABETH RHULMAN as a spinner and weaver February __, 1816. Indentures expired February 2, 1824. (F-60)

RILEY, HARRIET. Admitted August 14, 1819 aged thirteen years by JOSEPH RILEY, father. Born May 3, 1806. Indentured to LUCRETIA SMITH as a mantuamaker September 19, 1822. Indentures expired May 3, 1824. (I-41)

RILEY, MARGARET (MARTHA PENDERGRESS.) Admitted August 14, 1819 aged five years by JOSEPH RILEY, father. Born June 13, 1814. (I-43) Died April 4, 1826 of convulsive fits complicated by worms. Buried in the COH Burial Ground. (ROSP, April 5, 1826)

RILEY, MORGAN. Admitted August 14, 1819 aged seven years by JOSEPH RILEY, father. Born November 20, 1811. Indentures expired November 20, 1832. (I-42) Absconded, nd. (ROSP, January 23, 1828)

RIVERS, JOSEPH. Admitted October 4, 1812 aged twelve years by Warden of Charleston. Indentures expired October 1, 1821. (G-3) Dismissed from the Institution because he "committed an indecent outrage on one of the female Infants of the Institution." (Minutes, July 21, 1814)

ROU, ANDREW C. Admitted August 26, 1819 aged nine years by GEORGE D. ROU, father. Indentured to FRANCIS D. POYAS as a gunsmith September 30, 1824. Indentures expired January 1, 1831. (I-45)

ROU, CHARLES B. Admitted August 26, 1808 aged eleven years by GEORGE D. ROU, father. Born August 31, 1808. Indentured to JOHN P. LLOYD as a venetian blindmaker November 9, 1821. Indentures expired August 31, 1829. (I-44)

SCHENFIELD (SHENFIELD), MARY ELIZABETH. Admitted January 18, 1816 aged twelve years by FREDERICKE SCHENFIELD, mother. Indentured to ELIZABETH M. BLEWER as a domestic June 19, 1817. Indentures expired January 18, 1822. (G-104)

SCHENFIELD, WILLIAM. Admitted January 18, 1816 aged six years by FREDERICKE SCHENFIELD, mother. Indentured to JOHN HOLLAND (of Laurens District) as a blacksmith December 12, 1822. Indentures expired January 18, 1831. (G-105)

SCOTT, ISAAC. Admitted June 16, 1814 aged nine years by ANN ABRAMS, mother. Indentures expired June 16, 1826. (G-63) "Absconded...said to be carried off to Savannah by his mother." (ROSP, March 23, 1816)

SEAMAN, CHARLOTTE. Admitted May 27, 1814 aged seven years by SARAH SEAMAN, mother. Delivered to her mother April 25, 1816. Indentures expired May 27, 1825. (G-50)

SEPECHEY, CATHERINE. Admitted May 2, 1816 aged ten years by MICHEL SEPECHEY, father. Born July 6, _____. (G-113) Indentured to WILLIAM LAW (of Chester District) as a spinner and weaver March 12, 1818. (BO) Mother, unknown, was dead and father, a former USA soldier, was a member of the City Guard. (AtoA)

SEPECHY, WILLIAM LEWIS. Admitted May 2, 1816 aged six years by MICHEL SEPECHY, father. Born May 14, _____. Indentured to JOHN HOLLAND (of Laurens District) as a blacksmith December 12, 1822. (G-112)

SHANNON, JOHN. Admitted November 30, 1810 aged fourteen years by ELIZABETH SHANNON, mother. Indentured to FRANCIS COBIA as a house carpenter December 1, 1810. Indentures expired September 14, 1817. (F-63)

SHENFIELD (SCHENFIELD), WILLIAM. Admitted January 18, 1816. (BO) aged six years by FREDERICKE SHENFIELD, mother. Indentures expired December 12, 1832. (G-105)

SHEPPERD, ANN (ANNA). Admitted March 26, 1812 aged seven years by ELIZA SHEPPERD, mother. Delivered to her mother March 23, 1815. Indentures expired March 26, 1823. (F-100)

SHEPPERD, THOMAS. Admitted March 26, 1812 aged five years by ELIZA SHEPPERD, mother. Delivered to his mother August 5, 1818. Indentures expired March 26, 1828. (F-101)

SHETS (SHOTS), WILLIAM MOULTRIE. Admitted March 6, 1817 aged seven years by CHLOE SHETS, mother. Born December 22, 1809. Delivered to his mother May 22, 1817. Returned to the Institution June 11, 1818. Delivered to his mother October 16, 1823. Indentures expired December 22, 1830. (H-18) Born on Sullivan's Island. Father, unknown, killed in the War of 1812. (AtoA)

SIMONS, REBECCA. Admitted June 13, 1816 aged seven years by MARY SIMONS, mother. Indentured to MARY JOHNSON as a tayloress June 10, 1824. Transferred to her mother August 5, 1825. (G-120) Grandmother, REBECCA NEAL. (AtoA)

SKILLEN, JAMES. Admitted April 2, 1818 aged five years by JAMES SKILLEN, father. Indentured to THOMAS S. BUDD as a seaman and navigator November 4, 1824. Transferred to CHRISTOFF SWIMWE as a mariner June 23, 1825. Transferred to A.P. REEVES as a carpenter August 31, 1826 due to death of the master. Indentures expired April 2, 1834. (G-68)

SKILLEN, JOHN. Admitted April 2, 1818 aged eight years by JAMES
SKILLEN, father. Died October 6, 1818. (H-67)

SMITH, ELIZA. Admitted August 1, 1816 aged four years by Warden of
Charleston. Indentured to ANN DALEY as a domestic December 23, 1824.
Indentures expired August 1, 1830. (H-30)

SMITH, ELIZA. Admitted December 18, 1817 aged eleven years by Warden
of Charleston. Indentured to MANNING BELCHER for instruction and
learning before being taught ornamental needlework October 29, 1818.
Released from her indentures by T.S. RICHARDSON of the Office of
Common Pleas June 27, 1821. Transferred to S.L. REEVES, occupation
unknown, July 5, 1821. Indentures expired December 18, 1824. (H-52)

SMITH, JACOB. Admitted April 12, 1811 aged nine years by JOHN SMITH,
father. Indentured to WILLIAM VANVELSEY as a wheelwright June 22,
1815. Indentures expired April 12, 1823. (F-73)

SMITH, JAMES. Admitted October 27, 1814 aged five years by Warden of
Charleston. Died February 21, 1816 of pleurisy complicated by worms.
(ROSP, February 17, 1816)

SMITH, JANE. Admitted June 2, 1814 aged seven years by HANNAH SMITH,
mother. Indentured to LEWIS SMITH as a seamstress December 9, 1819.
Indentures expired June 2, 1825. (G-62)

SMITH, JOHN. Admitted September 24, 1818 aged eight years by ELIZA
SMITH, mother. Indentured to DR. ____ GOLDING (of Laurens District)
(indentures signed by ALLEN ANDREWS) as a farmer April 5, 1818.
Indentures expired September 24, 1831. (I-5)

SOZES, JOHN FRANCIS JOSEPH. Admitted March 26, 1812 aged seven years
by Warden of Charleston. Indentured to JOHN EGLESTON as a storekeeper
December 31, 1818. Indentures expired March 26, 1826. (F-102)

SPALDING, ALBERT MATHUS. Admitted September 15, 1814 aged seven years
by JANE SPALDING, mother. Indentures expired June 15, 1828. (G-68)
Sent to college at Columbia. (Minutes, November 1, 1821) "Passed
through the hands of the Medical Board of Georgia (and was) ...admitted
to practice in 1828...resigned in 1831...was publicly ordained to the
work of the Ministry." (Minutes, August 1, 1833)

SPENCER, ARCHELAUS. Admitted December 30, 1813 aged six years by
ARCHAELAUS SPENCER, father. Indentured to PETER AITMAN as a coachmaker August 9, 1821. Indentures expired December 30, 1828. (G-29)

SPENCER, JOHN. Admitted December 30, 1813 aged three years by ARCHELAUS
SPENCER, father. Born May __, 1811. Indentured to THOMAS S. LEAK
(of Laurens District) as a farmer January 27, 1825. Indentures expired
May 30, 1831. (G-30)

SPENCER, THOMAS. Admitted April 16, 1818 aged five years by ARCHELAUS
SPENCER, father. Indentured to JOHN MAYNARD as a baker October 13,
1828. Indentures expired July 4, 1833. (H-70)

SPILLARD (SPILYERDS), DANIEL. Admitted December 8, 1810 aged seven
years by Church Wardens of St. Philip's Church. Indentured to DAVID
AIKEN (of Winnsborough) as a storekeeper November 2, 1815. Indentures
expired December 8, 1824. (F-64)

STODDARD, ELISHA. Admitted May 21, 1812 aged six years by Warden of
Charleston. Delivered to his parents February 4, 1819. Indentures
expired May 21, 1827. (F-106)

SUIT, MARY A. Admitted June __, 1819 aged four years by Warden of
Charleston. Indentured to DR. THOMAS PRIOLEAU as a needlewoman March
16, 1826. Indentures expired January 3, 1833. (I-35)

THOMAS, CAROLINE. Admitted August 16, 1811 aged three years by BRIDGET THOMAS, mother. Born February __, 1808. Indentured to SARAH ARNOLD as a domestic June 1, 1820. Indentures expired February 10, 1826. (F-89)

THOMAS, ELEANOR. Admitted May 22, 1811 aged six years by JOHN THOMAS, father. Indentured to CHARLES H. MIOT as a domestic January 6, 1820. Indentures expired May 22, 1823. (F-76)

THOMSON, MARGARET. Admitted March 9, 1815 aged ten years by Warden of Charleston. Indentured to WILLIAM SIMONTON (of Fairfield District) as a spinner and weaver December 5, 1816. Indentures expired March 9, 1823. (G-83)

THOMSON, THOMAS. Admitted June 8, 1815 by LEWIS THOMSON, father. Born July 17, 1807. (G-89) No further information.

VANDRAPER (VANRIPPER), MARINUS. Admitted March 25, 1819 aged four years by Warden of Charleston. Indentured to JOHN J. SHERIDAN as a cabinet-maker September 12, 1829. Indentures expired September 12, 1843. (I-30) In 1843, his sister, MARY, wrote the Commissioners and stated that Marinus "had not been heard of for 13 or 14 years and that she had reason to believe he was dead, that she proposed to take out Letters of Administration on his Estate, but she had not been able to procure Securities to the Bond." (Minutes, August 10, 1843)

VANDRAPER (VAN RIPER), MARY. Admitted March 25, 1819 aged eight years by Warden of Charleston. Indentured to ANN PORTER, occupation unknown, May 11, 1820. Transferred to GEORGE NORMAN as a domestic October 16, 1823. Indentures expired December 5, 1830. (I-29)

WALKER, MARY. Admitted November 22, 1810 aged eight years by Warden of Charleston. Delivered to her uncle, WILLIAM J. PETERS, April 22, 1814. Returned to the Institution because of cruelty by her aunt. Transferred to JOHN HAGOOD (HAYGOOD), of Fairfield, occupation unknown, May 12, 1815. Indentures expired November 22, 1820. (F-62)

WALLACE, FRANCIS. Admitted February 11, 1813 aged four years by ELIZABETH WALLACE, mother. Delivered to her father, ANDREW WALLACE, November 28, 1816. Indentures expired February 11, 1830. (G-16)

WARD, CAROLINE. Admitted June 14, 1810 aged two years by SUSANNAH WARD, mother. (F-55) Died June 2, 1810 of a bowel complaint. (ROSP, June 16, 1810)

WATSON, JAMES. Admitted May 18, 1816 aged five years by Warden of Charleston. (G-109) "Absconded...last Sunday morning." (ROSP, February 13, 1825) Returned July 1, 1825. (ROSP, July 1, 1825) Indentured to JOSHUA BROWN (of Laurens District) as a farmer February 1, 1826. (ROSP, February 1, 1826) An orphan. (AtoA)

WELCH, MAZIMIN. Admitted April 24, 1817 aged seven years by NATHANIEL WELCH, father. Indentured to PETER MOOD and JOHN EVAN as a gold and silversmith September 30, 1824. Transferred to his mother, unknown, December 9, 1824. (H-26) Grandfather, M. CLASTVER. (AtoA)

WILLIAMS, GEORGE. Admitted January 13, 1814 aged five years by JANE WILLIAMS, mother. Delivered to his brother-in-law, HENRY CROSS, May 24, 1821. Indentures expired January 13, 1830. (G-39) Admitted from the Poor House. (ROSP, January 15, 1814)

WILSON, JAMES. Admitted March 7, 1811 aged eleven years by ANN WILSON, mother. From Philadelphia. Sent to the Poor House September 21, 1812. Indentures expired March 7, 1821. (F-67) "Cripple and idiot." ROSP, September 19, 1812)

WILSON, JOSEPH. Admitted April 10, 1817 aged nine years by MARY BUCKINGHAM, mother. Delivered to his mother December 23, 1819. Indentures expired January 10, 1829. (H-25)

WILSON, MARY JANE. Admitted March 9, 1815 aged five years by ANN WILSON, mother. Born February 28, 1810. Delivered to her mother, MARY POWERS, November 1, 1821. Indentures expired February 28, 1828. (G-84)

WILSON, ROBERT. Admitted March 7, 1811 aged nine years by ANN WILSON, mother. (F-68) Indentured to A. CARRUTH (of Greenville District) as a gunsmith June 8, 1815. (ROSP, June 10, 1815) Indentures expired March 7, 1821. (F-68)

WILSON, WILLIAM. Admitted March 7, 1811 aged five years by ANN WILSON, mother. Indentured to PETER GARTH (GAUTH) as a bricklayer July 24, 1817. Transferred to A. CARRUTH as a gunsmith September 6, 1819. Indentures expired March 7, 1827. (F-69)

WOLLEY, CHARLES. Admitted February 4, 1819 by ELIZABETH WOLLEY, mother. Delivered to his mother June 24, 1819. (I-24)

WOTTEN, ALFRED. Admitted January 25, 1810 aged eleven years by CHLOE WOTTEN, mother. Indentured to WILLIAM THOMPSON as a ship chandler March 18, 1813. Indentures expired January 25, 1820. (F-42)

WRIGHT, DANIEL. Admitted December 8, 1814 aged three years by S.L. WRIGHT, mother. Born January 5, 1811. Indentured to RICHARD VAN BRUNT as a bookbinder March 14, 1828. Indentures expired January 5, 1832. (G-79) Parents married in 1801; father died September 1814. (AtoA)

WRIGHT, HENRY. Admitted October 1, 1819 aged twelve years by Warden of Charleston. Born September 30, 1807. (I-48) Indentured to THOMAS FULTON, SR. (of Laurens District) as a farmer July 29, 1824. Indentures expired September 30, 1828. (I-48)

WRIGHT, HEZEKIAH. Admitted October 10, 1816 aged thirteen years by CHRISTIANA WRIGHT, mother. Indentured to THOMAS CARROLL as a painter and glazier July 10, 1817. Indentures expired January 13, 1825. (H-8)

WRIGHT, LITTLEBURY JOHN. Admitted October 10, 1816 aged ten years by CHRISTIANA WRIGHT, mother. Delivered to his mother June 3, 1819. Indentures expired December 27, 1827. (H-9)

WRIGHT, MARGARET. Admitted February 13, 1817 aged three years by SUSANNAH WRIGHT, mother. Indentured to MATTHEW BRAID as a domestic December 7, 1820. Transferred to RICHARD VAN BRUNT, occupation unknown, April 18, 1829. Indentures expired April 18, 1829. (H-15)

WRIGHT, NORMAN. Admitted December 8, 1814 aged seven years by S.L. WRIGHT, mother. Born September 6, 1807. Indentured to CHARLES EDMONSTON as a merchant October 19, 1820. Indentures expired September 6, 1828. (G-78)

ZIEHEN, LEWIS. Admitted September 23, 1819 aged nine years by Warden of Charleston. Born April 22, 1809. Indentured to C.C.SEBRING as a printer December 16, 1824. Indentures expired April 22, 1830. (I-47) From Prussia; arrived about two years before. (AtoA)

ZYLK, MARGARET. Admitted March 31, 1814 aged six years by ANNE ZYLK, mother. Died September 15, 1817. Indentures expired March 31, 1826. (G-48)

ZYLK, THOMAS. Admitted March 31, 1814 aged three years by ANNE ZYLK, mother. Indentured to PAUL PRITCHARD as a ship carpenter May 19, 1825. Indentures expired March 31, 1832. (G-49)

ABRAHAM, ROSANNA. Admitted April 15, 1829 aged six years by JOSEPH PREVOST, unknown. Indentured to JOSEPH PREVOST as a domestic November 27, 1834. Indentures expired April 15, 1841. (L-99)

ADAMS, JOHN. Admitted August 24, 1826 aged six years by Warden of Charleston. Indentured to E.H. WHITING as a turner July 26, 1832. Indentures expired August 24, 1841. (K-133) Admitted from the Poor House. (AtoA)

ADAMS, JOHN. Admitted June 17, 1824 aged four years by SUSAN ADAMS, mother. Delivered to his mother, SUSAN RIDLEY, April 20, 1826. Indentures expired June 17, 1841. (K-63) Father, unknown, lost at sea. (AtoA)

ADAMS, RICHARD. Admitted June 17, 1824 aged six years by SUSAN ADAMS, mother. Delivered to his mother, SUSAN RIDLEY (RIDBY), April 20, 1825. Indentures expired June 17, 1839. (K-82)

ADAMS, RICHARD. Admitted August 24, 1826 aged seven years by Warden of Charleston. Indentured to JOSEPH McCULLOUGH (of Greenville District) as a farmer May 7, 1833. Indentures expired August 24, 1840. (K-132)

ADAMS, WILLIAM C. Admitted March 2, 1826 aged seven years by BRIDGET ADAMS, mother. Indentures expired March 2, 1840. (K-116) Absconded, nd. Dropped from the list of children August 18, 1830. (ROSP, August 18, 1830) Father, WILLIAM BRONSON ADAMS, dead. (AtoA)

ALLEN, CHARLES. Admitted June 19, 1823 aged ten years by JOHN T. BOWLES, uncle. Indentured to JOHN CONNOR as a saddler February 22, 1827. Indentures expired June 19, 1836. (K-49) Grandmother, ANN BOWLES, was the COH schoolmistress. (AtoA)

ALLEN, JAMES. Admitted March 18, 1824 aged four years by CHRISTIANA JONES, aunt. (K-70) Indentured to his uncle, JOHN T. BOWLES, as a printer December 18, 1834. Transferred to SAMUEL T. MAXEY as a bricklayer November 25, 1835. (BO) Indentures expired March 18, 1841. (K-70)

ALLINE, WILLIAM. Admitted April 26, 1821 aged ten years by DOMINIQUE ALLINE, father. Delivered to his grandmother, MAD. C. RAVIN, November 25, 1824. Indentures expired August 16, 1832. (K-7)

ALLISON, GEORGE. Admitted July 3, 1823 aged eight years by MARIA ALLISON, mother. Delivered to his mother leaving for Philadelphia. Indentures expired July 3, 1836. (K-51) Father, ROBERT ALLISON, from Philadelphia. Grandfather, _____ VANDERCHIEN, a soldier. (AtoA)

ALLISON, JAMES. Admitted July 3, 1823 aged eleven years by MARIA ALLISON, mother. Delivered to his mother going to Philadelphia. Indentures expired June 3, 1833. (K-50)

BAKER, GEORGE. Admitted February 24, 1825 aged five years by Warden of Charleston. (L-47) Died August 11, 1828 of dysentary and buried in the COH Burial Ground. (ROSP, August 13, 1828)

BAKER, HORATIO W. Admitted February 24, 1825 aged nine years by Warden of Charleston. Indentured to WILLIAM STAGGERS (of Williamsburg District) as a storekeeper February 19, 1829. Indentures expired February 24, 1847. (L-46)

BARNES, SARAH SUSANNAH. Admitted December 19, 1822 aged four years by Warden of Charleston. Indentured to BENJAMIN THEUS as a seamtress February 10, 1831. Indentures expired December 19, 1839. (L-26)

BARTO (BERTEAU), SELINA. Admitted February 24, 1825 aged eight years by Warden of Charleston. Delivered to her father, NICHOLAS BARTO of Baltimore May 18, 1826. Indentures expired February 24, 1835. (K-100)

BASSETT, JOHN. Admitted February 12, 1829 aged six years by SARAH
BASSETT, mother. (ROSP, February 18, 1829) Admitted from the Poor
House. (AtoA) Died October 31, 1830 of Tabes Mesenterica. (ARP, 1831)

BASSETT, ORAN. Admitted February 12, 1829 aged eight years by SARAH
BASSETT, mother. Indentured to BENJAMIN GILDERSLEEVE as a printer
October 25, 1832. Indentures expired February 12, 1842. (M-30) Born
in New Orleans and admitted from the Poor House. (AtoA)

BEATSON, DAVID. Admitted April 25, 1822 aged thirteen years by SARAH
BEATSON, mother. Indentured to RICHARD H. GRADICK as a blacksmith
November 27, 1823. Indentures expired July 8, 1829. (K-29)

BECK, FRANCIS. Admitted July 3, 1823 aged eight years by REBECCA BECK,
mother. Indentured to CHARLES CHURCH as a copperplate printer March 22,
1827. Transferred to his mother March 13, 1828. Indentures expired
July 3, 1836. (K-52)

BECK, JOHN (FRENCHY). Admitted July 3, 1823 aged four years by REBECCA
BECK, mother. Delivered to his mother March 15, 1827. Indentures
expired July 3, 1840. (K-53)

BEDON, STEPHEN (DANIEL). Admitted May 27, 1824 aged ten years and eight
months by Warden of Charleston. Indentured to EDWARD SEBRING as a
tailor October 13, 1828. Indentures expired May 27, 1834. (K-81)

BETTERSON, DAWSON. Admitted March 30, 1826 aged seven years by FRANCES
BETTERSON, unknown. (K-118) Died October 13, 1829 of measles compli-
cated by convulsions. (ARP, 1829) Buried in the COH Burial Ground.
(ROSP, October 20, 1829)

BETTERSON, FRANCIS (WILLIAM). Admitted March 30, 1826 aged four years by
FRANCES BETTERSON, unknown. Indentured to JOHN S. RIGGS as a harnessmaker April 2, 1835. Indentures expired March 30, 1842. (K-119)

BETTERSON, THOMAS. Admitted May 25, 1826 aged ten years by WILLIAM
BETTERSON, father. Indentured to CLELAND BELIN (of Willtown) as a
merchant October 13, 1829. Indentures expired May 25, 1837. (K-122)
Father lived on West side of Wall Street, four doors from the corner
of Boundary. (AtoA)

BETTON, JEWEL (JOEL). Admitted March 22, 1827 aged four years by ELIZA
BETTON, mother. (M-3) Died December 5, 1829 of dysentary and cholera.
(Medical Matters, Illnesses and Treatments, 1829) Mother was a cook
in the Poor House and later worked for WILLIAM ROBINSON who lived on
the corner of Elliott and East Bay Streets. (AtoA)

BOG, KITTY. Admitted August 10, 1826 aged eight years by Warden of
Charleston. Delivered to her mother, MARGARET BOG, May 10, 1826.
Indentures expired August 10, 1836. (L-59) Born in New York. (Minutes,
August 10, 1826)

BOG, JOHN. Admitted August 10, 1826 aged six years by Warden of
Charleston. Delivered to his mother, MARGARET BOG, May 16, 1827.
Indentures expired August 10, 1841. (K-128) Born in Philadelphia.
(Minutes, August 10, 1826)

BOGGS, (BOG) CATHERINE. Admitted August 20, 1829 aged twelve years by
the Poor House. From New York. Indentured to ANN S. FABIAN as a domestic March 26, 1831. (L-90) Transferred to F.M. MULLER, occupation
unknown, March 1, 1832. (BO) Delivered to her mother, MARGARET BOGGS,
May 16, 1827. (ROSP, May 16, 1827) Indentures expired August 20,
1835. (L-90) "Mrs. Boggs resides in a house in French Alley - is a
scold and nuisance to the Neighborhood; is always drunk and disorderly,
admitting into her abode all sorts and colors of People...She has no
visible means of a livelihood. She beats her children cruelly, so as
to endanger their lives. She is an Irish woman but the Children were
born here." (Minutes, September 1, 1825)

BOGGS, JOHN. Admitted August 20, 1829 aged ten years by the Poor House. Indentures expired August 20, 1840. (M-39) Delivered to his mother, MARGARET McCULLOUGH, April 25, 1832. (Minutes, April 25, 1832)

BOONE, WILLIAM. Admitted December 27, 1827 aged nine years by ELIZA BOONE, mother. Indentured to R. VAN BRUNT as a bookbinder July 14, 1831. Indentures expired December 27, 1839. (M-17)

BOURDENSTINE, ELIZABETH. Admitted August 16, 1821 aged eight years by City Warden. (L-8) Delivered to her uncle, JOHN A. RIESTER, February 22, 1823. (ROSSC)

BRADICKS, THOMAS. Admitted August 24, 1826 aged seven years by Warden of Charleston. Indentured to JOHN C. SIMONS as a painter May 30, 1833. Indentures expired August 24, 1840. (K-131) Admitted from the Poor House. (AtoA)

BROTHERS, JAMES. Admitted July __, 1826 by MARGARET GRENAKER, unknown. (ROSP, July 5, 1826) Indentured to STEPHEN McCULLEY as a shoemaker, nd. (ROSP, April 25, 18-3)

BROUNDING, HAMPTON. Admitted November 9, 1821 aged eight years by Warden of Charleston. Indentures expired November 9, 1834. (K-19) Absconded January 23, 1828. (ROSP, January 23, 1828)

BRUGNIEN, AUGUSTE (AUGUSTUS). Admitted May 24, 1821 aged two years by Warden of Charleston. Born May __, 1819. Indentured to MOSES C. HYAMS as a merchant October 4, 1832. Indentures expired May 24, 1840. (K-11)

BRUGNIEN, GENTIL. Admitted April 26, 1821 aged six years by Warden of Charleston. Indentured to GEORGE LOCKE as a merchant January 26, 1829. Transferred to MOSES D. HYAMS, occupation unknown, September 1, 1831. Indentures expired December 27, 1835. (K-10)

BRUGNIEN, GLANDET. Admitted April 26, 1821 aged seven years by City Warden. Indentured to STEPHEN S. TARDY as a painter May 31, 1827. Indentures expired October 11, 1834. (K-9)

BRUGNIEN, PROSPER. Admitted April 26, 1821 aged eight years by Warden of Charleston. Indentures expired October 24, 1834. Delivered to MARIE ANNE BRUGNIEN, sister, to go to P. ALBIAGNAC as a tailor October 24, 1822. (BO)

BULL, CATHERINE. Admitted October 22, 1829 aged eight years by Poor House. (L-94) Delivered to her aunt, MARY BARNES, as a domestic November 30, 1834. (BO) Indentures expired October 22, 1839. (L-94)

BULL, MARTHA. Admitted October 22, 1829 aged ten years by Poor House. Indentured to MARIA F. RUSSELL as a domestic May 12, 1831. Indentures expired October 22, 1837. (L-93) Mother was MRS. MARTHA CANTWELL of Leonard Street in New York. (BO, rejected)

BULL, MARY. Admitted October 22, 1829 aged six years by Poor House. (L-95) Died November 25, 1829 of measles. (ROSP, November 25, 1829)

BUNCH, MARY. Admitted September 13, 1821 aged ten years by Warden of Charleston. Indentured to SARAH H. VANDAL as a domestic December 6, 1821. Transferred to MRS. C.C. SMITH, occupation unknown August 24, 1826. Indentures expired September 13, 1829. (L-9)

BURBRIDGE, ALFRED. Admitted January 27, 1820 aged ten years by RACHEL BURBRIDGE, mother. Born September 11, ____. Indentures expired September 11, 1830. (I-60) Father died of consumption, 1820. (AtoA) No further information.

BURBRIDGE, HARRIET. Admitted January 27, 1820 aged eight years by RACHEL BURBRIDGE, mother. Born August 16, 1811. Indentures expired August 16, 1829. (I-61) Father died of consumption, 1820. (AtoA) No further information.

BURKE, JOHN. Admitted April 1, 1824 aged seven years by NELLY BURKE, mother. Indentured to JAMES DONEGAN as a shoemaker May 20, 1831. Indentures expired April 1, 1838. (K-73) Admitted from the Poor House. (AtoA)

BURKE, MICHAEL. Admitted March 2, 1826 aged four years by ELEANOR BURKE, mother. (K-115) Died September 6, 1828 of dysentary and whooping cough, aggrevated by worms and buried in the COH Burial Ground. (ROSP, September 10, 1828) Father, DAVID BURKE, died in July 1820 of Yellow Fever. (AtoA)

BURMINSTER, JACOB. Admitted June 27, 1826 aged nine years by Warden of Charleston. Indentures expired June 27, 1838. (K-129) Absconded and taken from the list of children August 18, 1830. (ROSP, August 18, 1830)

BURNS, ANN. Admitted February 7, 1822 aged nine years by JOHN BURNS, father. Indentured to OLIVE PELLISIER as a domestic July 31, 1823. Indentures expired February 7, 1831. (L-11)

BURNS, JOHN. Admitted February 7, 1822 aged three years by JOHN BURNS, father. Born January 7, 1819. Indentured to F. WARLEY (of St. Matthews Parish) as a storekeeper June 1, 1832. Indentures expired January 7, 1840. (K-23)

BURRILL, HENRY. Admitted February 14, 1828 aged five years by the Poor House. Indentured to WILLIAM MERRITT (of Barnwell District) as a farmer and miller June 9, 1836 (M-18) Transferred to PETER ERNARD as a baker May 17, 1838 (BO) Indentures expired February 14, 1844. (M-18)

BUSBY, HARRIET. Admitted May 2, 1822 aged ten years by Warden of Charleston. Indentured to EDWARD W. BOURNETHEAU as a domestic August 22, 1822. (L-17)

CALVERT, WILLIAM. Admitted May 10, 1827 aged nine years by MARTHA MUNROE mother. Born in Georgetown. Indentured to N.G. ALLEN as a bricklayer and plasterer November 12, 1835. Indentures expired May 10, 1839. (M-5)

CAMPBELL, ALEXANDER. Admitted September 9, 1824 aged nine years by Warden of Charleston. Indentured to CHARLES O'NEALE as a merchant October 13, 1828. Indentures expired September 9, 1836. (K-86) Mother died of a fever and three sisters were taken in by "charitable friends." (AtoA)

CAMPBELL, JAMES. Admitted September 9, 1824 aged four years by Warden of Charleston. Indentured to J.R. and W. CUNNINGHAM (of Columbia) as a bookbinder February 19, 1835. Indentures expired September 9, 1841. (K-87)

CANADAY (KENNEDY), JAMES. Admitted October 2, 1828 aged ten years by Warden of Charleston. Indentured to WILLIAM ENSTON as a cabinetmaker and fancy painter December 17, 1835. Indentures expired October 2, 1839. (M-26)

CARLISLE, JAMES. Admitted May 16, 1822 aged seven years by WILLIAM CARLISLE, father. Delivered to his mother, MARGARET CARLISLE, August 17, 1826. Indentures expired December 25, 1835. (K-28)

CARLTON, ABRAHAM (ALEXANDER). Admitted April 25, 1821 aged ten years by MARGARET CARLTON, mother. Indentured to ISRAEL MILLER as a farmer, March 8, 1827. Indentures expired April 10, 1832. (K-5)

CARLTON, ELIZABETH. Admitted July 24, 1823 aged seven years by MARY CARLTON, mother. Indentured to MRS. CATHERINE P. STOCKER as a domestic July 22, 1830. Indentures expired July 24, 1834. (L-30)

CARLTON, JAMES. Admitted April 26, 1821 aged eleven years by MARGARET CARLTON, mother. Indentured to ROBERT CALDWELL and CO. (of the Charleston Neck on King Street Road) as a merchant October 2, 1823. Indentures expired April 20, 1831. (K-4)

CARLTON, MARGARET. Admitted April 25, 1822 aged eleven years by MARY CARLTON, mother. Indentured to ISAAC A. and JANE H. JOHNSON as a domestic January 29, 1824. Indentures expired March 14, 1829. (L-16)

CARLTON, MARY ANN. Admitted October 7, 1822 aged two years by MARGARET CARLTON, mother. Born October 14, 1820. Indentured to ELIZA BONNER as a milliner December 3, 1835. Indentures expired October 14, 1838. (L-24)

CARLTON, RICHARD. Admitted April 26, 1821 aged nine years by MARGARET CARLTON, mother. Indentured to WILLIAM McC. YOUNG (of York District) as a farmer April 19, 1827. Indentures expired July 1, 1833. (K-6)

CLARK, DRURY WILBURN. Admitted March 21, 1822 aged five years by MARY B. BALDWIN, mother. Indentures expired July 18, 1838. (K-24) Absconded, nd. (ROSP, January 23, 1828)

CLARK, JOSEPH ALEXANDER. Admitted August 21, 1828 aged eight years by ELIZABETH CLARK, mother. Indentured to FREDERICK FORD as a planter October 28, 1831. Indentures expired August 21, 1841. (M-24)

CLARKE, LYDIA CATHERINE. Admitted December 21, 1820 aged four years by E. CLARKE, mother. Born December 4, 1816. Indentured to JOHN C. WALKER, bookseller, occupation unknown, March 12, 1829. Transferred to JOHN P. JONES, brother-in-law, October 22, 1829. Indentures expired December 4, 1834. (I-89)

CLARK, SUSAN JUDITH. Admitted March 21, 1822 aged eight years by MARY B. BALDWIN, mother. Indentured to MARY WOOD as a domestic January 27, 1825. Indentures expired August 13, 1831. (L-12)

CLEMENTS, ROBERT. Admitted July 13, 1826 aged four years by CATHERINE CLEMENTS, mother. Delivered to his mother, CATHERINE LOWRY, July 30, 1829. Ordered to be received again into the COH September 15, 1831. (K-124) Indentured to TITUS L. BISSELL (of Alabama) as a tanner and currier September 15, 1836. Sent by the brig, Argo. (ROSP, November 9, 1836) Indentures expired July 13, 1843. (K-124)

CONKLIN, HARRIET. Admitted October 10, 1829 aged ten years by CAROLINE HOOD, unknown. Indentured to ESTHER BELIN as a domestic August 18, 1831. Indentures expired October 10, 1837. (L-92)

CONNELLY, JAMES. Admitted June 12, 1829 aged seven years and four months by SARAH CONNELLY, mother. Indentures expired February 12, 1843. (M-36) Born in Dorcetshire. (AtoA) Delivered to his mother, SARAH ADAMS, May 1834. (ROSP, May 1, 1834)

CORKER, GEORGE W. Admitted March 25, 1824 aged twelve years by THOMAS CORKER, father. Indentured to JOSIAH PHYNCEY as a pilot for the river and bar of Charleston. Indentures expired March 18, 1833. (K-71)

CORKER, ROBERT C. Admitted March 25, 1824 aged nine years by THOMAS CORKER, father. Indentures expired March 25, 1836. (K-72) Absconded, nd. (ROSP, January 23, 1828)

CRAFTS, JOHN. Admitted June 19, 1828 aged five years by LYDIA CRAFTS, mother. Indentured to THOMAS R. CHEW as a blacksmith August 25, 1836. Indentures expired June 19, 1844. (M-22) Born in Georgetown District (AtoA)

CRAFTS, LYDIA. Admitted June 19, 1828 aged seven years by LYDIA CRAFTS, mother. Delivered to her mother June 20, 1833. Indentures expired June 19, 1839. (L-72) Born in Georgetown District. (AtoA)

CRAFTS, WILLIAM. Admitted December 11, 1828 aged two years and five months by LYDIA CRAFTS, mother. Indentured to JOHN C. MILLER as a factor and commission merchant October 1, 1840. Indentures expired July 29, 1847 (M-28) Born in Georgetown. (AtoA)

CRAIG, WILLIAM. Admitted November 15, 1827 aged between three and four years by the Warden of Charleston. A foundling. (M-15) Delivered to his grandmother, ISABELLA KENNEDY, June 26, 1828. (ROSSC) Indentures expired November 15, 1844. (M-15)

CREIGER (CRUGER), CHARLES. Admitted August 12, 1824 aged eight years by ELIZA SHEKE, grandmother. Indentured to HENRY W. NEVILLE as a cabinetmaker and joiner March 18, 1831. Indentures expired August 12, 1837. (K-85) ELIZA CREIGER, mother, a former inmate. (Minutes, July 10, 1823)

CREIGER, FRANCES. Admitted August 12, 1824 aged eleven years by ELIZA SHEKE, grandmother. Delivered to her grandmother July 7, 1825. Indentures expired August 12, 1831. (L-39) ELIZA CREIGER, mother, a former inmate. (Minutes, July 10, 1823) Religion - Presbyterian. (ROSP, August 15, 1824)

CUTLER (CUTTER), GEORGE. Admitted December 28, 1820 aged eight years by JOHN F. CUTLER, father. Indentured to EDWARD FRANCIS as a grocer August 24, 1825. Transferred to JOHN REDFORD as a shoemaker October 6, 1825. Indentures expired December 28, 1833. (I-91) Absconded April 14, 1824 and returned July 25, 1824. (ROSP, July 25, 1824)

CUTLER, (CUTTER), HANNAH. Admitted December 28, 1820 aged six years by JOHN F. CUTLER, father. Indentured to GEORGE and BEULAH CRAMER as a domestic February 8, 1827. Indentures expired December 28, 1832. (I-92) Transferred to JANE M. EASTERBY, occupation unknown, May 15, 1828. (BO)

CUTLER (CUTTER), JOSEPH. Admitted December 28, 1820 aged three years by JOHN F. CUTLER, father. (I 93) Died September 23, 1826 of gangrene and buried in the COH Burial Ground. (ROSP, September 27, 1826)

CUTLER (CUTTER), JULIANNA. Admitted December 28, 1820 aged ten years by JOHN F. CUTLER, father. Indentured to JAMES HAMILTON as a domestic January 3, 1821. Indentures expired December 28, 1828. (I-90)

DANIEL, CAROLINE ANN. Admitted May 27, 1824 aged three years by Warden of Charleston. Indentured to B.W. RICHARD as a confectioner March 2, 1832. Indentures expired May 27, 1839. (L-34)

DARNES, EMILY. Admitted August 16, 1821 aged seven years by Warden of Charleston. Indentured to CATHERINE E. BIGGS as a domestic November 23, 1827. Indentures expired August 16, 1832. (L-6) October 17, 1831 and returned to the COH and sent to her sister, unknown, of Augusta, Georgia. (ROSSC)

DAVIS, RICHARD. Admitted November 14, 1822 aged seven years by MARY A. DAVIS, mother. Indentured to M. ANTONIO [indenture signed by HENRY W. CONNER] (of Columbia) as a merchant February 5, 1829. Indentures expired April 20, 1836. (K-38)

DAVIS, WILLIAM. Admitted November 14, 1822 aged ten years by MARY ANN DAVIS, mother. Delivered to his mother April 26, 1825. Indentures expired September 7, 1833. (K-37)

DAVIS, WILLIAM. Admitted January 20, 1825 aged six years by ELIZABETH BETTAN, mother. Delivered to his mother, ELIZA A.C. MUIRHEAD, January 7, 1830. Indentures expired January 20, 1840. (K-95)

DEAN, CHARLES. Admitted November 14, 1822 aged four years by SUSANNAH DEAN, mother (K-41) Indentured to A. JOHNSON (of Columbia), editor of the Telescope (ROSSC) as a printer November 24, 1831. Indentures expired April 4, 1839. (K-41)

DEAN, WILLIAM. Admitted March 5, 1829 aged six years by ANN DEAN, mother. Born in Bacon's Bridge, S.C. Indentured to RICHARD GLADNEY (of Columbia) as a printer July 9, 1835. Indentures expired March 5, 1844. (M-32)

DEBLIN (DEVLIN), THOMAS. Admitted May 20, 1824 aged four years by Warden of Charleston. Indentures expired May 20, 1841. (K-80) "11 June 1829, sent to Philadelphia in Brig Langdon Cheves to his father HUGH DEBLIN." (ROSSC)

DeBONNEFONS, ALONZO. Admitted October 11, 1821 aged four years by ANN DeBONNEFONS, mother. Died June 18, 1822. Indentures expired February 22, 1838. (K-18)

DICKS, HENRY. Admitted September 13, 1824 aged nine years by Warden of Charleston. Indentured to D.E. SWEENEY as a baker December 15, 1831. Indentures expired September 13, 1826. (ROSSC)

DIGNAN (DIEGNAN), CATHERINE. Admitted April 25, 1822 aged six years by MARY DIGNAN, mother. Delivered to her mother July 3, 1823. Indentures expired December 24, 1833. (L-18)

DIXON (DICKSON), MARTHA. Admitted July 7, 1825 aged nine years by JOHN DANIEL, uncle. Indentured to MARY SCHIRER as a domestic April 18, 1829. Transferred to SOPHIA MESSERVY (L-52), sister of MARY SCHIRER, (BO) occupation unknown, August 25, 1830. Indentures expired July 7, 1834. (L-52)

DIXON, MARY JANE. Admitted July 7, 1825 aged two years by JOHN DANIEL, uncle. Indentured to MARY ANN MICHELL as a domestic December 24, 1834. Transferred to ELIZA MICHELL, occupation unknown, April 20, 1836. Indentures expired July 7, 1841. (L-54)

DIXON, SUSANNAH ELIZABETH. Admitted July 7, 1825 aged four years by JOHN DANIEL, uncle. (L-53) Died February 6, 1826 of dropsy and visceral obstructux and buried in the COH Burial Ground. (ROSP, February 8, 1826)

DODD, JAMES. Admitted December 6, 1821 aged eight years by ANN DODD, mother. Delivered to his mother April 18, 1822. Indentures expired March 29, 1834. (K-20)

DODD, JOHN. Admitted December 6, 1821 aged five years by ANN DODD, mother. Delivered to his mother April 18, 1822. Indentures expired February 14, 1837. (K-21)

DONALDSON, CHARLES EDMONSTON. Admitted November 23, 1827 aged four years by JAMES A. DONALDSON, brother. Delivered to his brother living in Newark, New Jersey July 21, 1836. Indentures expired November 23, 1844. (M-16)

DOWNIE, ELIZABETH. Admitted August 16, 1821 aged eight years by Warden of Charleston. Indentured to CEPHAS WHITTEMON, occupation unknown, April 28, 1824. (L-5)

DUNLAP, LUCINDA. Admitted December 4, 1829 aged four years by WILLIAM DUNLAP, father. Delivered to her father June 24, 1831. Indentures expired December 4, 1843, (L-96) Admitted from the Poor House. (AtoA)

DUNLAP, SAMUEL. Admitted December 4, 1829 aged ten years by WILLIAM DUNLAP, father. Delivered to his father June 2, 1831. Indentures expired December 4, 1840. (M-41) Admitted from the Poor House. (AtoA)

EGGERTON, ELIZA. Admitted June 1, 1826 aged nine years by Warden of Charleston. Indentured to CATHERINE JOHNSON as a domestic June 29, 1826. Indentures expired June 1, 1835. (L-57)

EGRINCUTTER, FREDERICK. Admitted August 4, 1825 aged five years by MARGARET SMITH, unknown. Indentured to THOMAS McCULLOUGH (of Fairfield District) as a storekeeper May 28, 1830. Indentures expired August 4, 1841. (K-111) Died March 11, 1831. (ROSSC)

EIGENKOTTER, CHARLES. Admitted August 24, 1826 aged nine years by Warden of Charleston. Indentured to THOMAS W. McCULLOUGH (of Fairfield District) as a storekeeper May 27, 1830. Indentures expired August 24, 1838. (K-130) Admitted from Poor House. (AtoA)

ENGLEBERT, FREDERICK. Admitted June 20, 1822 aged nine years by Warden of Charleston. (K-32) Indentured to FRANCIS HANDSBERRY of 65 Queen Street as a painter and glazier February 8, 1827. (BO) Indentures expired July 17, 1834. (K-32)

EVERARD, JOHN. Admitted January 10, 1822 aged nine years by WILLIAM EVERARD, father. Indentured to HENRY S. BIGGS as a house painter October 11, 1827. Indentures expired January 4, 1834. (K-22) Absconded nd. supposedly gone to New York. (Minutes, July 22, 1830)

FAIRBROTHER, JAMES M. Admitted February 17, 1820 aged nine years by MARY ANN FAIRBROTHER, unknown. Born November 17, 1810. Indentures expired November 17, 1831. (I-63) Delivered to his mother August 24, 1820. (BO) Father - JOHN. (AtoA)

FERNALD, WILLIAM. Admitted May 20, 1824 aged five years by DENNIS FERNALD father. Indentured to JOHN SMITH (of Laurens District) as a merchant February 18, 1832. Indentures expired May 20, 1840. (K-77)

FLACK, JAMES (THOMAS).Admitted December 15, 1825 aged five years by Warden of Charleston. Indentures expired December 15, 1841. (K-112) Absconded, nd. (ROSP, March 14, 1833)

FOLEY, GEORGE. Admitted January 15, 1824 aged nine years by ELIZABETH FOLEY, mother. Delivered to his mother, ELIZABETH KEARN, March 13, 1828. Indentures expired January 15, 1836. (K-63)

FOLEY, JOSHUA. Admitted January 15, 1824 aged seven years by ELIZABETH FOLEY, mother. Delivered to his mother, ELIZABETH KEARN, March 13, 1828. Indentures expired January 15, 1838. (K-64)

FORDHAM, JOHN. Admitted October 3, 1822 aged eleven years by Warden of Charleston. Indentured to JOHN LEAK (of Laurens District) as a farmer and blacksmith March 18, 1824. Indentures expired October 3, 1832. (K-34)

FRASER, ELIZA. Admitted September 19, 1822 aged eleven years by SARAH FRASER, mother. Indentured to LOUISA WILLIS as a domestic January 16, 1823. Transferred to AARON CURTISS, occupation unknown, April 25, 1823. Transferred to her mother July 17, 1823. Indentures expired October 9, 1828. (L-21)

FRASER, ELLEN (ELEANOR).Admitted September 20, 1827 aged seven years by SARAH C. FRASER, mother. (L-68) Delivered to EDWARD and SARAH FOLGER, step-father and mother, May 2, 1833. (BO) Indentures expired September 20, 1838. (L-68)

GALLAHER, DOROTHY. Admitted September 28, 1820 aged three years by DOROTHY GALLAHER, mother. Born November 12, 1816. Indentured to DANIEL BOINIST as a domestic December 12, 1829. Indentures expired November 12, 1834. (I-84) Born in New York. (AtoA) Transferred to ALEXANDER BERRY, occupation unknown, January 1832. (BO)

GALLAHER, JOHN. Admitted September 28, 1820 aged five years by DOROTHY GALLAHER, mother. Born March 1, 1815. Delivered to his mother June 1, 1826. Indentures expired March 1, 1826. (I-83) Born in Ireland. (AtoA)

GALLAHER, WILLIAM. Admitted May 21, 1821 aged two years by DOROTHY GALLAHER, mother. Born October 1, 1818. Indentured to JOHN A. AMAND as a coachmaker February 13, 1834. Indentures expired June 1, 1829. (K-12)

GASKINS, EMMA. Admitted June 17, 1824 aged ten years by Warden of Charleston. Indentured to ZADOCK VOLLEME as a folder and sewer of books January 4, 1827. Indentures expired June 17, 1832. (L-36)

GILBERT, CAROLINE (ADELINE). Admitted November 9, 1821 aged six years by Warden of Charleston. Delivered to her mother, OLIVIA GILBERT, July 31, 1823. Indentures expired July 9, 1833. (L-10)

GILBERT, WASHINGTON. Admitted November 9, 1820 aged ten years by OLIVIA GILBERT, mother. Born April 11, 1810. Delivered to his mother November 27, 1823. Indentures expired April 10, 1831. (I-86)

GRADY, CATHERINE. Admitted January 13, 1822 aged six years by Warden of Charleston. Indentured to HELOISE (MRS. N.) BONDO as a jeweller May 26, 1831. Transferred to E. BELIN, occupation unknown, August 18, 1831. Indentures expired January 13, 1837. (L-45)

GRADY, CATHERINE. Admitted January 13, 1825 aged six years by Warden of Charleston. Indentured to CATHERINE HOGAN as a domestic November 8, 1832. (L-117) Transferred to MRS. M.E. FLAGG, occupation unknown, nd. Transferred to MRS. C. HOGARTH, occupation unknown, nd. (BO) Indentures expired January 13, 1837. (L-117) Parents died in Savannah. (AtoA)

GRAY, ELIZA. Admitted July 16, 1829 aged eight years by Warden of Charleston. Indentured to ROBERT D. and HANNAH LAWRENCE as a domestic February 6, 1834. Indentures expired July 16, 1839. (L-89) Died September 9, 1838 and buried in the COH Burial Ground. (ROSP, September 13, 1830) Father, WILLIAM GRAY, was a blacksmith. (AtoA)

GRAY, ISABELLA. Admitted March 24, 1825 aged six years by Warden of Charleston. Indentured to SARAH KNUST as a domestic April 7, 1825. Indentures expired March 24, 1837. (L-48) Father, WILLIAM GRAY, a blacksmith died and child adopted by MRS. GODFREY who then gave the child to NATHANIEL M. MARIONER. (AtoA)

GRAY, JANE. Admitted March 6, 1823 aged six years by Warden of Charleston. (L-29) Indentured to MARY E. PHELPS, COH Matron, as a seamtress April 27, 1830. (ROSP, April 28, 1830) Indentures expired April 27, 1834. (L-29)

GRAY, MARY. Admitted March 6, 1823 aged eight years by Warden of Charleston. Indentured to ISABELLA C. LOCKE as a domestic October 30, 1828. Indentures expired March 6, 1833. (L-28)

GREGORY, WILLIAM H.B. Admitted March 14, 1828 aged six years by WILLIAM H. GREGORY, father. Died March 4, 1829. (M-20) Father in Poor House. Born in Sumpter District. (AtoA)

GRIFFIN, JAMES. Admitted November 23, 1826 aged eleven years by Warden of Charleston. Delivered to his mother, JANE GRIFFIN, July 10, 1828. Indentures expired November 23, 1836. (K-138)

GRIMES, JAMES. Admitted April 13, 1820 aged five years by ELIZABETH CHRISTIAN, mother. Born July 14, 1814. Indentured to CHARLES STURAT as a shoe and bootmaker August 10, 1826. Transferred to ROBERT F. STEPHENS (of Laurens District) as a farmer January 3, 1838. Indentures expired July 14, 1838. (I-69)

GROVES, AMANDA. Admitted March 8, 1827 aged six years by ELIZABETH LAMAR, mother. Delivered to her mother March 29, 1832. Indentures expired March 8, 1839. (M-2) Mother owned drygoods store at 219 King Street (BO)

GROVES, EUGENE. Admitted March 8, 1827 aged eight years by ELIZABETH LAMAR, mother. Delivered to his mother March 29, 1832. Indentures expired March 8, 1837. (M-1)

GUERIN, VIRGINIA. Admitted March 26, 1829 aged three years and three months by ANN GUERIN, mother. (L-88) Died May 20, 1829 of diarrhea. (ARP, 1829) Admitted from the Poor House. (ROSSC)

GURFIN, ROBERT. Admitted September 18, 1823 aged six years by Warden of Charleston. Indentures expired September 18, 1838. (K-60) Absconded, nd. (ROSP, February 2, 1832) Had two sisters, MARY and SARAH GURFIN, deaf and dumb who were sent to school in Philadelphia. (COH Inmates' Files)

HAGAN, HUGH. Admitted June 29, 1820 aged two years by ROSANNA HAGAN, mother. Born December 24, 1817. Delivered to his mother October 5, 1826. Indentures expired June 29, 1838. (I-79)

HAGEN, JAMES R. Admitted April 15, 1824 aged eight years by RICHARD HAGEN, father. Indentured to WHITE, BRICKELL and WHITE (K-75) of Columbia (ROSSC) as a manufacturer of paper February 18, 1830. Indentures expired January 16, 1837. (K-75)

HAGEN, THOMAS F. Admitted April 15, 1824 aged ten years by RICHARD HAGEN, father. Indentured to F.G.H. GUNTHER as a grocer May 24, 1827. (K-74) Transferred to JOHN P. LEGRISE as a clerk July 3, 1828. (BO) Indentures expired April 15, 1835. (K-74)

HANCOCK, CHARLES. Admitted February 20, 1823 aged two years by GEORGE HANCOCK, father. Indentured to SAMUEL WEIR (of Columbia) as a printer February 27, 1834. Indentures expired July 12, 1841. (K-45)

HANCOCK, JANE. Admitted June 13, 1822 aged nine years by GEORGE HANCOCK, father. Indentured to SOPHIA KINGMAN as a milliner November 4, 1824. Transferred to MARGARET FLEMMING as a domestic February 23, 1826. Indentures expired June 13, 1831. (L-19)

HANSON, JOHN. Admitted February 9, 1826 aged three years and six months by Warden of Charleston. Indentures expired August 9, 1843. (K-113) Born in Scotland. (AtoA) Mother died of a fever in 1824 and father missing for several months. Father born in Norway. (AtoA) No further information.

HAZZARD, ELIZABETH. Admitted April 25, 1822 aged seven years by MARY TSCHUDY, mother. Delivered to her mother January 29, 1824. Indentures expired December 2, 1822. (L-15)

HAZZARD, OLIVER. Admitted April 25, 1822 aged nine years by MARY TSCHUDY, mother. Indentured to RICHARD VAN BRUNT as a bookbinder June 3, 1824. Indentures expired September 14, 1833. (K-26)

HAZZARD, PAUL. Admitted April 25, 1822 aged five years by MARY TSCHUDY, mother. Indentures expired August 21, 1837. (K-27) No further information.

HENRY, JOHN. Admitted October 19, 1820 aged twelve years by Warden of Charleston. Born December 20, ____. Indentured to WILLIAM PERONNEAU as a miller and lumber merchant December 20, 1821. (I-85)

HEYDENFELD, ELKIN. Admitted June 28, 1827 aged six years by ESTHER HEYDENFELD, mother. Born in Norfolk, Virginia. (M-10) Indentured to WILLIAM KINCAID (of Fairfield) as a merchant February 23, 1832. (ROSSC) Indentures expired June 28, 1842. (M-10) Commissioners donated $200.00 for his admission to the Georgia Bar. (Minutes, May 5, 1842)

HEYDENFELD, SAMETINE (SAMUELINE).Admitted June 28, 1827 aged nine years by ESTHER HEYDENFELD, mother. Delivered to her mother November 15, 1827. Indentures expired June 28, 1827. (L-66)

HEYDENFELD, SOLOMON. Admitted June 28, 1827 aged ten years by ESTHER HEYDENFELD, mother. Indentured to DR. NOHR (of Walterborough) as an apothecary November 12, 1829. Indentures expired June 28, 1838. (M-9) The Commissioners gave "$40.00 from MRS. GREGORIE'S fund for present aid to enable him to go to his friends in Waynesborough, Georgia to prepare himself for the Ministry." (Minutes, May 8, 1834)

HODGE, ALEXANDER. Admitted September 7, 1820 aged five years by BRIDGET HODGE, mother. Born March 1, 1815. Delivered to JOSEPH and BRIDGET SWARTZ, step-father and mother, April 26, 1827. Indentures expired March 1, 1836. (I-82)

HODGE, JOHN. Admitted September 7, 1820 aged nine years by BRIDGET RYAN, mother. Born May 1, 1811. Indentured to THOMAS FULTON, JR. as a farmer July 29, 1824. Indentures expired May 1, 1832. (I-81)

HUTCHINS, ANNA (ANGELINA).Admitted February 8, 1821 aged four years by SAMUEL HUTCHINS, father. (L-2) Delivered to her aunt, MRS. MANSON, (of Sullivan's Island) September 2, 1830. (BO) Indentures expired February 8, 1835. (ROSSC)

HUTCHINS, HILMAN. Admitted February 8, 1821 aged nine years by SAMUEL S. HUTCHINS, father. Born November 4, 1811. Indentured to WILLIAM H. FULTON (of Laurens District) as a farmer and blacksmith March 17, 1825. Transferred to ANDREW MANSON, uncle, January 17, 1828. Indentures expired November 4, 1832. (K-1)

HUTCHINS, MARTHA. Admitted February 8, 1821 aged five years by SAMUEL HUTCHINS, father. Indentured to EBENEZER and EVELINA THAYER, occupation unknown, March 27, 1828. Indentures expired February 8, 1834. (L-1)

HUTCHINS, WASHINGTON (GEORGE).Admitted February 8, 1821 aged seven years by SAMUEL S. HUTCHINS, father. Born July 4, 1813. Delivered to his uncle, ANDREW MANSON, (of Laurens District) June 16, 1825. Indentures expired July 4, 1834. (K-2) "This boy is now with A.E. MOLLER, printer." (ROSSC)

HUTCHINSON, MARY. Admitted May 18, 1820 aged four years by MARY HUTCHIN-SON, mother. Born May 24, 1816. Delivered to her mother September 21, 1820. Indentures expired May 24, 1834. (I-78)

IRVINE, JOSEPH. Admitted September 25, 1829 aged seven years by JOHN A. TULLOCK, step-father. Born in Columbia. (AtoA) Indentured to N.G. ALLEN as a bricklayer and plasterer November 12, 1835. Indentures expired September 25, 1844. (M-40)

JOHNSON (JOHNSTON), CAROLINE LETITIA. Admitted October 10, 1829 aged two years by CHARLES STARK, unknown. (L-91) Indentured to CHARLES STARK (of Laurens Street near the Bathing House) as a domestic July 23, 1835. (BO) In 1842, she was with MRS. GREY earning wages. Indentures expired January 8, 1845. (ROSSC)

JOHNSON, CATHERINE. Admitted August 3, 1820 aged four years by ANN JOHNSON, mother. Born September 1, 1815. Indentured to ZADOCK VOLLUME as a seamstress August 31, 1826. Indentures expired September 1, 1833. (I-80)

JOHNSON, WILLIAM. Admitted January 18, 1827 aged ten years by ELIZA JOHNSON, mother. Indentured to W.S. NELL as a baker February 25, 1830. Transferred to JAMES DONEGAN as a shoemaker May 20, 1831. Transferred to THOMAS O'BRIEN as a baker June 9, 1831. Indentures expired January 18, 1788. (K-139)

JONES, EDWARD JOHN. Admitted November 15, 1827 aged five years, seven months and eighteen days by ELIZABETH JONES, mother. From Edgefield District. Indentured to WILLIAM ENSTON as a cabinetmaker and fancy painter December 17, 1835. Indentures expired April 12, 1842. (M-14) Father, unknown, raised in the COH. (AtoA)

JONES, ORMSBY. Admitted May 18, 1826 aged nine years by STEPHEN MOORE, guardian. Delivered to his father, ROYCE JONES, of Havanna January 31, 1828. Indentures expired May 18, 1838. (K-120) Born in New York. (AtoA)

JONES, WILLIAM. Admitted May 18, 1826 aged seven years by STEPHEN MOORE, guardian. Delivered to his father, ROYCE JONES, of Havanna January 31, 1828. Indentures expired May 18, 1840. (K-121)

JOWITT (JEWITT), EDWIN. Admitted July 16, 1829 aged five years by ELIZA JOWITT, mother. (ROSP, July 22, 1829) Delivered to his mother January 30, 1834. (ROSSC) Indentures expired July 16, 1845. (M-37)

JOWITT, JOHN. Admitted May 24, 1827 aged six years by ELIZA JOWITT, mother. Indentured to W. CANUET (of Savannah) as a shipbuilder August 21, 1834. Indentures expired May 24, 1842. (M-6)

KEOWIN, JOSEPH. Admitted October 30, 1828 aged six years by JOHN A. KEOWIN, father. Indentured to WILLIAM P. GORMAN as a boot and shoe-maker November 6, 1834. Indentures expired October 30, 1842. (M-27) Born July 8, 1822. (AtoA)

KNIEFF, ELIZABETH. Admitted November 9, 1820 aged five years by FREDERICKE KNIEFF, father. Born March 8, 1815. Indentured to ELIZABETH KERRISON as a domestic October 11, 1827. Indentures expired March 8, 1833. (I-87) JOHN PEAGLES, step-brother. (AtoA)

KORTMAN, MARY. Admitted October 24, 1822. (L-23) Delivered to her mother July 25, 1833. (ROSSC)

LAIDLER, WILLIAM. Admitted March 16, 1820 aged eight years by Warden of Charleston. Born July 30, 1812. Indentured to JAMES HAIG as a printer June 9, 1825. (I-65) Transferred to A.S. WILLINGTON, his guardian July 31, 1828. (BO) Indentures expired July 30, 1833. (I-65)

LAMAR, ADELA. Admitted June 14, 1827 aged four years by ELIZABETH LAMAR, mother. Delivered to her mother January 5, 1828. Indentures expired June 14, 1841. (L-65)

LAWTON, CHARLES. Admitted June 16, 1825 aged eight years by SAMUEL PAGE, unknown. Delivered to his grandfather, ISAAC LAWTON, of Rhode Island May 11, 1826. Indentures expired June 16, 1838. (K-103) Born September 2, 1717. (Minutes, June 16, 1825)

LAWTON, JOSEPH. Admitted June 16, 1825 aged six years by SAMUEL PAGE, unknown. Delivered to his grandfather, ISAAC LAWTON, of Rhode Island May 11, 1726. Indentures expired June 16, 1838. (K-103) Born September 2, 1817. (Minutes, June 16, 1825)

LAWTON, NELSON. Admitted June 16, 1825 aged four years by SAMUEL PAGE, unknown. Delivered to his grandfather, ISAAC LAWTON, of Rhode Island May 11, 1826. Indentures expired June 16, 1842. (K-105) Born May 17, 1821. (Minutes, June 16, 1825)

LEEKS, ANN. Admitted February 24, 1825 aged five years by Warden of Charleston. Delivered to her aunt, JANE BUCHANAN, July 7, 1825. Indentures expired February 24, 1838. (K-98)

LEEKS, ELIZABETH. Admitted February 24, 1825 aged three years by Warden of Charleston. Delivered to her aunt, JANE BUCHANAN, July 7, 1825. Indentures expired February 24, 1840. (K-99)

LEMOTT, SUSAN. Admitted August 16, 1821 aged eight years by Warden of Charleston. Indentured to ANNA SMALL as a milliner February 10, 1825. (L-7)

LISTER, THOMAS. Admitted June 4, 1829 aged ten years by Warden of Charleston. Indentured to DR. JACOB DeLaMOTTA as an apothecary November 12, 1832. Indentures expired June 4, 1840. (M-35) Born in Waccamaw. (AtoA)

LONG, OWENS. Admitted February 19, 1824 aged twelve years by Warden of Charleston. Indentured to LARKIN WALDROP (of Newberry District) as a farmer June 1, 1826. Indentures expired February 19, 1833. (K-65) Admitted from the Poor House. (AtoA)

LOVEMAN, MARGARET. Admitted December 20, 1827 aged eight years by ANN LOVEMAN, mother. Delivered to her aunt, MRS. BARBARA CHANDLESS, April 15, 1830. Indentures expired December 20, 1837. (L-70)

LOVEMAN, SALLY. Admitted December 20, 1827 aged three years by ANN LOVEMAN, mother. Indentures expired December 20, 1842. (L-71) Died November 10, 1829 of pneumonia. (ARP, 1830)

LYNCH, ANNA MARIA. Admitted December 11, 1828 aged nine years and eight months by Warden of Charleston. Indentures expired March 29, 1837. (L-78) Delivered to her grandmother, MRS. JANE LYNCH, January 24, 1833. (BO) Born March 29, 1819 and lived in Ellery Street. (AtoA)

LYNCH, ELIZABETH. Admitted December 6, 1828 aged eight years by Warden of Charleston. Indentured to ELIZABETH STAFFORD as a domestic November 27, 1834. Indentures expired December 6, 1846. (L-77)

LYNCH, JAMES. Admitted April 18, 1829 aged five years by JANE LYNCH, mother. Died June 11, 1829 of dysentary. (ARP, 1829) Admitted from the Poor House. (ROSSC)

LYNES, BENJAMIN. Admitted July 23, 1829 aged nine years by MARY ANN LYNES, mother. (ROSP, August 12, 1829) Delivered to his mother April 10, 1834. Indentures expired July 23, 1841. (M-38)

McCAFFREY, (McCAFFEY), JOHN. Admitted June 28, 1827 aged five years by HUGH McCAFFREY, father. (M-8) Died May 30, 1829 of dysentary. (ARP, 1829)

McCANDLISH, LESLIE. Admitted January 9, 1825 aged seven years by SARAH McCANDLISH, mother. Indentures expired January 20, 1829. (K-94) Admitted from the Poor House. (AtoA) Graduated from South Carolina College December 6, 1837. (ROC , 1821) Brother, no name, died by an accident of the railroad. (Minutes, February 19, 1835)

McCANDLISH, ROBERT. Admitted January 20, 1825 aged nine years by SARAH McCANDLISH, mother. Indentured to WILLIAM B. and G. WILKIE as a ship-chandler March 25, 1830. Indentures expired February 20, 1837. (K-93) Admitted from the Poor House. (AtoA)

McCORY, JOSHUA. Admitted November 25, 1824 aged seven years by Warden of Charleston. Delivered to BORRIET ROMA, uncle, December 23, 1824. Indentures expired November 25, 1838. (K-91)

McCORY, JOHN. Admitted November 25, 1824 aged seven years by Warden of Charleston. Delivered to his uncle, B. ROMA, of New York. Indentures expired November 25, 1838. (K-91)

McGRANNIKER, JOHN. Admitted August 16, 1827 aged eleven years by Warden of Charleston. Born in Ireland. (M-11) Indentured to W.S. NELL (of Walterborough District) as a planter November 4, 1830. (ROSSC) Transferred to JAMES DONEGAN, occupation unknown, nd. Transferred to LOUIS PAPSILAIQUIS as a baker June 9, 1831. Indentures expired August 6, 1837. (M-11)

McGREGOR, HARRIETT. Admitted February 26, 1824 aged seven years by Warden of Charleston. Delivered to her brother-in-law, WILLIAM H. ELLIOTT (of Georgetown) April 29, 1824. Indentures expired February 26, 1835. (L-33)

McGUIRE (MAGUIRE), MARY ANN. Admitted October 19, 1827 aged four years by Warden of Charleston. Indentured to NICHOLAS BURGER, occupation unknown, October 23, 1834. Indentures expired October 19, 1841. (L-69) Admitted from the Poor House. (ROSP, October 24, 1827)

McKAY, HUGH. Admitted February 17, 1825 aged three years by ANN McKAY. Indentured to O.H. WELLS (of Greenville District) as a printer April 23, 1835. Indentures expired February 17, 1843. (K-97)

McKAY, JOHN. Admitted March 6, 1823 aged nine years by ANN McKAY, mother. Indentured to JOSEPH McCULLOGH (of Greenville District) as a storekeeper May 10, 1826. Indentures expired November 14, 1834. (K-46) Born November 14, ____. Mother, born in Scotland, arrived November 1819. Father died in 1821. (AtoA) In 1860, he was employed as a railroad agent in Greenville. (AtoA Brownell children)

McKAY, ROBERT. Admitted March 6, 1823 aged six years by ANN McKAY, mother. Indentured to O.H. WELLS (of Greenville District) as a printer ___, 1829. Indentures expired March 14, 1838. (K-47) Born March 14, ___. (AtoA) In 1860, he took CHARLES MORRISON as an apprentice. (BO)

McKAY, WILLIAM. Admitted December 31, 1823 aged four years by ANN McKAY, mother. Born May 9, 1819. Indentured to ANDREW BERRY (of Georgia) as a farmer March 10, 1832. Indentures expired May 9, 1840. (K-62)

McPHERSON, ELIZA. Admitted September 2, 1824 aged four years by SUSAN McPHERSON, mother. Delivered to her mother May 29, 1828. (L-41) Religion: Presbyterian. (ROSP, September 5, 1824)

McPHERSON, JOHN. Admitted May 20, 1824 aged nine years by SUSANNAH McPHERSON, mother. Indentured to DAVID HAIG as a cooper October 31, 1829. Indentures expired May 20, 1836. (K-79)

McPHERSON, PETER. Admitted May 20, 1824 aged ten years by SUSANNAH McPHERSON, mother. (K-78) Indentured to JACOB DeLaMOTTA as an apothecary and chemist October 13, 1828. Master died (ROSP, July 22, 1829) and transferred to ANDREW BLAIR as a wheelwright July 16, 1829. Indentures expired May 20, 1835. (K-78)

McPHERSON, SARAH. Admitted September 2, 1824 aged seven years by SUSAN McPHERSON, mother. Delivered to her mother May 29, 1838. Indentures expired September 2, 1832. (L-40)

McQUEEN (McQUIEN), DONALD. Admitted September 7, 1826 aged nine years by Warden of Charleston. Indentured to WILLIAM N. GIBSON as a grocer June 9, 1831. Transferred to ELISHA CARSON (of King Street) as a merchant July 11, 1833. Indentures expired September 7, 1838. (K-135) Born in Scotland. (AtoA)

MARINER, FREDERICK. Admitted March 11, 1824 aged three years and six months by SUSANNA MARINER, mother. (K-69) Delivered to his father, WILLIAM, of New York February 14, 1833. (BO) Indentures expired March 11, 1842. (K-69) Mother born in England. (AtoA)

MARINER, JAMES. Admitted March 11, 1824 aged five years by SUSANNAH MARINER, mother (K-68) Delivered to his father, WILLIAM, of New York February 14, 1833. (BO) Indentures expired March 11, 1840. (K-68)

MARINER, SUSAN. Admitted September 9, 1824 aged eight years by Warden of Charleston. Indentured to JANE MYLES as a needlewoman May 31, 1827. Transferred to FREDERICK A. FORD, occupation unknown July 7, 1831. Indentures expired September 31, 1834. (L-42) Mother, SUSAN MARINER, died September 5, 1824. (AtoA)

MARINER, WILLIAM. Admitted March 11, 1824 aged seven years and six months by SUSANNA MARINER, mother. Indentured to WHITE, BRICKELL, and WHITE as a manufacturer of paper February 18, 1830. Transferred to HENRY DAVIS (of Columbia), occupation unknown, September 11, 1834. Indentures expired March 18, 1837. (K-67)

MARSHALL, ELIZA. Admitted February 4, 1829 aged five years by SARAH MARSHALL, mother. Indentured to BENJAMIN GILDERSLEEVE as a domestic June 26, 1834. Transferred to JANE McKENZIE, occupation unknown, April 16, 1834. Indentures expired February 4, 1845. (L-81) Admitted from the Poor House. (ROSP, February 11, 1829)

MARTIN, JOHN VALANTINE. Admitted Oczober 20, 1825 aged thirteen years by ANN MOORE, mother. Indentures expired October 20, 1826. (I-94) No further information.

MESKER, GEORGE. Admitted May 11, 1820 aged eleven years by MARY STARK, mother. Born August 8, 1820. Died August 8, 1820. Indentures expired March 15, 1830. (I-72)

MESKER, SAMUEL (JAMES). Admitted May 11, 1820 aged nine years by MARY STARK, mother. Born April 30, 1811. Delivered to his mother June 5, 1824. Indentures expired May 30, 1832. (I-73)

MILLER, ELIZA. Admitted August 14, 1823 aged five years by ELIZABETH MILLER, mother. Delivered to her mother November 25, 1824. Indentures expired August 14, 1836. (L-31)

MILLIGAN, EDWARD. Admitted July 20, 1826 aged six years by Warden of Charleston. Indentured to STROTHER D. SHUMATE (of Greenville) as a farmer May 7, 1833. Born December 30, 1820. Father, a cripple, in the Poor House. Mother dead. (AtoA)

MILLIGAN, JOHN. Admitted August 26, 1826 aged ten years by WILLIAM MILLIGAN, father. Delivered to his father November 4, 1829. Indentures expired August 10, 1837. (K-127)

MILLIGAN, MARY E. Admitted July 20, 1826 aged nine years by Warden of Charleston. Indentured to J.E. EMERY, occupation unknown, April 3, 1829. Indentures expired July 20, 1835. (L-58) Born April 19, 1817. (AtoA)

MILLIGAN, WILLIAM. Admitted August 26, 1826 aged eleven years by WILLIAM MILLIGAN, father. Delivered to his father May 8, 1828. Indentures expired August 10, 1836. (K-126)

MORGAN, PETER. Admitted October 17, 1822 aged six years by Warden of Charleston. (K-36) Absconded, nd. (ROSP, March 12, 1828)

MORRISON, HENRIETTA MONUMIA. Admitted September 30, 1824 aged three years by Warden of Charleston. Indentured to JOHN and SARAH MORRISON as a domestic October 1, 1834. Indentures expired September 30, 1839. (L-43)

MURPHY, EDWARD HAMPTON. Admitted April 21, 1825 aged eight years by ISABELLA MURPHY, mother. Delivered to his grandmother, HENRIETTA MURPHY, of Philadelphia April 12, 1827. Indentures expired April 21, 1838. (K-101) Mother an English woman. (Minutes, March 24, 1825)

MURPHY, HENRY JOHN. Admitted April 21, 1825 aged five years by ISABELLA MURPHY, mother. Delivered to his grandmother, HENRIETTA MURPHY, of Philadelphia April 12, 1827. Indentures expired April 21, 1841. (K-102)

NEHLE, JOHN. Admitted June 8, 1820 aged ten years by Warden of Charleston. Indentured to HENRY ADDISON as a blacksmith December 11, 1823. Indentures expired December 15, 1830. (I-77) An orphan. (AtoA)

O'HEARN, JOHN JAMES. Admitted May 20, 1824 aged eight years by JOHN O'HEARN, father. Delivered to his father April 19, 1827. Indentures expired May 20, 1837. (K-76)

O'REILLY, FRANCIS. Admitted August 21, 1828 aged four years by SARAH O'REILLY, mother. Sent to the U.S. Naval School June 29, 1841. Indentures expired August 21, 1844. (M-25) Born in London. (AtoA)

O'REILLY, JAMES. Admitted May 15, 1828 aged ten years by SARAH O'REILLY, mother. Indentured to A. JOHNSON (of Columbia) (M-21), the editor of the Telescope (ROSSC) as a printer November 24, 1831. Indentures expired May 15, 1839. (M-21) Born May 27, ____ on Church Street. Lived on Linguard Street. (AtoA)

O'SULLIVAN, CHARLES. Admitted August 16, 1827 aged eight years by Warden of Charleston. Indentured to JOHN, Bishop of Charleston as a printer of books and papers June 5, 1828. Indentures expired Axgust 16, 1840. (M-12) Born February 15, 1819. (AtoA)

O'SULLIVAN, CHRISTIANNA. Admitted August 16, 1827 aged ten years by Warden of Charleston. Indentured to the RT. REV. BISHOP ENGLAND as a seamtress October 4, 1827. Indentures expired August 16, 1835. (L-67) Born March 13, 1817. (AtoA)

O'SULLIVAN, THOMAS. Admitted August 16, 1827 aged six years by Warden of Charleston. Indentured to JAMES BURGES as a printer January 29, 1835. Indentures expired August 16, 1842. (M-13) Born November 26, 1821. (AtoA)

PARKER, CATHERINE. Admitted March 28, 1822 aged three years by JAMES PARKER, father. Delivered to MRS. DOROTHY DEMPSEY, guardian, February 18, 1830. Indentures expired March 19, 1837. (L-14)

PARKER, MARY. Admitted March 28, 1822 aged five years by JAMES PARKER, father. Indentured to MYLES and DOROTHY DEMPSEY as a domestic December 22, 1829. Indentures expired October 14, 1835. (L-13)

PARKER, THOMAS. Admitted March 28, 1822 aged seven years by JAMES CLARK, father. Delivered to his father of Maranjies in the Island of Cuba, to be sent by MRS. DEMPSEY of Charleston January 27, 1825. Indentures expired February 26, 1836. (K-25)

PARLER, HARRIET. Admitted April 13, 1820 aged six years by MARY MARIA PARLER, mother. Born October 1, 1813. Indentured to MARTHA HARVEY as a domestic October 17, 1822. Transferred to her mother April 3, 1823. Indentures expired October 1, 1831. (I-68) Father, unknown, was a coachmaker. (AtoA)

PARLER, MILTON. Admitted April 13, 1820 aged eight years by MARY MARIA PARLER, mother. Born January 1, 1812. Indentured to JOHN CONNER as a saddler October 20, 1825. Indentures expired January 1, 1833. (I-67)

PAYNE, FRANCIS. Admitted September 20, 1821 aged eight years by WILLIAM P. PAYNE, father. Indentured to JOHN BONNER as a cabinetmaker September 11, 1828. Transferred to WILLIAM MEEKER as a blacksmith January 21, 1830. Transferred to SAMUEL MEEKER, occupation unknown, February 10, 1831. (K-16)

PAYNE, GEORGE. Admitted September 20, 1821 aged five years by W.P. PAYNE, father. Indentured to DR. ROBERT S. OAKLEY as an apothecary and druggist May 6, 1830. (K-17)

PAYNE, RACHEL. Admitted August 5, 1824 aged three years by ELIZABETH PAYNE, mother. Delivered to her mother November 27, 1828. Indentures expired August 5, 1839. (L-38) Religion: German Lutheran. (ROSP, August 8, 1824)

PAYNE, SARAH WALKER. Admitted August 5, 1824 aged six years by ELIZABETH PAYNE, mother. Delivered to her mother June 22, 1826. Indentures expired August 5, 1836. (L-37) Religion: German Lutheran. (ROSP, August 8, 1824)

PEAGLES, JOHN. Admitted November 9, 1820 aged eight years by Warden of Charleston. Born October 2, 1812. Indentured to WILLIAM ABRAMS (of Laurens District) as a farmer December 14, 1826. Indentures expired October 2, 1833. (I-88) FRANCIS KNIEFF, step-father. Step-sister, ELIZABETH KNIEFF. (AtoA)

PEAU, AMBROSE. Admitted June 24, 1824 age eleven years by MARY FATTEAU, mother. Indentures expired June 24, 1834. (K-84) Absconded, nd. (ROSP, January 23, 1828)

PETIT, EDWIN. Admitted September 21, 1826 aged nine years by CATHERINE PETIT, mother. Indentured to P. CARRE' (of Augusta), occupation unknown, February 8, 1827. Indentures expired September 21, 1835. (K-136) Transferred to his mother April 17, 1828. (BO)

PETIT, JAMES. Admitted July 17, 1828 aged nine years by CATHARINE PETIT, mother. Delivered to his mother October 9, 1828. Indentures expired July 17, 1840. (M-23)

POLAND, SARAH. Admitted May 25, 1820 aged two years by MOURNING POLAND, mother. Born March 11, 1818. Delivered to her mother MOURNING CARTER, February 8, 1821. Indentures expired March 11, 1836. (I-76) Father, GEORGE, dead. (AtoA)

91

PURSE, EDWARD JOHN. Admitted January 27, 1825 aged nine years by MARY PURSE, mother. Delivered to his mother April 10, 1828. Indentures expired January 27, 1837. (K-96) Born August 14, 1816. (AtoA)

QUINN, ELEANOR. Admitted July 31, 1828 aged three years by Warden of Charleston. Indentures expired July 31, 1843. (L-74) "Delivered to J.W. MITCHELL who was authorized by the child's mother, MRS. RALEIGH, residing in New York" on April 30, 1829. (ROSSC)

RAPP, ANN ELIZA. Admitted April 26, 1827 aged seven years by CATHARINE RAPP, mother. (L-64) Born in New York. (AtoA) Delivered to her father, ADAM WILLIAM RAPP, of Philadelphia August 5, 1831. (ROSSC) Indentures expired April 26, 1838. (L-64) Father was a prisonor of the Spanish. (BO)

RICHARDSON, JOHN HARDY. Admitted January 13, 1823 aged ten years by EDDY RICHARDSON, mother. Delivered to his mother, EDDY GAFFIN, February 17, 1825. Indentures expired November 13, 1833. (K-44) Father, HARDY R., dead. Born in Horry District November 13, 1812. (AtoA)

ROBINSON, THOMAS. Admitted June 7, 1821 aged seven years by Warden of Charleston. Born September 7, 1813. Indentures expired September 7, 1834. (K-13) Absconded, nd. (ROSP, January 23, 1828)

RYAN, ANN. Admitted January 15, 1824 aged four years by CATHARINE ANN RYAN, mother. Delivered to her mother April 31, 1825. Indentures expired January 15, 1828. (L-32)

SCHAFFER (SHAFFER), CAROLINE. Admitted January 26, 1829 aged eight years by SOPHIA SCHAFFER, mother. Indentured to WILLIAM VERAM (of Camden) as a domestic March 15, 1833. Indentures expired January 30, 1839. (L-80) Born in Alsac near Strasbourg. Mother immigrated in the spring of 1828 from Switzerland. Father died of yellow fever, nd. (AtoA)

SCHAFFER, CATHARINE. Admitted January 26, 1829 aged ten years by SOPHIA SCHAFFER, mother. Indentured to ELIZA MURDEN as a domestic January 2, 1834. Indentures expired January 30, 1837. (L-79)

SCHAFFER, ROSINA. Admitted February 26, 1829 aged three years by SOPHIA SCHAFFER, mother. Indentured to ISABELLA PORTER as a domestic February 23, 1837. (L-87) "Returned to O.H. a few months after her binding out -from suffering- and was duly received into the institution supported and educated, and after having attained to great moral and intellectual advancement, was again bound out to MR. GEO. W. OLNEY of this City on the 19th May 1842 aged 16 years." (Ibid.)

SCHOECHOLIN, MARIA. Admitted October 2, 1828 aged five years by Warden of Charleston. Indentured to WILLIAM GILL, warrant officer in the army of the USA, brother-in-law November 5, 1831. Indentures expired October 2, 1841. (L-75) Born in Germany. (AtoA)

SCHOECOHLIN, ROZA. Admitted October 2, 1828 aged three years by Warden of Charleston. Indentured to C. DeGLANNES as a domestic September 22, 1831. Indentures expired October 2, 1843. (L-76) Born in Germany. (AtoA)

SCHERER (SHIRER), MARY. Admitted August 4, 1825 aged five years by ELIZA FURSMAN, sister. Indentured to G.W. GOODRICH, occupation unknown, December 19, 1833. Transferred to JOHN B. LaFOURCADE, occupation unknown, January 22, 1835. Transferred to AMELIA ELMORE, occupation unknown, August 20, 1835. Indentures expired August 4, 1838. (L-56) Married in August 1845 and given a dowry of $50.00 (Minutes, June 19, 1845)

SCHULTZ, GEORGE HENRY. Admitted November 14, 1822 aged five years by ELIZABETH SCHULTZ, mother. Delivered to his mother April 5, 1827. Indentures expired November 2, 1838. (K-39

SCHULTZ (SHULTZ), MARTHA. Admitted October 28, 1824 aged six years by ELIZA SCHULTZ, mother. Delivered to her mother April 5, 1827. Indentures expired October 28, 1836. (L-44) Religion: Baptist. (ROSP, October 31, 1824)

SCURRY, JOHN. Admitted May 10, 1827 aged eleven years by ROBERT BOYCE, friend. Indentured to PETER GALAHER (of Laurens District) as a farmer March 5, 1829. Indentures expired May 10, 1837. (M-4)

SHERE(SHIRER), JOHN. Admitted September 6, 1821 aged six years by JOHN SHERE, father. (K-15) Died October 5, 1823 of worms and buried in the COH Burial Ground. (ROSP, October 4, 1823)

SHERE (SHERER), FRANCIS. Admitted July 17, 1823 aged five years by JOHN SHERER, father. (K-54) Died July 6, 1824 of worms and buried in the COH Burial Ground. (ROSP, July 4, 1824)

SHERER, WILLIAM JOHN. Admitted September 6, 1821 aged nine years by JOHN SHERE, father. Indentured to DR. AUGUSTUS FITCH as an apothecary and physician April 16, 1825. (K-14) Transferred to ELPHRIAM PECK (of Columbia) as a taylor October 27, 1825. Died October 20, 1831. (ROSSC)

SHORT, STEPHEN. Admitted January 13, 1825 aged four years by CHARLOTTE SHORT, mother. Indentured to JOHN SALE (of Hamburg, S.C.) as a carpenter May 27, 1834. Indentures expired January 13, 1842. (K-92)

SHOULTON, HENRY. Admitted October 3, 1822 aged eleven years by MARGARET SHOULTON, mother. Indentured to HORATIO G. STREET as an innkeeper April 28, 1825. Indentures expired October 3, 1832. (K-35)

SKILLIN, MARY. Admitted September 14, 1826 aged ten years by Warden of Charleston. Indentured to JAMES FIFE as a domestic December 2, 1830. Indentures expired September 14, 1834. (L-60) Born in St. Johns Parish. (AtoA)

SMITH, HENRY. Admitted December 13, 1827 aged six years. Indentured to STEPHEN McCULLY as a shoemaker April 19, 1833. Indentures expired January 10, 1841. (M-19)

SMITH, JOSEPH MARTIN THOMAS. Admitted March 9, 1820 aged six years by CHARLOTTE SMITH, mother. Born September 28, 1814. Delivered to his mother, CHARLOTTE HATCH, October 19, 1827. Indentures expired March 9, 1835. (I-64)

SMITH, MARTHA. Admitted March 31, 1825 aged six years by SARAH ANN SMITH, mother. (L-49) Died "Tuesday last of a highly diseased state of the bones." (ROSP, January 12, 1837)

SMITH, MARY HARRIET HEYWARD. Admitted May 24, 1821 aged ten years by Warden of Charleston. Born November 7, 1810. Indentured to S.L. REEVES as a domestic September 27, 1821. Transferred to W.T. ROYNEL, occupation unknown, June 7, 1827. Indentures expired November 7, 1828. (L-3)

SMITH, WILLIAM. Admitted February 26, 1824 aged four years by MEHITALLE SMITH, mother. Indentured to JOSEPH McCULLOUGH (of Greenville District) as a farmer May 7, 1833. Indentures expired February 26, 1841. (K-65) Ran away to Kentucky because of ill-treatment by the master. (BO-O.H. WELLS applying for ROBERT McKAY)

STEVENSON, WASHINGTON. Admitted November 5, 1829 aged six years. Indentured to SAMUEL WEIR (of Columbia) as a printer February 27, 1834. Indentures expired November 4, 1844. (M-41) Transferred to A.H. and W.F. PEMBERTON (of Columbia) as a printer September 27, 1838. (BO)

STEWART, JAMES. Admitted July 14, 1822 aged six years by MARY STEWART, mother. Delivered to his mother, MARY THORN, December 13, 1824. Indentures expired January 10, 1837. (K-40)

SUTTON, MARY ANN. Admitted December 12, 1820 aged three years by
Warden of Charleston. Indentured to JOHN FRASER, factor, as a domestic
April 24, 1833. Indentures expired September 22, 1837. (L-25)

SWORDS, JOHN T. Admitted April 25, 1822 aged nine years by MARIE
SWORDS, mother. Indentured zo ALEXANDER McMULLIN (of Newberry District)
as a farmer February 14, 1827. Indentures expired November 15, 1833.
(K-31)

TAYLOR, ALEXANDER. Admitted December 19, 1822 aged six years by MARY
TAYLOR, mother. Indentured to D.G. HAVILAND and CO. as an apothecary
December 2, 1830. Indentures expired April 16, 1837. (K-42)

TAYLOR, BENJAMIN. Admitted May 11, 1812 aged seven years by CATHARINE
TAYLOR, mother. Indentured to J.N. CARDOZO, editor of the Southern
Patriot, as a prinzer March 10, 1825. Indentures expired October 2,
1833. (I-75) Father, JOSEPH, dead. (AtoA)
"MR. B.F. TAYLOR...a candidate for Orders in the Ministry of the Prot.
Epis. Church, recently transferred from the diocese of New York to that
of South Carolina...Mr. Taylor has a wife & children and is in very
indigent circumstances...A committee...to make appropriation was formed."
(Minutes, January 11, 1849)

TAYLOR, JOHN. Admitted September 16, 1824 aged nine years by CATHARINE
SHILBECK, mother. Indentured to ANDREW BERRY (of Georgia) as a merchant
April 24, 1828. Indentures expired September 16, 1836. (K-88)

TAYLOR, JOSEPH. Admitted May 11, 1820 aged ten years by CATHARINE
TAYLOR, mother. Born September 4, 1809. Indentured to WILLIAM WILBURN
as a combmaker June 3, 1824. Indentures expired September 4, 1830.
(I-74) Father, JOSEPH, dead. (AtoA)

TAYLOR, LYDIA. Admitted December 19, 1822 by MARY TAYLOR, mother.
Delivered to her mother June 30, 1825. Indentures expired February 14,
1836. (L-27)

TAYLOR, PROSPER. Admitted December 19, 1822 aged two years by MARY
TAYLOR, mother. Indentured to D.G. HAVILAND and CO. as an apothecary
December 19, 1833. Indentures expired April 17, 1841. (K-43)

TAYLOR, WILLIAM. Admitted July 25, 1822 aged eight years by CATHARINE
SHILBECK, mother. Indentured to WILLIAM W. WILBURN as a combmaker
June 8, 1827. Indentures expired May 10, 1835. (K-33)

THOMSON, MARY ANN. Admitted July 5, 1821 aged six years by Warden of
Charleston. Indentured to RICHARD (a cabinetmaker) and ANN SMITH as
a mantuamaker and milliner October 11, 1827. Indentures expired
April 12, 1833. (L-4)

THOMSON, SARAH ANN. Admitted July 18, 1822 aged six years by Warden
of Charleston. Indentured to MARY C. THOMSON, occupation unknown,
April 23, 1829. Indentures expired October 1, 1834. (L-20)

TOPHAM, LUCY. Admitted May 11, 1820 aged six years by ELIZABETH TOPHAM,
mother. Born July 1, ____. Delivered to her mother July 27, 1820.
Indentures expired July 1, 1832. (I-72)

TOPHAM, MARY. Admitted May 11, 1820 aged nine years by ELIZABETH
TOPHAM, unknown. Delivered to her mother July 27, 1820. Indentures
expired December 2, 1829. (I-70)

TSCHUDY, MARY JANE. Admitted June 10, 1824 aged three years by MARY
TSCHUDY, mother. Indentures expired June 10, 1839. (L-35) No further
information.

UTES, JOHN. Admitted March 30, 1826 aged five years by LOUISA UTES,
mother. (AtoA) Indentured to B. GILDERSLEEVE as a printer August 20,
1835. Delivered to his grandmother, ELIZA WOTTON, March 26, 1836.
Indentures expired March 30, 1842. (K-117)

VANHAGEN, JOHN W. Admitted April 13, 1820 aged seven years by SARAH
VANHAGEN, mother. Born July 4, 1812. Indentured to DANIEL RIDER as
a house carpenter September 2, 1824. Indentures expired July 4, 1833.
(I-66)

WALL, WILLIAM. Admitted October 12, 1826 aged eight years by ELIZABETH
QUIRK, mother. Indentured expired October 12, 1839. (K-137) Born
in Baltimore. (AtoA) Indentured to THOMAS HAMMILL as a wheelwright
June 14, 1832. (ROSSC)

WALLACE, ROBERT. Admitted January 1, 1829 aged eight years by L. WALLACE,
mother. (ROSP, January 6, 1829) Indentured to A. ROULAIN as a blacksmith October 9, 1834. Indentures expired January 1, 1842. (M-29)

WELCH, HARRIET BUNCH. Admitted July 31, 1828 aged seven years by ELIZA-
BETH WELCH, mother. Delivered to her mother January 16, 1834. Inden-
tures expired July 31, 1839. (L-73) Father, NATHANIEL, in Poor House.
(AtoA)

WELCH, JACOB. Admitted February 10, 1820 aged three years by NATHANIEL
WELCH, father. (AtoA) Born December 20, 1816. Indentured to HENRY L.
PINCKNEY, editor of the Charleston Mercury, as a printer April 22,
1831. Indentures expired December 20, 1837. (I-62) Mother, ELIZABETH
(AtoA)

WILLIAMSON, JOHN. Admitted November 20, 1823 aged seven years by
MARGARET (MARY) WILLIAMSON, sister. Indentured to W.S. NELL as a
baker February 18, 1830. Indentures expired November 20, 1837. (K-61)

WISE, CHARLOTTE. Admitted February 12, 1829 aged eleven years by ELIZA
WISE, mother. Indentured to ASHAEL SLATE as a domestic May 26, 1832.
Indentures expired February 12, 1836. (L-82) Of Sumpter District.
(AtoA)

WISE, LOUISA. Admitted February 12, 1829 aged seven years by ELIZA
WISE, mother. Indentured to DAVID P. LANDERSHINE as a domestic
December 18, 1834. Indentures expired February 12, 1840. (L-85)

WISE, MARGARET. Admitted February 12, 1829 aged eight years by ELIZA
WISE, mother. Of Sumpter District. Indentured to JAMES KEOUGH as
a milliner and strawbonnetmaker March 21, 1833. Indentures expired
February 12, 1839. (L-84)

WISE, MARTHA. Admitted February 12, 1829 aged four years by ELIZA
WISE, mother. Of Sumpter District. (L-86) Died June 1831 of a bowel
complaint complicated by whooping cough. (ROSP, June 8, 1831)

WISE, MARY. Admitted February 12, 1829 aged nine years by ELIZA WISE,
mother. Of Sumpter District. (L-83) Died August 6, 1829 of dropsy.
(ARP, 1829)

WISH, BENJAMIN F. Admitted June 16, 1825 aged seven years by HARRIET
WISH, mother. (ROSP, June 15, 1825) Indentured to H. and D. HAIG
as a cooper November 2, 1832. Indentures expired June 16, 1839. (L-50)

WISH, EMMA. Admitted June 16, 1825 aged eight years by HARRIET WISH,
mother. Delivered to her mother November 18, 1831. Indentures
expired June 16, 1838. (L-51)

WISH, WILLIAM. Admitted July 21, 1825 aged three years by ANN MORTON,
grandmother. Indentured to DR. JAMES P. JERVEY as a druggist and
apothecary December 7, 1837. Indentures expired July 21, 1843. (L-55)
Grandmother aged fifty-five. Father, BENJAMIN, died in 1822 during
the gale when a house fell on him on the North Inlet. (AtoA)

WOOD, MARTHA. Admitted November 23, 1826 aged six years by MARY WOOD,
mother. Indentured to JOHN OSWALD (of Jacksonborough) as a domestic
June 23, 1831. Indentures expired November 23, 1838. (L-62) Mother
a former inmate. Born on the Charleston Neck. (AtoA)

WOOD, MARY. Admitted November 23, 1826 aged eight years by MARY WOOD, mother. Delivered to her sister, MRS. ELIZA D. BYTHWOOD, September 11, 1834. Indentures expired November 23, 1836. (L-61) A cripple. (BO)

WOOD, SAMUEL. Admitted March 26, 1829 by ELIZA BYTHWOOD, sister. (M-33) Born on the Charleston Neck. Born October 8, 1822. Indentured to AMASA BORTON as a bricklayer and plasterer July 23, 1838. Indentures expired October 8, 1843. (M-33) His sister, the wife of a Methodist minister, about to leave the City. (AtoA)

WRAY, ELLEN ELIZA. Admitted November 30, 1826 aged eight years by Warden of Charleston. Indentured to MARY RICH as a seamtress April 20, 1830. Indentures expired November 30, 1836. (L-63)

WRAY, HENRY. Admitted September 4, 1823 aged six years by SARAH D. WRAY, mother. Delivered to his mother July 10, 1829. Indentures expired September 4, 1838. (K-59)

WRAY, JAMES. Admitted September 4, 1823 aged nine years by SARAH D. WRAY, mother. Died January 17, 1824. (K-58)

ZEMP, FRANCIS. Admitted September 30, 1824 aged six years by Warden of Charleston. Indentured to DR. GEORGE REYNOLD (of Camden) through his attorney, JOHN HASLETT, as an apothecary and druggist April 22, 1830. Indentures expired September 30, 1839. (K-89)

ABRAHAMS, ALEXANDER. Admitted April 15, 1830 aged six years by JOSEPH PREVOST, unknown. Indentured to HERIOT, CURRY and PETSCH as a blacksmith and engineer June 1, 1838. Transferred to JOSEPH PREVOST, occupation unknown, nd. Indentures expired April 15, 1844 (corrected). (M-51)

ABRAHAMS, CHARLES THEODORE. Admitted April 15, 1830 aged five years by JOSEPH PREVOST, unknown. Indentured to JOSEPH PREVOST, occupation unknown, May 13, 1841. Indentures expired April 15, 1846. (M-52)

AIRS, ANTHONY. Admitted May 1, 1834 aged nine years by THOMAS AIRS, father. (ROSP, May 1, 1834) Sent to the U.S. Naval School October 1840. Indentures expired May 1, 1846. (N-56)

ALLAN, ELIZA. Admitted August 27, 1835 aged ten years by WILLIAM W. ALLAN, father. Indentures expired August 27, 1843. (O-40) Indentured to GEORGE GARRET as a milliner December 14, 1843. (ROSP, January 4, 1844)

ALLAN, HANNAH. Admitted December 10, 1835 aged five years by WILLIAM W. ALLAN, father. (O-42) Died December 26, 1839 of consumption and buried in the COH Burial Ground. (ROSP, December 27, 1838)

ALLAN, GEORGE. Admitted December 10, 1835 aged seven years by WILLIAM W. ALLAN, father and the Poor House. Sent to the U.S. Naval School June 29, 1841. Indentures expired December 10, 1849. (N-90)

ALLAN, HARRIET ANN. Admitted August 27, 1835 aged nine years by WILLIAM W. ALLAN, father. Indentured to GEORGE MOFFAT, merchant, as a domestic December 8, 1842. Indentures expired August 27, 1844. (O-41) Transferred to G.B. MOSES (of Pendleton) occupation unknown, July 20, 1843. (BO) Allowed fifty dollars as a dowry in 1848. (Minutes, January 17, 1848)

ASSALIE (ASSALIT), ELIZABETH. Admitted May 6, 1830 aged seven years by HARRIET ASSALIE, mother. Indentured to F. COSTAMAGNA as a mantuamaker February 26, 1835. Indentures expired May 6, 1844. (L-100) Father, unknown, a member of City Guard. (AtoA)

ASSALIE, MATILDA. Admitted May 6, 1830 aged four years by HARRIET ASSALIE, mother. Delivered to her uncle, W.J. ASSALIE, July 8, 1830. Indentures expired May 6, 1847. (L-101)

BACO, ANTOINE. Admitted November 26, 1835 aged six years and six months by ANN BACO, mother. Died May 10, 1836 of typhoid fever and buried in the COH Burial Ground. (ROSP, May 12, 1836) Religion: Methodist. (AtoA)

BAGNEL, JOHN. Admitted May 25, 1832 aged ten years by SARAH RUTLEDGE, unknown. (N-19) Died March 12, 1833 of dropsy (ARP, 1833) and buried in the COH Burial Ground. (ROSP, March 14, 1833) Born near Pocataligo. Father, unknown, a shoemaker. (AtoA)

BALANTINE, MARY JANE. Admitted March 24, 1836 aged three years by Poor House. Indentured to N. ALDRICK (of Savannah) as a housekeeper and nurse June 5, 1845. Indentures expired March 24, 1851. (O-43)

BARNO, ISAAC. Admitted October 11, 1838 aged fourteen years by Poor House. Born in Williamsburg, S.C. Indentured to SAMUEL PEARSE (N-123) of Columbia (ROSSC) as a tinplate worker November 15, 1838. Indentures expired October 11, 1845. (N-123) Absconded August 1839. (BO)

BARRETT, JOSEPH. Admitted January 29, 1835 aged six years by LUCY BARRETT, mother. (ROSP, February 5, 1835) Religion: Methodist. (AtoA) Died April 22, 1836 of a bowel complaint and buried in the COH Burial Ground. (ROSP, April 27, 1836)

BARRETT, MARIA KING. Admitted March 30, 1832 aged five years by ISABELLA AMANDA BARRETT, mother. Delivered to her father-in-law, MR. MEREDITH B. OWENS, (of Gadsden County, Florida) February 9, 1837. Indentures expired March 30, 1845. (O-10) Religion: Methodist. (AtoA)

BARRETT, MARY ANN. Admitted March 30, 1832 aged seven years by ISABELLA AMANDA BARRETT, unknown. Delivered to her father-in-law, MR. MEREDITH B. OWENS, (of Gadsden County, Florida) February 9, 1837. Indentures expired March 30, 1843. (O-9) Religion: Methodist. (AtoA)

BARTON, ANTHONY. Admitted August 14, 1834 aged twelve years by JANE BARTON, unknown. Indentured to JOHN W. HODGES as a merchant March 16, 1837. Indentures expired Axgust 14, 1843. (N-64)

BASSETT, AGNES. Admitted July 19, 1832 aged eight years by ELIZABETH LYONS, mother. Delivered to her mother, MRS. ELIZABETH KENT, April 16, 1835. Indentures expired July 19, 1845. (O-15) Religion: Methodist. (AtoA)

BASSETT, ROBERT. Admitted July 19, 1832 aged ten years by ELIZABETH LYONS, mother. Delivered to his mother, ELIZA KENT, January 9, 1834. Indentures expired July 19, 1843. (N-25) Step-father E. KENT. (BO) Religion: Methodist. (AtoA)

BEAMAN, AMELIA. Admitted February 27, 1832 aged eleven years by EDWARD and MARY WILSON, unknown. Indentured to JOHN W. WIGHTMAN as a domestic December 4, 1834. Indentures expired February 27, 1839. (O-5)

BIGGS, EMMA CATHARINE. Admitted Jxne 9, 1831 aged eight years by CATHARINE E. BIGGS, mother. Delivered to her mother May 29, 1834. Indentures expired June 9, 1844. (L-111) Mother lived with MRS. MACKY at the corner of Church and Linguard Streets. (AtoA)

BIGGS, HENRY K. Admitted May 22, 1831 aged nine years by CATHERINE BIGGS, mother. (ROSP, May 18, 1831) Delivered to his mother May 31, 1832. (ROSSC) Indentures expired May 12, 1843. (M-70)

BIGGS, WILLIAM L. Admitted June 9, 1831 aged six years by CATHARINE E. BIGGS, mother. Died of a bowel complaint (ARP, 1833) and buried in the COH Burial Ground. (ROSP, January 17, 1833)

BLAKELY, CHARLES HENRY COTESWORTH. Admitted September 19, 1832 aged six years by ELIAS BLAKELY, father. Indentured to WILLIAM KIRKWOOD as a shipbuilder August 25, 1842. Indentures expired September 19, 1847. (N-31) Born in Georgetown. (AtoA)

BLAKELY, WILLIAM GEORGE WASHINGTON. Admitted September 19, 1832 aged nine years by ELIAS BLAKELY, father. (N-50) Indentured to TITUS L. BISSELL (of Alabama) as a tanner and currier September 15, 1836. (ROSP, November 9, 1836) Indentures expired September 19, 1844. (N-50)

BLOCKER, DANIEL. Admitted February 19, 1835. (N-75) Absconded, 1840. (ROSSC)

BLOCKER, ELIZABETH. Admitted July 2, 1835 aged three years by Poor House. Died February 14, 1837 of hydrocephelus. (ARP, 1837)

BOURKE, WILLIAM. Admitted December 19, 1839 aged twelve years by Poor House. Indentured to WILLIAM BUTLER as a blindmaker August 4, 1842. Indentures expired December 19, 1848. (N-146) Born in Ireland. Religion: Catholic. (AtoA)

BRADLEY, HENRY. Admitted April 16, 1835 aged six years. Indentured to JOHN BRADY as a brickmason April 16, 1835. Indentures expired April 16, 1850. (N-77)

BRADLEY, LOUISA. Admitted April 16, 1835 aged ten years by SARAH BRADLEY, mother. Indentured to L. REIGNE, occupation unknown, January 29, 1835. Indentures expired March 10, 1840. (O-6)

BRADLEY, MARY ANN ELIZABETH. Admitted March 10, 1832 aged seven years by SARAH BRADLEY, mother. Indentured to JOHN BRADY as a domestic November 12, 1835. Indentures expired March 10, 1843. (O-7)

BRADY, HUGH. Admitted June 13, 1833 aged ten years, eleven months and fourteen days by ANN BRADY, mother. Delivered to his mother June 4, 1835. Indentures expired June 13, 1843. (N-42)

BRADY, MARY. Admitted June 13, 1833 aged six years, ten months and twenty days by ANN BRADY, mother. Delivered to her mother June 4, 1835. Indentures expired August 3, 1844. (O-26)

BROWN, GEORGE R.D. Admitted January 21, 1832 aged six years by MARY BROWN, mother. Delivered to his mother January 10, 1833. Indentures expired January 21, 1847. (N-9)

BROWN, ROBERT WILLIAM. Admitted December 18, 1834 aged nine years by MARTHA BROWN, mother. (ROSP, January 1, 1835) Delivered to S. NORRIS, father, May 14, 1839. (ROSP, May 21, 1839) Indentures expired December 18, 1846. (N-69)

BURGRINE (BERGRINE) MARY SARAH. Admitted August 18, 1836 aged eight years by Poor House. Indentured to SAMUEL CHAPMAN, occupation unknown, January 26, 1843. (O-46) Transferred to AMELIA ZACHARIAH as a milliner December 8, 1843. (BO) Indentures expired August 18, 1846. (O-46) Allowed fifty dollars as a dowry 1852. (Minutes, October 7, 1852)

CAMPBELL, JOHN. Admitted September 19, 1832 aged eight years. Indentured to RICHARD GLADNEY (of Columbia) as a printer July 9, 1835. Indentures expired September 19, 1847. (N-32) An orphan. Religion: Protestant. (AtoA) Delivered to his brother, ALEXANDER CAMPBELL (of Columbia) a merchant, October 25, 1838. (Minutes, October 25, 1838)

CANFIELD, THOMAS P. Admitted May 22, 1834 aged seven years by ANDREW KIRKPATRICK, unknown. Indentures expired May 22, 1848. Suffers from fits. (ROSP, February 28, 1839) Sent to the Poor House, 1844. (ROSSC)

CANTLEY, JAMES. Admitted May 29, 1834 aged five years by EMELINE CANTLEY, mother. (ROSP, June 5, 1834) Indentured to THOMAS WEST BOLGER as a saddler and harnessmaker July 22, 1842. Indentures expired May 29, 1850. (N-60)

CANTLEY, WILLIAM. Admitted May 29, 1834 aged nine years by EMELINE CANTLEY, mother. (ROSP, June 5, 1834) Indentured to DR. J. HUME SIMONS as an apothecary and druggist July 23, 1840. Indentures expired May 29, 1846. (N-59)

CARPENTIER (CARPENTER), ELLEN. Admitted April 8, 1833 aged five years by J. and MARY CARPENTER, parents. Indentured to REV. WILLIAM H. SMITH as a nurse and housekeeper October 21, 1842. (O-23) Transferred to T. W. FOWLER as a domestic June 9, 1843. (BO) Indentures expired April 8, 1846. (O-23)

CARPENTIER (CARPENTER), PETER. Admitted July 6, 1832 aged seven years by PETER CARPENTIER, father. Sent to the U.S. Naval School October 10, 1840. Indentures expired July 6, 1846. (N-22)

CARTER, THOMAS. Admitted August 23, 1832 aged nine years by ELIZABETH HESSE, mother. Delivered to his mother May 16, 1833. Indentures expired August 23, 1844. (N-27) Born in St. James Parish. Religion: Baptist. (AtoA)

CASSIN, WASHINGTON K. Admitted November 10, 1832 aged ten years by CONLY CASSIN, father. Indentures expired November 10, 1843. (N-34) Absconded, nd. (ROSP, May 15, 1834) Religion: Catholic. (AtoA)

CAULFIELD (CAULDFIELD), JAMES SAMUEL. Admitted January 21, 1830 aged five years by MARIA CAULFIED, mother. Delivered to his mother, MARY M. KIRKPATRICK, February 27, 1834. Indentures expired January 21, 1846. (M-44)

CAULFIELD, JAMES S. Admitted May 29, 1834 aged ten years by MARGARET BUTLER, sister. (ROSP, June 5, 1834) Indentured to J. OBERHAUSSER as an apothecary and druggist April 23, 1835. Indentures expired May 29, 1845. (N-61) Delivered to his mother, MARY KIRKPATRICK March 1834. (ROSP, March 14, 1834)

CELAFF (SIELAFF) CHARLES WILLIAM. Admitted April 25, 1839 aged seven years by Poor House. Indentured to DR. F.W. SYMMES (of Pendleton, S.C.) as a printer June 11, 1846. Indentures expired April 25, 1853. (N-136)

CHAMPLIN, ROBERT. Admitted April 26, 1838 aged six years by Poor House. Indentured to WILLIAM J. KNAUFF (of Pendleton, Anderson District) as a cabinetmaker October 2, 1845. Indentures expired April 26, 1853. (N-125)

CHANNEL, WILLIAM JAMES. Admitted June 13, 1833 aged nine years by ADELAIDE E. GIBBES, unknown. Of St. Bartholomew's Parish. Indentures signed by R. BARNWELL SMITH but not filled out or dated. Indentures expired June 13, 1845. (N-41) Indentured to MR. MARSH as a shipbuilder, 1837. (ROSP, May 17, 1837)

CHIVNELL, WILLIAM. Admitted July 2, 1835 aged three years by the Poor House. Sent to the Poor House, nd. Indentures expired July 2, 1853. (N-82) Admitted from the Poor House. (AtoA)

CLARENDON, CECELIA. Admitted February 18, 1832 aged nine years by ELIZABETH O'NEAL, unknown. (O-4) Delivered to her aunt, MARY McNEAL, November 15, 1841. (ROC, 1821)

CLARK, (CLARKE), JAMES HENRY. Admitted July 19, 1832 aged four years by ELIZABETH CLARK, mother. (N-24) Died August 14, 1834 of a bowel complaint. (ARP, 1834)

CLARK, JOHN MICHELL (MITCHELL). Admitted January 27, 1835 aged twelve years by HUGH CLARK, father. (ROSP, January 29, 1835) Indentured to SOLOMON L. REEVES as a turner November 22, 1838. Indentures expired January 27, 1844. (N-70) Allowed ten dollars "on account of his illness and distressed condition" in 1852. (Minutes, March 18, 1852)

CLARK, LYDIA ANN. Admitted June 19, 1837 aged three years. Indentured to J.B. NIXON occupation unknown, May 11, 1848. Indentures expired June 29, 1852. (O-52) Born in Georgetown. Religion: Baptist. (AtoA)

CORBETT, HENRY. Admitted October 23, 1834 aged nine years by MARGARET CORBETT, mother. Indentured to MICHAEL WAGNER (of Augusta, Georgia) as a baker May 12, 1836. Indentures expired October 23, 1846. (N-66) Delivered to his mother, 1840. (ROSP, March 26, 1840)

CORBETT, WASHINGTON. Admitted October 23, 1834 aged three years by MARGARET CORBETT, mother. Indentures expired October 23, 1852. (N-68) Delivered to his relatives, nd. (ROC, 1821)

CORBETT, WILLIAM. Admitted October 23, 1834 aged five years by MARGARET CORBETT, mother. Delivered to his mother, MARGARET KEAST, November 9, 1837. Indentures expired October 23, 1850. (N-67)

CRAWFORD, ELLEN. Admitted January 19, 1837 aged eight years by Poor House. Indentured to REV. THOMAS SMYTH, occupation unknown, November 10, 1842. Indentures expired January 19, 1847. (O-54)

CRAWFORD, WILLIAM ELIAS. Admitted January 19, 1837 aged five years by Poor House. Indentured to DAVID MURPHY as a storekeeper October 16, 1845. Indentures expired January 19, 1853. (N-102)

CUTTER, MARGARET. Admitted May 26, 1831 aged eleven years by HANNAH THOMPSON, mother. Indentured to WILLIAM ESTELL as a bookbinder July 21, 1831. Indentures expired May 26, 1841. (L-110)

DAVIS, JOHN SYLVESTER. Admitted August 20, 1835 aged nine years by Poor House. Indentured to A.S. JOHNSON (of Columbia) as a printer February 25, 1836. Indentures expired August 20, 1847. (N-88)

DEHAY, ROBERT. Admitted October 14, 1830 aged eight years by MARTHA LUND, mother. Indentured to DR. EDWARD H. FISHER as a manufacturer January 26, 1833. Indentures expired October 14, 1843. (M-54) Delivered to his mother, MRS. MARTHA MILLIGAN, February 1834. (ROSP, February 5, 1834) Born in St. John's Parish, Berkeley County. (AtoA)

DEHAY, ZACHARIAH. Admitted October 14, 1830 aged nine years by MARTHA LUND, mother. Indentured to EDWARD H. FISHER (of Columbia) as a manu- facturer January 25, 1833. Indentures expired October 14, 1842. Transferred to DR. SILL as an apothecary July 17, 1835. (BO) Born in St. John's Parish, Berkeley County. (AtoA)

DEIGNAN, CHARLES. Admitted January 14, 1832 aged nine years by a Commisioner and the Warden of Charleston because the mother was deranged. Indentures expired January 14, 1844. (N-7) Absconded nd. (ROSP, May 15, 1834)

DEIGNAN, FRANCIS. Admitted January 14, 1832 aged seven years by a Commisioner and the Warden of Charleston because the mother was deranged. Indentures expired January 14, 1846. (N-8) Absconded, nd. (ROSP, May 15, 1834)

DELANY, ANN. Admitted March 22, 1832 aged ten years by ANN BURNS, mother. (O-8) Indentured to DR. WILLIAM MAGILL (of Waccamaw), occupation unknown, January 16, 1834. (BO) Indentures expired March 23, 1840. (O-8) Born in Nova Scocia (sic) (AtoA)

DENOON, HENRY. Admitted January 19, 1837 aged six years by LILLIAS DENOON, mother. (ROSP, January 26, 1837) Indentures expired January 19, 1852. (N-101) Delivered to his uncle, C. DOUGLAS, November 8, 1838. (ROC, 1821)

DENOON, MARGARET. Admitted January 19, 1837 aged ten years by LILIAS DENOON, mother. (ROSP, January 26, 1837) Indentures expired January 19, 1846 (O-50) Delivered to her uncle, D. DOUGLAS, 1836. (ROC, 1821)

DOWNING, MARTHA. Admitted June 6, 1833 aged eight years by ELIZABETH DOWNING, mother. Indentures expired June 6, 1843. (O-25) Delivered to her mother, CATHARINE E. DOWNING, July 1838. (BO)

DOYLE, BERNARD (WILLIAM). Admitted April 23, 1835 aged ten years by DOYLE, mother. Delivered to his mother, ISABELLA DOYLE, April 7, 1837. Readmitted February 22, 1838. Indentures expired April 23, 1846. (N-83) Delivered to his mother June 18, 1840. (ROSP, June 18, 1840)

DOYLE, CAROLINE FRANCES. Admitted January 11, 1838 aged between three and four years by ISABELLA DOYLE, mother. Indentures expired January 11, 1853. (O-54) Delivered to her mother, nd. (ROC, 1821) Parents were Irish. (AtoA)

DOYLE, GEORGE. Admitted August 22, 1839 aged two years and two months by JAMES DOYLE, father. Indentured to JOHN MOOD as a gold and silver- smith October 17, 1850. Indentures expired June 10, 1858. (N-138) "Died in Mexico", nd. (ROC, 1821)

DOYLE, JAMES ALEXANDER. Admitted April 23, 1835 aged eight years by ISABELLA DOYLE, mother. Indentures expired April 23, 1848. (N-84) Delivered to his mother, 1841. (BO) Absconded March 27, 1841 (ROSP, April 1, 1841) and returned April 2, 1841. (ROSP, April 8, 1841)

DOYLE, MARY ANN. Admitted October 11, 1838 aged seven years and three months by Poor House. (AtoA) Indentured to O.L. DOBSON, occupation unknown, September 11, 1845. (ROC, 1821) Allowed fifty dollars as a dowry for her marriage to MR. CANNON of Lancaster District. (Minutes, November 27, 1856)

DOYLE, THOMAS L. Admitted October 11, 1838 aged four years by JAMES DOYLE, father, and the Poor House. Indentured to JAMES GRADY as a taylor August 22, 1850. Indentures expired October 11, 1855. (N-124)

DUFF, VINCENT. Admitted November 14, 1839 aged twelve years by CATHARINE DUFF, mother. Indentured to WILLIAM ENSTON as a cabinetmaker June 3, 1842. Indentures expired November 14, 1848. (N-143) Lived at the corner of Boundary and Wall Streets. Religion: Catholic. (AtoA)

EVANS, AMITY. Admitted November 25, 1831 aged eight years by MARY EVANS, mother. Indentured to D. JEWELL as a cabinetmaker January 15, 1835. Indentures expired November 25, 1844. (N-4)

EVANS, CHARLES WILLIAM EDWARD. Admitted November 19, 1831 aged six years by MARY ANN EVANS, mother. Indentured to O.H. WELLS, editor of the Greenville Mountaineer (of Greenville District) as a printer May 11, 1840. Indentures expired November 19, 1846. (N-2)

EVANS, JAMES H. Admitted November 19, 1831 aged four years by MARY ANN EVANS, mother. Indentured to PETER G. GERARD as a merchant tailor December 1, 1842. Indentures expired November 19, 1848. (N-3)

EVANS, JOSEPH (JAMES). Admitted August 9, 1838 aged two years and five months by Poor House. Indentured to F.H. ELMORE, W. HAMPTON and R.A. BROWN (of the Nesbit Iron Works of Spartanburgh) as an iron worker April 8, 1847. Indentures expired March 9, 1857. (P-66) Born on Sullivan's Island. Mother a Catholic; father an Episcopalian. (AtoA)

EVANS, MARY ANN. Admitted August 9, 1838 aged five years by ANN EVANS, mother. Born in Virginia. Indentured to JOHN W. STORY as a domestic June 10, 1847. Indentures expired August 9, 1851. (O-59)

EVANS, REBECCA. Admitted November 25, 1831 aged eleven years by MARY EVANS, mother. Indentured to ELIZABETH JOHNSTON (JOHNSON) as a storekeeper June 27, 1833. Transferred to MARY EVANS, mother, December 12, 1833. Indentures expired November 25, 1840. (O-2)

EVANS, SAMUEL. Admitted November 25, 1831 aged four years by MARY EVANS, mother. Sent to the U.S. Naval School October 1840. Indentures expired November 28, 1848. (N-5)

FAY, MARY ANN. Admitted November 14, 1839 aged two years by Poor House. Indentures expired November 14, 1855. (O-65) Delivered to her mother July 1844. (ROC, 1821) Application to Admit signed by MAYOR PINCKNEY.

FAY, WILLIAM. Admitted November 14, 1839 aged five years by Poor House. Indentures expired November 14, 1855. (N-144) Died June 30, 1844 of congestion of the chest. (ROSP, July 4, 1844) Application to Admit signed by MAYOR PINCKNEY.

FRANCIS, GEORGE MANNING. Admitted March 14, 1838 aged ten years by R. JENNEY, mother. Indentured to his uncle, ROBERT JENNEY, as a saddler November 6, 1845. Indentures expired March 14, 1850. (N-133) Father born in Irland. (AtoA)

FRIEDEBERG, JOSEPH. Admitted March 28, 1830 aged six years by PHILIP FRIEDEBERG, father. Indentured to A.S. JOHNSON (of Columbia) as a printer February 25, 1836. Indentures expired March 25, 1845. (M-48)

GABEAN, ANN VINCENT. Admitted May 7, 1835 aged eight years by ANN F. GABEAN, mother. (ROSP, May 14, 1835) Indentures expired May 7, 1845. (O-37) Taken by her mother December 1814. (ROC, 1821)

GABEAN, SUSAN FRASER. Admitted May 7, 1835 aged four years by ANN F. GABEAN, mother. (ROSP, May 14, 1835) Died June 22, 1838 of scarlatina and buried in the Burial Ground of St. Stephen's Chapel. (O-38)

GASKINS, THOMAS C. Admitted March 18, 1831 aged seven years by GEORGE CHUN, unknown. (M-62) Born in St. Paul's Parish. (AtoA) Died May 11, 1836 of cholera and buried in the COH Burial Ground. (ROSP, May 12, 1836)

GETSINGER (GITSINGER), HARRIET. Admitted August 30, 1832 aged seven years by ELEANOR E. GETSINGER, grandmother. Indentured to MARY E. PHELPS as a domestic February 18, 1836. Indentures expired August 30, 1846. (O-18) Religion: Episcopalian. (AtoA) Allowed fifty dollars as a dowry in 1844. (Minutes, April 18, 1844)

GRAINGER, CHARLES. Admitted April 3, 1834 aged eight years by MARY GRAINGER, mother. Delivered to his mother May 1842. Indentures expired April 3, 1847. (N-55) Religion: Methodist. (AtoA)

GRAINGER, HENRY E. Admitted April 3, 1834 aged ten years. Indentured to A. BORTON, occupation unknown, July 23, 1838. Indentures expired April 3, 1845. (N-54) Religion: Methodist. (AtoA)

GUERRIN, MARY LOUISE. Admitted May 2, 1833 aged five years by ANN STANTON, mother. Indentured to JOSEPH THOMLINSON, occupation unknown, July 20, 1843. Indentures expired May 2, 1846. (O-24) Religion: Catholic. (AtoA)

HAGGAMYER, ANDREW. Admitted December 6, 1838 aged ten years by Poor House. (N-130) Abducted by his mother Tuesday September 15, 1840. (ROSP, September 17, 1840) Indentures expired December 6, 1849. (N-130)

HAGGAMYER, CHRISTIAN. Admitted December 6, 1838 aged nine years by the Poor House. Indentures expired December 6, 1850. (N-131) Abducted by his mother Tuesday September 15, 1846. (ROSP, September 17, 1840)

HAGGAMYER, ELIZA GEORGE. Admitted December 6, 1838 aged three years by the Poor House. (O-62) Died July 18, 1839 of dropsy and buried in St. Patrick's Burial Ground. (ROSP, July 24, 1839)

HANSON, JOHN. Admitted August 26, 1831 aged four years by Warden of Charleston. Indentures expired August 31, 1843. (K-134) Graduated from Charleston College February 22, 1842. (ROC, 1821) In 1842 was Principal of Pineville Academy. (Minutes, September 8, 1842)

HAWES, HONORA. Admitted July 21, 1831 aged six years by JANE HAWES, mother. Indentures expired July 21, 1847. (L-114) Delivered to MRS. KINSEY June 7, 1838 who would send the child to her mother. (BO)

HAWES, PETER. Admitted June 16, 1831 aged six years by JANE HAWES, mother. Indentured to WILLIAM H. RIMROD as a bookbinder December 17, 1835. Indentures expired June 16, 1844. (M-75) Mother lived on State Street. (AtoA)

HAYES, MARGARET ANN. Admitted January 5, 1837 aged eleven years by the Poor House. Indentured to JULIA ELLARD as a domestic June 22, 1837. Indentures expired January 5, 1844. (O-49)

HEADDEN, AMELIA. Admitted March 26, 1831 aged six years and six months by CHARLES HEADDEN, father. Indentured to THOS. E. ABERGORRIE and wife as a domestic January 23, 1840. Indentures expired September 26, 1843. (M-64) Born in Surrey, England and arrived in Charleston May 1, 1829. (AtoA) Allowed fifty dollars as a marriage dowry to ABRAHAM W. LIMBAKER, a bricklayer, in 1845. (Minutes, October 9, 1845)

HEADDEN, CHARLES. Admitted March 26, 1831 aged eight years and six months by CHARLES HEADDEN, father. Indentures expired September 26, 1843. (M-63) Born in Surrey, England. (AtoA) Absconded, nd. (ROC, 1821)

HEADDEN, JOSEPH. Admitted March 26, 1831 aged five years by CHARLES HEADDEN, father. Indentured to WILLIAM BUTLER as a painter, paper hanger and venitian blindmaker August 5, 1842. Indentures expired March 26, 1843. (M-65) Delivered to JOSEPH HEADDEN, grandfather, (of Greenville) in 1844. (Minutes, March 21, 1844) Born in Surrey, England. (AtoA)

HENDRICKS, LAWRENCE. Admitted June 11, 1835 aged five years by CAROLINE B. HENDRICKS, mother. (ROSP, June 25, 1835) Indentured to J.A. STEVENSON (of Mount Taber, Union District) as a merchant February 21, 1844. Indentures expired June 11, 1850. (N-80) Transferred to WILLIAM J. LITTLE, occupation unknown, April 20, 1846. (BO)

HENDRICKS, HENRY. Admitted February 23, 1833 aged six years by F. and CAROLINE HENDRICKS, parents. Indentures expired February 23, 1848. (N-39) Sent to the U.S. Naval School June 29, 1841. (ROC, 1821) Religion: Lutheran. (AtoA)

HENDRICKS, RICHARD (STEPHEN). Admitted February 23, 1833 aged nine years by F. and CAROLINE HENDRICKS, parents. Indentured to FINLEY and PHIN as an apothecary and druggist June 1, 1838. Transferred to the U.S. Naval School June 29, 1841. Indentures expired February 23, 1842. (N-38) Religion: Lutheran. (AtoA)

HENNESIC, JOHN. Admitted May 19, 1832 aged three years and eight months by the City Council. (N-18) Died February 4, 1835 of a wasting disease. (ROSP, February 5, 1835) Admitted from the Poor House. (AtoA)

HENRY, ROBERT. Admitted February 1, 1833 aged seven years by THOMAS HINSON, unknown. Indentured to JOHN C. KERR, occupation unknown, February 18, 1841. Indentures expired February 1, 1847. (N-35) Parents' religion: Roman Catholic. (AtoA)

HESLEY, ALFRED. Admitted August 22, 1833 aged five years by MARY SMITH, mother. (N-45) Died October 1, 1834 at his mother's house of Tabes Mesentarica. (ROSP, October 2, 1834)

HESLEY, MARGARET ANN. Admitted August 22, 1833 aged seven years by MARY SMITH, mother. Indentured to SAMUEL NEWBOLD as a domestic November 11, 1841. Indentures expired August 22, 1844. (O-27)

HOLMES, JAMES HENRY. Admitted September 12, 1839 aged twelve years by J.J. MURRILL, friend. Sent to the U.S. Naval Academy October 1840. Indentures expired September 12, 1848. (N-139) Born in Portsmith, Virginia. Religion: Methodist. Father, insane, in the Poor House. (AtoA)

HOPKINS, ALONZO. Admitted March 8, 1838 aged four years by SUSAN HOPKINS, mother. Indentures expired March 8, 1838. (N-117) Delivered to his mother October 1838. (ROC, 1821) Mother in the Poor House. (AtoA) Father in Cuba. (Minutes, March 8, 1838)

HOPKINS, SAMUEL H. Admitted March 8, 1838 aged eight years by SUSAN HOPKINS, mother. Indentured to ISAAC LEVY (of Augusta, Georgia) as a merchant July 13, 1843. Indentures expired March 8, 1851. (N-116) Father in Cuba. (Minutes, March 8, 1838)

HOPKINS, SUSAN F. Admitted March 8, 1838 aged six years by SUSAN HOPKINS, mother. Delivered to her mother, nd. Indentures expired March 8, 1850. (O-56)

JERMON, CAROLINE. Admitted May 15, 1834 aged seven years by DESUN JERMON, grandmother. Indentured to CAPTAIN E. KEYES (of Moultriville, Sullivan's Island), occupation unknown, June 15, 1843. Indentures expired May 15, 1845. (O-32) Religion: Catholic. Lived on Ellery Street. (AtoA)

JOHNS, GEORGE. Admitted August 30, 1832 aged eight years by JOEL JOHNS, uncle. Sent to the U.S. Naval School, nd. Indentures expired August 30, 1845. (N-28) Born in New York. Parents born in Connecticut. (AtoA)

JOHNSON, ANDREW (VIRGIL). Admitted February 16, 1833 aged seven years by JOHN and MARY JOHNSON, parents. Sent to the U.S. Naval School, June 29, 1841. Indentures expired February 16, 1846. (N-36)

JOHNSON, ARCHIBALD. Admitted January 13, 1831 aged eight years by JOSEPH TYLER, unknown. Indentured to JOSEPH McCOLLOUGH (of Greenville District) as a farmer April 30, 1835. "A letter was received from Mr. Joseph McCullough postmarked 20th Feb. 1843 favorable to the character and conduct of A. Johnson his apprentice and stating that he had released Johnson from his indentures and set him up in business." (M-60)

JOHNSON, CHARLOTTE. Admitted February 16, 1833 aged eight years by JOHN and MARY JOHNSON, parents. Indentured to HANNAH BROWNING as a domestic February 18, 1836. Readmitted February 22, 1838. Indentures expired February 16, 1843. (O-21) No further information.

JOHNSON, CLARENCE. Admitted August 3, 1837 aged seven years by Poor House. Indentured to WILLIAM ASSMAN (of Lexington District) as a merchant January 26, 1843. Indentures expired August 3, 1851. (N-134)

JOHNSON, ELIZABETH. Admitted February 16, 1833 aged nine years by MARY and JOHN JOHNSON, unknown. Indentured to HANNAH BROWNING as a domestic July 9, 1835. Indentures expired February 16, 1842. (O-20) Delivered to her mother, MARY JOHNSON, August 13, 1835. (BO)

KANES, MARY. Admitted September 1, 1836 aged eight years by JOHN FORREST, friend. Indentured to SIMON (SIMEON) FRANKFORD as a seamstress, January 19, 1843. Transferred to JACOB ROSENFELD, occupation unknown, May 15, 1845. Indentures expired September 1, 1846. (O-48) Allowed thirty dollors as dowry for her marriage to MR. SPIERIN in 1845. (Minutes, August 28, 1845)

KELSO, ARCHIBALD. Admitted February 18, 1832 aged ten years by ELIZABETH ANGUS, mother. Delivered to his mother November 21, 1833. Indentures expired February 18, 1843. (N-13)

KENNEDY, CAROLINE M. Admitted September 20, 1838 aged nine years by Poor House. Indentured to REV. WILLIAM WRIGHT as a nurse and house-keeper January 1, 1842. Indentures expired September 10, 1847. (O-61)

KING, GEORGE H. Admitted March 12, 1838 aged twelve years by ELIZABETH KING, mother. Indentured to JAMES B. DUVAL as a tinplate worker June 18, 1840. Indentures expired March 12, 1847. (N-118) Delivered to his father GEORGE M. KING June 5, 1841. (BO) In 1838, father was a maniac in the City Asylum. (Minutes, March 8, 1838)

KNIGHT, THOMAS. Admitted February 14, 1839 aged ten years by R.W. SEYMOUR, unknown. Indentured to SAMUEL PEARSE (of Columbia) as a tinplate worker December 1, 1841. Indentures expired February 14, 1850. (N-132)

KYALL, THOMAS, R. Admitted August 18, 1831 aged seven years by MARTHA KYALL, mother. Indentured to THOMAS CHEW as a blacksmith May 26, 1836. Indentures expired August 18, 1845. (M-80)

LACY, ELIZABETH S. Admitted January 29, 1835 aged nine years by Poor House January 29, 1835. (O-34) Born in Goose Creek. (AtoA) Died March 1835 "Dibility consequent on disease previous to her admission." (ARP, 1835) Buried in the COH Burial Ground. (ROSP, March 4, 1835)

LAMBERS, BERNARD FREDERICK. Admitted May 11, 1837 aged eight years and seven months by CATHERINE LAMBERS, unknown. Indentured to JAMES H. McINTOSH (of Society Hill, Darlington District) as a merchant November 16, 1843. Indentures expired September 12, 1849. (N-107)

LAMBERS, FRANCIS J. Admitted May 11, 1837 aged six years. Indentured to WILLIAM P. SEELEY as a jeweller December 31, 1846. (ROSP, January 7, 1847) Indentures expired July 21, 1852. (N-108)

LAMBERS, MARY ELIZABETH. Admitted September 7, 1837 aged two years and five months by CATHERINE LAMBERS, mother. Born April 17, 1835. Indentures expired September 7, 1853. (O-58) Delivered to her mother August 28, 1845. (ROC, 1821)

LAMBERS, REBECCA LEONORA. Admitted September 7, 1837 aged nine years and ten months by CATHERINE LAMBERS, mother. Indentured to ROBERT T. CHISOLM as a nurse and housekeeper October 22, 1840. Indentures expired September 7, 1846. (O-57) Delivered to her mother March 16, 1843. (ROC, 1821) Allowed fifty dollars as a dowry in 1848. (Minutes, September 28, 1848)

LeCLERC (LUCLERC), ADOLPHUS. Admitted April 5, 1838 aged seven years by CAROLINE LeCLERC, mother. Indentured to THOMAS KIRKPATRICK (of Laurens District) as a merchant March 27, 1845. Indentures expired August 18, 1851. (N-119)

LLOYD, BENJAMIN. Admitted July 11, 1833 aged seven years by ANN LLOYD, mother. Indentured to SANDERS GLOVER (of Orangebrugh District) as a storekeeper May 1, 1846. Indentures expired July 11, 1847. (N-44) Sent to the High School of Charleston. (ROC,1821) Sent to Charleston College. (Minutes, March 25, 1845) "At his own request was withdrawn from Charleston College." (ROSP, May 7, 1846)

LLOYD, ELMIRA. Admitted June 29, 1832 aged eight years by ANN LLOYD, mother. Indentured to E. BRIDGES as a domestic November 15, 1833. Indentures expired June 29, 1842. (O-14) Religion: Presbyterian. Lived at corner of Guignard and Maiden Lane. (AtoA)

LOCHLEA, WILLIAM. Admitted June 13, 1831 aged ten years by ANN LOCHLEA, unknown. Born in St. John's Parish. (M-76) Indentured to TITUS L. BISSELL (of Alabama) as a boot and shoemaker September 15, 1836. (ROSP, September 9, 1836) Indentures expired June 30, 1842. (M-76)

LOWRY, EMMA (EMMELINE) C. Admitted February 23, 1833 aged six years by WILLIAM and CATHERINE LOWRY, parents. Indentures expired February 23, 1845. (O-22) Delivered to her mother, MRS. THROWAR, April 16, 1835. (BO)

LOWRY (LOWERY), WILLIAM. Admitted February 21, 1833 aged six years by WILLIAM and CATHERINE LOWRY, parents. Delivered to his mother, MRS. CATHERINE THROWAR, December 15, 1842. Indentures expired February 23, 1848. (N-37)

LYNCH, NORA. Admitted May 19, 1832 aged four years by City Council. Indentured to JAMES R. MOORER (of Orangeburgh District), occupation unknown, February 21, 1839. Indentures expired May 19, 1846. (O-13) Admitted from the Poor House. (AtoA)

LYONS, MARTHA. Admitted July 26, 1832 aged three years by ELIZABETH LYONS, mother. Delivered to her mother, MRS. ELIZABETH KENT, April 16, 1835. Indentures expired July 26, 1850. (O-16)

McCLUSKY, CHARLES. Admitted June 22, 1837 aged twelve years by BRIDGET McCLUSKY, mother. Sent to the U.S. Naval School October 1840. Indentures expired June 22, 1846. (N-109) Father a "member of Irish Volunteers in the Seminole campaign in Florada...and...(who) died in the Fort of St. Augustine." (AtoA)

McCLUSKY, ELIZABETH. Admitted June 22, 1837 aged four years by BRIDGET McCLUSKY, mother. Indentured to DR. T.R. COUTUTIER (of Hamburgh, Edgefield District) as a domestic April 16, 1846. Indentures expired June 22, 1851. (O-53)

McCLUSKY, WILLIAM. Admitted June 22, 1837 aged nine years by BRIDGET McCLUSKY, mother. (N-110) Delivered to his mother October 12, 1843 to be sent to Savannah to learn the carpentry trade with his uncle, ARTHUR McCLUSKY. (BO) Indentures expired June 22, 1849. (N-110)

McCOLLIM, HENRY. Admitted May 28, 1832 aged five years by ROBERT McCOLLIM, father. Sent to the U.S. Naval School June 29, 1841. Indentures expired May 28, 1847. (N-21)

McCOLLIM (McCULLUM), JAMES. Admitted July 3, 1833 aged three years by Poor House. Indentures expired July 3, 1851. (N-43) Religion: Episcopalian. Lived with his aunt, MARY CLEMENTS. (AtoA) Indentured to WILLIAM NASH as a baker October 13, 1842. (ROC, 1821) Absconded July 1840 (ROSP, July 30, 1840) and returned September 1840. (ROSP, September 17, 1840)

McCOLLIM (McCOLLUM), ROBERT. Admitted March 9, 1832 aged five years by ANN McCOLLIM, mother. Indentured to A. WILLINGTON and CO., proprietors of the Courier, as a printer February 15, 1844. Indentures expired March 9, 1848. (N-15) Sent to the High School of Charleston July 1841. (ROC, 1821) In 1843 it was "ordered that Robert McCollim be withdrawn from the High School, in consequence of his ill conduct." (Minutes, December 28, 1843)

McCOLLIM, ROBERT. Admitted May 28, 1832 aged seven years by ROBERT McCOLLIM, father. (N-20) Died May 30, 1837 of an accident while playing (ROSP, June 1, 1837) and was buried in the COH Burial Ground. (N-20)

McCOLLIM (McCULLOM), THOMAS. Admitted March 11, 1830 aged seven years by ANN McCOLLIM, mother. Indentures expired March 11, 1844. (M-47) Absconded May 1834. (ROSP, May 15, 1834)

McCOY, JAMES. Admitted March 10, 1831 aged eleven years by Warden of Charleston. Indentures expired March 10, 1841. (M-61) Born in Santee District. Admitted from the Poor House. (AtoA) Absconded April 1831. (ROC, 1821)

McCOLLUM (McCOLLIM), CATHERINE. Admitted March 11, 1830 aged five years by ANN McCOLLUM, mother. (L-97) Delivered to her aunt, MARY CLEMMONS, May 14, 1835. (BO) Indentures expired March 11, 1846. (L-97)

McDONALD, MALCOLM. Admitted April 18, 1839 aged twelve years by Poor House. Sent to the U.S. Naval School October 1840. Indentures expired April 18, 1848. (N-135)

MAHONEY, CORNELIUS. Admitted December 5, 1839 aged five years by Poor House. Abducted by his father, nd. Indentures expired December 5, 1855. (M-88) Father - JOHN. (BO)

MAHONEY, JOHN. Admitted December 5, 1839 aged nine years by Poor House. Abducted by his father, nd. Indentures expired December 5, 1851. (M-87) Father - JOHN. (BO)

MERAY, HARRIET. Admitted May 7, 1835 aged eleven years by MARY MERAY, mother. (Minutes, May 11, 1835) Indentured to SAMUEL N. HART, occupation unknown, March 19, 1841. Indentures expired May 7, 1842. (O-35) Born St. John's Parish, Berkeley County. Father dead, was an overseer to WILLIAM HEYWARD near Grahamville. (AtoA)

MERAY, JOHN (JAMES). Admitted May 7, 1835 aged nine years by MARY MERAY, mother. (ROSP, May 11, 1835) Indentured to REV. B. GILDERSLEEVE as a printer June 17, 1841. Indentures expired May 7, 1847. (N-79)

MERAY, MARGARET. Admitted May 7, 1835 aged five years by MARY MERAY, mother. (ROSP, May 11, 1835) Indentured to S.B. BERNARD and wife as a milliner July 18, 1844. Indentures expired May 7, 1848. (O-36) Allowed fifty dollars as a dowry in 1851. Married name MRS. MARGARET PRINCE. (Minutes, January 30, 1851)

MERAY, WILLIAM. Admitted May 7, 1835 aged thirteen years by MARY MERAY, mother. (ROSP, May 11, 1835) Indentured to WILLIAM E. HUGHSON (of Camden, Kershaw, S.C.) as a merchant March 12, 1840. When indentures expired he remained with Hughson. Indentures expired May 7, 1843. (N-78)

MOORE, JAMES. Admitted September 29, 1831 aged seven years by THOMAS
MOORE, father. Indentured to EDWARD JORDAN as a sailmaker December 24,
1835. Indentures expired September 29, 1845. (M-84)

MOORE, THOMAS. Admitted September 29, 1831 aged eight years by THOMAS
MOORE, father. Indentured to N.G. ALLEN as a bricklayer and plasterer
November 12, 1835. Indentures expired September 29, 1844. (M-83)

MUNDAY (MONDAY) JANE. Admitted December 17, 1831 aged eleven years by
MARY MUNDAY, mother. Delivered to her mother July 11, 1833. Indentures
expired December 17, 1838. (O-3)

MUNDAY (MONDAY), JOHN. Admitted December 17, 1831 aged twelve years by
MARY MUNDAY, mother. Indentured to JAMES E. WALKER as a stone cutter
May 2, 1833. Indentures expired December 17, 1840. (N-6)

MUNDAY (MONDAY), MARY. Admitted June 23, 1831 aged five years by MARY
MUNDAY, mother. Indentured to E. REDFERN, occupation unknown, November
2, 1832. Indentures expired June 23, 1844. (L-113)

MURPHY, ROBERT HEYWARD. Admitted December 22, 1836 aged three years by
MARY C. MURPHY, mother. Indentured to F. DUPONT as a paper hanger and
upholsterer October 1, 1846. Indentures expired December 22, 1855.
(N-104)

MURPHY, WILLIAM LEWIS. Admitted December 22, 1836 aged five years by
MARY C. MURPHY, mother. Indentured to JAMES ARTOPE (of Macon, Georgia)
as a stone cutter September 3, 1846. Indentures expired December 22,
1853. (N-103)

MYATT, EDWARD C. Admitted September 1, 1831 aged ten years by CATHERINE
and EDWARD MYATT, parents. Delivered to his parents December 23, 1831.
Indentures expired September 1, 1842. (M-81)

MYATT, EDWARD. (readmit) Admitted January 16, 1834 aged twelve years
by CATHERINE MYATT, unknown. Indentures expired January 16, 1843.
(N-49) Delivered to his sister, MARY ANN MYATT, May 8, 1834. (ROC, 1821)

MYATT, LEWIS. Admitted September 1, 1831 aged six years by EDWARD MYATT,
father. Delivered to his parents, December 23, 1831. Indentures expired
September 1, 1847. (M-82)

MYATT, LEWIS. (readmit) Admitted January 16, 1834 aged nine years by
CATHERINE MYATT, mother. Indentures expired January 16, 1846. (N-50)
Delivered to his sister, MARY ANN MYATT, May 8, 1834.(ROSP, May 15, 1834)

NEIL, HENRY E. Admitted June 15, 1837 aged fourteen years and eight
days by JANE NEIL, mother. Indentured to G.M.F. LAWKINS (of Lawrence-
ville, Gwinnet County, Georgia) as a merchant March 7, 1839. Sent to
the U.S. Naval School June 29, 1841. Indentures expired June 7, 1844.
(N-111)

NEIL, RUSSELL ALEXANDER. Admitted January 10, 1839 aged thirteen years
by ADELAIDE GIBBES, unknown. Indentured to JONATHAN N. McELIVEE, JR.
(of York District) as a merchant March 14, 1839. Indentures expired
January 10, 1847. (N-128)

NEIL, THOMAS BENJAMIN. Admitted June 15, 1837 aged twelve years and eight
months by JANE NEIL, mother. Indentures expired September 28,.1845.
(N-112) Born in South Carolina. Religion: Episcopalian. (AtoA) Sent
to the High School of Charleston July 1839. (Minutes, July 11, 1839)
Graduated from the College of South Carolina December 1845. (ROC, 1821)
In January 1851 he was a student of Ministry for the Presbyterian Church
in Covington, Louisiana. (Minutes, January 30, 1851) In November 1851
he was accepted at Princeton Theological Seminary. (Minutes, November
20, 1851) He transferred to South Carolina Theological Seminary in
Columbia in February 1852. (Minutes, February 19, 1852)

NEIL, WILLIAM BOYD. Admitted September 6, 1838 aged four years and seventy-two days by JANE NEIL, mother. Indentured to ROBERT P. OAKLEY as an apothecary and druggist April 8, 1847. Indentures expired June 26, 1855. (N-122) Transferred to CAPTAIN CONNER of the ship Caroline February 1853. (BO)

NELLES, PHILIP DAVID. Admitted October 14, 1830 aged ten years by JANNET PEARCE, mother. Delivered to his mother August 7, 1834. Indentures expired October 14, 1841. (M-56) Born in New York. AtoA)

NELSON, GEORGE. Admitted November 21, 1839 aged eleven years by ELIZA NELSON, mother. Sent to the U.S. Naval School October 1840. (N-145) Indentures expired November 21, 1848. (ROC, 1821)

NELSON, JOHN E. Admitted October 25, 1838 aged six years by ELIZA NELSON, mother. Indentured to GENERAL JAMES GILLIAM (of Lodi in Abbeville District) as a merchant January 28, 1847. Indentures expired October 28, 1853. (N-126)

NELSON, MARGARET. Admitted September 8, 1836 aged four years by HENRY JAGLER, unknown. Born in New York. Delivered to her step-grandfather, Henry Jagler, April 16, 1835. Indentures expired September 8, 1850. (O-47)

NELSON, WASHINGTON. Admitted October 25, 1838 by ELIZA NELSON, mother. Indentured to J.E. MORGAN (of Columbia) as a printer April 11, 1850. (N-127) Indentures expired October 25, 1857. (ROC, 1821)

NELSON, WILLIAM HENRY. Admitted September 8, 1836 aged seven years by HENRY JAGLER, unknown. Sent to the U.S. Naval School June 29, 1851. Indentures expired September 8, 1850. (N-97)

NETTLES, WILLIAM ELLISON. Admitted July 24, 1824 aged six years by Poor House. Died May 12, 1838 (ROC, 1821) of a helpatic derangement. Buried in the COH Burial Ground. (ROSP, May 17, 1838)

NORTON, JOHN. Admitted January 27, 1832 aged eight years by SUSAN NORTON, mother. Delivered to his mother January 29, 1835. Indentures expired January 27, 1842. (N-12) Born in North Santee, South Carolina. (AtoA)

O'BRIEN, ELIZA. Admitted January 13, 1831 aged five years by JANE O'BRIEN, mother. Indentured to JANE WHITING as a domestic December 10, 1835. Indentures expired January 13, 1844. (L-109) Transferred to MRS. SAMUEL WRAGG, occupation unknown, August 9, 1840. (BO)

O'BRIEN, JOHN. Admitted June 29, 1837 aged seven years by MARY (NANCY) HODGSON, unknown. Indentured to THOMAS WEST BOLGER as a saddler January 5, 1843. Indentures expired June 29, 1851. (N-106) Born in Marion District. Religion: Methodist. (AtoA)

O'BRIEN, MARY. Admitted January 13, 1831 aged five years by JANE O'BRIEN, mother. (L-108) Indentured to HANNAH BROWNING, COH School Mistress, (ROSP, May 7, 1835), occupation unknown, April 13, 1835. Transferred to J.F. STEINMEYER, occupation unknown, July 7, 1835. Indentures expired January 13, 1845. (L-108)

O'HANLON, DOYLE. Admitted May 12, 1831 aged twelve years by ELIZA O'HANLON, mother. Indentures expired May 12, 1840. (M-71) Absconded, 1831. (Minutes, September 22, 1831) Lived on Anson Street. (AtoA)

O'HANLON, ROBERT. Admitted May 12, 1831 aged eight years by ELIZA O'HANLON, mother. Indentures expired May 12, 1844. (M-72) Absconded, 1832. (ROSP, February 2, 1832)

PAGE, GEORGE WASHINGTON. Admitted March 10, 1836 aged three years by JOHN PAGE, father. Born August 20, 1832. (N-94) Died July 8, 1838 of a convulsive fit and buried in the COH Burial Ground. (ROSP, July 12, 1838)

PAGE, SAMUEL FREEMAN. Admitted March 10, 1836 aged seven years by JOHN PAGE, father. Indentured to E.R. STOKES as a bookbinder February 2, 1843. Indentures expired October 14, 1850. (N-93)

PETERSON, SUSANNAH. Admitted August 16, 1832 aged ten years by ANN PETERSON, mother. Indentured to CHRISTOPHER ROUSE as a tailoress August 9, 1838. Indentures expired August 9, 1839. (O-17) Married name POWERS. (Minutes, September 2, 1852)

PINCKNEY, WILLIAM. Admitted December 31, 1835 aged twelve years by Poor House. Indentured to DAVID McCULLOUGH (of Greenville District) as a farmer May 23, 1856. Indentures expired December 31, 1844. (N-92)

PRATT, WILLIAM B. Admitted May 12, 1831 aged five years by MARY A. FROBUS, mother. (ROSP, May 18, 1831). Delivered to his mother leaving for the North May 9, 1833. (BO) Indentures expired May 12, 1847. (M-73) Born New York. (AtoA)

RAGSDALE, ELIZA C. Admitted May 19, 1832 aged five years by City Council. Indentured to FREDERICK WITTPENN, a storekeeper, as a domestic January 30, 1840. Indentures expired May 19, 1845. (O-11) Returned to the COH December 10, 1841. (ROSP, December 10, 1840) Indentured to N.R. MIDDLETON, ESQ., occupation unknown, June 9, 1842. (ROSP, June 9, 1842). Admitted from the Poor House. (AtoA) Returned to the COH September 1842. (ROSP, September 22, 1842) "Found a situation with a MRS. SOLEE in Tradd Street." (ROSP, September 29, 1842)

RAGSDALE, JAMES N. Admitted May 19, 1832 aged one year by City Council. (N-16) Indentured to JAMES B. CLENNAHAN, as a bricklayer, April 13, 1843. (BO) Indentures expired May 19, 1852. (N-16) Admitted from the Poor House. (AtoA)

RAGSDALE, NARCISA (NARSISA). Admitted May 19, 1832 aged four years by City Council. Indentured to E.R. CALHOUN, a physician. (of Abbeville District) as a domestic April 15, 1841. Indentures expired May 19, 1846. (O-12) Admitted from the Poor House. (AtoA)

RANSFORD, HENRY. Admitted January 30, 1830 aged five years by MARGARET RANSFORD, mother. Delivered to his mother June 5, 1834. (M-45) Indentures expired January 30, 1846. (ROC, 1821)

RANTIN, JOHN DAWSON. Admitted April 1, 1831 aged nine years by JOHN RANTIN, unknown. Indentured to BENJAMIN C. SUARES as a tailor December 12, 1833. Indentures expired April 1, 1843. (M-67) Born in Spartanburgh. (AtoA)

RANTIN, RICHARD MUNRO. Admitted August 2, 1832 aged eight years by CAROLINE ANN RANTIN, mother. Delivered to his mother January 9, 1834. Indentures expired August 2, 1853. (N-26) Born in Spartanburgh. Religion: Baptist. (AtoA)

RANTIN, WILLIAM M. Admitted April 1, 1831 aged eleven years by JOHN RANTIN, unknown. Indentured to JOHN A. STURAT (M-66), editor of the Evening Post, (ROC, 1821) as a printer October 28, 1831. Indentures expired April 1, 1841. (M-66) Born in Ireland. (AtoA)

REETHY (ROTHE), JULIUS AUGUSTUS. Admitted February 19, 1835 by Poor House and CHARLES REETHY, father. (N-76) Delivered to his uncle, DANIEL A. DOBSON, July 30, 1840. (Minutes, July 30, 1840) Mother lived in Cheraw. (BO)

RIDGEWAY, LAWRENCE. Admitted October 14, 1830 aged seven years by CHARLES RIDGEWAY, father. Delivered to his mother, ELIZABETH SMITH, to be bound to PREGNALL and BARTON as a house carpenter August 7, 1832. Indentures expired October 14, 1844. (M-57)

RIDGEWAY, MARTHA. Admitted October 14, 1830 aged eleven years by CHARLES RIDGEWAY, father. Indentured to PETER READHIMER (moving to the upper country) as a domestic December 23, 1831. Indentures expired October 14, 1840. (L-105) Mother ELIZA. (AtoA)

RIVERS, DAVID S. Admitted January 21, 1832 aged twelve years by E.F. RIVERS, mother. Indentured to WILLIAM KUNHARDT as a factor and general agent June 26, 1834. Indentures expired January 21, 1841. (N-10)

RIVERS, WILLIAM. Admitted January 21, 1832 aged nine years by E.F. RIVERS, mother. Indentures expired January 21, 1844. (N-11) Graduated December 6, 1841 from South Carolina College. (ROC, 1821) Wrote a history of South Carolina and the Commisioners purchased fifty copies. (Minutes, August 31, 1843)

RYBURN, CATHARINE. Admitted February 27, 1834 aged eleven years by Poor House. (O-29) Delivered to her mother April 1834. (ROSP, April 24, 1834) Father, MATTHEW, died in the Poor House. Religion: Presbyterian. Born in Argleshire, Scotland. (AtoA)

RYBURN, JOHN. Admitted February 27, 1834 aged eight years by Poor House. Sent to the U.S. Naval School October, 1840. Indentures expired February 27, 1847. (N-52) Mother MRS. WARRENTON. (Minutes, October 29, 1840) "Upon being reproved by the Nurse, MRS. McPHERSON, for drawing a knife upon another boy, had struck her several blows, so violently as to require the attendance of the Physician who had to bleed her. Ordered that...the boy...(be kept) in confinement." (Minutes, October 22, 1840)

RYBURN, MARY. Admitted February 27, 1834 aged six years by Poor House. Indentured to REV. WILLIAM MOULTRIE REID (of Sumpter District), occupation unknown, December 1, 1842. Indentures expired February 27, 1846. (O-30) Returned to the COH as an assistant teacher. (Minutes, May 4, 1850)

RYBURN, PETER. Admitted February 27, 1834 aged four years by Poor House. Indentures expired February 27, 1851. (N-53) Sent to the High School of Charleston in 1844. (Minutes, January 25, 1844) Graduated February 25, 1851 from Charleston College. (ROC, 1821) In 1855 he requested money for a Theological Library. (Minutes, 25, 1855)

RYBURN, WILLIAM. Admitted February 27, 1834 aged ten years by Poor House. Indentured to THOMAS MORRISON as a cabinetmaker July 2, 1838. Indentures expired February 27, 1845. (N-51)

SCOTT, ROBERT. Admitted July 16, 1835 aged twelve years by REBECCA S. SCOTT, mother. Indentured to JAMES KEAN (of Greenville District) as a boot and shoemaker July 7, 1836. Indentures expired July 16, 1844. (N-85) Born in Georgetown District. Religion: Episcopalian. (AtoA)

SCOTT, WILLIAM. Admitted July 16, 1835 aged eleven years by REBECCA SCOTT, mother. Indentured to _____ CRUIKSHANK as a tanner July 7, 1836. Indentures expired July 16, 1836. (N-86) Transferred to JAMES KEAN as a boot and shoemaker July 14, 1836. (ROSP, July 14, 1836) Born in Georgetown District. Religion: Episcopalian. (AtoA)

SCRAM, JOHN. Admitted October 10, 1833 aged four years by CHLOE MILLER, unknown. Indentured to ELIAS ROGERS (of Spartanburg District) as a farmer January 5, 1843. Indentures expired October 10, 1850. (N-48)

SHEIVENEL, JEREMIAH HENRY. Admitted September 17, 1830 aged six years by MRS. SHEIVENEL, unknown. Indentured to A.S. JOHNSON (of Columbia) as a printer February 25, 1836. Indentures expired September 17, 1845. (M-53)

SHIVERNALL, ALMIRA LUCRETIA, JANE. Admitted July 24, 1834 aged eight years by Poor House. Indentured to W.H. HILLIARD, occupation unknown, July 20, 1838. Indentures expired July 24, 1844. (O-33)

SIVIL, ALEXANDER. Admitted August 14, 1834 aged eleven years by JANE BARTON, unknown. (N-65) Indentured to HENRY PREGNALL as a carpenter July 25, 1837. (BO) Indentures expired August 14, 1844. (N-65)

SMITH, BENJAMIN FRANKLIN. Admitted May 31, 1838 aged six years by E. RHODES, grandmother. Indentured to CHARLES B. MOSES (of Pendleton, Anderson District) as a store-keeper January 14, 1847. Indentures expired May 31, 1853. (N-120) Allowed forty dollars to go to his parents in Alabama because of his illness and financial situation. (Minutes, March 4, 1852)

SMITH, HAMILTON BLACKWELL. Admitted June 19, 1834 aged twelve years by HARRIOTT PINCKNEY, unknown. Indentures expired June 19, 1834. (N-62) Baptized in St. Philip's Church. (AtoA) No further information.

SOMPAYRAC, THEODORE (FREDERICK). Admitted September 19, 1832 aged ten years by MARY McNEAL, aunt. Indentured to JAMES H. McINTOSH (of Society Hill) as a merchant June 3, 1834. Indentures expired September 19, 1843. (N-29) Religion: Catholic. (AtoA)

SPECHT, JOHN. Admitted February 11, 1830 aged nine years by ANN SPECHT, mother. (M-46) Born December 29, ____ (AtoA) Died August 7, 1831 of tetanus. (ARP, 1831)

STENTON, HUGH. Admitted September 15, 1836 aged three years by ROBERT Y. HAYNE, Mayor. Indentured to W. HAMPTON and R.A. BROWN, of the Nesbit Iron Works, (Spartanburg District) as an iron worker, nd. Indentures expired September 15, 1854. (N-100) Father, HUGH, and mother, ELIZABETH GILMORE, born in Derry, Ireland. Arrived in 1831. Father, in the City Guard, died March 17, 1835. Mother, married THOMAS MATTHEWS, of Ireland, and died September 13, 1836 of cholera. (AtoA)

STENTON, ROBERT. Admitted September 15, 1836 aged six years by ROBERT Y. HAYNE, mayor. Indentured to JOHN POOLE (of Spartanburg District) as a merchant May 13, 1842. Indentures expired September 15, 1851. (N-99)

STENTON, THOMAS. Admitted September 15, 1836 aged thirteen years by ROBERT Y. HAYNE, Mayor. Indentured to JOSEPH POWELL (of Greenville) as a merchant May 11, 1837. Indentures expired September 15, 1844. (N-98)

STEWART, HENRY. Admitted July 21, 1831 aged nine years by ANN STEWART, mother. Delivered to his mother ANN MARSO, January 23, 1834. Indentures expired July 21, 1843 (M-78) Born in John's Island. (AtoA)

STEWART, THOMAS. Admitted July 21, 1831 aged seven years by ANN STEWART, mother. Indentures expired July 21, 1845. (M-79) Delivered to his mother, ANN MOUSSEAU, September 5, 1833. (ROSP, September 5, 1833)

STINTORE, (STINTON), ANDREW. Admitted August 9, 1838 aged two years by Poor House. Indentured to JAMES B. ARTOPE (of Macon, Georgia) as a stone cutter and quarrier February 15, 1849. Indentures expired August 9, 1857. (N-140)

STREET, JOSEPH. Admitted August 20, 1835 aged eleven years by JOSEPH STREET, father. Indentured to G. GOOD (of Edgefield, South Carolina) as a merchant January 26, 1837. Indentures expired August 20, 1845. (N-87) Mother ELIZA. Religion: Methodist. (AtoA)

STROBEL, CHARLES. Admitted January 22, 1835 aged five years by Poor House. Sent to the U.S. Naval School June 29, 1841. Indentures expired January 22, 1851. (N-72)

TARRY, CORNELIA CATHERINE. Admitted March 1, 1838 aged ten years by MARY TARRY, mother. Indentured to THOMAS C. DUPONT as a domestic September 23, 1841. Indentures expired March 1, 1846. (O-55) Mother in the Poor House. (AtoA)

TARRY, CYRUS CHAPMAN. Admitted March 1, 1838 aged eight years by MARY TARRY, mother. Indentured to J.B. NIXON as an engraver and carver February 23, 1843. Indentures expired March 1, 1851. (N-113)

TARRY, ESAU L. Admitted March 1, 1838 aged three years by MARY TARRY, mother. Indentured to JOHN B. COTTERELL (of Lentonville, Anson County, North Carolina) as a merchant March 30, 1848. Indentures expired March 1, 1856. (N-115) Mother in the Poor House. (AtoA)

TARRY (TARREY), RUEBEN L. Admitted March 1, 1838 aged six years by MARY TARRY, mother. Indentured to WILLIAM KNAUF (of Anderson District, village of Pendleton) as a cabinetmaker October 2, 1845. Indentures expired March 1, 1853. (N-114) Mother in the Poor House. (AtoA)

TAYLOR, ISHAM WILLIAM. Admitted May 5, 1831 aged eight years. Indentured to DR. T.Y. SIMONS, occupation unknown, December 22, 1836. Indentures expired May 10, 1844. (M-68)

TAYLOR, RICHARD AVERY. Admitted May 10, 1831 aged six years by ANN TAYLOR, mother. Indentured to THADDEUS C. BOLLINGS (of Greenville District) as a merchant February 24, 1838. Indentures expired May 10, 1845. (M-69)

THOMASON, JOHN GEORGE. Admitted September 5, 1833 aged three years by Poor House. Indentures expired September 5, 1849. (N-47) Absconded, nd. (ROC, 1821) Mother in the Poor House subject to fits and the father in gaol. (AtoA)

THOMASON, MARK. Admitted July 2, 1835 aged four years by S.T. THOMASON, unknown. Indentures expired July 2, 1852. Absconded November 16, 1842 and returned July 17, 1845. (Minutes, July 17, 1845) Absconded again, nd. (ROC, 1821) Admitted from the Poor House. (AtoA)

THOMASON, STEPHEN. Admitted September 5, 1833 aged four years by Poor House. (N-46) Died August 1839 of worms and convulsive fits. (ROSP, August 15, 1839)

THOMPSON, CAROLINE. Admitted October 14, 1830 aged eight years by MRS. THOMPSON (MRS. RIDGEWAY). Indentured to MARY ANN JUDGE as a storekeeper June 29, 1837. Indentures expired October 14, 1840. (L-106) A cripple. (ROSP, October 20, 1830)

THORNLEY, GEORGE W. Admitted November 4, 1830 aged seven years by ELIZABETH ALLEN, mother. Indentured to JAMES MACK as a merchant November 15, 1838. Indentures expired November 4, 1844. (M-59)

THORNLEY, JANE E. Admitted November 4, 1830 aged eleven years by ELIZABETH ALLEN, mother. Indentured to JAMES D. KNIGHT and wife as a domestic November 2, 1832. Indentures expired November 4, 1877. (L-107)

THORNLEY, SAMUEL. Admitted November 4, 1830 aged nine years by ELIZABETH ALLEN, mother. Indentured to DR. THOMAS M. LOGAN as an apothecary December 18, 1834. Indentures expired November 4, 1842. (M-58) Absconded 1837 and believed to be with relatives in Wassamasaw. (BO)

TINKHAM, ELIZABETH. Admitted November 15, 1831 aged nine years by Poor House. (O-1) Delivered to her sister, EUNICE DENNIS, October 2, 1834. (BO) Transferred to ELIZABETH GILLIARD, occupation unknown, March 12, 1835. Transferred to MRS. ELIZABETH BAGSHAW, nd. Indentures expired November 15, 1840. (O-1) Requested money to move to Beaufort and allowed fifty dollars. (Minutes, June 25, 1846) Father a sailor. (AtoA)

TINKHAM, JOHN. Admitted November 15, 1831 aged seven years by Poor House of the Charleston Neck. Indentured to MARTIN LEWIS as a bricklayer December 6, 1839. Indentures expired November 15, 1846. (N-1)

VAN HOLTON, JOHN. Admitted May 8, 1834 aged eight years by Poor House. (N-47) Died February 20, 1835 of fever and pneumonia. (ARP, 1835) An orphan. Religion: Methodist. (AtoA)

VAN HOLTON, MARTHA. Admitted May 8, 1834 aged twelve years by Poor House. Indentured to HENRY BRISBANE and wife as a domestic January 21, 1836. Indentures expired May 8, 1840. (O-31) An orphan. Religion: Methodist. (O-31)

WALLACE, CHARLES A. Admitted January 26, 1837 aged four years. Indentured to JAMES B. ARTOPE (of Macon, Georgia) as a stonecutter September 3, 1846. Indentures expired January 26, 1854. (N-105)

WALLACE, WILLIAM JOHN. Admitted January 7, 1830 aged seven years by SARAH WALLACE, mother. Indentured to B.C. SUARES as a tailor November 20, 1834. Indentures expired January 7, 1844. (M-43)

WELCH, MARY. Admitted November 15, 1832 aged five years by ELIZABETH WELCH, mother. Delivered to her mother January 16, 1834. Indentures expired November 15, 1845. (O-19) Religion: Methodist. (AtoA)

WHITE, WILLIAM. Admitted November 10, 1832 aged eleven years by MARGARET WALLIS, unknown. Indentured to THOMAS FELL as a tinsmith November 10, 1836. Indentures expired November 10, 1836. Indentures expired November 10, 1842. (N-33). Religion: Catholic. (AtoA)

WILCOX, JANE. Admitted June 24, 1830 aged nine years by MARY ANN WILCOX, mother. Indentured to WILLIAM WHITTEMORE as a domestic March 7, 1833. Indentures expired June 24, 1840. (L-103)

WILCOX, MARY. Admitted June 24, 1830 aged ten years by MARY ANN WILCOX, mother. Indentured to WILLIAM LLOYD and WIFE (1-102), about to move to New York (BO) as a domestic April 12, 1833. Indentures expired June 24, 1838. (L-102)

WILLIAMS, CALEB. Admitted May 19, 1832 aged three years by City Council. Indentured to JOHN POTTS (of Chester District), occupation unknown, March 24, 1836. Indentures expired May 19, 1850. (N-17) Admitted from the Poor House. (AtoA) "Caleb Williams, who had been apprenticed to Mr. Potts in 1836, and who was now residing in that County (Louisville, Winston County, Mississippi) had had devised to him by Mr. Potts, a tract of Land of 480 acres and ten Negroes." (Minutes, January 12, 1843)

WILLIAMS, HENRY. Admitted August 11, 1836 aged four years by KOSIA WILLIAMS, mother. Indentured to WILLIAM H. GRUVER as a plasterer August 15, 1844. (N-96)

WILLINGHAM, HENRY. Admitted February 5, 1835 aged four years by DICEY WILLINGHAM, mother. (ROSP, February 11, 1835) Died August 14, 1836 of Tabes Mesenterica and buried in the COH Burial Ground. (ROSP, August 18, 1836)

WILLINGHAM, JAMES. Admitted February 5, 1835 aged eight years by DICEY WILLINGHAM, mother. (ROSP, February 11, 1835) Sent to the U.S. Naval School June 29, 1841. Indentures expired February 5, 1848. (N-73)

WILSON, CONRAD. Admitted February 27, 1832 aged four years by EDWARD and MARY WILSON, unknown. Indentured to CHARLES W. GRAVES as a bricklayer November 10, 1842. Indentures expired February 27, 1849. (N-14)

WINNINGHAM, ISAAC. Admitted December 13, 1838 aged five years by DICEY WINNINGHAM, mother. (N-129) Delivered to his mother, MRS. WILLIAMS (of Rantolls) June 3, 1841. (ROSP, June 3, 1841) Indentures expired December 13, 1854. (N-129)

WINSLIFE, MARY ANN. Admitted May 2, 1839 aged seven months by Poor House. Adopted by ANDREW MILNE, planter, June 2, 1842. Indentures expired October 2, 1856. (O-63) Mother, an epileptic, in the Poor House. (AtoA)

WISE, JAMES. Admitted July 28, 1836 aged seven years by CATHERINE WISE, mother. Sent to the U.S. Naval School June 29, 1841. Indentures expired July 28, 1850. (N-95)

WISE, MARY ANN. Admitted July 28, 1836 aged four years by CATHERINE WISE, mother. Sent to the U.S. Naval School June 29, 1841. Indentures expired July 28, 1850. (N-95)

WISE, SARAH. Admitted July 27, 1836 aged nine years by CATHERINE WISE, mother. Indentured to WILLIAM BUTLER as a domestic July 22, 1842. Indentures expired July 28, 1845. (O-44)

WOOLCOOK, ELIZABETH. Admitted September 8, 1831 aged six years by JOHN WOOLCOCK, father. Indentured to B.E. HABERSHAM as a domestic April 15, 1841. Indentures expired September 8, 1846. (L-115) Allowed fifty dollars as a marriage dowry in 1846. (Minutes, February 16, 1846)

WOOLCOCK, JANE. Admitted September 8, 1831 aged eight years by JOHN WOOLCOCK, father. Delivered to her mother April 25, 1837. Indentures expired September 8, 1841. (L-116)

WOOLCOCK, MARY ANN. Admitted January 23, 1834 aged two years and eight months by JOHN WOOLCOCK, unknown. Delivered to her mother, MRS. SARAH PAGE, December 4, 1845. Indentures expired May 23, 1849. (O-28) Allowed fifty dollars as a marriage dowry in 1850. (Minutes, April 4, 1850)

* * * * * *

ADAMS, CORNELIUS. Admitted May 4, 1843 aged four years by Poor House. (P-13) Indentured to C. CANNING of the Southern Christian Advocate as a printer March 4, 1852. (BO) Indentures expired May 4, 1860. (P-13)

ANDERSON, JOSEPH. Admitted May 27, 1847 aged five years by E. ANDERSON, mother. Indentured to GEORGE KINLOCH and SON as a merchant March 10, 1859. Indentures expired May 27, 1863. (P-70) Sent to the High School of Charleston. (ROC, 1821)

ANDERSON, SARAH ELLEN. Admitted May 7, 1846 aged seven years by Poor House. Indentured to REV. FERDINAND JACOBS as a domestic, November 8, 1849. Indentures expired May 7, 1857. (C-106) Born May 4, 1839. Father, W.P. ANDERSON, blind. (AtoA)

ANDERSON, Z. YEARDON. Admitted May 14, 1846. (ROSP, May 14, 1846) aged nine years. Indentured to J.B. RICHARDSON, occupation unknown, September 29, 1853. Indentures expired May 7, 1858. (P-50) Born February 9, 1837. Father, W.P. ANDERSON, blind. (AtoA) Allowed one hundred dollars a year to study for the Ministry of the Protestant Episcopal Church at Camden. (Minutes, April 5, 1860)

BACKHILL (BACKILL), WILLIAM EDWARD. Admitted October 5, 1848 by the Poor House. (P-98) Died May 23, 1849. (ROC, 1821)

BAILE, ELIZABETH A. Admitted November 14, 1844 aged seven years by MARY BAILE, mother, and the Poor House. (O-103) Delivered to her mother, MRS. MARY GAGE, wife of JAMES GAGE, December 14, 1848. (Minutes, December 14, 1848) Indentures expired November 14, 1855. (O-103) Religion: Methodist. (AtoA)

BAILE, FRANCIS (JOHN). Admitted November 14, 1844 aged ten years by MARY BAILE, mother, and the Poor House. Indentured to B. ARTOPE (of Macon, Georgia) as a stonecutter February 15, 1849. Indentures expired November 14, 1855. (P-32) Religion: Methodist. (AtoA)

BAILE, HENRY. Admitted March 25, 1847 aged four years by MARY KNIGHTS, mother. Indentures expired March 25, 1864. (P-65) Delivered to his mother, 1847. (ROC, 1821)

115

BAILE, JAMES E. Admitted November 14, 1844 aged eight years by MARY BAILE, mother and the Poor House. Indentured to A.S. WILLINGTON and CO., publishers of the Charleston Courier, as a printer December 3, 1852. Indentures expired November 14, 1857. (P-33) Religion: Methodist. (AtoA)

BAILE, WILLIAM. Admitted November 14, 1844 aged four years by MARY BAILE, mother, and the Poor House. Indentured to CAMERON and CO., machinists, as a boilermaker November 18, 1856. Indentures expired November 14, 1861. (P-34) Religion: Methodist. (AtoA)

BARKERDING, DORIS. Admitted September 30, 1847 aged two years and six months by the Poor House. Born in Germany. Indentures expired March 30, 1863. (O-116) Delivered to her mother and step-father, MR. and MRS. MILLER, May 1850. (Minutes, May 16, 1850)

BARKERDING, HENRY. Admitted September 30, 1847 aged eight years by Poor House. Born in Germany. Indentures expired September 30, 1860. (P-79) Delivered to his mother and step-father, MR. and MRS. MILLER, May, 1850. (Minutes, May 16, 1850)

BARTH, FREDERICK. Admitted August 6, 1846 aged eight years and six months by father and the Poor House. Born December 16, 1836 from an affadavit submitted by his brother, WILLIAM H.C. BARTH. Indentured to ZACHARIAH deHAY (of Kershaw District) as an apothecary June 19, 1851. Indentures expired December 16, 1857. (P-56) Father, DR. WILLIAM BARTH. (AtoA)

BEHRE, FREDERICK GUSTAVUS. Admitted April 30, 1846 aged nine years by his mother and the Poor House. Born near Hamburgh, Germany January 7, 1837. Indentures expired April 30, 1858. (P-47) Sent to the High School of Charleston January 22, 1852. (Minutes, January 22, 1852) Sent to South Carolina College, 1858. (COH Inmates' Files) Suspended from school until October 1, 1858. (Minutes, April 8, 1858) Allowed to stay at the Orphan House while studying for the Bar. (Minutes, December 16, 1858) Offered a job at the Academy of Walterboro and accepted it. (Minutes, December 30, 1858)

BEHRENS, FREDERICK. Admitted May 25, 1848 aged seven years by Poor House. Indentures expired May 25, 1862. (P-90) Delivered to his father and sent to Germany on board the Bark Johann Frederick with CAPTAIN WERTING in 1849. (Minutes, June 14, 1849)

BEHRENS, HENRY. Admitted May 25, 1848 aged nine years by Poor House May 25, 1848. Indentures expired May 25, 1860. (P-89) Delivered to his father and sent to Germany on board the Bark Johann Frederick with CAPTAIN WERTING in 1849. (Minutes, June 14, 1849)

BENTON, LOUISA. Admitted August 1, 1844 aged eleven years by Poor House. Indentured to SARAH CADLE, widow, (of Granitteville, Edgfield) as a manufacturer, nd. Returned to COH January 1850. Transferred to JOHN SYMONS (of St. Philip's Parish), occupation unknown, March 13, 1851. Indentures expired August 1, 1851. (O-99) Born in Walterborough. Religion: Methodist. (AtoA)

BOURDIN, EUGENE. Admitted November 26, 1846 aged three years by Poor House. Indentures expired September 17, 1864. (P-62) Born September 17, 1843 in the Poor House. Mother VIRGINIA BOURDIN. (Minutes, November 26, 1846) Delivered to his father, nd. (ROC, 1821)

BOYCE, JOHN H. Admitted October 4, 1849 aged five years by Poor House. Indentures expired October 4, 1865. (Q-5) Delivered to his mother October 16, 1857. (ROC, 1821)

BREMER, CHARLES. Admitted November 12, 1841 aged twelve years by Poor House. Indentured to BENJAMIN GILDERSLEEVE as a printer March 24, 1842. Indentures expired November 12, 1849. (M-106) Transferred to B. JENKINS, occupation unknown, November 13, 1845. (BO)

BREMER (BREUER), ELIZA. Admitted November 12, 1840 aged ten years by Poor House. Indentured to JOHN G. FLYNN as a domestic December 24, 1846. Indentures expired November 12, 1848. (O-73)

BREMER, HENRY J. Admitted November 12, 1840 aged six years by Poor House. Indentured to CHARLES CANNING as a printer November 15, 1849. Indentures expired November 12, 1855. (M-105)

BRITTON, JOHN FRANCIS. Admitted May 18, 1843 aged eight years by HARRIET BRITTON, mother, and the Poor House. Delivered to his mother January 11, 1844. Indentures expired May 18, 1856. (P-14)

BUCKHEISTER, EDWARD P. Admitted March 19, 1841 aged three years by parents, . Indentures expired March 19, 1859. (M-107) Absconded, 1849. (ROC, 1821)

BUCKHEISTER, JAMES ANDREW. Admitted October 1, 1840 aged eight years by FRANCES BUCKHEISTER ., mother. Indentured to J.T. SLOAN (of Pendleton, Anderson District) as a tanner and currier February 13, 1845. Indentures expired October 1, 1853. (M-101) "The father a Guardsman and Constable. From the latter office he was dismissed on account of his violent and tyrannical conduct to a poor female debtor. It is supposed he is occasionally dereanged...The wife almost confined is now in bed where she has been for the last five days from a severe beating inflicted by her husband. Apprehensions for her life were entertained and he has been arrested and now lies in Gaol." (AtoA)

BUCKHEISTER, JOHN. Admitted October 1, 1840 aged eleven years by FRANCES BUCKHEISTER, mother. Indentured to J.T. SLOAN (of Pendleton, Anderson District) as a tanner and currier February 13, 1845. Indentures expired October 1, 1850. (M-100)

BUCKHEISTER, ROBERT JOEL. Admitted October 1, 1840 aged six years by FRANCES BUCKHEISTER, mother. Indentured to F.H. ELMORE, W. HAMPTON, and R.A. BROWN of the Nesbitt Iron Works (of Spartenburgh District) as an iron worker April 8, 1847. Indentures expired October 1, 1855. (M-102)

BUCKHEISTER, WILLIAM CHRISTIAN. Admitted October 9, 1845 aged three years by F. BUCKHEISTER, mother, and the Poor House. Indentured to J.C.H. CLAUSSEN as a baker August 27, 1857. Indentures expired October 9, 1863. (P-61) Father, JOHN BUCKHEISTER, in the Poor House. Mother lived on the north side of Laurens Street, second door from Anson Street. (AtoA)

BUIST, EDWARD H. Admitted April 29, 1847 aged nine years by the Poor House. Delivered to his uncle, the REV. EDWARD BUIST, April 20, 1848. Indentures expired April 29, 1859. (P-67)

BUIST, JAMES F. Admitted April 19, 1847 aged eight years by the Poor House. Delivered to his uncle, the REV. EDWARD BUIST, April 20, 1848. Indentures expired April 29, 1860. (P-68)

BULL, WILLIAM ROBERT. Admitted May 28, 1846 aged eleven years by his mother and the Poor House. Indentured to GEORGE D. BECKHAM (of Lancaster District) as a merchant May 20, 1852. Indentures expired March 9, 1856. (P-51) Born in Barnwell District. Religion: Episcopalian. (AtoA)

BURTON, CHARLES HENRY. Admitted February 1, 1849 aged four years and six months by ELIZA BURTON, mother, and the Poor House. Indentures expired August 1, 1865. (P-99) Abducted by his mother, nd. (ROC, 1821)

CALVITT, WILLIAM LOWNDES. Admitted September 20, 1849 aged twelve years by JANE J. MISCALLY, aunt, and the Poor House. Indentured to CHARLES LESLIE of the Barque Harriet and Martha, as a mariner December 12, 1850. Indentures expired September 20, 1858. (Q-4)

CAMPANA, CHARLES. Admitted December 7, 1843 aged nine years by the Poor House and his mother, unknown. Indentures expired December 7, 1855. (P-17) Delivered to his mother going to New York April 4, 1844. (Minutes, April 11, 1844)

CAMPANA, GEORGE ALEXANDER. Admitted December 7, 1843 aged eleven years by the Poor House, and his mother, unknown. Indentures expired December 22, 1853. (P-16) Delivered to his mother going to New York April 4, 1844. (Minutes, April 11, 1844) KATHERINE RINGENT aunt. (BO)

CAMPANA, NAPOLEON B. Admitted December 7, 1843 aged seven years by the Poor House and his mother, unknown. Indentures expired December 7, 1857. (P-18) Delivered to his mother going to New York April 4, 1844. (Minutes, April 11, 1844)

CANTLEY, JAMES W. Admitted April 8, 1847 aged six years by the Poor House. (P-75) Died June 28, 1848 of a cold and fever at his mother's house on Montague Street near Rutledge Street. (ROSP, June 22, 1848)

CASEY, THOMAS. Admitted July 29, 1841 aged four years by MRS. CASEY, mother. Delivered to his mother (M-124), MRS. THOMAS (ROSP, September 15, 1842) September 8, 1842. Indentures expired July 29, 1858. (M-124)

CONLON, THOMAS. Admitted May 12, 1842 aged four years by the Poor House. Indentured to AUGUST IUSTI (JUSTI) as a black and locksmith December 29, 1850. Indentures expired May 12, 1859. (P-5)

CONNELL, ELLEN. Admitted May 10, 1849 aged eleven months by ANN CONNELL, mother and the Poor House. (O-126) Died July 26, 1849. (Minutes, July 26, 1849)

CONOLLY (CONOLY), JOHN. Admitted May 20, 1841 aged ten years by MARY RYAN, mother. Indentures expired May 20, 1851. (M-113) Delivered to his mother September 14, 1842. (ROC, 1821) Admitted from the Poor House. (AtoA)

COOK, HENRY. Admitted August 12, 1841 aged seven years by Poor House. Delivered to MRS. HOLBROK, unknown, 1846. Indentures expired August 12, 1855. (M-125) Born in Williamsburg. (AtoA)

COOK, JAMES. Admitted May 8, 1845 aged two years by Poor House. (P-39) Delivered to his mother, MARYANN BURNS, and his step-father, JOHN, a seaman and rigger, December 31, 1845. (BO) Readmitted June 8, 1848. (ROC, 1821) Indentured to J.C.H. CLAUSSEN as a baker August 27, 1857. Indentures expired May 8, 1864. (P-39)

COVERT, HENRY. Admitted January 23, 1840 aged ten years by CORNELIA COVERT, mother and the Poor House. Indentured to THOMAS KIRKPATRICK and RICHARD MATTOX, his father-in-law, (of Laurens District) as a merchant March 27, 1845. Indentures expired January 23, 1851. (M-94) Born in St. Augustine. Religion: Methodist. (AtoA)

COVERT, MICHAEL (MIKELL). Admitted January 23, 1840 aged eight years by CORNELIA COVERT, mother and the Poor House. Indentures expired January 23, 1853. (M-95) Born in St. Augustine. Religion: Methodist. (AtoA) Sent to the High School of Charleston, January 1846. (ROC, 1821) Graduated from Charleston College, 1853. (Minutes, January 20, 1853) Allowed to stay in the Institution while completing medical school. (Ibid.) Graduated from the Medical College, 1855. (Minutes, March 15, 1855)

COVERT, THOMAS. Admitted January 23, 1840 aged twelve years by C. COVERT, mother and the Poor House. Indentured to LEWIS M. HATCH as a merchant December 24, 1842. Indentures expired August 26, 1848. (M-93) Born in St. Augustine. Religion: Methodist. (AtoA)

DAWSON, ALFRED. Admitted June 7, 1849 aged two years by SUSAN DAWSON, mother, and the Poor House. (P-107) Died, nd. (ROB, 1856)

DAWSON, ANN. Admitted June 7, 1849 aged six years by SUSAN DAWSON, mother and the Poor House. Indentures expired February 25, 1861. (O-127) Delivered to her aunt, MRS. JOSEPH CHURCH, February 21, 1856. (BO)

DAWSON, FRANCIS. Admitted June 7, 1849 aged eight years by SUSAN DAWSON, mother, and the Poor House. Indentured to G. and F. DAWSON as a merchant March 25, 1858. Indentures expired June 15, 1862. (P-105) Sent to the High School of Charleston January 1, 1856. (ROC, 1821) Discharged from the High School December 17, 1857. (Minutes, December 17, 1857)

DAWSON, RICHARD. Admitted June 7, 1849 aged four years by SUSAN DAWSON, mother and the Poor House. Indentures expired January 23, 1866. (P-106) Delivered to H.F. DAWSON, unknown, July 19, 1860. (ROB, 1856)

DeBEAUGRINE, DOROTHEA. Admitted November 28, 1844 aged six years by AMELIA HEADEN, sister. Indentured to MRS. N.R. DOBSON as a domestic November 16, 1848. Indentures expired November 28, 1856. (O-104) Religion: Methodist. (AtoA)

DeBEAUGRINE, WILLIAM. Admitted November 28, 1844 aged eight years by AMELIA HEADEN, sister. Indentured to JAMES H. McINTOSH (of Society Hill, Darlington District) as a merchant November 29, 1849. Indentures expired November 28, 1857. (P-35) Religion: Methodist. (AtoA)

DeCARETER, (CARTER) ESTHER (HESTER). Admitted June 16, 1842 aged eight years by Poor House. Indentured to H. CAMINADE, occupation unknown, June 11, 1846. Indentures expired June 16, 1852. (O-90) Mother, MRS. ANN WILSON. Step-father was a mariner. (AtoA)

DeCARTER, REUBEN. Admitted June 16, 1842 aged seven years by Poor House. (P-7) Died February 20, 1846. (ROSP, February 20, 1846) "Labours under paralysis, induced by pressure of the body of the last cervical vertebra upon the medulla spinalis...when eighteen months old, a dislocation of the spine took place." (ROSP, February 20, 1845)

DEVEAUX, EDWARD SINCLAIR. Admitted May 7, 1846 aged six years by his mother and the Poor House. Indentured to CAMERON and CO. Machinists as a machinist August 6, 1855. Indentures expired May 7, 1861. (P-49) Born April 5, 1840 in the Charleston Neck. (AtoA)

DEVEAUX, THOMAS L. Admitted May 7, 1846 aged ten years by CAROLINE DEVEAUX, mother, and the Poor House. Indentures expired August 6, 1856. (P-48) Born August 6, 1835 in the Charleston Neck. (AtoA) Sent to the High School of Charleston, January 1849. (ROC, 1821) Sent to Charleston College, 1854. (COH Inmates' Files) In 1855 he signed a petition against the faculty of the College of Charleston. When he refused to relent, the Commissioners did not permit him to return. (Minutes, April 26, 1855 to June 7, 1855)

DEXTER, GEORGE. Admitted May 23, 1844 aged fourteen months by SARAH McCOLLIN, mother, and the Poor House. Indentured to N.C. SCOTT (of Whitfield County, Georgia) as a blacksmith December 3, 1857. Indentures expired March 23, 1864. (P-23) Religion: Methodist. (AtoA)

DICKS, HENRY WILEY. Admitted January 20, 1848 aged eight years by HARRIET DICKS, mother. Indentured to NIMROD STEWART (of Ninety-Six, Abbeville District), occupation unknown, November 23, 1854. Indentures expired March 1, 1860. (P-84)

DICKS, WILLIAM RUFUS. Admitted January 20, 1848 aged eleven years by HARRIET DICKS, mother, and the Poor House. Indentured to E.R. STOKES as a bookbinder November 7, 1850. Indentures expired February 26, 1858. (P-83)

DIXON, CHAPMAN. Admitted November 5, 1840 aged seven years by Poor House. Indentured to JOHN PATERSON as a boot and shoemaker September 3, 1846. Indentures expired November 5, 1854. (P-9)

DOAR, MARY. Admitted November 18, 1841 aged eleven years by Poor House. Indentured to J.H. KALB, baker, as a domestic April 24, 1845. Indentures expired November 18, 1848. (O-80)

DUNOVANT, MICHAEL. Admitted January 13, 1848 aged two years and eleven months by ANN DUNOVANT, mother, and the Poor House. Indentured to THOMAS STEIN (of Greenville) as a merchant November 7, 1861. Indentures expired February 7, 1866. (P-82)

EDEN, JOHN. Admitted October 28, 1841 aged nine years by Poor House. Delivered to his mother, nd. Indentures expired October 28, 1853.(M-130)

EGEN, GEORGE. Admitted May 27, 1841 aged five years by Poor House. (M-127) Delivered to his grandmother, MRS. MARGARET CHAMBERS, 1846. (BO) Indentures expired May 27, 1847. (M-127) Lived on Gadsden Wharf. Father, HENRY, was a common drunkard. (AtoA)

EGEN, JOHN. Admitted May 27, 1841 aged nine years by Poor House. Delivered to his grandmother, 1847. Indentures expired May 27, 1853. (M-126) Religion: Episcopalian. (AtoA)

EVANS, CATHARINE. Admitted September 19, 1844 aged four years and six months by ANN EVANS, mother and the Poor House. Indentured to WILLIAM M. REID as a domestic October 12, 1848. Indentures expired March 15, 1858. (O-100)

FEHRENBACH, JOHAN HIMRIK RICHARD. Admitted November 14, 1844 aged six years by MARY A. FEHRENBACH, mother, and the Poor House. Delivered to his parents October 30, 1845. Indentures expired November 14, 1859. (P-31) Born July 18, 1838. (AtoA)

FEHRENBACH, NIKHOLAS. Admitted September 5, 1844 aged eleven years by Poor House and his mother. Delivered to his parents October 30, 1845. Indentures expired September 5, 1854. (P-28) Father, NICKOLAS, from Baden, Germany. (AtoA)

FERRINE, WILLIAM EDWARD. Admitted December 11, 1845 aged thirteen years and four months by Poor House. Indentures expired August 27, 1853. (P-43) Born in New York. Father, PETER. Religion: Lutheran. (AtoA) Sent to the High School of Charleston. (ROC, 1821) Sent to South Carolina College. (COH Inmates' Files)

FLEISHMAN, HENRY. Admitted June 22, 1848 aged seven years by Poor House. Indentures expired June 22, 1862. (P-92) Absconded February 1853. (Minutes, April 14, 1853)

FLYNN, JAMES. Admitted March 19, 1840 aged eight years by Poor House. (M-104) Died February 23, 1847 of cancer, complicated by worms. (ROSP, February 25, 1847)

FLYNN, WILLIAM. Admitted March 19, 1840 aged ten years by Poor House. (M-103) Delivered to his grandmother March 1847. (ROSP, March 25, 1847) Indentures expired March 19, 1851. (M-103)

FORBES, WILLIAM. Admitted July 21, 1842 aged nine years by Poor House. Indentures expired July 21, 1854. (P-8) Absconded 1846. (ROC, 1821)

FOSTER, ROBERT. Admitted May 18, 1848 aged twelve years by ELIZABETH FOSTER, mother, and the Poor House. Indentures expired May 18, 1857. (P-87) Absconded, nd. (ROC, 1821)

FOURCHE (FOURCHER), JAMES. Admitted January 18, 1844 aged seven years by SUSAN FOURCHE and the Poor House. Indentures expired January 18, 1858. (P-19) Delivered to his mother July 1, 1852. (ROC, 1821) Stepfather GEORGE LYNNES. (BO) Religion: Episcopalian. (AtoA)

FOURCHE, VICTOR HENRY. Admitted January 18, 1844 aged five years by SUSAN FOURCHE, mother, and the Poor House. Indentured to ROBERT WING as a bell hanger and locksmith May 5, 1853. Indentures expired January 18, 1860. (P-20) Religion: Episcopalian. (AtoA)

FRIEND, GEORGE D. Admitted August 1, 1844 aged twelve years by Poor House. Indentures expired August 1, 1853. (P-27) Delivered to his mother January 7, 1847. (ROC, 1821) Religion: Episcopalian. (AtoA)

GALLAGHER, PHOEBE ANN. Admitted April 25, 1844 aged eleven years by Poor House. Indentured to MISS MARY JANE TAYLOR as a milliner November 18, 1847. Indentures expired April 25, 1851. (O-97)

GILBERT, ADELINE. Admitted December 23, 1841 aged eight years by ELIZABETH GILBERT, mother, and the Poor House. Indentured to MRS. SARAH CADLE, widow, (of Graniteville, Edgefield, S.C.) as a cotton manufacturer November 9, 1848. Indentures expired December 23, 1851. (O-81) Returned to the COH June 1849. (Minutes, June 14, 1849) Delivered to her mother January 24, 1850. (Minutes, January 24, 1850) Allowed fifty dollars as a marriage dowry in 1850. (Minutes, August 1, 1850)

GILBERT, JOHN WALTER. Admitted December 23, 1841 aged ten years by ELIZABETH GILBERT, mother, and the Poor House. Indentured to JAMES P. CALDWELL (of Newberry District) as a merchant November 30, 1843. Indentures expired December 23, 1852. (M-133)

GILBERT, SARAH JANE. Admitted December 23, 1841 aged twelve years by ELIZABETH GILBERT, mother, and the Poor House. Indentures expired December 23, 1847. (O-83) Delivered to her mother and step-father, PETER and ELIZABETH MANGAN, November 30, 1843. (BO)

GILBERT, STEPHEN CAPERS. Admitted December 23, 1841 aged three years by ELIZABETH GILBERT, mother. Indentures expired December 23, 1859. (P-2) Absconded July 1852. (ROC, 1821)

GILBERT, THOMAS EDWARD. Admitted December 23, 1841 aged five years by ELIZABETH GILBERT, mother. Indentured to GEORGE W. FABIAN (of St. George's, Colleton) as a farmer June 7, 1849. Indentures expired December 23, 1857. (P-1)

GRAY, HENRY D. Admitted July 15, 1841 aged three years and seven months by ISABELLA CHAPMAN, mother and the Poor House. Indentures expired December 5, 1858. (M-123) Sent to the High School of Charleston February 1852. (ROC, 1821) Sent to Charleston College, nd. (ROB, 1856) In declining health, sent to Albany, New York in 1857. (Minutes, October 8, 1857) Died, nd. (ROB, 1856) Religion: Episcopalian. (AtoA)

GRAY, JOHN L. Admitted July 15, 1841 aged four years by ISABELLA CHAPMAN, mother, and the Poor House. Indentured to JOHN RUSSELL as a bookseller May 26, 1853. Indentures expired December 5, 1858. (M-122) Religion: Episcopalian. (AtoA)

GREEN, EMILY H. Admitted September 13, 1849 aged seven years by EMILY GREEN, mother, and the Poor House. Indentures expired September 13, 1860. (R-1) Delivered to her mother, nd. (ROG, 1856)

GREEN, WILLIAM. Admitted September 13, 1849 aged nine years by EMILY E. GREEN, mother, and the Poor House. Indentures expired September 13, 1861. (Q-1) Sent to the Military Academy January 1, 1856. (ROC, 1821) Discharged for academic reasons in 1857. (Minutes, December 10, 1857)

GREEN, SARAH E. Admitted September 13, 1849 aged five years by EMILY GREEN, mother, and the Poor House. Indentures expired September 13, 1862. (R-2) Delivered to her mother, nd. (ROG, 1856)

GUTHRIE, JAMES. Admitted July 8, 1841 aged three years and six months by Poor House and his grandmother, CATHERINE KAIN. Indentures expired January 8, 1858. (M-119) Delivered to his grandmother March 6, 1845. (ROC, 1821)

GUTHRIE, WILLIAM PATRICK. Admitted July 8, 1841 aged nine years and three months by the Poor House and his grandmother, CATHERINE KAIN. Delivered to his grandmother, MRS. M. KING, 1845. Indentures expired April 8, 1853. (M-118)

HAFER, ROBERT. Admitted July 1, 1841 aged ten years by Poor House. Indentures expired July 1, 1852. (M-115) Because of his idiotism and paralysis was sent to the Poor House January 18, 1849. (Minutes, January 18, 1849)

HAFER, WILLIAM. Admitted July 1, 1841 aged seven years by Poor House. Indentured to F.H. ELMORE, W. BROWN, and W. HAMPTON, of the Nesbit Iron Works, (of Spartanburg District) as an iron worker April 8, 1847. Indentures expired July 1, 1855. (M-116)

HANNON (HANNAU), JOHN. Admitted September 20, 1849 aged two years and six months by JOHN HANNON, father, and the Poor House. Indentured to DR. O.C. RHAME as a farmer, December 11, 1862. Indentures expired March 20, 1868. (Q-3)

HAYES, JOHN (CAESAR). Admitted December 13, 1849 aged six years by Poor House. Indentured to J.S.C. MOORE (of North Carolina) as a farmer, March 24, 1859. Indentures expired December 13, 1864. (Q-10)

HEINSOATH, HARMON. Admitted September 13, 1849 aged four years by REBA HEINSOATH, mother, and the Poor House. (Q-2) Died 1850 of worms and dropsy. (ARP, 1850)

HEINSOATH (HEINSOOTH), HENRY. Admitted April 5, 1849 aged six years by his mother and the Poor House. Indentured to WILLIAM STRATTON as a baker December 9, 1858. Indentures expired April 5, 1864. (P-102)

HEINSOATH, JOHN FREDERICK. Admitted April 5, 1849 aged eight years by his mother and the Poor House. Indentured to ISHAM W. TAYLOR (of Anderson Courthouse) as a druggist February 1, 1855. Indentures expired April 5, 1862. (P-101)

HIDRICKS, MARTHA E. Admitted October 5, 1848 aged eight years by T.A. HIDRICKS, mother, and the Poor House. Indentured to JOHN BENJAMIN MORGAN as a domestic November 6, 1851. Indentures expired October 5, 1818. (O-120)

HIDRICKS, WASHINGTON THOMAS. Admitted October 5, 1848 aged ten years by T.A. HIDRICKS, mother, and the Poor House. Indentures expired October 5, 1859. (P-97) Absconded, nd. (ROC, 1821)

HITZFELDT, DOROTHEA (DORIS). Admitted May 4, 1848 aged six years by Poor House. Adopted by J.T. LISSAK, hatter, August 30, 1849. Indentures expired March 3, 1860. (O-118) Born March 3, 1842. (AtoA)

HITZFELDT, JOHN FREDERICK. Admitted May 4, 1848 aged ten years by his father and the Poor House. Indentured to JOHN BROADFOOT as a boot and shoemaker April 7, 1853. Indentures expired March 29, 1860. (P-86)

HODGE, ERASMUS. Admitted December 31, 1845 aged four years by FRANCES HODGE, mother, and the Poor House. Indentures expired December 31, 1862. (P-42) Born in St. Stephen's Parish. Religion: Methodist. (AtoA) Delivered to his father, nd. (ROC, 1821) Mother born in Georgetown; maiden name MURPHY. (AtoA)

HODGE, MARY ANNE. Admitted December 31, 1845 aged five years by FRANCES HODGE, mother, and the Poor House. Indentures expired December 31, 1858. (O-105) Born in St. Stephen's Parish. Religion: Methodist. (AtoA) Delivered to her mother, nd. (ROC, 1821)

HUTSON, JOHN. Admitted January 27, 1842. (P-4) A derelict. (AtoA) Died June 25, 1842 of dropsy (ARP, 1842) and buried in the COH Burial Ground. (ROSP, June 30, 1842)

JOHNSON, JANE. Admitted August 5, 1841 aged thirteen years by Poor House. Indentured to PETER ROTUREAU as a tailoress January 2, 1843. Indentures expired October 5, 1845. (O-76) Allowed fifty dollars as a marriage dowry in 1844. (Minutes, August 22, 1844)

KARNES, VIRGINIA. Admitted September 23, 1841 aged six months by M. COBIA, grandmother, and the Poor House. Indentured to ANDREW MILNE, planter, occupation unknown, October 30, 1845. Indentures expired March 23, 1859. (O-78) Religion: Episcopalain. Parents abandoned her. (AtoA)

KAVANEAUGH (KAVINAUGH), EDWARD. Admitted November 18, 1841 aged six years by ALICE KAVANEAUGH, mother, and the Poor House. (M-131) Died April 8, 1844 of scarlet fever and buried in the Roman Catholic Church of the Charleston Neck. (ROSP, April 11, 1844)

KENNEY, JAMES C. Admitted June 27, 1844 aged six years by Poor House and ANN KENNEY, mother. Delivered to his mother February 27, 1845 and returned April 8, 1847 upon her death. Indentured to J.E. MORGAN (of Columbia) as a printer April 11, 1850. Indentures expired June 27, 1859. (P-26) Mother born in Ireland. Religion: Church of England. Father died of yellow fever, nd. (AtoA) Step-father JOHN CURRAN. (BO) Born June 1, 1838. (Minutes, June 27, 1844)

KILROY, JAMES. Admitted December 6, 1849 aged five years by MARGARET KILROY, mother, and the Poor House. Indentured to CAMERON and CO. (CAMERON and JOHNSON) as a machinist January 6, 1859. Indentures expired December 6, 1865. (Q-9)

KILROY, JOHN. Admitted December 6, 1849 aged seven years by MARGARET KILROY, mother, and the Poor House. Indentured to CAMERON and CO. (JOHN JOHNSON and JOHN F. TAYLOR) as a machinist November 7, 1856. Indentures expired December 6, 1863. (Q-8)

KILROY, THOMAS. Admitted December 6, 1849 aged eight years by MARGARET KILROY, mother, and the Poor House. Indentured to HENRY PREGNALL as a carpenter June 7, 1855. Indentures expired December 6, 1862. (Q-7)

KIMMEY, ANN ELIZABETH. Admitted April 23, 1840 aged eleven years by ELIZABETH KIMMEY, mother. Delivered to her mother January 23, 1842. Indentures expired April 23, 1847. (O-67) Born in Georgetown. Religion: Methodist. (AtoA)

KIMMEY, AUGUSTUS ABRAHAM. Admitted May 25, 1843 aged seven years by A. KIMMEY, mother, and the Poor House. Born May 16, 1837. Father, JOHN. Indentures expired May 25, 1857. (P-15) Delivered to his sister, ELIZA F. KIMMEY, September 23, 1852. (BO)

KIMMEY, ELIZA. Admitted January 9, 1840 aged ten years by Poor House. Delivered to her mother March 22, 1844. Returned to the COH August 22, 1844. Indentured to ANNA COE (of Newport, Rhode Island) as a domestic July 19, 1845. Indentures expired January 9, 1848. (O-66) Allowed fifty dollars because of her illness in Providence, Rhode Island. (Minutes, October 2, 1848) Married JOHN GILL, a journeyman carpenter, in January.

KIMMEY, JAMES. Admitted January 9, 1840 aged four years by Poor House. Indentured to JOHN P. GILL as a carpenter November 8, 1849. Indentures expired January 9, 1857. (M-91) While living in Atchinson, Kansas he requested aid which was refused. (Minutes, October 9, 1856)

KIMMEY, JOHN. Admitted January 9, 1840 aged seven years by Poor House. Indentured to WILLIAM F. DURISOE (DORISOE), by his attorney, W. RILEY, (of Edgefield) as a printer July 20, 1843. Indentures expired January 9, 1853. (M-90)

KING, ELEANOR. Admitted October 3, 1844 aged two years by Poor House. Indentures expired October 3, 1860. (O-101) Mother, "a dumb person" now in the Poor House. (AtoA) Became a COH teacher. Died February 5, 1917. (ROG, 1856)

KING, MARY, (ETEELIA). Admitted January 23, 1840 aged nine years by Poor House. Indentured to J. CLAUDIUES MILLER as a domestic May 14, 1846. Indentures expired January 23, 1849. (O-70) Admitted by order of H.L. PINCKNEY, Mayor. (AtoA) Allowed fifty dollars as a marriage dowry to FREDERICK KREMER in 1849. (Minutes, February 22, 1849)

KNAPP, MARY FRANCIS. Admitted February 1, 1849 aged twelve years by Poor House and F. KNAPP, mother. Indentures expired February 1, 1855. (O-121) Delivered to her mother January 22, 1852. (ROC, 1821)

KRUM, CAROLINE. Admitted June 9, 1842 aged three years and ten months by CAROLINE KRUM, mother. Indentures expired August 9, 1856. (O-88) Delivered to MRS. JOHN HARRISON (of Winnsborough, Fairfield District), occupation unknown, February 8, 1844. (ROSP, March 7, 1844) Religion: Catholic. (AtoA)

KRUM, JOSEPHINE. Admitted June 9, 1842 aged two years and ten months by CAROLINE KRUM, mother. Indentured to JESSIE P. FOWLER as a milliner May 1, 1856. Indentures expired December 9, 1857. (O-89) Religion: Catholic. (AtoA)

LAWLER, MATTHEW O. Admitted April 15, 1841 aged ten years by the Poor House. Indentured to WILLIAM H. GRUVER (GRUVER) as a plasterer August 15, 1844. Indentures expired April 15, 1852. (M-110) Born in Savannah. Religion: Catholic. (AtoA)

LEGGETT, JOHN. Admitted October 11, 1849 aged four years by JOHN PATTERSON, unknown, and the Poor House. Indentures expired October 11, 1866. (Q-6) No further information.

LENOX, RICHARD. Admitted July 30, 1840 aged two years by A. HUBBARD, mother, and the Poor House. (M-99) Indentured to C. CANNING of the Southern Christian Advocate as a printer March 4, 1852. (BO) Indentures expired July 30, 1859. (M-99)

McCABE, GEORGE ADAM. Admitted February 15, 1849 aged three years by SUSAN McCABE, mother, and the Poor House. (P-100) Died September 3, 1850 of worm fever. (ARP, 1850)

McCABE, LOUISA. Admitted February 15, 1849 aged two years by SUSAN McCABE, mother, and the Poor House. Indentured to MRS. MARY TREZEVANT (of Mineral Spring, Florida), occupation unknown, September 26, 1850. Indentures expired February 15, 1865. (O-123)

McCABE, SARAH ANN. Admitted February 15, 1849 aged six years by SUSAN McCABE, mother, and the Poor House. Indentures expired February 15, 1861. (O-122) Delivered to her mother January 12, 1859. (BO)

McGINNIS, PATRICK. Admitted January 9, 1840 aged nine years by Poor House. Indentures expired January 9, 1852. (M-92) No further information.

McINTYRE, JOHN. Admitted November 25, 1840 aged two years by Poor House. Indentures expired November 25, 1860. (M-132) Absconded, 1850. (ROC, 1821) "Absconded for the third or fourth time in March." (Minutes, April 14, 1853)

McINTYRE, JULIA. Admitted October 1, 1840 aged six years by Poor House. Indentured to JAMES H. ANDERSON (of Hamburgh, Edgefield District) as a domestic August 13, 1846. Indentures expired October 1, 1852. (O-71)

McINTYRE, LOUISA. Admitted October 1, 1840 aged four years by MARY McINTYRE, unknown, and the Poor House. Indentures expired October 1, 1854. (O-72) Delivered to her mother, nd. (ROC, 1821) Suffered from epilepsy. (ROSP, April 25, 1844)

McKENZIE, JAMES L. Admitted April 29, 1841 aged eight years by Poor House. Indentures expired April 29, 1852. (M-111) Delivered to his mother, MRS. CAMMER, January 25, 1844. (ROSP, February 1, 1844)

McKENZIE, JOHN W. Admitted April 29, 1841 aged four years by Poor House. Indentures expired April 29, 1858. (M-112) Delivered to his mother March 24, 1842. (BO)

McNICHOLAS, DOMINIQUE. Admitted December 14, 1843 aged three years by BRIDGET McNICHOLAS, mother, and the Poor House. Indentured to DR. JOHN S. WEAR, a physician, (of Columbia) for adoption December 6, 1849. Indentures expired December 14, 1861. (P-22)

MACBETH, CHARLES (JAMES). Admitted May 14, 1840 aged three years by
MRS. HERRON, sister, and the Poor House. Indentures expired May 14,
1858. (M-96) Mother a lunatic and the father deserted the child.
(Minutes, May 14, 1840)

MAGINNIS, MARY DUNN. Admitted December 20, 1849 aged seventeen months
by JAMES MAGINNIS, father, and the Poor House. (R-2) Mother in the
Lunatic Asylum of the Poor Hospital. (AtoA) Died August 29, 1850 of
Marasmus. (ARP, 1850)

MANNING, ELIZABETH. Admitted February 11, 1847 aged ten years by
Poor House. Indentured to DR. EZRA M. GREGG (of Sumter District) as
a domestic November 30, 1848. Indentures expired February 11, 1855.
(O-109) Transferred to REV. MOULTRIE REID, occupation unknown, November
22, 1849. (BO)

MANNING, JAMES. Admitted February 11, 1847 aged six years by MRS. ANN
M. HENRY, aunt, and the Poor House. Indentured to AUGUST IUSTI (JUSTI)
as a black and locksmith December 19, 1850. Indentures expired February
11, 1862. (P-64)

MILLER, JESSEY. Admitted October 7, 1847 aged four years by PRISCILLA
MILLER, mother, and the Poor House. Indentures expired October 7, 1864.
(P-81) Delivered to his mother, nd. (ROB, 1856)

MILLER, JOHN BRADFORD. Admitted October 7, 1847 aged eleven years by
PRISCILLA MILLER, mother, and the Poor House. Indentured to JAMES P.
ROBERTS as a shoe store worker July 18, 1850. Indentures expired
October 7, 1857. (P-80)

MILLER, MARY. Admitted October 7, 1847 aged nine years by PRISCILLA
MILLER, mother, and Poor House. Indentures expired October 7, 1856.
(O-117) Delivered to her mother, MRS. P.A. WANNAMAKER, November 3,
1853. (BO)

MOOD, MARGARET. Admitted December 7, 1843 aged four months. Indentures
expired August 2, 1861. (O-96) Delivered to her mother, nd. (ROC, 1821)

MORRIS, CAROLINE. Admitted January 12, 1843 aged twelve years by Poor
House. Indentured to REV. C.W. HOWARD as a nurse and seamtress January
15, 1846. Indentures expired January 12, 1849. (O-93) Allowed fifty
dollars as a marriage dowry in 1860. (Minutes, May 3, 1860) Born in
Goose Creek. Religion: Episcopalian. (AtoA)

MULLEN, MICHAEL. Admitted May 3, 1849 aged zen years by ANN DONOHOE,
mother, and the Poor House. Indentured to JAMES B. RANDALL (of
Marietta, Georgia) as a printer November 3, 1853. Indentures expired
May 3, 1860. (P-104)

MULLEN, (MULLENS), JOHN. Admitted October 22, 1841 aged eighteen months
by Poor House. (M-129) Died April 15, 1842 of Marasmus. (ARP, 1842)

MULLEN (MULLENS), MATTHEW. Admitted October 22, 1841 aged three years
by Poor House. Indentured to JOHN VINYARD HOLMES as a gunsmith
November 7, 1850. Indentures expired October 22, 1859. (M-128)

MURPHY, WILLIAM HENRY. Admitted June 18, 1846 aged eight years by M.
MURPHY, mother. Indentured to RICHARD ARNOLD as a blacksmith May 5,
1853. Indentures expired June 18, 1859. (P-52)

MURRAY, HENRY. Admitted May 18, 1848 aged seven years by his mother and
the Poor House. Indentures expired May 18, 1862. (P-88) Mother, SUSAN.
Born in St. Stephen's Parish. Religion: Methodist. Lived at the
corner of Clifford and King Streets. (AtoA) Absconded, February 1853.
(Minutes, April 14, 1853)

NELSON, ELIZA ANN. Admitted June 8, 1843 aged eight years by Poor
House. Indentured to WILLIAM SHAW (of Sumter District) as a domestic
November 30, 1846. Indentures expired June 8, 1853. (O-94)

NELSON, EMILY CHRISTINA. Admitted May 3, 1849 aged ten years by Poor House. Indentures expired January 3, 1857. (O-125) Indentured to ROBERT ADGER, occupation unknown, nd. (ROC, 1821)

NELSON, JAMES. Admitted February 12, 1846 aged seven years and four months by MRS. SUSAN KIRK, mother, and the Poor House. (P-46) Indentured to EDWARD ALPHONSO BRONSON (of Barnwell District) as a printer January 28, 1853. Indentures expired October 12, 1859. (P-46) Religion: Methodist. Mother's first husband, JOHN NELSON, died in 1840. Her second husband, ROBERT KIRK, deserted her. (AtoA) Absconded to his mother who lived on Radcliffe Street in August 1855. (BO)

NICHOLAS, JOSEPH (also NICHOLAS JOSEPH). Admitted April 24, 1845 aged ten years by J.E. PASSAEILAGUE, unknown. Indentures expired April 24, 1856. (P-41) Absconded 1846. (ROC, 1821)

O'DWYER, ALEXANDER. Admitted June 7, 1849 aged two years and six months by ANN O'DWYER, mother, and the Poor House. Indentured to WILLIAM F. PADDON as a gas fitter September 10, 1864. Indentures expired December 7, 1867. (P.110)

O'DWYER, MARY ANN. Admitted June 7, 1849 aged four years by ANN O'DWYER, mother, and the Poor House. Indentures expired June 7, 1863. (O-129) Father, DENNIS O'DWYER. (Minutes, May 31, 1849) "Left." (ROG, 1856)

O'DWYER, THOMAS. Admitted June 7, 1849 aged six years by ANN O'DWYER, mother, and the Poor House. Indentured to D.O. HAWTHORNE (of Due-West, Abbeville District) as a merchant, April 10, 1857. Indentures expired June 7, 1864. (P-109)

O'NEILL, CHARLES CALHOUN. Admitted May 1, 1845 aged eight years by M.M. O'NEILL, mother, and the Poor House. Indentures expired May 1, 1858. (P-38) Born in New York. Religion: Baptist. (AtoA) Delivered to his mother November 26, 1846. (ROC, 1821)

O'NEILL, ROBERT JAMES. Admitted May 1, 1845 aged ten years by M.M. O'NEILL, mother, and the Poor House. Delivered to his mother November 26, 1846. Indentures expired May 1, 1856. (P-37) Born in New York. Religion: Baptist. (AtoA)

PERRY, JANE. Admitted January 28, 1847 aged ten years by Poor House. Indentured to G.W. OLNEY as a domestic January 24, 1850. Indentures expired January 1, 1855. (O-108)

POLSON, HESTER. Admitted September 7, 1843 aged ten years by Poor House. Indentured to JOHN HILL as a domestic November 13, 1845. Transferred to S.S. BROWNE, occupation unknown, August 22, 1846. Transferred to ISAAC HIBBES, occupation unknown, May 13, 1848. Indentures expired September 7, 1851. (O-95)

PRINCE, CHARLES JOSEPH. Admitted March 14, 1844 aged thirteen years and seven months by the Poor House. Indentured to WILLIAM M. DAVIS (of Sumter District) as a farmer December 31, 1845. Indentures expired August 29, 1851. (F-21)

PUCKMYER, MARTHA. Admitted November 14, 1844 aged six years by NORA PUCKMYER, mother, and the Poor House. Indentured to MARY JANE TAYLOR as a milliner January 13, 1848. Indentured expired November 14, 1856. (O-102) Born in Ireland. Religion: Catholic. (AtoA)

PURSE, ELIZA. Admitted June 18, 1840 aged nineteen months by Poor House. Indentures expired November 19, 1856. Delivered to her mother, LOUISA PURSE, March 11, 1841. (BO)

PURSE, SARAH. Admitted June 18, 1840 aged four years by Poor House. Indentures expired June 18, 1854. (O-68) Delivered to her mother, LOUISA PURSE, March 11, 1841. (BO)

QUINBY, ABIGAIL PEARSON. Admitted July 8, 1841 aged six years by FRANCES QUINBY, mother, and the Poor House. Indentures expired July 8, 1853. (O-75) Delivered to her mother, nd. (ROC, 1821)

QUINBY, BENJAMIN. Admitted July 8, 1841 aged nine years by FRANCES QUINBY, mother. Indentures expired July 8, 1853. (M-120) Delivered to DANIEL and FRANCES WELLS, parents, 1846. (BO)

QUINBY, EDWIN JOSEPH. Admitted March 16, 1843 aged two years and four months by Poor House. Indentures expired November 16, 1861. (P-10) Religion: Circular Congregational Church. AtoA) Delivered to his step-father, DANIEL WELLS, April 26, 1855. (ROC, 1821)

QUINBY, JAMES RODYMIAN. Admitted July 8, 1841 aged three years by FRANCES QUINBY, mother. Indentured to JAMES MARLOW (of Selma, Alabama) as a druggist and apothecary July 28, 1853. Transferred to GEORGE F. MARLOW (brother of JAMES), occupation unknown, August 5, 1853. Indentures expired July 8, 1859. (M-121)

QUINBY, SUSANNAH ADLER. Admitted October 14, 1841 aged eleven years by FRANCES QUINBY, mother. Delivered to her aunt, MRS. S.C. WHITE (of Georgetown) April 6, 1843. Indentures expired October 14, 1848. (O-79) Allowed fifty dollars as a marriage dowry to J.W. COLLINS in 1846. (Minutes, August 6, 1846) Admitted from the Poor House. (AtoA)

RATCLIFFE, ARCHIBALD. Admitted March 3, 1842 aged nine years by Poor House. Indentured to S.S. SOLOMONS (of the North Eastern Railroad Co.) occupation unknown, October 21, 1858. Indentures expired February 22, 1853. (P-12)

REARDON, JOHN. Admitted September 28, 1848 aged three years by JANE REARDON, mother, and the Poor House. (P-95) Indentured to WILLIAM M. THOMAS an attorney, (of Greenville District) as a clerk in his office December 29, 1859. (BO) Indentures expired September 28, 1866. (P-95)

REARDON, ROBERT. Admitted September 28, 1848 aged two years by JANE REARDON, mother, and the Poor House. Indentured to F.P. SEIGNIOUS as a farmer October 5, 1860. Indentures expired September 28, 1867. (P-96)

REDDING, MARY JANE. Admitted June 1, 1848 aged three years by ELIZA REDDING, mother, and the Poor House. Indentures expired June 1, 1863. (O-119) Delivered to her mother January 31, 1850. (ROC, 1821)

REILLY (RILEY), JOHN. Admitted September 30, 1847 aged four years by Poor House. Indentured to ARCHIBALD CAMPBELL, editor and printer, as a printer September 25, 1856. Indentures expired September 30, 1864. (P-77)

REILLY, MARY ANN. Admitted September 30, 1847 aged eight years by Poor House. Indentured to ARCHIBALD CAMPBELL as a domestic November 22, 1855. Indentures expired September 30, 1857. (O-115)

REILLY, PATRICK. Admitted September 30, 1847 aged two years and six months by the Poor House. Indentured to CHARLES H. HANCOCK (of Americus, Georgia) as a printer February 11, 1858. Indentures expired March 30, 1866. (P-78)

REILLY, WILLIAM. Admitted September 30, 1847 aged six years by the Poor House. Born April 22, 1839 in Liverpool, England. Indentured to JAMES B. RANDALL (of Marietta, Georgia) as a printer November 3, 1853. Indentures expired September 30, 1862. (P-76)

RICHTER, ANGELINA. Admitted August 5, 1841 aged two years and six months by the Poor House. (O-77) Died March 16, 1842 of a gangrenous ulcer of the mouth and buried in the COH Burial Ground. (ROSP, March 17, 1842) Born during passage from Germany. Her parents deserted her. (AtoA)

RIGGS, ISAAC DeLEON HAYNE. Admitted November 5, 1846 aged eight years by MRS. M.L. RIGGS, mother, and the Poor House. Delivered to his mother May 1850. Indentures expired July 18, 1859. (P-58)

RIGGS, LANGDON CHEVES. Admitted November 5, 1846 aged two years by MRS. R.L. RIGGS, mother, and the Poor House. Indentured to S.A. LYON (Of Donaldsville) as a merchant December 16, 1858. Returned to the COH June 9, 1859. Indentures expired December 15, 1865. (P-60) Transferred to JAMES McINDOO as a baker August 10, 1859. (BO) Absconded, nd. (ROC, 1821)

RIGGS, THOMAS LEHRE. Admitted November 5, 1846 aged six years by MRS. R.L. RIGGS, mother, and the Poor House. Indentures expired October 1, 1861. (P-59) Absconded, nd. (ROC, 1821)

RIGGS, WILLIAM BAILEY. Admitted November 5, 1846 aged ten years by MRS. R.L. RIGGS, mother, and the Poor House. Indentured to R.T. RIGGS, brother-in-law as a farmer March 15, 1849. Indentures expired September 6, 1857. (P-57)

ROACH, JOHN. Admitted July 15, 1847 aged five years by MARIA ROACH, unknown, and the Poor House. Indentures expired July 15, 1863. (P-71) Delivered to his mother August 22, 1850. (ROC, 1821)

ROACH, THOMAS. Admitted July 15, 1847 aged three years by MARIA ROACH, unknown, and the Poor House. Indentures expired July 15, 1865. (P-72) Delivered to his mother August 22, 1850. (ROC, 1821)

ROSS, ANNA MARIA (ETELIA).Admitted May 12, 1842 aged six years and nine months by the Poor House. Born August 15, 1835. Indentured to SARAH CADLE, widow, (of Graniteville, Edgefield, S.C.) as a cotton manufacturer November 9, 1848. Indentures expired August 15, 1853. (O-87) Returned to the Orphan House because of the ill-health of Mrs. Cadle and delivered to her mother and brother 1850. (Minutes, January 24, 1850) Born in Columbia. Religion: Episcopalian. (AtoA) Allowed fifty dollars as a marriage dowry 1855. (Minutes, November 15, 1855)

RUTLAND, JOSEPH. Admitted March 19, 1841 aged nine years by MARY RUTLAND, mother, and the Poor House. Indentured to MARTIN E. MUNRO, editor and proprietor of a daily newspaper, as a printer September 3, 1846. Indentures expired March 19, 1853. (M-108)

RUTLAND, LEWIS. Admitted March 19, 1841 aged five years and six months by the Poor House. Indentured to MARTIN MUNRO as a printer November 19, 1846. Indentures expired September 19, 1856. (M-109)

RUTLAND, WILLIAM H. Admitted January 20, 1842 aged thirteen years and eight months by the Poor House. (P-3) Delivered to his aunt and uncle, ELIZABETH and LUKE P. SWAIN, (of North Carolina), September 8, 1842. (BO) Indentures expired May 19, 1849. (P-3)

RYAN, AUGUSTUS K. Admitted July 22, 1846 aged eleven years by JULIA A. RYAN, mother, and the Poor House. Indentured to W.F. JONES (of Rutherford County, North Carolina) as a merchant May 9, 1850. Indentures expired July 22, 1856. (P-53)

RYAN, GEORGE K. Admitted July 22, 1846 aged nine years by JULIA K. RYAN, mother, and the Poor House. Indentured to HENRY S. TEW (of Mount Pleasant in Christ Church Parish) as a merchant March 31, 1853. Indentures expired July 22, 1858. (P-54)

RYAN, THEODORE. Admitted July 22, 1846 aged seven years by JULIA RYAN, mother, and the Poor House. Indentures expired July 22, 1860. (P-55) Delivered to his mother April 26, 1855. (P-55)

SCOTT, JAMES STEPHEN. Admitted March 6, 1845 aged nine years by REBECCA SCOTT, mother, and the Poor House. Indentures expired March 6, 1857. (P-36) Absconded, March 12, 1846. (ROSP, March 12, 1846) Delivered to his mother, nd. (ROC, 1821)

SHAW, JAMES. Admitted January 2, 1840 aged four years by Poor House. (M-89) Indentured to D.H. POOL (POOLE) (of Sumpter District), uncle, to be educated May 4, 1843. Indentures expired January 2, 1857. (M-87) Religion: Episcopalian. (AtoA)

SHECUT, FRANCIS. Admitted June 27, 1844 aged five years by his mother and the Poor House. Indentures expired June 27, 1860.(P25) Born July 23, 1839. (Minutes, June 27, 1844) Born in Georgetown. Religion: Methodist. (AtoA) Delivered to his parents, MARY and WILLIAM SHECUT, who lived on King Street opposite Ann Street. (BO)

SHECUT, WILLIAM. Admitted July 27, 1844 aged seven years by his mother and the Poor House. Indentures expired June 27, 1858. (P-24) Born December 25, 1837. (Minutes, July 27, 1844) Religion: Methodist. (AtoA) Delivered to his parents, WILLIAM and MARY SHECUT, nd. (BO)

SILCOX, JOSEPH. Admitted June 14, 1849 aged ten years by MARIA SILCOX, mother, and the Poor House. Placed aboard the U.S. Cutter Crawford, September __, 1849. Indentures expired June 14, 1860. (P-108)

SILCOX, MARIA L. Admitted June 14, 1849 aged three years by L. SILCOX, mother, and the Poor House. (O-128) Died April 1854. (ROC, 1821)

SIMMS, AMELIA JANE. Admitted May 6, 1847 aged nine years. Indentured to WILLIAM BLANDING, occupation unknown, November 24, 1853. Indentures expired May 6, 1856. (O-111) Allowed sixty dollars as a marriage dowry 1856. (Minutes, June 17, 1856)

SIMMS, WILLIAM. Admitted May 6, 1847 aged three years by the Poor House. Indentured to GEORGE CAULIER as a druggist April 29, 1858. Indentures expired May 6, 1865. (P-69)

STREATTON, GEORGE. Admitted April 12, 1849 aged nine years by ANN CASKINS, mother, and the Poor House. Indentures expired April 12, 1861. (P-103) Abducted by his mother May 5, 1850. (ROC, 1821)

STREATTON, JULIA. Admitted April 12, 1849 aged eleven years by ANN CASKINS, mother, and the Poor House. Indentures expired April 12, 1856. (O-124) Abducted by her mother January 5, 1850. (ROC, 1821)

STREET, CAROLINE MARTHA. Admitted December 2, 1841 aged nine years by Poor House. Indentured to ROBERT CUNNINGHAM as a domestic October 5, 1848. Indentures expired December 2, 1850. (O-82) Born in New York State. (AtoA)

TAYLOR, MARY JANE. Admitted March 4, 1841 aged eleven years by the Poor House. Indentured to BENJAMIN F. SMITH, a merchant, as a domestic November 14, 1844. Indentures expired March 4, 1848. (O-74) After her marriage to MR. WOODALL, she requested fifty dollars "to assist them in an establishment which they were about to make in the City for their future." (Minutes, February 7, 1850)

UDALL, ANDREW. Admitted June 29, 1848 aged two years and six months by MINA UDALL, mother, and the Poor House. Delivered to J.H. HOLLY, occupation unknown, June 14, 1849. Indentures expired December 29, 1866. (ROC, 1821)

UDALL, JACOB. Admitted June 29, 1848 aged one year and three months by MINA UDALL, mother, and the Poor House. Indentures expired March 29, 1868. (P-94) Delivered to J.H. HOLLY, occupation unknown, June 14, 1849. (ROC, 1821)

UDALL, MARGARET. Admitted July 22, 1847 aged six years by the Poor House. Indentured to CHARLES E. BAKER, occupation unknown, January 1, 1857. Indentures expired July 22, 1859. (O-114) Her aunt, MRS. CAROLINE BUCHANAN, stated she was born February 10, 1842 at 7:00 in the evening. Religion: Protestant. An orphan. (AtoA)

VANTINE, PHOEBE ANN. Admitted December 1, 1842 aged four years by the Poor House. (O-92) Died January 16, 1845 of Marasmus. (ARP, 1845)

WALDEN, JACOB. Admitted March 9, 1848 aged eight years and two months by RACHEL WALDEN, mother, and the Poor House. Indentures expired January 19, 1861. (P-85) Delivered to his mother June 15, 1848. (ROC, 1821)

WALLACE, JULIUS. Admitted February 26, 1846 aged five years by the Poor House. Indentures expired February 26, 1846 (P-45) Delivered to his mother March 22, 1849. (ROC, 1821) Grandmother ANN WALLACE. (AtoA)

WALLACE, PETER M. Admitted February 26, 1846 aged ten years by the Poor House. Indentures expired February 26, 1857. (P-44) Absconded, February 1849 (ROC, 1821) Grandmother ANN WALLACE. (AtoA)

WARD, THOMAS JEFFERSON. Admitted June 23, 1843 aged three years and one month by the Poor House. Indentures expired March 23, 1861. (P-11) Admitted from the Poor House. (AtoA) Delivered to his mother, MARY WARD, December 5, 1844. (ROC, 1821)

WHITE, CATHERINE ANN. Admitted April 28, 1842 aged six years by MARTHA WHITE, mother, and the Poor House. (O-85) Born St. Thomas Parish. Religion: Presbyterian. (AtoA) Died March 25, 1844 of scarlet fever and buried in the COH Burial Ground. (ROSP, March 28, 1844)

WHITE ELIZA JANE. Admitted April 28, 1842 aged four years by MARTHA WHITE, mother. Delivered to her mother, MRS. LEOPOLD, June 13, 1844. Indentures expired April 28, 1856. (O-86) Born in St. Thomas Parish. Religion: Presbyterian. (AtoA)

WHITE, MARY ANN. Admitted April 28, 1842 aged eight years by MARTHA WHITE, mother. Indentures expired April 28, 1852. (O-84) Delivered to her mother, MARTHA LEOPOLD, June 13, 1844. Step-father, JOHN LEOPOLD, a fireman on the railroad. (Minutes, June 13, 1844) Born in St. Thomas Parish. Religion: Presbyterian. (AtoA)

WILLIAMS, HENRY. Admitted July 30, 1840 aged six years by DORCAS WILLIAMS, mother, and the Poor House. Indentured to DR. F.W. SYMMES (of Pendleton, Anderson District) as a printer June 11, 1846. Transferred to FRANCIS BUIST, occupation unknown, April 6, 1848. Indentures expired July 30, 1855. (M-98) Religion: Methodist. (AtoA)

WILLIAMS, JAMES. Admitted July 13, 1840 aged eleven years by DORCAS WILLIAMS, mother. Indentured to W.L. GRAHAM (of Ripley, Joppah County, Mississippi) as a merchant October 19, 1843. Indentures expired July 30, 1850. (M-97) Religion: Methodist. (AtoA)

WINGATE, ELIAS. Admitted July 15, 1847 aged four years by MARTHA WINGATE, mother, and the Poor House. Indentures expired July 15, 1864. (P-74) Delivered to his mother January 31, 1850. (ROC, 1821)

WINGATE, JOSEPH. Admitted July 15, 1847 aged eight years by MARTHA WINGATE, unknown, and the Poor House. Indentures expired July 15, 1860. (P-73) Delivered to his mother January 31, 1850. (ROC, 1821)

WINGATE, MARTHA. Admitted July 15, 1847 aged seven years by MARTHA WINGATE, mother, and the Poor House. Indentures expired July 15, 1858. (O-112) Delivered to her mother January 31, 1850. (ROC, 1821)

WINGATE, SARAH. Admitted July 15, 1847 aged seven years by MARTHA WINGATE, mother, and the Poor House. Indentures expired July 15, 1858. (O-113) Delivered to her mother January 31, 1850. (ROC, 1821)

WOOD, FRANCIS. Admitted October 3, 1844 aged thirteen years by his father, FRANCIS W. WOOD, and the Poor House. AtoA) Indentured to LOUIS H. DADIN as a silversmith and jeweller October 8, 1846. Indentures expired October 3, 1852. (P-29)

WOOD, JAMES. Admitted May 29, 1845 aged five years and six months by JANE WOOD, mother and the Poor House. Indentured to WELCH and HARRIS (SAMUEL B. WELCH and HIRAM HARRIS) as a bookbinder March 15, 1855. Indentures expired November 29, 1860. (P-40) Born in Sacket's Harbor, New York. Religion: Protestant. (AtoA)

WOOD, WILLIAM. Admitted October 3, 1844 aged nine years by FRANCIS W. WOODS, father, and the Poor House. (AtoA) Indentured to W.F. SIMMONS as a painter July 1, 1848. Indentures expired October 3, 1856. (P-30) Religion: Methodist. (AtoA)

YATES, AMELIA. Admitted November 26, 1846 aged six years by the Poor House. Indentures expired November 26, 1858. (O-107) Elected Assistant Teacher December 4, 1856. (Minutes, December 4, 1856) Married WILLIAM W. REILEY, a former inmate (Q-32), January 2, 1866. (Minutes, January 4, 1866)

YATES, JOHN. Admitted November 26, 1846 aged four years by the Poor House. Indentured to N.G. KNAUFF (of Pendleton, S.C.) as a cabinetmaker April 16, 1859. Indentures expired November 26, 1863. (P-63)

ADCOCK, CAROLINE. Admitted December 10, 1857 aged four years by JANE ADCOCK, mother. (U-107) Died August 11, 1860. (ROG, 1856)

ANDES, CONSTAND. Admitted December 8, 59 aged three years and six months by the Poor House. Delivered to his uncle, unknown, March 22, 1860. Indentures expired June 8, 1856. (ROB, 1856)

ANDREWS, GEORGE THOMAS. Admitted February 15, 1855 aged nine years and four months by JANE L. ANDREWS, mother. Born October 29, _____, in New Jersey. (AtoA) Indentured to DAVID JENNINGS as a saddler August 23, 1860. Indentures expired October 29, 1866. (S-34)

ARNOLD, JOHN. Admitted April 10, 1856 aged nine years. Indentures expired April 10, 1868. (S-93) Delivered to his mother November 27, 1863. (ROB, 1856) Father Methodist and mother Roman Catholic. (AtoA)

ARNOLD, WILLIAM. Admitted April 10, 1856 aged eleven years by ANN ARNOLD, mother. Indentured to B.G. HAPPOLDS as a gunsmith December 15, 1859. Indentures expired April 10, 1866. (S-92) Transferred to E. MERKER as a blacksmith June 20, 1860. (BO)

ATKINSON, JAMES. Admitted December 23, 1852 aged ten years and six months by the Poor House. Indentures expired June 23, 1863. (Q-75) Absconded, 1854. (ROC, 1821) Father in the Poor House. Formerly a fireman on the railroad, suffered from palsy. (AtoA)

ATKINSON WASHINGTON. Admitted December 23, 1852 aged eight years by the Poor House. Indentured to A. PUDIGON as a gardner February 2, 1860. Indentures expired December 23, 1865. (Q-76)

ATKINSON, WILLIAM. Admitted December 23, 1852 aged four years by the Poor House. Indentured to E.A. BRONSON as a printer November 15, 1866. Indentures expired December 23, 1869. (Q-77)

AYER, HENRY. Admitted April 5, 1855 aged three years by SUSAN A. AYER, mother. Indentures expired April 5, 1873. (S-42) Delivered to his grandmother, unknown, nd. (ROB, 1856) Religion: Methodist. Born in South Carolina. (AtoA)

AYER, MARTHA. Admitted April 5, 1855 aged seven years by SUSAN A. AYER, mother. Indentures expired April 5, 1866. (R-70) Delivered to her mother April 10, 1857. (ROG, 1856) Religion: Methodist. Born in South Carolina. (AtoA)

AYER, WILLIAM. Admitted April 5, 1855 aged four years by SUSAN A. AYER, mother. Indentures expired April 5, 1872. (S-41) Delivered to his grandmother, unknown, nd. (ROB, 1856) Religion: Methodist. Born in South Carolina. AtoA)

BAGLEY, CHARLES. Admitted April 10, 1857 aged five years by MARY BAGLEY, mother. (S-124) Died September 9, 18__. (ROB, 1856)

BAGLEY, MICHAEL. Admitted November 29, 1855 aged five years, ten months and thirteen days by MARY COSTELL BAGLEY, mother. Born January 16, 1850. (S-60) Died February 17, 1859. (ROB, 1856) Mother was born in Ireland. Married MICHAEL BAGLEY, a bookkeeper in Utica, New York. Father died in New Orleans of yellow fever about 1852. (AtoA)

BAHR, CATHARINE. Admitted March 18, 1858 aged seven years by CAROLINE BAHR, mother. Indentures expired March 18, 1869. (U-129) Delivered to her mother, nd. (ROG, 1856)

BAHR, ELIZA. Admitted May 5, 1859 aged five years by JULIA BAHR, unknown. Indentures expired May 5, 1875. (U-197) "Not in House." (ROG, 1856)

BAHR, FRANCIS HENRY. Admitted May 5, 1859 aged seven years by JULIA BAHR, unknown. Absconded, nd. Indentures expired May 5, 1873. (T-166)

BAHR, REBECCA. Admitted March 18, 1858 aged nine years by CAROLINE BAHR, mother. Indentured to J.A. ENGLEBACK as a domestic and storekeeper February 27, 1862. Indentures expired September 1, 1865. (corrected)

BAHR, WILLIAM. Admitted June 2, 1859 aged four years by CAROLINE BAHR, mother. Indentures expired June 2, 1876. (T-171) Delivered to his mother September 22, 1864. (ROB, 1856)

BARKERDING, ADOLPH. Admitted July 10, 1851 aged four years by H. MILLER, father-in-law. Indentures expired July 10, 1868. (Q-40) Delivered to his mother, 1852. (ROC, 1821) Religion: Lutheran. (AtoA)

BARKERDING, DOROTHEA (DORIS). Admitted July 10, 1851 aged six years by H. MILLER, father-in-law, and the Poor House. Indentures expired July 10, 1863. (R-16) Delivered to her mother, nd. (ROC, 1821) Born in Germany. Religion: Lutheran. (AtoA)

BARNO, JULIA ANN. Admitted April 27, 1854 aged five years by Poor House. Indentures expired April 27, 1867. (R-58) Delivered to her sister, MRS. ELIZABETH PRINTICO of 48 Queen Street, August 10, 1863. (BO)

BARNO (BARINO), PRISCILLA ELIZABETH. Admitted April 27, 1854 aged nine years by Poor House. Indentured to M.A. JORDAN (of Cheraw, South Carolina) as a milliner April 1, 1858. Indentures expired April 27, 1863. (R-57) Delivered to her mother April 25, 1858. (ROG, 1856)

BENNETT, CATHARINE. Admitted November 29, 1855 aged nine years by MARTHA BENNETT, mother. Indentures expired November 29, 1864. (R-95) Delivered to her mother November 10, 1860. (ROG, 1856)

BENNETT, HENRY ALEXANDER. Admitted May 22, 1857 aged seven years by THERESA A. BENNETT, mother. Indentures expired May 22, 1871. (S-135) Delivered to his mother, nd. (ROB, 1856)

BENNETT, HENRIETTA. Admitted November 29, 1855 aged seven years by MARTHA BENNETT, mother, and the Poor House. Indentures expired November 29, 1866. (R-96) Delivered to her mother, MRS. COX of Georgetown, November 10, 1860. (BO)

BENNETT, JAMES. Admitted May 22, 1857 aged ten years by THERESA A. BENNETT, mother. "Given to his mother from quarentin" nd. Indentures expired May 22, 1868. (S-134)

BENNETT, LAURA. Admitted November 29, 1855 aged six years by MARTHA BENNETT, mother, and the Poor House. Indentures expired November 29, 1867. (R-97) Delivered to her mother, MRS. COX of Georgetown, November 10, 1860. (BO)

BERKELEY (BURKLEY), ELLEN. Admitted August 2, 1855 aged three years by Poor House. Indentures expired August 2, 1870. (R-77) "Stayed in the House" (ROG, 1856). Religion: Catholic. (AtoA) Born 1853 "in the large House in Queen Street opposite Philadelphia Street (known as Cow Alley) called the "Toohey House" ...mother died of yellow fever...1854. Father, JOHN BURKLEY, died of yellow fever between 2 & 3 weeks after her mother." (Ibid.)

BETTERSON, ALFRED. Admitted August 10, 1854 aged four years by his mother and the Poor House. Indentured to B.P. POOSER (of Orangeburg District) as a farmer March 8, 1866. Indentures expired August 10, 1871. (S-30)

BETTERSON, BELTON. Admitted August 10, 1854 aged five years by his mother and the Poor House. Indentures expired August 10, 1870.(S-29) Indentured to JOHN HAMILTON, occupation unknown, nd. (ROB, 1856)

BETTERSON, FRANCES. Admitted August 10, 1854 aged ten years by FANNY BETTERSON, mother, and the Poor House. Indentured to MRS. H.A. LAWRENCE as a domestic March 24, 1859. Indentures expired August 10, 1862. (R-64)

BETTERSON, WILLIAM. Admitted August 10, 1854 aged eight years by his mother and the Poor House. Indentures expired August 10, 1867. (S-28) Indentured to GASS CO., occupation unknown, April 1, 1864. (ROB, 1856) In 1862 he received a silver watch for his work during the 1861 fire. (Minutes, July 17, 1862)

BEUSCH, CHARLES. Admitted August 10, 1854 aged four years by his mother and the Poor House. Indentures expired August 10, 1871. (S-31) Delivered to his father, unknown, nd. (ROB, 1856)

BIGGER, CHARLES. Admitted November 25, 1858 aged two years and four months by MARY BIGGER, mother. Indentures expired July 25, 1877. (T-126) Delivered to his mother, nd. (ROB, 1856)

BIGGER, ELLEN. Admitted November 25, 1858 aged six years and six months by MARY BIGGER, mother. Indentures expired May 25, 1869. (U-169) Delivered to her mother, nd. (ROG, 1856)

BLAKE, CATHARINE. Admitted February 6, 1857 aged seven years by the Poor House. Indentured to A.A. HEMINGWAY as a domestic December 28, 1865. Indentures expired February 6, 1868. (U-57)

BLAKE, JOHANNA. Admitted November 29, 1855 aged five years by Poor House. Indentured to ANNA T. LOGAN as a domestic March 8, 1866. Indentures expired November 26, 1868. (R-91) ANNA MARIA WILLSDEN - sister. (BO, rejected)

BLAKE, MARIA. Admitted November 29, 1855 aged twelve years by the Poor House. Indentured to A. TOOMER PORTER as a domestic March 1, 1860. Indentures expired November 29, 1861. (R-90)

BLANGUARD, WILLIAM. Admitted May 26, 1853 aged four years by the Poor House. Indentured to WILLIAM WAY (of Orangeburg District) as a farmer December 7, 1865. Indentures expired May 26, 1870. (Q-94) Mother died in the Poor House in 1853. (AtoA)

BOSMAN, LEMUEL. Admitted July 17, 1856 aged nine years by CATHARINE CONLON, unknown. Indentures expired July 17, 1868. (S-102) Delivered to PETER and CATHARINE CONLON, step-father and mother, nd. (BO)

BOURDON, MICHAEL. Admitted May 25, 1854 aged three years by Poor House. Indentures expired May 25, 1872. (S-18) Absconded, nd. (ROB, 1856) Mother died in the Poor House in 1854. (AtoA)

BOURKE (BURKE), JOHN. Admitted August 2, 1855 aged ten years by ORMSBY BOURKE, father. Indentures expired August 2, 1866. (S-55) Delivered to his siter, MRS. JAMES BURNSIDES (of Columbia), June 1857. (BO) "ORMSBY BOURKE, father of John Bourke resides (keeps a shop) west side of St. Philips one door south of Wentworth St. - opposite Mr. Honey's Stables." (AtoA)

BOWMAN, ELIZABETH. Admitted April 7, 1859 aged nine years by BRIDGET BOWMAN, mother. Indentures expired April 7, 1868. (U-191) Delivered to the Sisters of Mercy, nd. (ROG, 1856)

BRADY, JOSEPH. Admitted August 13, 1857 aged seven years by JAMES BRADY, father. Indentures expired August 13, 1871. (T-9) Sent to the School Ship February 24, 1863. (ROB, 1856)

BRANDUST, PETER HENRY. Admitted March 15, 1855 aged nine years by Poor House. Indentured to JAMES CLOTHWORTHY as an upholsterer January 19, 1860. Indentures expired March 1, 1867. (S-38)

BRIDGET. Admitted December 22, 1859 aged one year by MRS. JANE E. REES, unknown. Indentures expired December 22, 1876. (U-229) "Not in House." (ROG, 1856)

BRILLAUCEAU, (BRILLANCEAU), GUSTAVUS. Admitted July 17, 1856 aged twelve years by G. BRILLAUCEAU, father. Indentures expired July 17, 1865. (S-100) Sent to the Marine School December 1, 1859. (ROB, 1856)

BRONSON, FRANCIS WESTON. Admitted July 25, 1850 aged seven years by Poor House. (Q-17) Died November 6, 1852 of dropsy. (Minutes, November 13, 1853) A derelict. It was believed that he was born on the Edisto River. Mother died Sunday July 21, 1850. (AtoA)

BROWN, BENJAMIN. Admitted June 19, 1856 aged ten years by MATILDA BROWN, mother. (T-1) Indentured to J.M. EASON, occupation unknown, November 12, 1859. (ROB, 1856) Indentures expired June 19, 1867. (T-1)

BROWN, MARY ELIZABETH. Admitted June 19, 1856 aged three years by MATILDA BROWN, mother. Indentures expired June 9, 1871. (U-11) Delivered to her mother, nd. (ROG, 1856)

BROWN, SARAH A. Admitted June 19, 1856 aged six years by MATILDA BROWN, mother. Indentures expired June 19, 1868. (U-10) "Not in House." (ROG, 1856)

BROWNELL, GEORGE W. Admitted December 27, 1855 aged nine years by MRS. JANE BROWNELL, mother. Indentures expired December 27, 1867. (S-75) Indentured to F.W. BAILEY, occupation unknown, April 25, 1861. (ROB, 1856) Mother born in New York. Religion: Episcopalian. (AtoA)

BROWNELL, ISAAC B. Admitted December 27, 1855 aged eleven years by MRS. JANE BROWNELL, mother. Indentured to D.O. HAWTHORNE (of Due West, Abbeville District) as a coachmaker September 25, 1857. Indentures expired December 27, 1865. (S-74)

BROWNELL, NATHANIEL B. Admitted December 27, 1855 aged seven years by MRS. JANE BROWNELL, mother. Indentured to F.W. BAILEY (of Savannah, Georgia), occupation unknown, November 1, 1860. Indentures expired December 27, 1869. (S-76)

BRUCE, REBECCA. Admitted November 4, 1858 aged two years by MRS. ELLEN BRUCE, mother. Indentures expired November 4, 1874. (U-157) "Not in House." (ROG, 1856)

BUCH (BUCK), CATHERINE. Admitted March 1, 1855 aged six years by Poor House. Indentures expired March 1, 1867. (R-68) Stayed in the House until August 1869. (ROG, 1856)

BULLEN, AMANDA. Admitted April 26, 1855 aged ten years and six months and twelve days by CATHERINE BULLEN, mother, and the Poor House. Indentures expired October 14, 1862. (R-72) Employed in the Sewing Room as an assistant April 12, 1866. (Minutes, April 12, 1866) Allowed fifty dollars as a dowry in 1866. (Minutes, September 6, 1866) Religion: Presbyterian. (AtoA)

BULLEN, CATHARINE. Admitted April 26, 1855 aged six years and one month by CATHARINE BULLEN, mother, and the Poor House. April 26, 1855. Indentures expired March 26, 1867. (R-73) "Stayed in the House." (ROG, 1856)

BUNCH, JACOB NIPPER. Admitted January 20, 1853 aged eight years by DENNIS BUNCH, uncle. Indentures expired January 20, 1866. (Q-82) Sent to the High School of Charleston and taken out for misconduct November 22, 1860. (Minutes, November 22, 1860) Died in the army, nd. (ROB, 1856) Received a gold watch for his services to the Committee to Revamp the Rules and Regulations of the House. (Minutes, May 10, 1860) Enlisted in the "Bee Rifles." (Minutes, September 19, 1861)

BUNCH, SAMUEL F. Admitted January 20, 1853 aged ten years by DENNIS BUNCH, uncle. Indentured to ENOCH R. STOKES (of Columbia) as a bookbinder November 13, 1856. Indentures expired January 20, 1864. (Q-81) Grandmother lived on King Street, the second door below St. James Methodist Church. Dennis Bunch lived at 63 Queen Street. (AtoA)

BUTLER, JAMES ANDREW. Admitted May 1, 1855 aged seven years by MARY BUTLER, mother. Indentures expired May 17, 1869. (S-49) Mother a native of Ireland. Religion: Roman Catholic. (AtoA) Delivered to his uncle, July 29, 1864. (ROB, 1856)

BUTLER, JOHN SAMUEL. Admitted May 17, 1855 aged nine years by MARY BUTLER, mother. Indentured to JOHN WHITE as a stone cutter November 14, 1861. Indentures expired May 17, 1867. (S-48)

CAAN, HONORA. Admitted July 3, 1856 aged two years by HONORA CAAN, mother. Indentures expired July 3, 1872. (U-15) Delivered to her mother, nd. (ROG, 1856)

CALDER, HENRY. Admitted March 24, 1853 aged nine years and six months by JANE CALDER, mother. Indentured to the NORTH EASTERN RAILROAD CO., occupation unknown, October 21, 1858. Indentures expired October 1, 1864. (Q-87)

CALDER, GEORGE. Admitted March 24, 1853 aged six years by JANE CALDER, mother. Born February 14, 1847. Indentures expired February 14, 1868. (Q-88) Delivered to his mother, February 1, 1864. (ROB, 1856)

CALDER, JAMES. Admitted October 6, 1853 aged two years and seven months by JANE CALDER, mother, and the Poor House. (Q-104) Died, nd. (ROB, 1856)

CALDER, MARGARET. Admitted January 9, 1857 aged eleven years by JANE CALDER, mother. Indentures expired January 9, 1864. (U-49) No further information.

CALDER, WILLIAM. Admitted March 24, 1853 aged four years by JANE CALDER, mother. Born March 7, 1849. (Q-89) Died October 25, 1862. (ROB, 1856)

CALHOUN, JAMES. Admitted March 27, 1857 aged three years and six months by unknown. Indentures expired September 27, 1873. (S-123) Delivered to his mother May 1, 1857. (ROB, 1856)

CAMMER, EMANUEL CASIMIR. Admitted November 28, 1856 aged three years and five months by DR. JOHN BACHMAN, unknown. Indentures expired June 28, 1874. (AtoA) "Left." (ROB, 1856. (S-114)

CAMMER, EUGENE. Admitted June 8, 1854 aged seven years by JOHN CAMMER, father, and the Poor House. Indentures expired June 8, 1868. (S-22) Sent to the School Ship April 17, 1862. (ROB, 1856)

CAMMER, JAMES. Admitted June 8, 1854 aged five years by JOHN CAMMER, father, and the Poor House. Indentured to C.G. McCAY (of St. Stephens Parish) as a farmer July 19, 1866. Indentures expired June 8, 1870. (S-23)

CAMMER, JULIUS. Admitted June 8, 1854 aged four years by JOHN CAMMER, father, and the Poor House. Indentured to DR. J.R. SOLOMONS as a dentist November 15, 1866. Indentures expired June 8, 1874. (S-24) Dr. Solomons wrote the Commissioners and stated that Cammer was not able to become a dentist' instead he would be taught to be "a workman at the Mechanical Branch of dentistry." (BO)

CAMPBELL, CHARLES. Admitted February 18, 1858 aged eight years by SOPHIA CAMPBELL, mother. Indentures expired February 18, 1871. (T-68) Delivered to his mother October 12, 1864. (ROB, 1856)

CAMPBELL, ELLEN. Admitted March 4, 1858 aged eight years by CATHARINE DUNNAN, unknown. Indentures expired March 4, 1868. (U-117) Delivered to her father July 1, 1865. (ROG, 1856)

CAMPBELL, JOHN. Admitted February 18, 1858 aged six years by SOPHIA CAMPBELL, mother. Indentures expired February 18, 1873. (T-70) Delivered to his mother October 12, 1864. (ROB, 1856)

CAMPBELL, OWEN. Admitted March 4, 1858 aged five years by CATHARINE DUNNAN, mother. Indentures expired March 4, 1874. (T-74) No further information.

CANGHAY, MARY JANE. Admitted May 13, 1858 aged six years by JANE CANGHAY, mother. Indentures expired May 13, 1870. (U-143) No further information.

CANGHAY (CANPHAY), WILLIAM JOHN. Admitted May 13, 1858 aged eight years by JANE CANGHAY, mother. (T-90) Died March 4, 1862. (ROB, 1856)

CARSON, ANDREW MILLS. Admitted February 12, 1852 aged twelve years by JAMES CARSON, father. Indentures expired February 12, 1861. (Q-51) Absconded February 1853. (ROC, 1821) Born in Colleton District. Religion: Methodist. (AtoA)

CARSON, JOSEPH. Admitted February 12, 1852 aged four years and nine days by JAMES CARSON, father. Born February 3, 1848. Indentures expired February 3, 1869. (Q-52) Born in Colleton District. Religion: Methodist. (AtoA) Delivered to his father, nd. (BO)

CARTER, MARIA ANN. Admitted August 21, 1856 aged six years by LUCINDA KENNEDY, mother. Indentures expired August 21, 1868. (U-18) Delivered to her aunt, unknown, nd. (ROG, 1856)

CARTER, RICHARD PINCKNEY. Admitted August 21, 1856 aged nine years by LUCINDA KENNEDY, mother. Indentures expired August 21, 1868. (S-105) Delivered to his uncle, EDWARD MILLIGAN, November 7, 1861. (ROB, 1856)

CARTER, STARLING L. Admitted August 21, 1856 aged four years by LUCINDA KENNEDY, mother. Indentures expired August 21, 1873. (S-106) Delivered to his mother, nd. (ROB, 1856)

CASHMAN, BESS. Admitted August 27, 1857 aged three years by ANNE CASHMAN, mother. Indentures expired August 27, 1872. (U-47) No further information.

CASHMAN, MARY. Admitted August 27, 1857 aged five years by ANNE CASHMAN, mother. Indentures expired August 27, 1870. (U-46) Delivered to her mother, nd. (ROG, 1856)

CHAMBERS, MARTIN. Admitted November 6, 1857 aged seven years by MARY CHAMBERS, mother. Indentures expired November 6, 1871. (T-22) Delivered to his mother, nd. (ROB, 1856)

CHURCHILL, JOHN WILLIAM. Admitted October 27, 1853 aged four years by ANN CHURCHILL, mother, and the Poor House. Born April 1, 1849. Indentures expired October 27, 1870. (Q-106) Born in New York. Religion: Protestant. Mother lived at 3 Philadelphia Street. (AtoA) Absconded 1864. (ROB, 1856)

CHURCHILL, MARGARET. Admitted October 13, 1859 aged five years by the Poor House. Indentures expired October 13, 1872. (U-215) "Left." (ROG, 1856)

CHURCHILL, MARY. Admitted October 27, 1853 aged seven years by ANN CHURCHILL, mother. Indentured to DR. U.S. HANCKEL as a domestic January 1, 1863. Indentures expired October 27, 1864. (R-51) Born in New York. Religion: Protestant. (AtoA)

CLARK, HANNAH. Admitted October 7, 1858 aged seven years by WILLIAM B. YATES, unknown. Indentured to JAMES M. CALDWELL as a domestic December 12, 1867. Indentures expired October 7, 1869. (U-149)

CLARK, JOHN. Admitted February 24, 1859 aged one year and six months by the Poor House. Indentured to D.M.F. HUFF (of Orangeburgh) as a farmer February 1, 1872. Indentures expired October 24, 1878. (T-150)

CODY, SARAH. Admitted May 17, 1859 aged eight years by BRIDGET CODY, mother. (U-247) Died March 12, 1862. (ROG, 1856)

COLLINS, JANE. Admitted November 23, 1855 aged four years and eleven months by RICHARD COLLINS, father. Indentured to WILLIAM E. SIMMONS as a domestic December 28, 1865. Indentures expired December 23, 1868. (R-88) Religion: Protestant. (AtoA)

COLLINS, JOANNA. Admitted November 23, 1855 aged ten years and six months by RICHARD COLLINS, father. Indentured to THOMAS PARKER as a domestic April 12, 1860. Indentures expired May 23, 1863. (R-86) Born in County Kerry, Ireland. Religion: Protestant. Parents arrived in Charleston August 26, 1848. (AtoA)

COLLINS, MARY CATHARINE. Admitted November 23, 1855 aged eight years and seven months by RICHARD COLLINS, father. Indentures expired April 23, 1865. (R-87) Born in Baltimore. Religion: Protestant. (AtoA) "Stayed in House." (ROG, 1856)

CONDON, DAVID. Admitted September 25, 1857 aged five years by CATHARINE CONDON, mother. Indentures expired September 25, 1873. (T-18) "Left." (ROB, 1856)

CONNELLY, HENRY. Admitted July 7, 1859 aged five years by JAMES CONNELLY, father. Indentured to R.L. MORILLO as a cigarmaker May 26, 1869. Indentures expired July 7, 1873. (T-181)

CONNELLY, MELISSA ANN. Admitted July 7, 1859 aged three years by JAMES CONNELLY, father. Indentured to J. EVANS EDINGS (of Edisto), occupation unknown, March 3, 1874. (U-203)

CONNELLY, THOMAS (JAMES). Admitted July 7, 1859 aged seven years by JAMES CONNELLY, father. Indentured to DR. S.E. GRAHAM (of Williamsburg, South Carolina) as a farmer March 2, 1868. Indentures expired July 7, 1873. (T-179)

CONOHET (CONCHEY), EUGENE. Admitted December 23, 1852 aged eight years by VIRGINIA BOURDON, mother. Indentures expired December 23, 1865. (Q-78) No further information.

CONVOY, MARGARET. Admitted March 11, 1858 aged twelve years by DOMINICK CONVOY, father. Indentures expired March 11, 1864. (U-125) Absconded, nd. (ROG, 1856)

COOK, DAVID (DANIEL). Admitted February 4, 1848 aged eight years by MRS. MARTHA H. COOK, mother. Indentures expired February 4, 1871. (T-62) Delivered to his father May 7, 1859. (ROB, 1856)

COOK, SAMUEL. Admitted February 4, 1858 aged six years by MRS. MARTHA H. COOK, mother. Indentures expired February 4, 1873. (T-64) Delivered to his father May 7, 1859. (ROB, 1856)

COOK, WILLIAM. Admitted February 20, 1858 aged ten years and six months by MRS. MARTHA H. COOK, mother. Indentures expired August 4, 1868. (T-60) Delivered to his father May 7, 1859. (ROB, 1856)

CORDES, CATHARINE. Admitted November 4, 1858 aged nine years by DR. J. BUCHANAN, unknown. Indentured to ALBERT C. CORDES, occupation unknown, February 14, 1861. Indentures expired November 4, 1867. (U-162)

CORDES, HENRIETTA. Admitted November 4, 1858 aged eleven years by DR. JOHN BUCHANAN (BACKMAN), unknown. Indentures expired November 4, 1865. (V-262) Indentured to WILLIAM HUNTER, occupation unknown, November 14, ____. (ROG, 1856)

COSGROVE, FANNY. Admitted November 18, 1858 aged one year and eleven months by ELLEN COSGROVE, mother. Indentures expired December 18, 1874. (U-167) Delivered to her mother, nd. (ROG, 1856)

COTTAR, JOHN. Admitted October 14, 1852 aged eight years by the Poor House. Indentures expired October 14, 1865. (Q-70) Born in Ireland. Arrived 1849. Father died in Ireland five months previously. Mother went to New York. Grandmother, MRS. WOOD. Sister with a MRS. WILLIS. (AtoA) Delivered to his mother November 1852. (ROC, 1821)

COTTAR, PATRICK. Admitted October 14, 1852 aged nine years and six months by the Poor House. Indentures expired April 14, 1864. (Q-71) Born in Ireland. (AtoA) Delivered to his mother November 1852. (ROC, 1821)

CREWS, MARY ANN. Admitted June 16, 1856 aged eleven years by BRIDGET CREWS, mother. Indentured to GEORGE CHISOLM (of North Carolina) as a domestic February 28, 1861. Indentures expired June 19, 1863. (U-9)

CROGHAN, BRIDGET. Admitted May 25, 1854 aged nine years by the Poor House. Indentured to MISS M. GRIFFITH (of Greenville) as a milliner April 19, 1860. Indentures expired May 25, 1863. (R-61) Father in gaol. (AtoA) Transferred to MRS. BEATTEE as a dressmaker May 9, 1861. (BO)

CROGHAN, CATHARINE. Admitted May 15, 1856 aged four years by CATHARINE CROGHAN, mother. Indentured to W.D. WALLER as a domestic August 31, 1868. Indentures expired May 15, 1870. (U-6)

CROGHAN, ELLEN. Admitted January 10, 1856 aged nine years by CATHARINE CROGHAN, mother. Indentures expired January 10, 1865. (R-102) Delivered to her mother August 12, ____. (ROG, 1856)

CROGHAN, MARY ANN. Admitted December 15, 1853 aged eleven years by the Poor House. Born in Ireland. Indentures expired December 15, 1860. (R-55) "Stayed in House." (ROG, 1856)

CROGHAN, PATRICK. Admitted January 10, 1856 aged six years by CATHARINE CROGHAN, mother. Indentures expired January 10, 1871. (S-81) Delivered to MR. and MRS. HOFFMAN, unknown, October 9, 1864. (ROB, 1856)

CROWS, WILLIAM E. Admitted February 23, 1854 aged eleven years by Poor House. Indentures expired February 23, 1864. (S-2) Born in New Orleans. Religion: Protestant Episcopalian. (AtoA) Absconded, January 1856. (ROB, 1856)

CRUM, HENRY. Admitted February 24, 1859 aged seven years by CAROLINE CRUM, unknown. Indentured to MRS. ELLEN D. OLIVER (of Orangeburg) as a farmer March 20, 1868. Indentures expired February 24, 1873. (T-148)

CUDWORTH, ALICE. Admitted April 3, 1856 aged six years by MRS. C. CUDWORTH, mother. Indentures expired June 8, 1868. (R-108) Delivered to her mother February 27, 1857. (ROG, 1856)

CUDWORTH, EDWARD NORTH. Admitted July 25, 1850 aged eight years by CATHERINE CUDWORTH, mother. Indentures expired July 25, 1863. (Q-16) Delivered to his mother January 16, 1851. (ROC, 1821)

CUDWORTH, EDWARD NORTH. Admitted June 10, 1852 aged ten years by his mother and the Poor House. Indentures expired April 17, 1863. (Q-57) Born in Georgetown District. (AtoA) Absconded, nd. (ROC, 1821)

CUDWORTH, ELIZA. Admitted July 25, 1850 aged eight years by CATHARINE CUDWORTH, mother. Indentures expired April 17, 1860. (R-10) Delivered to her mother October 2, 1858. (ROG, 1856)

CUDWORTH, ELLA MARY. Admitted July 25, 1850 aged six years by CATHERINE CUDWORTH, mother, and the Poor House. Indentures expired December 5, 1862. (R-11) Delivered to her mother February 27, 1857. (ROG, 1856)

CUDWORTH, NATHANIEL THOMAS. Admitted June 10, 1852 aged five years and one month by MRS. C. CUDWORTH, mother, and the Poor House. Born May 27, 1847. Indentures expired May 27, 1868. (Q-58) No further information.

CURLEY (CORLEY), MICHAEL. Admitted December 27, 1855 aged eight years and five and one half months by MRS. MARCELLA HUGHES, mother. Indentured to COL. ROBERT BARNWELL RHETT as a printer January 1, 1863. Indentures expired July 12, 1868. (S-72) Delivered to his mother July 29, 1863. (BO) Religion: Roman Catholic. (AtoA)

CURLEY (CORLEY), THOMAS. Admitted December 27, 1855 aged six years and eleven months by MARCELLA HUGHES, mother. Indentures expired January 26, 1870. (S-73) Religion: Roman Catholic. (AtoA) A cripple. (Minutes, January 31, 1856) Sent to the Poor House May 1864. (ROB, 1856)

DANIEL, STEPHEN. Admitted January 20, 1853 aged eight years and seven months by EVELINE JEFFORDS, mother. Indentures expired June 20, 1865. (Q-79) Born on Anson Street. Religion: Methodist. (AtoA) Delivered to his mother 1853. (ROC, 1821)

DARBY, LAURETTA M. Admitted July 3, 1857 aged six years by her father, unknown. Indentured to B.W. WARNER as a domestic December 7, 1865. Indentures expired July 3, 1869. (U-36)

DARBY, MARY L. Admitted July 3, 1857 aged ten years by father, unknown. Indentures expired July 3, 1865. (U-35) Delivered to her aunt, unknown, nd. (ROG, 1856)

DAVIS, JACOB PRINGLE. Admitted January 3, 1856 aged ten years and four months by DORCAS DAVIS, mother. Indentured to WILLIAM STREATTON (STRATTON) as a baker December 9, 1858. Indentures expired September 3, 1866. (S-77)

DAVIS, LEMUEL. Admitted January 3, 1856 aged nine years and three months by DORCAS DAVIS, mother. Indentured to S. BREVANDE as a plasterer June 2, 1859. Indentures expired October 3, 1867. (S-78)

DAVIS, MARIA. Admitted December 15, 1853 aged twelve years by the Poor House. Indentured to PETER J. and LYDIA HUTSON, unknown, January 31, 1856. Indentures expired February 15, 1859. (R-65) Born in the North Santee District. (AtoA). Children admitted to COH: WILLIAM and LUCIUS June 4, 1868. (AtoA)

DAVIS, REBECCA. Admitted January 3, 1856 aged eight years by DORCAS DAVIS, mother. Indentured to N.R. DOBSON as a domestic December 26, 1861. Indentures expired January 3, 1866. (R-100)

DAVIS, WILLIAM AUGUSTUS. Admitted November 11, 1852 aged ten years by the Poor House. Indentures expired November 11, 1863. (Q-103) Absconded August 1855. (ROC, 1821)

DAWSON, WILLIAM. Admitted July 3, 1851 aged two years and four months by SUSAN DAWSON, mother, and the Poor House. (Q-38) Died October 28, ____. (ROB, 1856) Mother a COH nurse. (AtoA)

DeGAFFORELLY, THOMAS. Admitted March 11, 1858 aged eight years by JANE DeGAFFORELLY, mother. Indentures expired March 11, 1871. (T-76) Delivered to his mother, nd. (ROB, 1856)

DELESSELIEME (DESESSELIENE), ISAAC. Admitted April 6, 1854 aged thirteen years by MARTHA DELESSELIEME, mother. Indentures expired April 6, 1862. (S-7) Delivered to his mother March 1855. (ROC, 1821)

DELESSELIEME, JOHN. Admitted April 6, 1854 aged six years by MARTHA DELESSELIEME, mother. Indentures expired April 6, 1869. (S-8) Delivered to his mother, March 1855. (ROC, 1821)

DENIS, FRANCIS CAMILE. Admitted April 14, 1853 aged five years and six months by CAROLINE DENIS, mother, and the Poor House. Indentured to WELCH and HARRIS (HIRAM HARRIS and SAMUEL B. WELCH) as a bookbinder July 2, 1863. Indentures expired November 12, 1868. (Q-93)

DENIS, JOHN ALEXANDER. Admitted April 14, 1853 aged ten years and ten months by CAROLINE DENIS, mother. Indentures expired June 20, 1863. (Q-91) Delivered to his mother November 4, 1858. (BO)

DENIS, JOSEPH ADOLPHE. Admitted April 14, 1853 aged seven years and nine months by CAROLINE DENIS, mother. Indentured to B. FITZSIMMONS, occupation unknown, August 19, 1858. Indentures expired August 19, 1858. (Q-92) Transferred to MR. _____ HEFFRON as a saddler December 29, 1859. (BO)

DENNEN, EDWARD. Admitted March 9, 1854 aged six years by the Poor House. (S-6) Died October 1854. (ROC, 1821)

DENNEN, JOHN. Admitted March 9, 1854 aged twelve years and seven months by the Poor House. Born in New York. Indentured to W.J.KNAUFF (of Pendleton) as a printer February 28, 1856. Indentures expired August 10, 1862. (S-5)

DENNIS, CHARLES LEWIS CLARK. Admitted August 28, 1851 aged two years and nine months by EUNICE DENNIS and the Poor House. Born January 20, 1849. (Q-47) Died March 22, 1853 of varioloid complicated by worms. (Minutes, November 13, 1853) Religion: Episcopalian. (AtoA)

DENNIS, GEORGE WASHINGTON ALEXANDER. Admitted May 16, 1850 aged ten years by EUNICE DENNIS, mother, and the Poor House. Indentured to WILLIAM MATHIESSON as a tailor and clothier May 26, 1853. Indentures expired May 16, 1861. (Q-11) Born November 12, 1838. (corrected) (Minutes, September 1, 1851)

DENNIS, HENRY DRAYTON. Admitted August 28, 1851 aged seven years by EUNICE DENNIS, mother, and the Poor House. Born April 11, 1844. (Q-46) Died 1853 of varioloid complicated by pneumonia. (Minutes, November 13, 1853) Religion: Episcopalian. (AtoA)

DENNIS, NATHANIEL WILSON. Admitted May 16, 1850 aged eight years by EUNICE DENNIS, mother, and the Poor House. Born March 5, 1842. Indentures expired May 16, 1863. (Q-12) Absconded February 1853. (ROC, 1821)

DENNIS, WILLIAM B. Admitted January 6, 1859 aged nine years by MRS. C.M. DANIELS, mother. Indentures expired January 6, 1871. (T-136) Delivered to his brother, unknown, nd. (ROB, 1856)

DESMOND, JOHN. Admitted April 24, 1857 aged four years by BRIDGET DESMOND, mother. Indentures expired April 24, 1874. (S-127) "Left." (ROB, 1856)

DILLON, GEORGE. Admitted July 25, 1857 aged four years by ANN E. MILLER, mother. Indentured to S.E. SCANLON (of Orangeburg) as a blacksmith March 25, 1869. Indentures expired July 25, 1874. (T-5)

DILLON, THOMAS. Admitted July 25, 1857 aged seven years by ANN E. MILLER, mother. (T-4) Died August 12, ____ (ROB, 1856)

DOHLEN, CATHERINE ANN. Admitted February 13, 1857 aged two years and four months by ANNE DOHLEN, mother. Indentures expired August 13, 1872. (U-59) "Not in House." (ROG, 1856)

DOLAN, FRANCIS. Admitted September 26, 1850 aged six years and ten months by MARGARET DOLAN, unknown, and the Poor House. Indentured to D. HAWTHORNE (of Due West, Abbeville District) as a harnessmaker April 10, 1857. Indentures expired November 26, 1864. (Q-22)

DOLAN, PETER. Admitted March 13, 1851 aged three years and three months by his mother and the Poor House. (Q-33) Died 1858. (ROB, 1856)

DOLAN, WILLIAM. Admitted September 26, 1850 aged nine years and one month by MARGARET DOLAN, unknown, and the Poor House. Indentured to W.A. LEE and WILLIAM WILSON (of Abbeville District) as a printer December 12, 1856. Indentures expired August 26, 1862. (Q-21)

DONAHUE, BARNEY. Admitted September 30, 1852 aged five years and six months by ELIZA DONAHUE, mother, and the Poor House. Born March 20, 1847. Indentures expired March 20, 1868. (Q-67) Delivered to his father, HENRY DONAHUE, April 1853. (BO) Born in Bridgeport, Connecticut. (AtoA)

DONAHUE, JOHN D. Admitted November 10, 1853 aged eight years by MICHAEL DONAHUE, father, and the Poor House. Indentured to HENRY SIEGLING as a merchant November 24, 1859. Indentures expired November 10, 1866. (Q-107) Born in New York. Religion: Roman Catholic. (AtoA)

DONAHUE, VICTOR. Admitted November 10, 1853 aged five years by MICHAEL DONAHUE, father, and the Poor House. Indentured to JOSEPH BELLINGER (of Barnwell District) as a farmer December 28, 1865. Indentures expired November 10, 1869. (Q-108) Religion: Roman Catholic. (AtoA)

DONEGAN, LEWIS. Admitted August 18, 1859 aged eleven years by CATHERINE DUGAN, mother. Indentures expired August 18, 1869. (T-193) Sent to the School Ship. (ROB, 1856)

DOOLY, AUGUSTIN. Admitted February 14, 1856 aged nine years and six months by ANASTASIA DOOLY, mother. Indentured to JOHN A. MICHEL as a surveyor January 12, 1860. Indentures expired August 14, 1867. (S-84) Absconded November 19, 1861 to join the army. (BO) Mother born in Ireland. Child born in New York. Religion: Roman Catholic. Lived in Bedon's Alley. (AtoA)

DOSSEN, ELEANOR. Admitted January 3, 1850 aged eleven years by SOPHIA DOSSEN, mother, and the Poor House. Indentures expired January 3, 1857. (R-4) No further information.

DOUGHERTY, ISABELLA. Admitted November 28, 1856 aged three years by ANN DOUGHERTY, mother. Indentures expired November 28, 1871. (U-22) "Not in House." (ROG, 1856)

DUFFIE, JOHN. Admitted July 15, 1858 aged eight years by ROSE DUFFIE, mother. Indentured to DR. JOSEPH YATES as a physician November 16, 1866. Indentures expired July 15, 1873. (T-103)

DUGAN, BRIDGET. Admitted September 15, 1853 aged seven years and nine months by MARTIN DUGAN, father. Born in Charleston. (R-47) Lived in Cow Alley. (AtoA) Died April 28, 1860. (ROG, 1856)

DUGAN, JAMES. Admitted September 15, 1853 aged twelve years by MARTIN DUGAN, father. Indentured to JOHN WALCOTT as a blacksmith February 20, 1857. Indentures expired September 15, 1862. (Q-101)

DUGAN, MARTIN. Admitted September 15, 1853 aged ten years and six months by MARTIN DUGAN, father. Indentured to W.C. DAVIS and B. CREWS (of Abbeville District) as a printer December 24, 1857. Indentures expired March 17, 1864. (Q-102) Transferred to CHARLES CANNING, occupation unknown, November 9, 1859. (ROC, 1821)

DUGAN, WILLIAM. Admitted July 28, 1859 aged five years by Poor House. Indentures expired July 28, 1875. (T-185) "Left." (ROB, 1856)

DUNCAN, ALEXANDER. Admitted January 30, 1851 aged nine years and eight months by ARCHIBALD DUNCAN, father. Indentures expired May 30, 1862. (Q-27) Born in Scotland. Religion: Presbyterian. (AtoA) Delivered to his father August 1853. (ROC, 1821)

DUNCAN, JAMES. Admitted January 30, 1851 aged seven years and ten months by ARCHIBALD DUNCAN, father. Indentures expired March 30, 1864. (Q-28) Delivered to his father August 1853. (ROC, 1821) Religion: Presbyterian. (AtoA)

DUNCAN, MARGARET. Admitted January 30, 1851 aged four years and six months by her mother, unknown. Indentures expired July 30, 1864. (R-14) Delivered to her father 1852. (ROC, 1821) Religion: Presbyterian. (AtoA)

DUNCAN, SARAH. Admitted January 30, 1851 aged three years by ARCHIBALD DUNCAN, father. (R-15) Died 1852. (ROC, 1821) Religion: Presbyterian. (AtoA)

DUNLAP, JOHN. Admitted December 13, 1855 aged six years and fourteen days by LOUISA DUNLAP, mother. Indentures expired November 29, 1870. (S-70) A cripple. (Minutes, January 31, 1856) Delivered to S.G. DUNLAP, unknown, December 29, 1870. (ROB, 1856) Religion: Protestant Episcopalian. Lived in Spring Street at the corner of St. Philip Street. Father, SAMUEL, died November 21, 1855. Grandfather, WILLIAM ARMS, a bricklayer. (AtoA)

DUNLAP, SAMUEL. Admitted December 13, 1855 aged eight years, eight months, and twenty-two days by LOUISA DUNLAP, mother. Indentures expired March 21, 1868. (S-69) Sent to "Wayside House." (ROB, 1856) Received a silver watch for his services during the 1861 fire. (Minutes, July 17, 1862)

DUNLAP, WILLIAM. Admitted December 13, 1855 aged eleven years, two months, and five days by LOUISA DUNLAP, mother. Indentured to R.E. SEYLE and C.C. SEYLE (of East Florida) as a merchant February 3, 1859. Indentures expired October 8, 1865. (S-68) Delivered to his uncle, JOHN ORCHARD, February 19, 1861. (BO)

EASTERLING, GEORGE WASHINGTON. Admitted December 5, 1856 aged three years by RACHEL EASTERLING, mother. Indentures expired December 5, 1875. (S-117) Born in Georgia. Religion: Methodist. (AtoA) "Left." (ROB, 1856)

EBERLE, LOUISA ELLEN. Admitted April 17, 1858 aged four years by JANE D. EBERLE, mother. Indentures expired April 17, 1872. (U-137) Delivered to MRS. B.J. PARKER, unknown, March 18, 1869. (ROG, 1856)

EBERLE, MARY FLORENCE. Admitted April 17, 1858 aged five years by JANE D. EBERLE, mother. Indentures expired April 17, 1871. (U-135)

EHNEY, PETER THEODORE. Admitted January 8, 1852 aged nine years by ANN REDMON, mother, and the Poor House. Born June 19, 1842. Indentures expired June 19, 1863. (Q-50) Absconded February 1854. (ROC, 1821) Discovered at the home of his aunt, MRS. MARTHA DOWNEY, and allowed to stay with her July 20, 1854. (BO)

ELLIS, JOSEPH SAMUEL. Admitted September 30, 1852 aged nine years by ELIZABETH ELLIS, mother, and the Poor House. Indentures expired September 30, 1864. (Q-65) Delivered to her mother February 1855. (ROC, 1821) Religion: Episcopal. Mother lived in Bogard Street near corner of Rutledge Avenue. (AtoA)

ELLIS, JOSEPH S. Admitted October 4, 1855 aged twelve years by ELIZABETH ELLIS, mother. Indentures expired September 30, 1864. (S-58) Delivered to his mother February 20, 1857. (ROB, 1856)

ELLIS, JOSEPHINE ANN. Admitted December 28, 1854 aged eight years and ten months by ELIZABETH ELLIS, mother, and the Poor House. Born March 27, 1846. Indentures expired March 27, 1864. (R-66) Mother lived on Nassau Street, two doors south of Columbus Street. (AtoA)

ELLIS, JOSEPHINE ANN. Admitted October 4, 1855 aged nine years by ELIZABETH ELLIS, mother. Indentured to HUGH R. RUTLEDGE (of French Broad, North Carolina) as a domestic January 30, 1862. Indentures expired March 27, 1864. (R-84) Delivered to her aunt, MRS. SARAH KINGDON, March 12, 1863. (BO)

ELLIS, JULIA. Admitted October 4, 1855 aged seven years by ELIZABETH ELLIS, mother. Indentures expired October 4, 1866. (R-85) Delivered to her mother, nd. (ROG, 1856)

ELLIS, WILLIAM JOHN. Admitted September 30, 1852 aged eight years by ELIZABETH ELLIS, mother, and the Poor House. Indentures expired September 30, 1865. (Q-66) Delivered to his mother February 1855. (ROC, 1821)

ELLIS, WILLIAM J. Admitted October 4, 1855 aged eleven years by ELIZABETH ELLIS, mother. Indentures expired September 30, 1865. (S-59) No further information.

EMLYN, HORATIO NELSON. Admitted April 29, 1852 aged eight years and six months by MARTHA EMLYN, mother, and the Poor House. Indentured to ROBERT M. STOKES (of Laurens District) as a printer March 13, 1856. Indentures expired November 21, 1864. (Q-53) Born in St. Paul's Parish. Religion: Methodist. (AtoA)

EMLYN, WILLIE CLARENCE. Admitted April 29, 1852 aged six years by MARTHA EMLYN, mother, and the Poor House. Indentured to WILLIAM S. HENEREY as a machinist October 24, 1861. Indentures expired March 5, 1867. (U-12) Born in St. Paul's Parish. Religion: Methodist. (AtoA)

FERGERSON, JANE ELIZABETH. Admitted May 5, 1853 aged four years and three months by CAROLINE DENIS, grandmother. Indentures expired May 12, 1867. (R-36) Born January 12, 1849. Religion: Catholic. (AtoA) Delivered to her mother to be sent to her aunt, MRS. YGLESIAS, February 23, 1854. (BO)

FERGERSON (FERGUSON), JANE ELIZABETH. Admitted August 20, 1857 aged nine years by CATHARINE STRATTON, unknown. Adopted by AMADO and RUTH LaFOURCADE May 7, 1863. Indentures expired August 20, 1866. (U-43)

FERRELL, HENRY CLAY. Admitted March 13, 1856 aged nine years by ELIZABETH FERRELL, mother. Indentures expired March 13, 1868. (S-86) Delivered to his mother, ELIZABETH MURRAY, November 22, 1860. (BO) Religion: Methodist. (AtoA)

FICKENS, MARY. Admitted Marvh 6, 1857 aged eleven years. Indentured to WILLIAM BREDEMAN as a domestic June 16, 1863. Indentures expired March 6, 1864. (U-61)

FINK, SOPHIA. Admitted July 21, 1859 aged nine years by ELIZA ANN REILLS, unknown. Indentured to MRS. SAMUEL ROBERTSON as a domestic December 7, 1865. Indentures expired July 21, 1868. (U-206)

FINK, SUSANNA. Admitted July 21, 1859 aged seven years by ELIZA ANN REILLS, unknown. Indentures expired July 21, 1870. (U-207) "Adopted." (ROG, 1856)

FINN, EUGENIA LAVAL. Admitzed October 4, 1855 aged six years, four and one half months by HARRIETT EUGENIA FINN, mother. Indentures expired May 21, 1867. (R-82) Delivered to her mother, nd. (ROG, 1856) Born in Mississippi. Religion: Protestant Episcopalian. (AtoA)

FINN, FRANCES RIVERS. Admitted October 4, 1855 aged eight years and seven and three quarters months by HARRIETT EUGENIA FINN, mother. Indentures expired February 19, 1865. (R-81) Delivered to her mother August 2, 1860. (ROG, 1856) Born in Mississippi. Religion: Protestant Episcopalian. (AtoA)

FINN, PHILIP POWELL. Admitted October 4, 1855 aged three years and two months by HARRIETT EUGENIA FINN, mother. Indentures expired July 30, 1873. (S-57) Delivered to his mother, nd. (ROB, 1856) Born in Mississippi. Religion: Protestant Episcopalian. (AtoA)

FITZPATRICK, HORACE EDWARD. Admitted July 14, 1859 aged six years by ALICE GARDNER, grandmother. Indentured to TOBIN and MOSELEY (of Laurens) as a merchant December 13, 1869. Indentures expired July 14, 1874. (T-183)

FLEMING, ANN. Admitted July 30, 1857 aged five years by ANN HIGGINS, mother. Indentures expired July 30, 1857. (U-38) Delivered to her mother, nd. (ROG, 1856)

FLEMING, MARGARET. Admitted July 30, 1857 aged nine years and nine months by ANN HIGGINS, mother. Indentures expired October 30, 1865. (U-37) Delivered to her mother, nd. (ROG, 1856)

FLYN, MARY ANN. Admitted March 20, 1856 aged seven years by CATHARINE FLYN, unknown. Indentures expired March 20, 1867. (R-105) Delivered to her mother, MRS. HENRY ASH, July 22, 1862. (BO) Religion: Catholic. (AtoA) Born in New York. (R-105)

FRANKLIN, BENJAMIN. Admitted October 2, 1857 aged four years by MRS. EMILY ROBERTS, unknown. Indentures expired October 2, 1874. (T-20) Delivered to his mother, unknown, nd. (ROB, 1856)

ENGLAT, FRANK. Admitted July 3, 1856 aged ten years. Indentures expired July 3, 1867. (S-98) Delivered to his sister, unknown, nd. (ROB, 1856) Admitted from the Poor House. (AtoA)

ENGLAT, LOUISA. Admitted July 3, 1856 aged nine years. Indentured to NICHOLAS CALLERTON, occupation unknown, October 11, 1860. Indentures expired July 3, 1865. (U-12)

ENGLAT, MARY. Admitted July 3, 1856 aged four years. Indentured to DR. THOMAS S. GRIMKE as a domestic January 9, 1868. Indentures expired July 3, 1870. (U-13)

EVANS, ELIZABETH. Admitted November 10, 1859 aged eleven years by MRS. HARRIET EVANS, mother. (U-221) Died, nd. (ROG, 1856)

EVANS, HARRIET. Admitted March 25, 1858 aged eight years by MRS. H.B. EVANS, mother. Indentures expired November 10, 1869. (U-223) Delivered to her mother, nd. (ROG, 1856)

FALK, ELLEN JANE. Admitted March 25, 1858 aged seven years by MARY E. FALK, unknown. Indentures expired March 25, 1869. (U-133) Delivered to her sister, unknown, nd. (ROG, 1856)

FALK, HENRY. Admitted March 25, 1858 aged six years by MARY E. FALK, mother. Indentures expired March 25, 1873. (T-78) Delivered to his sister, unknown, nd. (ROB, 1856)

FALK, ISRAEL. Admitted March 25, 1858 aged eight years by MARY E. FALK, mother. Indentures expired March 25, 1871. (T-80) Delivered to his sister, unknown, nd. (ROB, 1856)

FARLEY, CHARLES JAMES. Admitted August 2, 1855 aged two years, eight months, and fourteen days. Indentures expired November 15, 1873. (S-56) Religion: Catholic. (AtoA) "Left." (ROB, 1856)

FARMER, EDWARD. Admitted August 4, 1859 aged ten years by RICHARD
FARMER, father. Indentures expired August 4, 1870. (T-189) Delivered
to his father, nd. (ROB, 1856)

FARMER, JOHN. Admitted August 4, 1859 aged eight years by RICHARD
FARMER, father. Indentures expired August 4, 1872. (T-191) Delivered
to his father, nd. (ROB, 1856)

FARMER, MARY ANN. Admitted August 4, 1859 aged five years by RICHARD
FARMER, father. Indentures expired August 4, 1872. (U-209) Delivered
to her step-mother, nd. (ROG, 1856)

FARRELL, CATHERINE. Admitted June 30, 1853 aged six years by MARY
FARRELL, mother, and the Poor House. Indentures expired June 30, 1865.
(R-41) Delivered to her father, EDWARD FARRELL, of 22 Queen Street,
July 10, 1856. (BO)

FARRELL, ELLEN. Admitted June 30, 1853 aged eleven years by MARY
FARRELL, mother, and the Poor House. Indentures expired June 30, 1859.
(R-40) Delivered to her father, EDWARD FARRELL, of 22 Queen Street
July 10, 1856. (BO)

FAULLING, WILLIAM. Admitted October 14, 1852 aged seven years and nine
months by SARAH C. WOOD, mother, and the Poor House. Born January
8, 1845. Indentured to WILLIAM WILSON and W.A. LEE (of Abbeville
District) as a printer December 12, 1856. Indentures expired January
8, 1866. (Q-72) Born Charleston District. Religion: Methodist. (AtoA)

FREEMAN, WILLIAM JOSEPH. Admitted February 2, 1854 aged eight years
and five months by JANE KING, mother, and the Poor House. Indentures
expired September 2, 1867. (S-1) Born Horry District. Religion:
Methodist. (AtoA) "Dismissed." (ROB, 1856)

GAMBO, HENRY. Admitted June 10, 1858 aged four years by MARY GAMBO,
mother. Indentures expired June 10, 1875. (T-92) Delivered to his
mother, nd. (ROB, 1856)

GAMBO, LOUIS. Admitted June 10, 1858 aged three years by MARY GAMBO,
mother. Indentxres expired June 10, 1876. (T-94) Delivered to his
mother, nd. (ROB, 1856)

GERK, CHARLES. Admitted June 1, 1854 aged ten years and nine months
by ELIZA GERK, mother. Indentured to J.C.H. CLAUSSEN as a baker
November 18, 1858. Indentures expired September 1, 1864. (S-21)
Religion: Lutheran. (AtoA)

GERK, FRANCIS. Admitted June 1, 1854 aged eleven years by ELIZA GERK,
mother. Indentured to J.J. BONNER (of Due West, Abbeville District)
as a printer November 27, 1856. Indentures expired November 1, 1863.
(S-20) Religion: Lutheran. (AtoA)

GIBBONS, PATRICK. Admitted January 14, 1858 aged five years by MARY
GIBBES, mother. Indentures expired January 14, 1874. (T-54) Delivered
to his mother, nd. (ROB, 1856)

GIRVEN, (GARVIN), ADAM. Admitted October 20, 1853 aged ten years and
seven months by ELIZABETH GIRVEN, mother, and the Poor House. Indentured to J.S. BONNER (of Due West, Abbeville District) as a printer
November 22, 1856. Indentures expired March 20, 1864. (Q-105) Born
in Antrim, Ireland. Religion: Presbyterian. (AtoA)

GLEASON, JOHN. Admitted January 1, 1857 aged eight years by MARGARET
GLEASON, mother. Indentures expired January 1, 1870. (S-119) Delivered to his father May 2, 1857. (ROB, 1856)

GORY, JANE. Admitted March 3, 1853 aged nine years by JANE E. GORY,
mother. Indentures expired February 9, 1862. (R-35) Delivered to
her mother February 13, 1857. (ROG, 1856) Parents from Ireland.
Religion: Roman Catholic. (AtoA)

GRAHAM, JOSEPH HUGH. Admitted December 27, 1855 aged six years, four and one half months by MRS. ANN GRAHAM, mother. Indentures expired August 12, 1870. (S-71) Born Christ Church Parish. Religion: Episcopalian. (AtoA) Delivered to his mother, MRS. ANN RAINE, January 5, 1857. (BO)

GRAHAM, MARY JANE. Admitted December 27, 1855 aged nine years and nine months by ANN GRAHAM, mother. Indentures expired March 6, 1864. (R-99) Born in Christ Church Parish. Religion: Episcopalian. (AtoA) Delivered to her mother, MRS. ANN RAINE, January 5, 1857. (ROG, 1856)

GREEN, KETURAH. Admitted August 31, 1854 aged six years and six months by EMILY E. GREEN, mother. Born February 23, 1848. Indentures expired February 23, 1866. (R-65) Delivered to her mother May 27, 1858. (BO)

GRIFFITH, ANNIE. Admitted January 5, 1854 aged seven years by ELIZA GRIFFITH, mother, and the Poor House. Indentures expired January 5, 1864. (R-53) Elected teacher in the School March 1, 1866. (Minutes, March 1, 1866) Allowed one hundred dollars as a marriage dowry 1869. (Minutes, October 21, 1869) Religion: Presbyterian. (AtoA)

GRIFFITH, ELIZA. Admitted January 5, 1854 aged five years by ELIZA GRIFFITH, mother, and the Poor House. Indentures expired January 1867. (R-54) Elected assistant teacher November 29, 1866. (Minutes, November 29, 1866) Died December 27, 1877 at 2 AM of pneumonia. (DR, December 27, 1877) Religion: Presbyterian. (AtoA)

GRIFFITH, JOHN NELSON. Admitted January 5, 1854 aged five months by ELIZA GRIFFITH, mother. (Q-110) Died May 1854. (ROC, 1821) Religion: Presbyterian. (AtoA)

GRIFFITH, SARAH. Admitted January 5, 1854 aged nine years by ELIZA GRIFFITH, mother, and the Poor House. Indentures expired January 5, 1863. (R-52) Elected teacher in the School March 1, 1866. (Minutes, March 1, 1866) Religion: Presbyterian. (AtoA)

GROGAN (GROGHAN), THOMAS. Admitted November 7, 1850 aged one year and nine months and twenty-one days by MARGARET GROGAN, mother, and the Poor House. (Q-24) Born January 17, 1849. Religion: Protestant Episcopalian. (AtoA) Died December 9, 1851 of Marasmus. (ARP, 1852)

GRUBER, ALBERT. Admitted May 6, 1852 aged five years by SARAH GRUBER, mother, and the Poor House. Indentured to J.A. ENGLEBACK as a baker February 27, 1862. (Q-56) Mother born Tyrone County, Ireland. Father, ALBERT GRUBER, born Germany deserted the family. Child born New York. Lived in Charleston three years. (AtoA)

GUARDEN, ANN DOROTHEA AUGUSTA. Admitted November 4, 1858 aged eight years by J.C.H. CLAUSSEN, unknown. Indentures expired November 4, 1868. (U-156) Delivered to a relative, nd. (ROG, 1856)

HALLAM (HOLLOM), JOHN CHRISTOPHER. Admitted May 1, 1851 aged three years, nine months, and thirteen days by JANE FRANCES HALLAM, mother, and the Poor House. Indentures expired July 17, 1868. (Q-34) Born Sullivan's Island. Religion: Episcopalian. (AtoA) Delivered to his mother August 10, 1854. (ROC, 1821)

HAMSEN, CHARLES. Admitted May 6, 1858 aged seven years by ELIZABETH HAMSEN, mother. Indentured to E. ERHARDT (of Barnwell District) as a wheelwright and blacksmith August 28, 1866. Indentures expired May 6, 1872. (T-89)

HARNETT, HENRY JAMES. Admitted August 6, 1857 aged five years by ELLEN JOYCE, mother. Indentures expired August 6, 1873. (T-7) Delivered to his mother February 1858. (ROB, 1856)

HARPER, HANNAH. Admitted November 11, 1858 aged twelve years by REV. W.B. YATES, unknown. Indentured to D.P. DUNCAN (of Barnwell District) as a domestic June 20, 1864. Indentures expired November 11, 1864. (U-165)

146

HARPER, MARTHA. Admitted November 11, 1858 aged nine years by REV. W.B. YATES, unknown. Indentures expired November 11, 1867. (U-163) Delivered to her brother, unknown, nd. (ROG, 1856)

HARRIS, ANDREW J. Admitted July 30, 1857 aged five years by MRS. GEORGE HARRIS, mother. Indentures expired July 30, 1873. (T-6) Delivered to his mother, nd. (ROB, 1856)

HARRIS, GEORGE. Admitted March 3, 1859 aged three years by GEORGE F. HARRIS, father. (T-154) Died, nd. (ROB, 1856)

HARRIS, JAMES. Admitted December 22, 1853 aged eight years by the Poor House. Indentured to GEORGE W. EGAN as a carpenter October 11, 1860. Indentures expired December 22, 1866. (Q-109) Born North Carolina. Religion: Methodist. An orphan cared for by MRS. SUSAN HILL of 52 Beaufain Street. (AtoA)

HAYDEN, CATHARINE. Admitted July 24, 1856 aged eight years by ELIZABETH HAYDEN, mother. Indentures expired July 24, 1866. (U-16) Delivered to her mother December 6, 1860. (ROG, 1856)

HAYDEN, THOMAS WILLIAM. Admitted July 25, 1856 aged three years by ELIZABETH HAYDEN, mother. Indentures expired July 24, 1874. (S-103) Delivered to his mother January 23, 1869. (ROB, 1856) Religion: Methodist. (AtoA)

HAYS, ELIZABETH VICTORIA. Admitted September 27, 1855 aged eleven years and six months by HANNAH HAYS, mother. Indentures expired August 12, 1862. (R-79) Became a teacher in the School. (ROG, 1856) Religion: Episcopalian. (AtoA)

HAYS, GILBERT. Admitted April 10, 1856 aged eleven years by SARAH HAYS, mother. Indentures expired April 10, 1866. (S-89) Delivered to his uncle, unknown, March 7, 1861. (ROB, 1856)

HAYS, ISABELLA CLARA. Admitted October 9, 1856 aged seven years by MARY ANN HAYS, mother. Indentures expired October 9, 1867. (U-20) No further information.

HAYS, MARGARET ANNA. Admitted October 9, 1856 aged five years by MARY ANN HAYS, mother. Indentures expired October 9, 1869. (U-21) Delivered to her mother, nd. (ROG, 1856)

HAYS, MARGARET ELIZABETH. Admitted September 27, 1855 aged twelve years and eight months by HANNAH HAYS, mother. Indentures expired December 17, 1860. (R-78) Delivered to her mother August 5, 1858. (ROG, 1856) Religion: Episcopalian. (AtoA)

HAYS, MARY. Admitted April 10, 1856 aged thirteen years by SARAH HAYS, mother. Indentures expired April 10, 1861. (U-1) Delivered to her mother July 22, 1858. (ROG, 1856)

HAYS, RICHARD. Admitted April 10, 1856 aged nine years by SARAH HAYS, mother. Indentures expired April 10, 1868. (S-90) Delivered to his mother March 7, 1861. (ROB, 1856)

HAYS, RICHARDINE HAYCOCK. Admitted September 27, 1855 aged nine years, one month, and eight days by HANNAY HAYS, mother. Indentures expired August 19, 1864. (R-80) Delivered to her mother, January 21, 1864. (BO) Religion: Episcopalian. (AtoA)

HAYS, THOMAS HEYWARD. Admitted October 9, 1856 aged two years by MARY ANN HAYS, mother. Indentured to E.J. OLIVEROS (of Orangeburg) as a merchant December 29, 1870. Indentures expired October 9, 1875. (S-109) Religion: Episcopalian. Lived on America Street near Judith Street. (AtoA)

HAYS, WILLIAM WARREN. Admitted May 1, 1856 aged eleven years by MARY ANN HAYS, mother. Indentures expired May 1, 1866. (S-95) Sent to the School Ship, nd. (ROB, 1856) Father, THOMAS. Religion: Protestant Episcopalian (St. Stephens Chapel) Mother lived in Unity Alley. (AtoA)

HAZZARD, JAMES. Admitted November 29, 1855 aged nine years by SUSAN CONOLOY, aunt, and the Poor House. Indentured to ROBERT S. MAYS (of Maysville), occupation unknown, January 8, 1863. Indentures expired November 29, 1867. (S-62) Father, JOHN HAZZARD, deserted him. (AtoA) Received a silver watch for his services during the 1861 fire. (Minutes, July 17, 1862)

HAZZARD, JOHN. Admitted November 29, 1855 aged eleven years by SUSAN CONOLY, aunt, and the Poor House. Sent to the Marine School December 1, 1859. Indentures expired November 29, 1865. (S-61)

HAZZARD, RICHARD. Admitted November 29, 1855 aged four years by SUSAN CONOLY, aunt, and the Poor House. (S-63) Died February 5, 1856. (ROC, 1821)

HEARGROVES, JOHN. Admitted July 15, 1852 aged seven years by MARY HEARGROVES, mother and the Poor House. Indentured to WILLIAM SMITH (of Abbeville District) as a farmer February 10, 1859. Indentures expired July 15, 1866. (Q-60) Born in Walterboro. Religion: Methodist. (AtoA)

HEARGROVES, MARY JANE. Admitted July 15, 1852 aged four years by MARY HEARGROVES, mother, and the Poor House. Indentured to JOHN T. WIGHTMAN, JR. as a domestic June 4, 1863. Indentures expired July 15, 1866. (R-24) Religion: Methodist. (AtoA)

HEILBURN, AUGUSTUS R. Admitted November 4, 1852 aged two years and four months by ELIZA HEILBURN, mother, and the Poor House. (Q-73) Delivered to his mother December 30, 1852. (ROC, 1821) Readmitted January 6, 1853. (AtoA) Indentured to C. EHRHARDT (of Barnwell District) as a millwright and blacksmith August 28, 1866. Indentures expired July 4, 1871. (Q-73) Born in Georgia. Father, ROBERT S. HEILBURN, born in Maine and died October 1852, was a machinist. Religion: Baptist. (AtoA)

HEINEY, MARY ANN. Admitted July 31, 1856 aged two years and eight months by BRIDGET HEINEY, mother. Indentures expired November 30, 1871. (U-71) Delivered to her mother March 8, 1859. (ROG, 1856)

HEINSOHN, ERNEST CHARLES. Admitted January 9, 1851 aged ten years by BETTE HEINSOHN, mother, and the Poor House. Born in Hanover, Germany. Indentures expired January 9, 1862. (Q-25) Delivered to his mother, MRS. DUNNEMAN, November 4, 1852. (Minutes, November 4, 1852) Religion: Lutheran. Had been living in Charleston for three years. Mother lived in Reid Street. (AtoA)

HEINSOHN, WILLIAM. Admitted January 9, 1851 aged six years by BETTE HEINSOHN, mother, and the Poor House. Born in Hanover, Germany. Indentures expired January 9, 1866. (Q-26) Delivered to his mother, MRS. DUNNEMAN, November 4, 1852. (BO)

HENDERSON, ELIZABETH. Admitted December 16, 1858 aged seven years by ISABELLA HENDERSON, mother. Indentures expired December 16, 1869. (U-171) An Advanced Girl. (ROG, 1856)

HENDERSON, WILLIAM. Admitted November 16, 1858 aged three years by ISABELLA HENDERSON, mother. Indentures expired February 16, 1876. (T-134)

HERRITAGE, WILLIAM. Admitted December 9, 1858 aged three years by MRS. THOMAS HOLLAND HERRITAGE, mother. Indentures expired December 9, 1876. (T-128) Delivered to his mother, nd. (ROB, 1856)

HIDRICKS, MARION. Admitted September 4, 1851 aged six years by SARAH HIDRICKS, mother, and the Poor House. Indentured to CHARLES H. HANCOCK (of Americus, Georgia) as a printer February 11, 1858. Indentures expired September 4, 1866. (Q-48)

HIGGINS, DANIEL. Admitted May 25, 1854 aged eight years by the Poor House. Indentured to J.K. FREY (of Spartanburg District) as a tanner February 3, 1859. Indentures expired May 25, 1867. (S-17)

HIGGINS, ELIZA. Admitted March 20, 1856 aged seven years by HANNAH HIGGINS, mother. Indentures expired March 20, 1867. (R-106) Religion: Catholic. (AtoA) No further information.

HIGGINS, ROSEANNA. Admitted September 2, 1852 aged eleven years by the Poor House. Indentured to WADE J. and CECILIA A. MARKLEY as a needle-worker March 12, 1856. Indentures expired September 2, 1859. (R-25) Returned to the COH June 19, 1856 (BO) Elected Assistant Nurse December 17, 1856. (Minutes, December 17, 1856) Died January 3, 1861. (ROG, 1856)

HOLWAY, MARY E. Admitted November 29, 1855 aged three years and two days by AURA A. HOLWAY, mother. Indentures expired November 27, 1871. (R-89) Born October 27, 1852. Religion: Methodist. (AtoA) Delivered to her mother May 15, 1856 because she had a "peculiar disease." (BO)

HOWARD, CATHARINE. Admitted May 26, 1853 aged four years by JOANNA HOWARD, mother, and the Poor House. Indentures expired May 26, 1867. (R-38) Delivered to her mother, April 8, 1864. (BO) Religion: Roman Catholic. (AtoA)

HOWARD, MARY ANN. Admitted May 26, 1853 aged five years by JOANNA HOWARD, mother, and the Poor House. Indentures expired May 26, 1853 (R-37) Delivered to her uncle and aunt, MR. and MRS. MANNING (of Helena, Newberry District) July 20, 1863. (BO) Religion: Roman Catholic. (AtoA)

HUGHES, JESSE. Admitted June 12, 1857 aged six years by ELIZA HUGHES, mother. Indentures expired June 12, 1872. (S-139) Delivered to his mother, nd. (ROB, 1856)

HUGHES, LOUISA. Admitted June 12, 1857 aged seven years by ELIZA HUGHES, mother. Indentures expired June 12, 1868. (U-67) Delivered to her mother December 14, 1865. (ROG, 1856)

HUMBELL, HENRY. Admitted August 31, 1854 aged two years and six months by the Poor House. (S-33) A derelict. Religion: Lutheran. (AtoA) Died, nd. (ROB, 1856)

HYAMS, W.P. Admitted October 13, 1859 aged nine years by the Poor House. Indentured to C. HICKEY as a gilder May 9, 1868. Indentures expired October 13, 1871. (T-200)

ICARD, CAROLINE. Admitted December 2, 1852 aged ten years by JOHANNA ICARD, mother. Indentures expired December 2, 1852. (R-29) Delivered to her mother August 17, 1856. (ROG, 1856) Born in New York State. Grandfather THOMAS A. BRANDT. Religion: Methodist. (AtoA)

ICARD, CATHARINE. Admitted June 16, 1859 aged nine years by JOHANNA PATUSE, mother. Indentures expired June 16, 1868. (U-201) Delivered to her mother, nd. (ROG, 1856)

ICARD, ELIZABETH. Admitted December 2, 1852 aged five years by JOHANNA ICARD, mother. Indentures expired December 2, 1865. (R-32) Delivered to her mother, nd. (ROG, 1856) Born in New York State. Religion: Methodist. (AtoA)

INGHAM, JAMES C. Admitted April 16, 1859 aged six years by ELIZABETH INGHAM, mother. Indentures expired April 16, 1874. (T-158) Delivered to his mother March 10, 1870. (ROB, 1856)

INGHAM, JANE H. Admitted April 16, 1859 aged twelve years by ELIZABETH INGHAM, unknown. Indentures expired April 16, 1865. (U-165) "Teacher." (ROG, 1856)

INNIS, HUGH. Admitted April 10, 1857 aged eight years by BRIDGET INNIS, unknown. Indentures expired April 10, 1870. (S-125) "Left." (ROB, 1856)

IRVIN, ALICE. Admitted December 19, 1856 aged two years. Indentures expired December 19, 1872. (U-24) Delivered to her mother, unknown, nd. (ROG, 1856)

IRONMONGER, JANE A. Admitted December 29, 1859 aged six years by MRS. A.M. IRONMONGER, mother. Indentured to MRS. W.B. BAYNARD (of Edisto Island), occupation unknown, February 20, 1868. Indentures expired December 29, 1871. (U-233)

IRONMONGER, SARAH R. Admitted December 29, 1859 aged nine years by MRS. A.M. IRONMONGER, mother. Indentures expired December 29, 1868. (U-231) No further information.

IRONMONGER, WILLIAM G. Admitted December 29, 1859 aged two years by MRS. A.M. IRONMONGER, mother. Indentures expired December 29, 1878. (T-210) No further information.

JACKSON, JAMES. Admitted May 15, 1857 aged nine years by ANN JACKSON, mother. Indentures expired May 15, 1869. (S-133) Delivered to his mother, nd. (ROB, 1856)

JARROLD, JOHN HENRY. Admitted January 20, 1853 aged three years by SARAH JARROLD, mother, and the Poor House. Indentured to THOMAS A. JOHNSON as a butcher January 11, 1866. Indentures expired January 20, 1871. (Q-80) Mother, an inmate of the Poor House, had consumption. (AtoA)

JENERETT (JEANNERETT), WILLIAM FRANKLIN. Admitted February 6, 1851 aged eight years by REBECCA JENERETT, mother, and the Poor House. Indentured to ROBERT M. STOKES (of Laurens District) as a printer March 13, 1856. Indentures expired February 6, 1864. (Q-29)

JOHANS, ANNA MATILDA. Admitted December 17, 1857 aged two years by SARAH ANN JOHANS, unknown. (U-109) Died April 16, 1858. (ROB, 1856)

JOHNSON, JANE. Admitted October 10, 1858 by the Poor House. Indentured to JAMES R. GILLAND, occupation unknown, December 21, 1865. (U-119)

JONES, MARION. Admitted December 22, 1853. Adopted by JOHN R. HARRISON March 20, 1856. Indentures expired December 22, 1874. (S-87)

JONES, THOMAS. Admitted September 23, 1852 aged six years and three months by MARY JONES, mother, and the Poor House. Indentured to CAMERON & CO. as a moulder September 23, 1860. Indentures expired September 23, 1867. (Q-63) Born Dublin, Ireland. Religion: Protestant. Lived at 126 Church Street, the corner of Linguard Street. (AtoA)

KAOUGH, MARGARET. Admitted August 4, 1853 aged eleven years by ELLEN KAOUGH, mother, and the Poor House. Indentured to MRS. JAMES MAGILL, occupation unknown, February 27, 1857. Indentures expired August 4, 1860. (R-44) Father, PATRICK KAOUGH, a blacksmith died in Savannah. (AtoA)

KAOUGH, THOMAS. Admitted August 4, 1853 aged three years by ELLEN KAOUGH, mother, and the Poor House. (Q-100) Died May 1854. (ROC, 1821)

KEARNEY, ROBERT. Admitted October 6, 1856 aged ten years by CATHARINE JOHNSON, mother. Indentures expired October 9, 1867. (S-110) Delivered to his sister, unknown, nd. (ROB, 1856) Born Ireland. Religion: Protestant Episcopalian. Mother lived at 8 Philadelphia Alley. (AtoA)

KEEFE, CORNELIUS. Admitted July 7, 1853 aged three years and six months by SARAH KEEFE, mother. Indentures expired January 7, 1871. (Q-98) Delivered to his mother November 8, 1860. (BO)

KEEFE, JOHN. Admitted July 7, 1853 aged five years by SARAH KEEFE, mother. Indentures expired July 7, 1869. (Q-97) Delivered to his mother November 8, 1860. (BO)

KENNEDY, JOHN. Admitted July 25, 1850 aged seventeen months by ELLEN KENNEDY, mother, and the Poor House. Born Ireland. (Q-15) Died September 1850 of dysentary. (ARP, 1850)

KENNEDY, MICHAEL CONWAY. Admitted July 25, 1850 aged five years by
ELLEN KENNEDY, mother, and the Poor House. Indentures expired July 25,
1866. (Q-14) Delivered to his mother 1853. (ROC, 1821)

KENNEDY, THOMAS. Admitted June 17, 1858 aged ten years by JULIA KENNEDY,
sister. Indentured to HERRMANN KOPPEL as a tailor February 16, 1860.
Indentures expired June 17, 1869. (T-97)

KING, MARY. Admitted January 29, 1852 aged three years and one month
by the Poor House. (R-20) Died January 27, 1853 of Marasmus. (Minutes,
June 13, 1853) Born in the Poor House. Mother, deaf and dumb, an inmate of the Poor House. Religion: Roman Catholic. (AtoA)

KING, THOMAS. Admitted March 24, 1859 aged eight years by ELIZABETH
McLAUGHLIN, unknown, and the Poor House. Indentures expired March 24,
1872. (T-156) Delivered to his father January 5, 1864. (ROB, 1856)

KONROY, JAMES. Admitted January 12, 1859 aged four years by JULIA
KENNEDY, aunt. Indentures expired January 12, 1876. (T-152) Delivered
to his mother, nd. (ROB, 1856)

KOTCH, AMELIA. Admitted March 1, 1855 aged four years by the Poor House.
Indentures expired March 1, 1869. (R-67) Indentured to J. ADGER SMYTHE,
occupation unknown, November 2, 1866. (ROG, 1856) Mother, an inmate of
the Poor House "is subject to occasional weakness of mind amounting
almost to harmless derangement." (AtoA)

KOTCH (KOSCH), ROBERT. Admitted July 27, 1854 aged seven years by the
Poor House. Indentured to CHARLES W. HANCOCK (of Americus, Georgia)
as a printer January 30, 1863. Indentures expired July 27, 1868. (S-26)

KUFFNIER (KAUFNER), JACOB. Admitted May 1, 1851 aged five years by
JOHANNA KUFFNIER, mother, and the Poor House. Indentures expired May
1, 1867. (Q-35) Delivered to his mother October 23, 1863. (ROB, 1856)
Religion: Lutheran. Mother lived at the corner of King and Ann Streets.
(AtoA)

KUFFNIER, JOHN. Admitted May 1, 1851 aged four years by JOHANNA KUFFNIER,
mother, and the Poor House. Indentures expired May 1, 1868. (Q-36)
Delivered to his mother, nd. (ROB, 1856) Religion: Lutheran. Mother
lived at the corner of Ann and King Streets. (AtoA)

LAKE, EDWARD. Admitted March 4, 1851 aged eight years by NICHOLAS LAKE,
father. Indentures expired June 15, 1863. (Q-30) Delivered to his
father September 18, 1851. (BO) Born Halifax County, Virginia June 15,
1842. Religion: Congregationalist. (AtoA)

LAKE, JOHN. Admitted March 4, 1851 aged five years by NICHOLAS LAKE,
father. Indentures expired October 28, 1845. (Q-31) Delivered to his
father September 18, 1851. (BO) Born Halifax County, Virginia October
28, 1845. Religion: Congregationalist. (AtoA)

LAMBLE, ALEXANDER MARION. Admitted April 13, 1854 aged three years and
ten months by LOUISA C. LAMBLE, mother. (S-10) Delivered to his uncle,
JOSEPH LAMBLE, to be trained as a machinist November 15, 1866. (BO)
Indentures expired May 20, 1871. (S-10) Religion: Episcopalian. (AtoA)

LAMBLE, HENRY. Admitted August 4, 1859 aged three years by MRS. L.C.
LAMBLE, unknown. Indentured to WILMOT G. DeSAUSSURE as a clerk June 23,
1870. Indentures expired August 4, 1877. (T-188)

LAMBLE, WILLIAM JAMES. Admitted April 13, 1854 aged eight years and four
and one half months by LOUISA C. LAMBLE, mother. Sent to the School
Ship March 29, 1860. Indentures expired November 30, 1866. (S-9)
Religion: Episcopalian. (AtoA)

LATHROP, GEORGE WASHINGTON. Admitted March 24, 1853 aged three years
by SARAH LATHROP, mother. Indentures expired January 23, 1871. (Q-86)
Delivered to his mother going to Savannah August 1853. (BO) Born
January 23, 1850 in Savannah. Religion: Episcopalian. (AtoA)

LATHROP, JOSEPH JACKSON. Admitted March 24, 1853 aged eight years and six months by SARAH LATHROP, mother. Indentures expired August 2, 1865. (Q-85) Delivered to his mother going to Savannah August 1853. (BO) Born August 2, 1844 in Buffalo, New York. Religion: Episcopalian. (AtoA)

LECKIE, JOHN. Admitted October 13, 1859 aged seven years by the Poor House. Indentures expired October 13, 1873. (T-195) Absconded while at Orangeburg. (ROB, 1856)

LECKIE, ROBERT. Admitted October 13, 1859 aged four years by the Poor House. Indentured to FRANCIS L. WALKER as a farmer January 13, 1871. Indentures expired October 13, 1876. (T-197)

LEITCH, THOMAS. Admitted January 7, 1858 aged eight years by CATHARINE LEITCH, mother. Indentured to W.B. ELKIN (of Gadsden, South Carolina), occupation unknown, January 7, 1871. (T-48)

LEMAN, BENJAMIN. Admitted January 31, 1856 aged seven years by JEANNETTE LEMAN, mother. Indentures expired January 31, 1870. (S-82) Delivered to his brother, DAVID LEMAN, June 17, 1862. (BO) Religion: Jewish. (AtoA)

LEMAN, HENRIETTA. Admitted March 15, 1855 aged ten years by JEANNETTE LEMAN, mother, and the Poor House. Indentures expired March 15, 1863. (R-69) Elected assistant teacher January 1, 1863. (Minutes, January 1, 1863) Delivered to her mother, nd. (ROG, 1856) Born Philadelphia. Religion: Jewish. (AtoA)

LEMAN, MITCHELL. Admitted March 15, 1855 aged twelve years by JEANNETTE LEMAN, mother, and the Poor House. Indentures expired March 15, 1864. (S-39) Delivered to his mother, nd. (ROC, 1821) Born Philadelphia. Religion: Jewish. (AtoA)

LEONARD, MARY ANN. Admitted December 10, 1857 aged nine years by MRS. JANE ADCOCK, mother. Indentured to N.R. DOBSON as a domestic August 14, 1862. (U-105)

LEONARD, PETER FREDERICK B. Admitted July 17, 1856 aged six years and three months by JANE LEONARD, mother. Indentures expired April 16, 1871. (S-101) Delivered to his mother, nd. (ROB, 1856) Religion: Episcopalian, St. Stephens Chapel. (AtoA)

LEQUEUX, MARY LOUISE. Admitted January 3, 1856 aged eight years and three months by S.F. LeQUEUX, father. Indentures expired October 10, 1865. (R-101) Elected teacher and later Superintendent. (ROG, 1856) Religion: Methodist. (AtoA) Grandmother, MARY MANNO. (Minutes, January 3, 1856)

LEQUEUX, WILLIAM BENJAMIN. Admitted January 3, 1856 aged twelve years and one month by S.F. LeQUEUX, father. Indentures expired December 7, 1864. (S-79) Delivered to his father November 23, 1858. (BO) Religion: Methodist. (AtoA)

LILLIS, MICHAEL. Admitted March 1, 1855 aged three years by the Poor House. Indentures expired March 1, 1873. (S-37) Religion: Roman Catholic. (AtoA) No further information.

LINDE, GOTTLIEB FREDERICK HANCOCK. Admitted April 19, 1855 aged three years and six months by FREDERICK WILLIAM LINDE, father. "The Masonic order has something for this boy and his brother." Indentures to BENJAMIN McINNES as a blacksmith March 6, 1868. Indentures expired October 19, 1872. (S-47) "A good boy. Wishes a clerkship, or anything respectable. Has a father, a Baker, and an Uncle with segan business, but no expectations from either." (Minutes, December 5, 1861) Religion: Luthern. Born in Augusta, Georgia. (AtoA)

LINDE, JOHN FREDERICK WILLIAM. Admitted April 19, 1855 aged four years and six months by FREDERICK WILLIAM LINDE, father. Indentured to JACOB SMALL & CO. as a baker October 5, 1866. Indentures expired October 19, 1871. (S-46)

LONERGAN, CATHARINE. Admitted November 29, 1855 aged two years by WILLIAM LONERGAN, father. Indentures expired November 29, 1871. (R-94) Delivered to her sister, unknown, nd. (ROG, 1856) Religion: Roman Catholic. Father "a laboring Irishman...a worthless Drunkard." (AtoA)

LONERGAN, JOHANNA. Admitted November 29, 1855 aged twelve years by WILLIAM LONERGAN, father. Indentured to MRS. JAMES BAILE, occupation unknown, December 9, 1858. Indentures expired November 29, 1861. (R-92) Requested a marriage dowry October 21, 1869. (Minutes, October 21, 1869)

LONERGAN, MARY. Admitted November 29, 1855 aged four years by WILLIAM LONERGAN, father. Indentured to JOSEPH E. ADGER, a merchant of this city, occupation unknown, October 31, 1867. Indentures expired November 29, 1869. (R-93)

LONERGAN, WILLIAM. Admitted November 29, 1855 aged seven years by WILLIAM LONERGAN, father. Indentured to W.S. DUDLEY (of Orangeburg District) as a farmer November 1, 1865. Indentures expired November 29, 1869. (S-67)

LUDERWIG, AMANDA. Admitted March 28, 1850 aged seven years by AMELIA LUDERWIG, mother, and the Poor House. (R-5) Adopted by MARSHALL THOMPSON (of Edgefield District) October 3, 1850. (ROC, 1821) Indentures expired March 28, 1861. (R-5) Born in Germany. Religion: Protestant. (AtoA)

McALVOY, CHARLOTTE. Admitted September 18, 1856 aged four years. Indentured to JOHN T. WIGHTMAN, occupation unknown, September 12, 1867. Indentures expired September 18, 1870. (U-19)

McCALVEY (McKELVEY), ANDREW CHARLES. Admitted September 11, 1856 aged eleven years by CATHARINE McCALVEY, mother. Indentured to JONATHAN FORD (of Tennessee) as a turner and cabinetmaker December 6, 1860. Indentures expired September 11, 1866. (S-107) Born in Newburgh, New York. Lived at 2 Queen Street. Father in a Northern lunatic asylum. Brother, EDWARD, recently died of yellow fever. (AtoA)

McCOLLUM, GEORGE. Admitted April 16, 1859 aged eleven years by JULIA McCOLLUM, mother. Indentures expired April 16, 1869. (T-160) Delivered to his mother, nd. (ROB,1856)

McCOLLUM, JOHN. Admitted July 8, 1858 aged three years by MARY McCOLLUM, mother. Indentures expired July 8, 1876. (T-100) Absconded May 1869. (ROB, 1856)

McCOLLUM, JULIA SMITH. Admitted August 27, 1857 aged three years by MARY McCOLLUM, mother. Adopted by her cousin, JAMES E. McCOLLUM, September 18, 1868. Indentures expired August 27, 1872. (U-45)

McCOLLUM, MARY C. Admitted August 27, 1857 aged five years by MARY McCOLLUM, mother. Adopted by her cousin, JAMES E. McCOLLUM, October 2, 1868. Indentures expired August 27, 1870. (U-45)

McCOLLUM, ROBERT. Admitted April 16, 1859 aged nine years by JULIA McCOLLUM, mother. Indentures expired April 16, 1871. (T-162) Delivered to his mother, nd. (ROB, 1856)

McCORMICK, JAMES. Admitted April 24, 1857 aged eight years by MARY McCORMICK, mother. Indentures expired April 24, 1870. (S-129) Delivered to his uncle, JAMES FITZPATRICK, January 20, 1859. (ROB, 1856)

McCORMICK, WILLIAM. Admitted April 24, 1857 aged ten years by MARY McCORMICK, mother. Indentures expired April 24, 1868. (S-128) Delivered to his uncle, JAMES FITZPATRICK, January 20, 1859. (ROB, 1856)

McDERMIE, JAMES. Admitted February 17, 1859 aged five years and six months by CECILIA McDERMIE, mother. Indentures expired August 17, 1875. (T-144) Indentured to ADAM BEILY, occupation unknown, August 12, 1869. (ROB, 1856)

McDONNOUGH, WILLIAM. Admitted August 14, 1851 aged four years by
SARAH McDONNOUGH, mother, and the Poor House. Born December 10, 1847.
Indentures expired August 14, 1868. Delivered to his mother going to
Philadelphia July 6, 1853. (BO) Religion: Roman Catholic. (AtoA)

McFEELEY, JOHN EDWARD. Admitted August 19, 1852 aged six years by MARY
A. McFEELEY, mother, and the Poor House. Indentured to O.A HAWTHORNE
(of Abbeville District) as a coachmaker September 25, 1857. Indentures
expired August 19, 1867. (Q-61) Religion: Roman Catholic. (AtoA)

McGRANAGAN (McGRANAGHAN), WILLIAM JOSEPH. Admitted June 9, 1853 aged
three years by HESTER McGRANAGAN, mother, and the Poor House. Indentures
expired June 9, 1871. (Q-95) "Left." (ROB, 1856) Born April 22, 1850
in Ireland. Religion: Methodist. (AtoA)

McLANE, ANN ELIZABETH. Admitted July 28, 1853 aged three years by the
Poor House. A derelict. Adopted by JOHN G. FORBES (of Columbia)
November 10, 1853. Indentures expired July 28, 1868. (R-43)

McLEAN (McLANE), GEORGE. Admitted July 28, 1853 aged seven years by
the Poor House. A derelict. Indentured to H.A. CAUBLE (of Greenville)
as a merchant and a farmer March 21, 1861. Indentures expired July
28, 1867. (Q-99)

McNAMARA, ANNA. Admitted July 3, 1856 aged five years and six months by
M.A. McNAMARA, mother. Born in New York. Indentures expired January
3, 1869. (U-14) No further information.

MACK, MICHAEL. Admitted November 12, 1857 aged nine years by MARY
MACK, mother. Indentures expired November 12, 1869. (T-23) Delivered
to his father, unknown, nd. (ROB, 1856)

MAHONEY, CHARLES. Admitted October 2, 1856 aged four years. (S-108)
Died, nd. (ROB, 1856) Admitted from the Alms House. Mother declared
to be unfit to keep him. (AtoA)

MAHONEY, CHARLES. Admitted August 19, 1858 aged six years by MRS. ANNE
MAHONEY, mother. Indentures expired August 19, 1873. (T-116) "Left."
(ROB, 1856)

MANNIHAN, MICHAEL. Admitted July 3, 1856 aged ten years by MARY STANLEY,
grandmother, of Ireland. (AtoA) Indentures expired July 3, 1867.
(S-99) "Left." (ROG, 1856) Religion: Catholic. (AtoA)

MARGART, GEORGE MARTIN. Admitted February 20, 1857 aged eight years by
MARGARET PALMERSTERR, mother. Indentures expired February 20, 1870.
(S-121) Delivered to his mother November 15, 1860. (ROB, 1856)

MARTIN, FRANCES ANN. Admitted December 6, 1855 aged three years and
two months by ELIZA JANE MARTIN, mother. Born September 19, 1852.
Indentures expired September 19, 1870. (R-98) Delivered to her mother
July 21, 1859. (ROG, 1856) Parents from North Carolina. Father died
of yellow fever during the summer of 1854. Religion: Methodist. (AtoA)

MASSALON, THOMAS H. Admitted June 26, 1857 aged five years by SARAH
MASSALON, mother. Indentures expired June 26, 1873. (S-140) Delivered
to his mother, nd. (ROB, 1856)

MAULL, EDWIN H. Admitted June 12, 1857 aged eight years and six months
by ANN MAULL, mother. Indentures expired June 12, 1869. (S-138)
No further information.

MAULL, JAMES. Admitted June 26, 1857 by ANN MAULL, mother. (T-3)
Delivered to his father, unknown, April 2, 1868. (ROB, 1856)

MAULL, MARTIN. Admitted June 26, 1857 aged six years and four months by
ANN MAULL, mother. Indentured to CHARLES W. SEIGNIOUS, occupation
unknown, December 6, 1866. Indentures expired June 26, 1871. (T-2)

MAZYCK, NINA. Admitted February 13, 1852 aged ten days by the Poor House. (R-21) A foundling left at the COH gate. (Minutes, February 19, 1852) Adopted by LYDIA and JOHN WITZ September 8, 1859. (ROG, 1856)

MERCIER, CHARLES. Admitted November 29, 1855 aged nine years by MARY ANN MERCIER, mother, and the Poor House. Indentures expired November 29, 1867. (S-65) Delivered to his mother August 25, 1859. (BO) Born in Ireland. (AtoA)

MERCIER, FREDERICK WILLIAM. Admitted May 1, 1856 aged five years and four months by JOSEPHINE MERCIER, mother. Indentures expired January 1, 1872. (S-96) Delivered to his mother June 23, 1859. (BO) Born in Ireland. Religion: Episcopalian. (AtoA)

MERCIER, GEORGE. Admitted November 29, 1855 aged seven years by MARY ANN MERCIER, mother, and the Poor House. Indentures expired November 29, 1869. (S-66) Delivered to his mother June 23, 1859. (BO) Born in Ireland. (AtoA)

MEYER, CORDE. Admitted June 14, 1855 aged ten years and six months by MARTIN MEYER, guardian. Indentured to E.A. BRONSON (of Barnwell District) as a printer April 8, 1858. Indentures expired December 14, 1865. (S-50) Born in New York. Religion: Lutheran. (AtoA) Absconded, nd. Transferred to I.H.F. WRAGGE (of Barnwell District) as a carpenter October 12, 1858. (BO)

MICHEL, BENJAMIN. Admitted June 21, 1855 aged five years by MARY A. MICHEL, mother. Indentures expired June 21, 1871. (S-52) Delivered to his mother (of Macon, Georgia) February 25, 1864. (BO) Religion: Episcopalian. (AtoA)

MICHEL, MAXIMILLIAN. Admitted June 21, 1855 aged twelve years by MARY A. MICHEL, mother. Indentured to ERNEST PRESHKE as a watchmaker June 3, 1858. Indentures expired June 21, 1861. (S-51) Transferred to his brother, EDMUND A. MICHEL, nd. (ROB, 1856) Served at Fort Sumter. (BO, MA. A. Michel applying for B. Michel) Religion: Episcopalian. (AtoA)

MICHEL, VIRGINIA. Admitted March 18, 1858 aged ten years by MARY A. MICHEL, mother. Indentures expired March 18, 1866. (U-131) Delivered to her mother July 19, 1860. (ROG, 1856)

MILLAR, LOUIS. Admitted March 6, 1857 aged two years and nine months by ANN MILLAR, mother. Indentures expired June 6, 1875. (S-122) "Not in House." (ROB, 1856)

MILLIGAN, HENRY. Admitted January 20, 1859 aged nine years by ALICE MILLIGAN, mother. Indentures expired January 20, 1871. (T-138) Delivered to his mother June 6, 1864. (ROB, 1856)

MILLIGAN, R.A. Admitted January 20, 1859 aged three years by ALICE MILLIGAN, mother. Indentures expired January 20, 1877. (T-140) Delivered to his mother June 6, 1864. (ROB, 1856)

MILLS, CAROLINE. Admitted December 4, 1851 aged nine years by MRS. ____ MILLS, mother, and the Poor House. Born March 12, 1842. Indentures expired December 4, 1860. (R-19) Delivered to her mother February 20, 1857. (ROG, 1856) Born St. James Parish, Santee District. Religion: Methodist; Glebe Street Church (AtoA) Allowed fifty dollars as a marriage dowry 1858. (Minutes, November 25, 1858)

MILLS, JAMES SEABROOK. Admitted June 17, 1852 aged two years by ELIZABETH W. MILLS, mother, and the Poor House. Indentures expired June 17, 1871. (Q-59) Delivered to his mother 1860. (BO) Born St. James Parish, Santee District. Lived in College Street.

MILLS, MARY JANE. Admitted June 17, 1852 aged six years by ELIZABETH W. MILLS, mother, and the Poor House. Indentures expired June 17, 1864. (R-22) Born in St. James Parish, Santee District. (AtoA) Delivered to her mother March 29, 1860. (BO)

MILLS, SARAH ANN. Admitted December 4, 1851 aged eleven years by MRS. _____ MILLS, mother, and the Poor House. Born December 6, 1840. Indentures expired December 4, 1858. (R-18) Delivered to her mother November 15, 1855. (BO) Born St. James Parish, Santee District. Religion: Methodist. (AtoA) Allowed fifty dollars as a marriage dowry 1857. (Minutes, February 19, 1857)

MILLS, WILLIAM. Admitted December 4, 1851 aged six years by MRS. _____ MILLS, mother, and the Poor House. Born April 6, 1845. Indentures expired December 4, 1866. (Q-49) Delivered to his mother February 10, 1859. (BO) Born St. James Parish, Santee District. Religion: Methodist. (AtoA)

MINUS, ANN. Admitted January 13, 1853 aged nine years by SAVAGE MINUS, father. Indentures expired January 13, 1862. (R-33) No further information.

MINUS, SUSAN. Admitted January 13, 1853 aged six years by SAVAGE S. MINUS, father. (R-34) Delivered to her cousin-in-law, LUKE DOHERTY (of Ridgeville, South Carolina) February 20, 1862. (BO) Indentures expired January 13, 1865. Born June 30, 1846. (R-34)

MONTGOMERY, JAMES HENRY. Admitted April 3, 1856 aged thirteen years by JOHN J. SYMONS, unknown. Indentured to N.C. SCOTT (of Dalton, Georgia) as a blacksmith December 3, 1857. Indentures expired April 3, 1864. (S-88)

MOORE, JAMES. Admitted September 22, 1853 aged six years by ELIZA MOORE, mother. Indentured to J.J. BONNER (of Due West, Abbeville District) as a printer October 31, 1861. Indentures expired September 22, 1868. (R-48) Father, MALCOLM MOORE, in Florida, deserted his family. Mother born in Ireland. Parents married in Pennsylvania. Religion: Episcopalian. (AtoA)

MORAN, JOHN. Admitted March 24, 1853 aged ten years by the Poor House. Indentures expired March 24, 1864. (Q-90) Absconded 1853. (ROB, 1856) "Mother...a lunatic in the cells of the Poor House." (AtoA)

MORAN, PATRICK. Admitted September 30, 1852 aged three years by the Poor House. Indentures expired September 30, 1870. (Q-69) Delivered to his brother, C.E. MORAN, to be trained as a blacksmith December 30, 1863. (BO)

MORRISON, CHARLES. Admitted May 22, 1857 aged twelve years. Indentured to ROBERT McKAY, occupation unknown, June 14, ____. Indentures expired May 22, 1866. (S-136)

MORIEN (MORAN), CATHARINE. Admitted May 3, 1855 aged nine years, four months and nine days by ANN DUN, mother. Indentures expired December 24, 1863. (R-74) Delivered to her step-father, JOHN DUN, of Washington Street February 13, 1857. (BO) Born December 24, 1845. Religion: Catholic. (AtoA)

MORRISON, JAMES. Admitted March 1, 1855 aged six years by the Poor House. Indentured to HIRAM HARRIS as a bookbinder January 11, 1866. Indentures expired March 1, 1870. (S-36) Born New York. Religion: Episcopalian. Mother died in New York in August 1853 and the father died in Charleston in September 1854. (AtoA)

MORRISON, WILLIAM. Admitted March 1, 1855 aged eight years by the Poor House. Indentures expired March 1, 1868. (S-35) Indentured to WILLIAM C. BEE, occupation unknown, nd. (ROB, 1856) Received a silver watch for his services during the 1861 fire. (Minutes, July 17, 1862)

MULKAHY, JAMES. Admitted April 24, 1857 aged six years by his parents, unknown. Indentures expired April 24, 1872. (S-126) Delivered to his mother, nd. (ROB, 1856)

MULLEN, ELIZA. Admitted February 6, 1857 aged three years by ELIZA MULLEN, mother. Indentures expired February 6, 1872. (U-55) Delivered to her mother July 21, 1859. (ROG, 1856)

MULLINS, MICHAEL. Admitted November 29, 1855 aged six years and nine months by ELIZA MULLINS, unknown. Born January 29, 1849. (S-64) Died February 27, 1862. (ROB, 1856) Born Limerick, Ireland. Religion: Roman Catholic. Mother lived on Philadelphia Street. (AtoA)

MURRAY, ANDREW BUIST. Admitted May 29, 1856 aged twelve years by JAMES MURRAY, father. (S-97) Indentured to J.J. TOON, occupation unknown, July 28, 1860. (ROB, 1856) Transferred to W.J. BENNETT, occupation unknown, November 22, 1860. Indentures expired May 29, 1865. (S-97) Born in South Carolina. (AtoA)

MURRAY, ELIZABETH ANN. Admitted November 17, 1859 aged ten years by SARAH MURRAY, mother. Indentured to M.C. GRISWALD, occupation unknown, March 22, 1866. Indentures expired November 17, 1867. (U-228)

MURRAY, JAMES. Admitted May 11, 1858 aged three years and six months by NANCY MURRAY, mother. Indentures expired May 11, 1876. (T-124) No further information.

MURRAY, JOHN. Admitted January 21, 1858 aged six years by NANCY MURRAY, mother. Indentured to C.S. McCAY (of St. Stephens Parish) as a farmer July 19, 1866. Indentures expired January 21, 1873. (T-57)

MURRAY, MARTHA ELIZA. Admitted November 17, 1859 aged six years by MRS. SARAH S. MURRAY, mother. Indentured to E.H. KELLER, s M.D. as a domestic December 19, 1867. Indentures expired November 17, 1871. (U-225)

MURRAY, MARY ELLEN. Admitted May 18, 1854 aged eleven years by the Poor House. (R-59) Delivered to her brother, TERRENCE MURRAY, to be sent to E.B. and E.S. STEPHENS as a dressmaker July 10, 1857. (BO) Indentures expired May 18, 1861. (R-59) Allowed fifty dollars as a marriage dowry 1861. (Minutes, February 28, 1861)

MURRAY, ROBERT. Admitted December 19, 1856 aged eleven years by CHARLOTTE MURRAY, mother. Indentured to J.K.FREY (of Spartanburg District) as a tanner and currier February 3, 1859. Indentures expired December 19, 1866. (S-118) Born Ireland. Religion: Roman Catholic. Lived at 4 Clifford Street. (AtoA)

MYERS, CHARLOTTE ELIZABETH. Admitted June 23, 1853 aged five years and six months by MARY MYERS, mother. Born Christmas Eve, 1847. Indentures expired December 24, 1865. (R-29) Born Ireland. Mother a Roman Catholic. Father a Unitarian. (AtoA) Delivered to her cousin, unknown, nd. (ROG, 1856)

NEUFFER, AUGUST. Admitted August 12, 1858 aged four years by ELIZA NEUFFER, mother. Indentures expired August 12, 1875. (T-112) Absconded, nd. (ROB, 1856)

NEUFFER, EDWARD. Admitted August 12, 1858 aged five years and six months by ELIZA NEUFFER, mother. Indentures expired February 12, 1871. (T-110) Absconded, nd. (ROB, 1856)

NEWCOME (NEWCOMEN), JOHN. Admitted September 26, 1850 aged eight years and two months by JOHN NEWCOME, father. Born July 20, 1842. Indentured to HARRAL NICHOLS and CO. as a bookkeeper February 20, 1857. Indentures expired July 20, 1863. (Q-19)

OAKLEY, JOHN R. Admitted April 27, 1854 aged six years and four months by JOSEPHINE OAKLEY, mother. Indentures expired December 27, 1869. (S-11) Delivered to his mother in Philadelphia September 1859. (ROB,1856) Born New York. Religion: Roman Catholic. (AtoA)

O'BRIEN, RICHARD. Admitted September 3, 1857 aged nine years by T. ROBINSON, unknown. Indentured to COL. ROBERT BARNWELL RHETT as a printer January 1, 1863. Indentures expired September 3, 1869. (T-13)

O'BRIEN, WILLIAM. Admitted September 3, 1857 aged seven years by T. ROBINSON, unknown. Indentures expired September 3, 1871. (T-12) Absconded, nd. (ROB, 1856)

OWENS, CLARA PATTON. Admitted April 17, 1856 aged three years and nine months by ANN ELIZABETH OWENS, mother. Indentures expired July 5, 1870. (U-5) Delivered to her mother, nd. (ROG, 1856)

OWENS, ELIZA EUGENIA. Admitted April 17, 1856 aged five years and nine months by ANN ELIZABETH OWENS, mother. Indentures expired July 25, 1868. (U-4) Delivered to her mother, nd. (ROG, 1856)

OWENS, JOHN. Admitted July 24, 1851 aged seven years by the Poor House. Indentured to N.L. COSTE as a mariner December 16, 1858. Indentures expired July 24, 1865. (Q-43)

OWENS (OWEN), JOHN BACHMAN. Admitted April 17, 1856 aged nine years and one month by ANN ELIZABETH OWENS, mother. Indentures expired March 12, 1868. (S-94) Delivered to his mother July 9, 1862. (BO)

OWENS, MARGARET ADELE. Admitted April 17, 1856 aged seven years and one month by ANN ELIZABETH OWENS, mother. (U-3) Died, nd. (ROG, 1856)

OWENS, MARY EMMA. Admitted April 17, 1856 aged ten years and nine months by ANN ELIZABETH OWENS, mother. Born August 28, 1845. Indentures expired July 17, 1863. (U-2) Delivered to her mother, nd. (ROG, 1856)

OWENS, THOMAS. Admitted July 24, 1851 aged ten years by the Poor House. Indentures expired July 24, 1862. (Q-42) Absconded 1854. (ROC, 1821)

PARKER, BENJAMIN THOMAS. Admitted July 15, 1858 aged six years by SUSAN ANN PARKER, mother. Indentures expired July 15, 1873. (T-104) "To a relative." (ROB, 1856)

PARKER, SARAH ANN. Admitted July 15, 1858 aged five years by SUSAN ANN PARKER, mother. (U-145) Died, nd. (ROG, 1856)

PENDARVIS, JACOB. Admitted August 6, 1857 aged five years by MARY PENDARVIS, mother. Indentures expired August 6, 1873. (T-8) Delivered to his mother December 4, 1857. (ROB, 1856)

PENDARVIS, MARTHA ANN. Admitted June 5, 1857 aged ten years by MARY PENDARVIS, mother. Indentures expired June 5, 1865. (U-65) No further information.

PETIT, OSCAR (FRANCIS). Admitted April 5, 1855 aged nine years by CHARLES P. PETIT, uncle. Indentures expired April 5, 1867. (S-40) Religion: Episcopalian. (AtoA) Entered the army, nd. (ROB, 1856)

PHILIPS, RAYMOND (ALIAS JAMES T. RAYMOND). Admitted July 11, 1850 aged seven years by the Poor House. (Q-13) Delivered to his mother, MRS. RAYMOND, who went to California in 1849 and returned in 1852. February 12, 1852. (BO) Indentures expired July 11, 1864. (Q-13)

PIERCE (PEARCE), JOHN. Admitted December 5, 1856 aged two years and four months. Indentured to H.A. WILSON (of Lexington District), occupation unknown, July 3, 1862. Returned to COH February 11, 1869. Transferred to J.J. KENNERTY as a farmer February 11, 1869. Indentures expired August 5, 1875. (S-115). Admitted from the Poor House. (AtoA)

POWERS, CHARLES HENRY. Admitted March 2, 1854 aged four years by SUSAN POWERS, mother and the Poor House. Indentures expired April 18, 1871. (S-4) Delivered to his mother July 27, 1854. (BO) Born April 18, 1850. Religion: Episcopalian. (AtoA) Mother a former inmate. (Minutes, September 25, 1852)

POWERS, CHARLES HENRY TOOMER. Admitted January 9, 1857 aged six years. Indentures expired January 9, 1872. (U-26) Delivered to his mother, unknown, nd. (ROB, 1856)

POWERS, ELLEN. Admitted October 13, 1859 aged seven years by the Poor House. Indentured to JAMES CALDWELL as a domestic December 4, 1867. Indentures expired October 13, 1869. (U-220)

POWERS, FRANCIS MARION. Admitted March 2, 1854 aged six years by SARAH (SUSAN) POWERS, mother. (S-3). Born Feb. 14, 1848. Religion: Episcopalian. (A to A). Died May, 1854. (ROG, 1821).

QUINN, CHARLES. Admitted January 22, 1853 aged twelve years by the Poor House. Indentured to W.J. KNAUFF (of Pendleton, S.C.) as a cabinetmaker February 28, 1856. Indentures expired January 27, 1862. (Q-84)

RANDLES, THOMAS. Admitted April 29, 1852 aged four years by WILLIAM B. YATES, guardian. (Q-55) Died April ___, 1856. (ROB, 1856) Father's religion: Protestant. Mother's religion: Roman Catholic. (AtoA)

REDMON, ANDREW. Admitted November 3, 1859 aged three years by NORA REDMON, mother. Indentures expired November 3, 1877. (T-203) Delivered to his mother, MRS. REILLEY, November 21, 1867. (ROB, 1856)

REDMON, PATRICK. Admitted November 3, 1859 aged six years by NORA REDMON, mother. Indentures expired November 3, 1874. (T-201) Absconded April ___, 1865. (ROB, 1856)

REEDY, EDWARD. Admitted June 30, 1853 aged eight years by the Poor House. Indentured to JOHN and T.S. HEFFRON as a saddle and harnessmaker May 30, 1861. Indentures expired June 30, 1866. (Q-96)

REGIN, ELEANOR. Admitted December 16, 1858 aged fourteen years by REV. A.P. PORTER, unknown. Indentures expired December 16, 1862. (U-173) "To a relative." (ROG, 1856)

REGIN, JOHN. Admitted December 16, 1858 aged six years by the Poor House. (T-130) Died, nd. (ROB, 1856)

REGIN, PETER. Admitted December 16, 1858 aged four years by REV. A. PORTER and the Poor House. Delivered to his brother-in-law, J.O. EDWARDS, March 4, 1869. Indentures expired December 16, 1875. (T-132)

REILLEY (RILEY), WILLIAM. Admitted March 13, 1851 aged seven years by the Poor House. Indentures expired March 13, 1865. (Q-32) Delivered to his mother, MRS. THOMAS MURPHY, November 10, 1858. (BO)

REITZLER, ENOCH. Admitted August 10, 1854 aged eight years and three months by the Poor House. Indentures expired May 10, 1867. (S-32) Delivered to someone in Philadelphia, nd. (ROB, 1856)

REMPP, CONRAD. Admitted July 5, 1855 aged ten years by F. ANSEL, uncle, and the Poor House. Delivered to his uncle to be trained as a cabinet-maker September 9, 1858. Indentures expired July 5, 1866. (S-53) An orphan. Religion: Lutheran. Born in Germany. (AtoA)

RETTMAN, EMILY. Admitted February 27, 1859 aged seven years by CAROLINE RETTMAN, sister. Indentures expired January 27, 1870. (U-184) Delivered to her brother-in-law, unknown, February 23, 1871. (ROG, 1856)

RETTMAN, MARY. Admitted January 14, 1859 aged ten years by CAROLINE RETTMAN, sister. Indentured to MARY E. and JAMES B. PORTER as a domestic October 27, 1865. Indentures expired January 27, 1867. (U-182)

RETTMAN, WILLIAM. Admitted January 27, 1859 aged eight years by the Poor House. Indentures expired January 27, 1872. (T-142) Absconded, nd. (ROB, 1856)

RIAN, ALICE G. Admitted May 2, 1850 aged ten years by C. RIANS, mother and the Poor House. Delivered to MRS. H. WRIGHT, occupation unknown, May 2, 1858. Indentures expired May 2, 1858. (R-6) Born Glasgow, Scotland. Religion: Presbyterian. (AtoA) Elected teacher, nd. (Minutes, January 31, 1856)

RIANS, ANNIE. Admitted May 2, 1850 aged seven years by C. RIANS, mother, and the Poor House. Indentures expired May 2, 1861. (R-7) Elected teacher September 13, 1860. (Minutes, September 6, 1860) Religion: Presbyterian. (AtoA) Married, nd. (ROG, 1856)

RIANS, JOHN FORREST. Admitted June 5, 1851 aged five years by CATHERINE BENNETT, mother, and the Poor House. Delivered to his mother December 9, 1852. Readmitted September -2, 1853. Indentured to WILLIAM SMITH (of Abbeville District) as a farmer February 10, 1859. Indentures expired June 5, 1866. (Q-37) Religion: Presbyterian. Lived at 4 Weims Court. (AtoA)

RICHARDS, THOMAS. Admitted February 21, 1856 aged twelve years by the Poor House. Indentured to LOVE and WIENGES (CHARLES LOVE and EDWARD WIENGES) as a saddler Februray 13, 1857. Indentures expired March 26, 1865. Born March 26, ____. An orphan. (AtoA)

ROBERTS, SAMUEL CAPERS. Admitted January 10, 1856 aged ten years by MRS. LOUISA ROBERTS, mother. Indentures expired January 10, 1867. (S-80) Born in Queen Street. Religion: Baptist (AtoA) Indentured to WILLIAM C. BEE, occupation unknown, nd. (ROB, 1856)

ROBINSON, STEPHEN CLARK. Admitted May 18, 1854 aged five years by MARTHA JANE ROBINSON, mother. Indentures expired April 26, 1870. (S-14) Delivered to his mother February 15, 1859. (BO)

ROBINSON, TIMOTHY HAMPTON. Admitted May 18, 1854 aged eight years and one month by MARTHA JANE ROBINSON, mother. Indentures expired April 10, 1867. (S-13) Delivered to his mother February 15, 1859. (BO)

ROBINSON, WILLIAM PINCKNEY. Admitted May 18, 1854 aged ten years and three months by MARTHA JANE ROBINSON, mother. Indentured to WILLIAM S. HENEREY and CO. as a machinist March 6, 1857. Indentures expired February 11, 1865. (S-12)

RUTH (ROUTH), JAMES. Admitted November 28, 1856 aged five years by ELLEN RUTH, mother. Indentures expired November 28, 1872. (S-112) Delivered to his mother, nd. (ROB, 1856) Admitted from the Poor House. (AtoA)

RUTH (ROUTH), JOHN. Admitted November 28, 1856 aged seven years by ELLEN RUTH, mother. Indentured to W.B. ELKIN (of Gadsden), occupation unknown, January 12, 1865. Indentures expired November 28, 1870. (S-111) Admitted from the Poor House. (AtoA)

RUTH (ROUTH), THOMAS. Admitted November 28, 1856 aged three years by ELLEN RUTH, mother. Indentures expired November 28, 1874. (S-113) Delivered to his parents, JAMES and ELLEN RUTH, July 30, 1857. (BO) Admitted from the Poor House. (AtoA)

RYAN, ALICE A. Admitted November 6, 1857 aged ten years by HENRY RYAN, father. Delivered to her aunt, MRS. SARAH ANN BRADLEY, June 11, 1863. Indentures expired November 6, 1865. (U-49)

RYAN, JAMES. Admitted April 19, 1855 aged five years by MARY RYAN, mother. Indentured to JAMES M. OSBORN as a photographer December 28, 1865. Indentures expired April 19, 1871. (S-45) Religion: Roman Catholic. (AtoA)

RYAN, JOHN. Admitted September 2, 1857 aged four years by MARY RYAN, mother. Indentures expired September 2, 1874. (T-11) Delivered to ____ SMITH, nd. (ROB, 1856)

RYAN, PATRICK. Admitted February 14, 1856 aged four years by MARGARET RYAN, mother. Indentures expired February 14, 1873. (S-83) Delivered to his mother, MRS. HICKEY, May 26, 1859. (BO) Religion: Roman Catholic. (AtoA)

RYAN, THOMAS. Admitted April 19, 1855 aged eleven years. Indentures expired April 19, 1865. (S-144) "Left." (ROB, 1856) Religion: Roman Catholic. (AtoA)

RYAN, WILLIAM H.Y. Admitted November 6, 1857 aged seven years by HENRY J. RYAN, father. Indentures expired November 6, 1871. (T-21) Delivered to his aunt, unknown, nd. (ROB, 1856)

SCHMIDT, ANDREAS MAGUIRE. Admitted May 25, 1854 aged four years and eight months by MARIA HENRIETTA SCHMIDT, mother. Indentures expired September 30, 1870. (S-15) Delivered to his mother May 15, 1856. (ROB, 1856) Father, SEBASTIAN, was a cabinetmaker. (AtoA)

SCOTT, CHRISTIANA. Admitted February 14, 1856 aged eleven years by LEWIS SCOTT, brother. Indentured to MRS. N.L. COSTE as a domestic March 10, 1859. Indentures expired March 20, 1863. (R-104) Born March 20, 1845 in Orangeburg. Religion: Episcopalian. Mother, MARGARET, died January 31, 1856. (AtoA)

SCOTT, RUTH ANN. Admitted February 14, 1856 aged thirteen years by LEWIS SCOTT, brother. Indentured to MRS. S. MORTIMER as a domestic May 5, 1859. Transferred to MRS. N.R. DOBSON, occupation unknown, October 5, 1859. Indentures expired February 15, 1861. (R-103) Born February 15, 1843 in Orangeburg. Religion: Episcopalian. (AtoA)

SEIFERT, CAROLINE. Admitted July 26, 1855 aged nine years by LOUIS ALBRECHT, uncle, and the Poor House. Indentures expired July 26, 1864. (R-75) Delivered to her father December 9, 1858. (BO) Born in Saxe Weimar, Germany. Religion: Lutheran. (AtoA)

SEIFERT, CHRISTIANA. Admitted July 26, 1855 aged six years by LOUIS ALBRECHT, uncle, and the Poor House. Indentures expired July 26, 1867. (R-76) Delivered to her father December 9, 1858. (BO) Born Saxe Weimar, Germany. Religion: Lutheran. (AtoA)

SEIFERT, KARL (CHARLES). Admitted July 26, 1855 aged twelve years by LOUIS ALBRECHT uncle, and the Poor House. Indentures expired July 26, 1864. (S-54) Delivered to his father 1858. (BO) Born Saxe Weimar, Germany. Religion: Lutheran. (AtoA)

SESSIONS, FERDINAND. Admitted May 25, 1854 aged eight years and four months by MARTHA SESSIONS, mother. (S-16) Born Horry District. Religion: Methodist. (AtoA) Died December 17, 1855. (ROC, 1821)

SESSIONS, JULIA. Admitted May 25, 1854 aged six years and one month by MARTHA SESSIONS, mother. Born April 13, 1848. Indentures expired April 13, 1866. (R-60) Delivered to her mother January 10, 1856. (ROC, 1821) Born Horry District. Religion: Methodist. (AtoA)

SHAW, JESSIE ANN. Admitted August 13, 1857 aged eight years by JAMES SHAW, father. Indentures expired August 13, 1867. (U-40) Delivered to her mother, nd. (ROG, 1856) Allowed twenty-five dollars as a marriage dowry 1869. (Minutes, June 5, 1869)

SHAW, JANE. Admitted August 13, 1857 aged seven years by JAMES SHAW, father. (U-41) Died February 17, 1862. (ROG, 1856)

SHAW, MARY E.W. Admitted August 13, 1857 aged nine years by JAMES SHAW, father. Indentures expired August 13, 1866. (U-39) Delivered to her mother, unknown, nd. (ROG, 1856)

SHAW, MELVINA. Admitted August 13, 1857 aged four years by JAMES SHAW, father. Indentures expired August 13, 1871. (U-42) Delivered to her mother, unknown, nd. (ROG, 1856)

SHAW, SUSIE ANN. Admitted August 13, 1857 aged eight years by JAMES SHAW, father. Indentures expired August 13, 1867. (U-40) Delivered to her mother, unknown, nd. (ROG, 1856)

SHEVLAND, LAWRENCE. Admitted January 26, 1854 aged three years and eight months by ROSA SHEVLAND, mother. Born May 27, 1850. Indentures expired May 27, 1871. (Q-111) Delivered to someone in the North. (ROB, 1856) Religion: Catholic. (AtoA)

SILCOX, HENRY. Admitted March 7, 1850 aged two years by LOUISA SILCOX, mother, and the Poor House. Indentured to F.H. DUC as a tinner December 17, 1865. Indentures expired March 7, 1869. (Q-23)

SLAVEAN (SLAVAAN), EDWARD. Admitted April 10, 1856 aged ten years by CATHARINE SLAVEAN, mother. Indentures expired April 10, 1867. (S-91) Absconded, nd. (ROB, 1836) Born Ireland. Religion: Roman Catholic. (AtoA)

SLAVEAN, JOHN. Admitted February 17, 1859 aged four years by CATHARINE CONROY, unknown. Delivered to his mother, unknown, nd. Indentures expired February 17, 1876. (ROB, 1856)

SMITH, CHARLES ALLEN. Admitted April 15, 1858 aged four years by MRS. MARTHA SMITH, mother. Indentures expired April 15, 1875. (T-84) "Left." (ROB, 1856)

SMITH, EHNERT HENRY MANLY. Admitted July 31, 1851 aged eight years by the Poor House. Delivered to his brother, WILLIAM M. SMITH, (of North Carolina) January 14, 1858. Indentures expired July 31, 1864. (Q-44) Sent to the High School of Charleston January 1856. (ROC, 1821) Discharged from the High School 1857. (Minutes, December 17, 1857) Admitted from the Poor House. Father, WILLIAM, a shoemaker died in the Poor House. Father born in England. Arrived in America around 1836. Mother died 1846 and was buried in St. John's Chapel cemetary. Sister, MARY ANN married to _____ McGARRITY, an engineer. Brother WILLIAM fifteen years old in 1851. (AtoA)

SMITH, HENRY. Admitted August 26, 1852 aged five and one half months by CHARLOTTE PHILIPS, mother, and the Poor House. (Q-62) Born March 15, 1847. (AtoA) Died 1853. (ROC, 1821)

SMITH, MARY. Admitted August 18, 1853 aged eight years by the Poor House. (R-45) Delivered to her aunt, EMELINE WISE, March 17, 1859. (ROG, 1856) Indentures expired August 18, 1863. (R-45)

SMITH, MARY J. Admitted April 5, 1855 aged seven years by WILLIAM SMITH, father. Indentures expired April 5, 1866. (R-71) Delivered to her aunt, EMELINE WISE, April 2, 1856. (BO)

SMITH, MARY SUSAN. Admitted June 27, 1850 aged four years and six months by MARY DOAR, friend, and the Poor House. Indentures expired December 28, 1863. (R-9) Delivered to her mother and step-father, CATHARINE and JOHN A. DAVIS (of New Orleans) July 31, 1851. (BO)

SMITH, WILLIAM H. Admitted April 5, 1855 aged nine years by WILLIAM SMITH, father. Indentured to CHARLES W. HANCOCK (of Americus, Georgia) as a printer January 30, 1863. Indentures expired April 5, 1867. (S-43)

SMYTH, DANIEL. Admitted January 26, 1854 aged four years by JOHN SMYTH, father, and the Poor House. Indentures expired January 26, 1870. (Q-112) Delivered to his father, nd. (ROB, 1856) Father a Catholic and mother Protestant. Lived on the southside of Queen Street. (AtoA)

SPEARS, THOMAS. Admitted October 14, 1858 aged two years by E.W. EDGERTON, unknown. Indentures expired October 19, 1877. (T-118) "Left." (ROB, 1856)

SPENCER, ALBERT. Admitted August 12, 1858 aged eleven years by CATHERINE R. SPENCER, mother. Indentures expired August 12, 1868. (T-106) Sent to the High School of Charleston, nd. (ROB, 1856) No further information.

SPENCER, JACOB. Admitted August 12, 1858 aged nine years by CATHERINE SPENCER, mother. Indentures expired August 12, 1870. (T-108) Delivered to his mother, nd. (ROB, 1856)

STIEFATER, JULIANA ESTEPHANIE. Admitted July 1, 1852 aged eight years and three months by the Poor House. Delivered to her mother and her uncle, F. JOSEOALLE, September 1, 1853. Indentures expired April 14, 1862. (R-23)

STOCK, JULIA JOHANNA. Admitted September 8, 1853 aged twelve years by the Poor House. Born Germany. Indentured to MRS. NAOMI DOBSON, occupation unknown, July 25, 1856. Indentures expired September 8, 1859. (R-46) An orphan. Religion: Lutheran. (AtoA)

STRAFFORD, ANN JULIA. Admitted January 14, 1858 aged four years and six months by ANN STRAFFORD, mother. Indentures expired July 14, 1871. (U-113) Delivered to her mother, nd. (ROG, 1856)

STRAFFORD, LOUISA CATHARINE. Admitted January 15, 1858 aged three years by ANN STRAFFORD, mother. Indentures expired January 14, 1873. (U-115) Indentured to F. HORSEY, occupation unknown, March 2, 1868. (ROG, 1856)

STRAFFORD, WILLIAM. Admitted January 14, 1858 aged six years and six months by ANN STRAFFORD, mother. Indentures expired July 14, 1872. (T-52) Delivered to his mother, nd. (ROB, 1856)

STRAUSS, GEORGE FRANCIS. Admitted August 13, 1857 aged twelve years by THOMAS C. LOGAN, unknown. Indentures to J.S. HYER, occupation unknown, January 26, 1860. Indentures expired August 13, 1866. (T-10)

SWEENEY, CATHERINE. Admitted August 1, 1850 aged nine years by E. SWEENEY, mother, and the Poor House. Indentures expired August 1, 1859. (R-12) Delivered to her mother, nd. (ROC, 1821)

SWEENEY, MILES. Admitted August 1, 1850 aged twenty-five months by ELIZABETH SWEENEY, mother, and the Poor House. (Q-18) Died of Tabes September 10, 1850. (ARP, 1850)

TALBOT, JANE. Admitted September 16, 1858 aged two years by MISS M.L. TRANHOLM, unknown. (U-147) Died September 1, 1859. (ROG, 1856)

TESKY, ROBERT. Admitted January 14, 1858 aged twelve years by JULIA DAVISON, grandmother. Indentured to EDWARD C. JONES as a bookseller July 19, 1860. Indentures expired January 14, 1867. (T-50)

THOMAS, DANIEL. Admitted June 23, 1859 aged five years by HARRIETT THOMAS, mother. Indentures expired June 23, 1875. (T-177) Delivered to his mother December 30, 1863. (ROB, 1856)

THOMAS, JAMES PINCKNEY. Admitted June 5, 1857 aged nine years by HARRIETT THOMAS, mother. Indentures expired June 5, 1869. (S-137) Joined (K) Company, SCV in 1863. (COH Inmates' Files)

TIERNEY, JULIA. Admitted June 8, 1854 aged six years by JAMES TIERNEY, father. Indentured to REV. A.M. CHRIESTZBERG (CHRIETZBERG), of Greenville, as a domestic August 16, 1864. Indentures expired June 8, 1866. (R-62)

TIERNEY, SARAH. Admitted June 8, 1854 aged three years by JAMES TIERNEY, father. Born July 23, 1852. Indentured to WILLIAM CHERRY, occupation unknown, December 26, 1867. Indentures expired June 8, 1869. (R-63)

TIERNEY, WILLIAM. Admitted June 8, 1854 aged eight years. Indentured to J.J. BONNER (of Due West, Abbeville District) as a printer October 31, 1861. Indentures expired June 8, 1867. (S-263)

TOY, EDWARD. Admitted April 1, 1858 aged three years and six months by MRS. MARY TOY, mother. Indentures expired October 1, 1875. (T-82) Delivered to his mother September 25, 1866. (ROB, 1856)

TOY, JAMES. Admitted September 17, 1857 aged nine years by MRS. MARY TOY, mother. (T-14) Died, nd. (ROB, 1856)

TOY, JOSEPH. Admitted September 17, 1857 aged eight years by MRS. MARY TOY, mother. Indentures expired September 17, 1870. (T-15) Delivered to his mother October 7, 1863. (ROB, 1856)

TOY, THOMAS. Admitted September 17, 1857 aged five years by MRS. MARY TOY, mother. (T-16) Died, nd. (ROB, 1856)

TOY, WILLIAM. Admitted September 17, 1857 aged five years by MRS. MARY TOY, mother. Indentures expired September 17, 1873. (T-17) Delivered to his mother, nd. (ROB, 1856)

TROUBLEFIELD, MARION. Admitted May 18, 1854 aged five years by CATHARINE TROUBLEFIELD, mother. Indentures expired May 18, 1870. (S-19) Delivered to his mother July 17, 1856. (ROB, 1856) Lived in Hanover Street. Religion: Methodist. (AtoA)

TUOMEY, JOHN A. Admitted June 17, 1858 aged four years by ELLEN TUOMEY, mother. Indentures expired June 17, 1875. (T-98) "Left." (ROB, 1856)

USHER, JAMES. Admitted September 23, 1852 aged six years by the Poor House. (Q-64) Died February 8, 1863. (ROB, 1856) A foundling, left at the home of MRS. ANN CREIGHTON in Cannonsboro on October 10, 1845. Christened by REV. WILLIAM BARNIVAL of St. Peter's Church. (AtoA)

UTTYS, MARGARET ANN. Admitted September 11, 1851 aged four years and three months by LOUISA UTTYS, mother, and the Poor House. Indentures expired June 16, 1865. (R-17) Delivered to her mother January 1, 1857. (ROG, 1856) Born June 16, 1847 in the Poor House. Religion: Methodist. (AtoA)

VON GLAHN, FREDERICK. Admitted July 3, 1851 aged three years by the Poor House. Indentured to P.W. PLEDGER (of Marlboro District) as a farmer July 14, 1864. Indentures expired July 4, 1869. (Q-39) Mother ELIZA MONTAG. Child illigitimate. Father, FREDERICK VON GLAHN. Born Lehe, Hanover. Religion: Lutheran. (AtoA)

WALLACE, JOSEPH. Admitted June 16, 1859 aged four years and six months by LETITIA WALLACE, mother. Indentures expired December 16, 1875. (T-75) Delivered to his mother, nd. (ROB, 1856)

WALLACE, MARY ANN. Admitted June 16, 1859 aged five years and six months by LETITIA WALLACE, mother. Indentures expired June 16, 1871. (U-199) No further information.

WARNER, FREDERICKA EMMA. Admitted May 15, 1857 aged three years by JANE WARNER, mother. Indentures expired May 15, 1872. (U-63) Delivered to her mother, nd. (ROG, 1856)

WATERS, ISAAC PALMER. Admitted November 18, 1852 aged five years and nine months by LUCY A. WATERS, mother. Indentured to E.R. STOKES (of Columbia) as a bookbinder July 3, 1862. Indentures expired February 18, 1868. (Q-74) Born St. Stephens Parish. Religion: Methodist. (AtoA)

WATERS (WARTERS), MARGARET ANN. Admitted November 18, 1852 aged nine years and two months by LUCY A. WATERS, mother. Indentures expired September 18, 1861. (R-26) Delivered to her mother, MRS. DAVIS, nd. (ROG, 1856) Born St. Stephens Parish. Religion: Methodist. (AtoA)

WATERS, MARIA. Admitted November 18, 1852 aged seven years and nine months by LUCY A. WATERS, mother. Indentures expired February 18, 1863. (R-27) Delivered to her mother, MRS. DAVIS, February 1859. (BO) Born St. Stephens Parish. Religion: Methodist. (AtoA)

WATERS, MARY JANE. Admitted November 18, 1852 aged two years and nine months by LUCY A. WATERS, mother. Indentures expired February 18, 1868. (R-28) Delivered to her mother, MRS. DAVIS, nd. (ROG, 1856) Born St. Stephens Parish. Religion: Methodist. (AtoA) Allowed twenty-five dollars as a marriage dowry, 1869. (Minutes, July 15, 1869

WEST, JAMES. Admitted August 7, 1856 aged two years and six months. A derelict. Indentures expired February 7, 1875. (S-104) "Left." (ROB, 1856)

WHITTEMORE, MARY R. Admitted June 20, 1850 aged six years and eight months by MARY A. JORDAN, grandmother, and the Poor House. (R-8) Indentured to ELLEN and WILLIAM R. NELSON (of Williamsburg District), occupation unknown, April 4, 1854. (BO) Indentures expired October 20, 1861. (R-8) Deaf. (Minutes, January 26, 1854) Died 1855. (ROG, 1856)

WIENGES, CATHARINE. Admitted March 24, 1859 aged four years by CATHARINE WIENGES, mother. Delivered to her father, GEORGE H. WIENGES, August 13, 1868. Indentures expired March 24, 1874. (U-190)

WIENGES, MARY. Admitted March 24, 1859 aged eight years by CATHARINE WIENGES, mother. Indentures expired March 24, 1869. (U-185) Delivered to her father, unknown, nd. (ROG, 1856)

WIENGES, SARAH AMELIA. Admitted October 4, 1855 aged twelve years and three months by SUSANNAH J. WIENGES, mother. Indentures expired October 4, 1861. (R-83) Elected an assistant in the Sewing Department June 24, 1858. (Minutes, June 24, 1858) Delivered to her mother August 12, 1858. (BO) Religion: Methodist. Born July 8, 1843. (AtoA) Allowed seventy-five dollars as a marriage dowry 1861. (Minutes, July 11, 1861)

WIENGES, SUSAN. Admitted March 24, 1859 aged six years by CATHARINE WIENGES, mother. Indentured to JOHN H. SAMS, occupation unknown, nd. Transferred to her father, GEORGE H. WIENGES, August 16, 1868. Indentures expired March 24, 1871. (U-188)

WILKINSON, E.G. Admitted April 22, 1858 aged ten years by M.E. WILKINSON, mother. Indentures expired April 22, 1866. (U-139) Delivered to her mother, nd. (ROG, 1856)

WILKINSON, M.A. Admitted April 22, 1858 aged eight years by MRS. M.E. WILKINSON, mother. Indentures expired April 22, 1868. (U-141) Delivered to her mother, nd. (ROG, 1856)

WILKINSON, W. Admitted April 27, 1858 aged five years by M.E. WILKINSON, mother. Indentures expired April 28, 1874. (T-86) Delivered to his mother, nd. (ROB, 1856)

WILLIAMS, ALICE. Admitted September 15, 1859 aged nine years by R.S. PARKER, guardian. Indentured to EPHRAIM BAILEY (of Orangeburg) as a domestic December 7, 1865. Indentures expired September 15, 1868. (U-211)

WILLIAMS, MARGARET D. Admitted December 15, 1856 aged nine years by ELIZABETH WILLIAMS, mother. Indentures expired December 5, 1865. (U-23) Delivered to her mother January 23, 1857. (ROG, 1856)

WILLIAMS, RICHARD W. Admitted December 5, 1856 aged seven years by ELIZABETH WILLIAMS, mother. (S-116) Born Alabama. Religion: Baptist. Lived on Percy Street. (AtoA) Died January 7, 1857. (ROB, 1856)

WITT, JOANNA AUGUSTA. Admitted September 29, 1853 aged six years and six months by A.M. WITT, uncle. Indentured to MISS CATHERINE AIMAR as a mantuamaker August 20, 1862. Indentures expired March 29, 1865. (R-50) Mother dead. Parents immigrated in 1844. Father, P.F. WITT, a shoemaker, deserted her. Parents from Mildorph in Holstein. (AtoA) Father requested her in 1858 because he was going to New York. Refused. (BO, rejected)

YOUNG, JANE. Admitted July 28, 1853 aged nine months by the Poor House. A derelict. Indentures expired October 28, 1870. (R-42) Delivered to her aunt, ELSIE BAKER, May 6, 1857. To be sent to her father, JAMES YOUNG, in New York. (BO) Born at Gadsden's Wharf. Religion: Protestant. (AtoA)

Charleston Orphan House Building

[1] *Minutes*, July 10, 1791

[2] *Minutes*, July 24, 1791

[3] *Minutes*, July 31, 1791

[4] *Minutes*, August 7, 1791

[5] *Minutes*, August 14, 1791

[6] *Minutes*, August 21, 1791

[7] *Minutes*, August 28, 1791

[8] *Minutes*, September 4, 1791

[9] *Minutes*, September 11, 1791

[10] *Minutes*, September 18, 1791

[11] *Minutes*, December 4, 1791

Charleston Orphan House Officers-General History

[1] *Minutes*, July 17, 1826

[2] *Minutes*, August 13, 1840

[3] *Digest of the Ordinances of the City of Charleston.* Charleston: Archibald E. Miller, 1818. p. 198

Charleston Orphan House Stewards

[1] *Minutes*, November 18, 1790

[2] *Minutes*, November 5, 1798

[3] *Minutes*, November 16, 1798

[4] ROSSC

[5] *Minutes*, November 15, 1810

[6] last page of Minutes, 1834 - 1841 (191)

[7] *Minutes*, July 17, 1835

[8] *Minutes*, October 19, 1841

[9] COH Officers' Files - Steward

[10] *Minutes*, August 8, 1850

[11] *Minutes*, January 10, 1856

[12] *Minutes*, January 17, 1856

[13] *Minutes*, December 14, 1865

Charleston Orphan House Matrons

[1] *Minutes*, October 28, 1790

[2] *Minutes*, November 1, 1791

[3] *Minutes*, November 1, 1791

[4] *Minutes*, March 14, 1793

[5] *Minutes*, March 28, 1793

[6] *Minutes*, September 14, 1795

[7] *Minutes*, November 5, 1795

[8] *Minutes*, October 10, 1796

[9] *Minutes*, November 10, 1796

[10] *Minutes*, April 30, 1801

[11] ROSSC

[12] *Minutes*, July 8, 1819

[13] *Minutes*, September 27, 1827

[14] *Minutes*, October 25, 1827

[15] *Minutes*, February 9, 1843

[16] *Minutes*, March 16, 1843

[17] *Minutes*, July 18, 1850

[18] *Minutes*, August 8, 1850

[19] *Minutes*, January 4, 1856

[20] *Minutes*, January 17, 1856

[21] *Minutes*, August 2, 1862

Charleston Orphan House Nurses

[1] *Minutes*, March 8, 1810

[2] ROSSC

[3] *Minutes*, August 2, 1860

[4] *Minutes*, July 15, 1869

[5] *Minutes*, February 21, 1811

[6] ROSP, October 2, 1828

[7] *Minutes*, October 28, 1790

[8] *Minutes*, November 18, 1790

[9] *Minutes*, October 4, 1819

[10] *Minutes*, January 5, 1809

[11] ROSSC

[12] Minutes, February 17, 1825

[13] ROSP, January 9, 1840

[14] Minutes, May 13, 1852

[15] ROSSC

[16] Ibid.

[17] Minutes, November 15, 1855

[18] Minutes, December 3, 1857

[19] ROSSC

[20] Minutes, January 30, 1823

[21] COH Officers' Files - Nurses

[22] Minutes, July 12, 1855

[23] Minutes, February 29, 1816

[24] Minutes, December 12, 1822

[25] Minutes, January 5, 1854

[26] ROSP, August 20, 1840

[27] Minutes, November 5, 1801

[28] Minutes, April 19, 1804

[29] Minutes, May 2, 1802

[30] Minutes, June 10, 1804

[31] Minutes, February 28, 1822

[32] ROSSC

[33] Minutes, November 5, 1798

[34] Minutes, March 29, 1799

[35] Minutes, January 29, 1807

[36] Minutes, February 26, 1807

[37] ROSSC

[38] Minutes, October 20, 1853

[39] Minutes, January 31, 1856

[40] Minutes, September 29, 1836

[41] Minutes, December 19, 1839

[42] Minutes, June 24, 1852

[43] Minutes, May 27, 1858

[44] Minutes, August 18, 1796

[45] Minutes, October 28, 1790

[46] Minutes, October 13, 1791

[47] Minutes, January 5, 1854

[48] Minutes, June 23, 1814

[49] Minutes, April 23, 1829

[50] Minutes, January 25, 1855

[51] Minutes, October 12, 1864

[52] Minutes, June 30, 1859

[53] COH Officers' Files - Nurses

[54] Minutes, December 17, 1856

[55] Minutes, March 21, 1861

[56] Minutes, November 17, 1791

[57] Minutes, May 17, 1792

[58] Minutes, May 8, 1801

[59] Minutes, March 18, 1802

[60] Minutes, December 23, 1857

[61] Minutes, July 21, 1859

[62] Minutes, November 26, 1840

[63] Minutes, June 23, 1859

[64] Minutes, October 7, 1824

[65] Minutes, February 3, 1825

[66] Minutes, December 24, 1835

[67] Minutes, February 15, 1838

[68] Minutes, June 30, 1853

[69] COH Officers' Files - Nurses

[70] ROSSC

[71] Minutes, June 6, 1822

[72] Minutes, June 24, 1858

[73] Minutes, July 15, 1858

[74] Minutes, July 28, 1859

[75] Minutes, June 24, 1864

[76] Minutes, March 27, 1806

[77] Minutes, March 31, 1817

[78] Minutes, August 19, 1858

[79] Minutes, September 5, 1861

[80] Minutes, June 17, 1824

[81]Minutes, June 10, 1852

[82]Minutes, June 17, 1824

[83]Minutes, February 17, 1825

[84]Minutes, August 25, 1791

[85]Minutes, November 15, 1791

[86]Minutes, April 30, 1829

[87]Minutes, December 24, 1835

[88]Minutes, August 12, 1797

[89]Minutes, October 7, 1797

[90]Minutes, August 6, 1802

[91]ROSSC

[92]COH Officers' Files - Nurses

[93]Minutes, July 19, 1860

[94]ROSSC

[95]Minutes, May 27, 1824

[96]Minutes, November 15, 1855

[97]ROSP, November 5, 1814

[98]Minutes, February 2, 1816

[99]Minutes, March 6, 1817

[100]ROSSC

[101]Minutes, January 20, 1803

[102]ROSSC

[103]Minutes, January 27, 1798

[104]Minutes, March 31, 1798

[105]Minutes, June 12, 1856

[106]Minutes, October 12, 1864

[107]Minutes, May 30, 1857

[108]Minutes, December 30, 1869

[109]Minutes, June 17, 1824

[110]Minutes, December 20, 1832

[111]Minutes, April 3, 1834

[112]Minutes, August 29, 1839

[113]ROSSC

[114]Ibid.

[115]Minutes, November 8, 1799

[116]Minutes, August 1, 1800

[117]Minutes, May 13, 1852

[118]Minutes, December 21, 1853

[119]Minutes, February 27, 1823

[120]ROSSC

[121]Minutes, January 10, 1833

[122]Minutes, June 15, 1843

[123]Minutes, November 22, 1855

[124]Minutes, October 28, 1869

[125]Minutes, September 12, 1800

[126]Minutes, August 19, 1802

[127]Minutes, June 1, 1801

[128]Minutes, August 6, 1802

[129]ROSSC

[130]Minutes, June 5, 1828

[131]ROSSC

[132]Minutes, 1834-1841, last page

[133]ROSSC

[134]Minutes, March 6, 1817

[135]Minutes, December 12, 1822

[136]Minutes, September 22, 1836

[137]Minutes, January 20, 1798

[138]Minutes, May 12, 1798

[139]Minutes, April 11, 1822

[140]Minutes, June 3, 1824

[141]ROSSC

[142]Minutes, January 29, 1807

[143]Minutes, June 21, 1855

[144]Minutes, May 30, 1861

Charleston Orphan House Sewing
  Mistresses

[1]ROSSC

[2]Ibid.

[3]Minutes, April 4, 1822

[4]ROSSC

[5]Minutes, November 1, 1827

[6]Minutes, December 12, 1835

[7]ROSSC

[8]Minutes, January 31, 1889

Charleston Orphan House School-masters

[1]Minutes, February 19, 1807

[2]Minutes, February 26, 1807

[3]Minutes, October 19, 1812

[4]ROSSC

[5]Minutes, February 22, 1799

[6]Minutes, June 9, 1853

[7]Minutes, January 22, 1795

[8]ROSSC

[9]Minutes, October 10, 1805

[10]Minutes, February 12, 1807

[11]Minutes, June 23, 1796

[12]Minutes, August 4, 1798

[13]ROSSC

[14]Minutes, November 16, 1837

[15]Minutes, November 23, 1837

[16]Minutes, October 9, 1856

[17]Minutes, August 20, 1798

[18]Minutes, November 16, 1798

[19]Minutes, March 5, 1807

[20]ROSSC

[21]Minutes, September 20, 1799

[22]Minutes, November 1, 1800

[23]Minutes, July 21, 1802

[24]Minutes, March 31, 1803

[25]Minutes, June 2, 1803

[26]Minutes, September 5, 1805

[27]Minutes, February 22, 1801

[28]Minutes, July 14, 1802

[29]Minutes, February 21, 1856

School Mistresses of the Charleston Orphan House, 1790-1860

[1]ROSSC

[2]Minutes, April 10, 1814

[3]Minutes, January 5, 1832

[4]Minutes, January 18, 1838

[5]Minutes, December 14, 1854

[6]Minutes, January 28, 1869

[7]Minutes, June 24, 1858

[8]ARC, 1910

[9]Minutes, February 15, 1838

[10]Minutes, April 6, 1854

[11]Minutes, March 31, 1814

[12]Minutes, May 1, 1828

[13]Minutes, June 5, 1828

[14]Minutes, January 5, 1832

[15]Minutes, December 28, 1854

[16]Minutes, January 10, 1856

Charleston Orphan House Assistant Teachers, 1790-1860

[1]Minutes, August 20, 1857

[2]Minutes, J-ne 17, 1860

[3]Minutes, June 24, 1858

[4]ROG, 1856

[5]Minutes, January 31, 1856

[6]Minutes, March 12, 1857

[7]Minutes, July 19, 1860

[8]Minutes, March 12, 1863

[9]Minutes, June 24, 1858

[10]ARC, 1917

[11]Minutes, February 19, 1857

[12]Minutes, August 2, 1860

[13]Minutes, January 31, 1856

[14]Minutes, February 19, 1857

[15]Minutes, May 4, 1850

[16]Minutes, May 27, 1869

[17]Minutes, August 20, 1857

[18]Minutes, April 3, 1884

[19]Minutes, December 4, 1856

[20]Minutes, January 4, 1866

Cooks of the Charleston Orphan
House, 1790-1860

[1]Minutes, January 15, 1846

[2]Minutes, July 16, 1840

[3]Minutes, August 19, 1802

[4]ROSSC

Porter/Gardeners of the Charleston
Orphan House, 1790-1860

[1]Minutes, January 17, 1850

[2]Minutes, May 22, 1869

[3]Minutes, May 29, 1834

[4]ROSSC

[5]COH Officers' Files - Porter/
Gardener

[6]Minutes, July 30, 1840

[7]Minutes, May 27, 1841

[8]ROSSC

[9]Minutes, July 17, 1835

[10]Minutes, December 22, 1836

[11]Minutes, June 17, 1841

[12]ROSSC

[13]COH Officers' Files - Porter/
Gardener

[14]Minutes, May 21, 1840

Charleston Orphan House Spinners/
Weavers, 1790-1860

[1]Minutes, January 5, 1809

[2]ROSSC

[3]Ibid.

[4]Minutes, April 19, 1804

[5]Minutes, November 4, 1813

[6]Minutes, June 9, 1814

[7]ROSSC

[8]Minutes, January 11, 1801

[9]ROSSC

[10]Ibid.

[11]Minutes, March 10, 1814

[12]ROSSC

Charleston Orphan House Washers,
1790-1860

[1]Minutes, February 1, 1855

[2]Minutes, December 15, 1859

[3]Minutes, July 12, 1866

[4]COH Officers' Files - Washers

[5]ROSSC

[6]Minutes, December 14, 1837

[7]Minutes, December 22, 1859

[8]COH Officers' Files - Washers

[9]ROSSC

WILLIS, JOHN. Admitted November 24, 1803, aged two years by
JANE DICKSON, mother. Died September 30, 1808. (E-15). Born
in Charleston. (ROSSC).

HANSON, SAMUEL. Admitted February 9, 1826 aged two years and
six months by Warden of Charleston. (K-114). Died Saturday,
July 21, 1827 of a stomach and bowel disorder. (ROSP, July 25,
1827). "This child was left in the House by a Mrs. BENNETT,
residing in Elliott St." (ROSSC).

POWERS, MARY. Admitted October 13, 1859 aged nine years by the
Poor House. Indentured to O.P. FITZSIMMONS (of Green Pond),
occupation unknown, January 16, 1868. Indentures expired
October 13, 1868. (U-217).

BRODERICK, William Thomas 36
BRODIE, Robert 18
BRONSON, E. A./Edward Alphonso 126,131,155
BRONSON, Francis Weston 134
BROOKMAN, Ann 20
BROOKMAN, Conrad 20
BROOKMAN, Elizabeth Rebecca 20
BROOKS, Ann 11,37
BROOKS, Ann Elizabeth 11
BROOKS, Henry 37
BROOKS, Mary 11,25
BROOKS, Rachel 59
BROSS, Benjamin 54
BROSS, Eliza 54
BROSS, Francis 55
BROSS, John 54,55
BROSS, Mary 54,55
BROTHERS, James 78
BROUNDING, Hampton 78
BROWER, Ann 11
BROWER, John 20
BROWER, Mary 20
BROWN, Alexander 37
BROWN, Benjamin 134
BROWN, Catherine 37
BROWN, Collin 55
BROWN, Eleanor 37
BROWN, Elizabeth 37
BROWN, George 33
BROWN, George R. D. 99
BROWN, James 55
BROWN, Jane 11,16,37
BROWN, John 31,37
BROWN, Joshua 62,74
BROWN, Martha 99
BROWN, Mary 37,99
BROWN, Mary Elizabeth 134
BROWN, Matilda 134
BROWN, Michael 55
BROWN, Mitchell 37
BROWN, Rebecca 55
BROWN, R. A. 108,112,117
BROWN, Robert William 99
BROWN, Sarah 37
BROWN, Sarah A. 134
BROWN, Thomas 37
BROWN, W. 122
BROWN, William 37,55
BROWNE, S. S. 126
BROWNELL, George W. 134
BROWNELL, Isaab. 134
BROWNELL, Mrs. Jane 134
BROWNELL, Nathaniel B. 134
BROWNING, Hannah 15,105,109
BROWNLEE, John 2
BRUCE, Mrs. Ellen 134
BRUCE, Mary 20
BRUCE, Rebecca 134
BRUGNIEN, Auguste 78
BRUGNIEN, Gentil 78
BRUGNIEN, Glandet 78
BRUGNIEN, Marie Ann 78
BRUGNIEN, Prosper 78
BRYAN, John 2
BRYAN, Susanna 34
BUCH, Catherine 135
BUCHANAN, Caroline 129
BUCHANAN, Catherine Caroline 55
BUCHANAN, James 37
BUCHANAN, Jane 11,87
BUCHANAN, John 37,55
BUCHANAN, Dr. (J.)ohn 138
BUCHANAN, Margaret 37
BUCK(see also BUCH)
BUCKHEISTER, Edward P. 117
BUCKHEISTER, Frances 117
BUCKHEISTER, James Andrew 117
BUCKHEISTER, John 117

BUCKHEISTER, Robert Joel 117
BUCKHEISTER, William Christian 117
BUCKINGHAM, Mary 74
BUDD, Thomas S. 72
BUFORD, Ann 24
BUFORD, Elizabeth 24
BUIST, Rev. Edward 117
BUIST, Edward H. 117
BUIST, Francis 130
BUIST, George 2
BUIST, James F. 117
BULIT, Catharine 20
BULIT, Peter 20
BULKLEY, James 70
BULL, Catherine 78
BULL, Martha 78
BULL, Mary 78
BULL, William 71
BULL, William Robert 117
BULLEN, Amanda 135
BULLEN, Catherine 135
BULOW, John J. 2
BUNCE, Jacob 26
BUNCH, Dennis 135
BUNCH, Elizabeth 55
BUNCH, Hezekiah 55
BUNCH, Jacob Nipper 135
BUNCH, Mary 78
BUNCH, Samuel F. 135
BUNCH, Timothy 55
BURBRIDGE, Alfred 78
BURBRIDGE, Harriet 78
BURBRIDGE, Rachel 78
BURCH, Elizabeth 20
BURCH, Naomi 21
BURCH, Thomas 20
BURCHALL, William 56
BURGER, David 22
BURGER, Nicholas 88
BURGES, James 91
BURGRIN, Mary Sarah 99
BURKE(see also BOURKE)
BURKE, David 79
BURKE, Eleanor 79
BURKE, John 79
BURKE, Michael 79
BURKE, Nelly 79
BURKLEY(see also BERKELEY)
BURKLEY, John 133
BURMINSTER, Jacob 79
BURN, Hugh 21
BURN, John Alexander 21
BURN, Sarah 21
BURNET, Foster 23
BURNICE, Daniel 67
BURNS, Ann 79,101
BURNS, John 79,118
BURNS, Maryann 118
BURNSIDES, Mrs. James 134
BURRILL, Henry 79
BURROW, Isaac 21
BURROW, Margaret 21
BURROW, Mary 21
BURROWS, James 55
BURROWS, Mary 55
BURROWS, Samuel 55
BURTON, Charles Henry 117
BURTON, Eliza 117
BUSBY, G. W. 7
BUSBY, Harriet 79
BUTCHER, Mary 37
BUTLER, Daniel 55,56
BUTLER, Edward William 55
BUTLER, James Andrew 135
BUTLER, John 56
BUTLER, John Samuel 135
BUTLER, Joseph 55
BUTLER, Joseph Pierce 56
BUTLER, Margaret 100
BUTLER, Maria 55,56
BUTLER, Martha 55,56

BUTLER, Mary 56,135
BUTLER, Sarah 64
BUTLER, Thomas James 56
BUTLER, William 98,104,115
BYERS, Elizabeth 38
BYERS, Margaret 38
BYRD, Oran D. 21
BYRD, Samuel 21
BYRNES, Joseph 38
BYRNES, Rebecca 38
BYRNS, Ann 21
BYRNS, Bridget 21
BRTHWOOD, Mrs. Eliza D. 96

CAAN, Honora 135
CABEEN, Alexander 51
CADLE, Sarah 116,121,128
CALDER, Alexander 22
CALDER, George 135
CALDER, Grieg 51
CALDER, Henry 135
CALDER, James 135
CALDER, Jane 135
CALDER, Margaret 135
CALDER, William 135
CALDWELL, James 159
CALDWELL, James M. 137
CALDWELL, James P. 121
CALDWELL, John 48
CALDWELL, Mary Ann 23
CALDWELL, Robert 79
CALHOUN, E. R. 110
CALHOUN, James 135
CALLERTON, Nicholas 144
CALVERT, James 38
CALVERT, Judith 38
CALVERT, William 38,79
CALVITT, William Lowndes 117
CALWELL, Bealentoe 70
CAMERON(see also CREAMER)
CAMERON, ___ 116,123
CAMERON, Alexander 21
CAMERON, Mary 21,49
CAMINADE, H. 119
CAMMER, Emanuel Casimir 135
CAMMER, Eugene 136
CAMMER, James 136
CAMMER, John 136
CAMMER, Julius 136
CAMMER, Mrs. 124
CAMPANA, Charles 117
CAMPANA, George Alexander 118
CAMPANA, Napoleon B. 118
CAMPBELL, Alexander 79,99
CAMPBELL, Ann 10
CAMPBELL, Archibald 9,127
CAMPBELL, Charles 136
CAMPBELL, Ellen 136
CAMPBELL, James 79
CAMPBELL, John 56,99,136
CAMPBELL, Joseph 56
CAMPBELL, Dr. J. M. 2
CAMPBELL, Owen 136
CAMPBELL, Sophia 136
CAMPBELL, Mrs. (see Laura E. WILBUR)
CANADY, James 79
CANAND, Frances 21
CANAND, John Peter Paul 21
CANE, Brian 32
CANFIELD, Thomas P. 99
CANGHAY, Jane 136
CANGHAY, Mary Jane 136
CANGHAY, William John 136
CANNING, (C)harles 115,117, 124,142
CANNON, ___ 6
CANNON, Mr. 101
CANTLEY, Emeline 11,99
CANTLEY, James 11,99
CANTLEY, James W. 118
CANTLEY, William 11,99

CANTWELL, Mrs. Martha 78
CANUET, W. 87
CAPERS, Thomas Farr 2
CAPERS, Rev. William 2
CAPERS, Rev. William T. 14
CAPRY, Henty 21
CAPRY, James 21
CAPRY, Mary Jovert 21
CAPRY, Stephen Joseph 21
CARDOZO, J. N. 94
CARDOZO, T. W. 54
CAREW, Ann 21
CAREW, Bridget 21
CAREW, Catharine 21
CAREW, John 21
CAREW, Joseph 21
CAREW, Mary 21
CAREW, Sarah 21
CARIVENE, Anthony 64
CARLISLE, James 79
CARLISLE, Margaret 79
CARLISLE, William 79
CARLTON, Abraham 79
CARLTON, Elizabeth 79
CARLTON, James 79
CARLTON, Margaret 79,80
CARLTON, Mary 79,80
CARLTON, Mary Ann 80
CARLTON, Richard 80
CARMINADE (see also CAMINADE)
CARMINADE, Henry 38
CARMINADE, John 56
CARMINADE, Peter 56
CARMINADE, Veronique 38,56
CARPENTER(see also CARPEN-
TIER)
CARPENTER, A. C.,27
CARPENTER, H. 22
CARPENTER, Mary 31
CARPENTIER, Ellen 99
CARPENTIER, J. 99
CARPENTIER, Mary 99
CARPENTIER, Peter 99
CARRE, P. 91
CARRERE, Eliza Frances 29,
31
CARROLL, Elizabeth 56
CARROLL, Mary Ann 56
CARROLL, Thomas 75
CARRUTH, A. (Major) 71,75
CARSON, Andrew Mills 136
CARSON, Elisha 89
CARSON, James 136
CARSON, Joseph 136
CART, John 41
CART, Susannah 41
CARTER(see also DeCARTER)
CARTER, Loisa 38
CARTER. Maria Ann 136
CARTER. Mary 26
CARTER, Mourning 70,91
CARTER, Richard Pinckney
136
CARTER, Sarah 38
CARTER, Starling L. 136
CARTER, Thomas 99
CARTER, William 38
CASEY, Benjamin 20,26
CASEY, Thomas 118
CASEY. Mrs. 118
CASHMAN. Anne 136
CASHMAN, Bess 136
CASHMAN, Mary 136
CASKINS, Ann 129
CASSIN, Conly 99
CASSIN, Washington K. 99
CATISTAL, Francois 21
CATISTAL, Jean Batista
Michael 21
CATONNET, Ann 46
CATONNET, W. P. 46
CAUBLE, H. A. 154
CAULDFIELD(see also CAULFIELD)

CAULFIELD, James (S)amuel
99,100
CAULFIELD, Maria 99
CAULIER, George 129
CELAFF, Charles William 100
CETOWELL(see also CALWELL)
CHADRIAC, Ursula C. 22
CHAMBERS, Mrs. Margaret 120
CHAMBERS, Martin 137
CHAMBERS, Mary 137
CHAMPLIN, Robert 100
CHAMPNEYS, John 2,28
CHANDLESS, Mrs. Barbara 87
CHANNEL, William James 100
CHANNER, Catherine Eliza 67
CHANNER, C. E. 60
CHANSON, Catherine 11,56
CHANSON, Charlotte 11,14,
56
CHANSON, Henrietta 11,56
CHANSON, Mary 11,56
CHAPMAN, Isabella 121
CHAPMAN, Samuel 99
CHATBURN, Frances Ann 57
CHATBURN, Mary 57
CHATELIN, M. A. 55
CHERRY, William 163
CHERRYTREE, Thomas 61
CHESNUT, David 40
CHESNUT, Jane 40
CHEVES, Langdon 2
CHEW, Thomas (R.) 80,105
CHILDS, Eliza 43
CHISOLM, George 138
CHISOLM, J. M. 60
CHISOLM, Robert T. 106
CHISOLM, Thomas 33
CHIVNELL, William 100
CHRETZBERG, George 60
CHRIESTZBERG, Rev. A. M.163
CHRIETZBERG(see also
CHRIESTZBERG)
CHRIETZBERG, Rev. H. 57
CHRISTBURG, Thomas 60
CHRISTIAN, Elizabeth 84
CHRISTIAN, John 38
CHRISTIAN, Rebeccah 38
CHUCKSHANKS, William 30
CHUN, George 103
CHURCH, Charles 57,77
CHURCH, Charles H. 54
CHURCH, Mrs. Joseph 118
CHURCH, Margaret 57
CHURCHILL, Ann 137
CHURCHILL, John William 137
CHURCHILL, Margaret 137
CHURCHILL, Mary 137
CLARENDON, Cecelia 100
CLARK, Ann 16,22
CLARK, Charles 38
CLARK, Charlotte Catherine
38
CLARK, Drury Wilburn 80
CLARK, Edward 21,38
CLARK, Elizabeth 38,80,100
CLARK, Hannah 137
CLARK, Hannah Maria 38
CLARK, Hugh 100
CLARK, James 32,91
CLARK, James Henry 100
CLARK, John 38,137
CLARK, John Michell 100
CLARK, Joseph Alexander 80
CLARK, Lydia Ann 100
CLARK, Margaret 21,22
CLARK, Mary 21,38
CLARK, Sarah 38
CLARK, Susan Judith 80
CLARK, Susannah 38
CLARK, Zachariah 38
CLARKE, Cornelius Vander-
built Henry 57
CLARKE, Elizabeth 57

CLARKE, E. 80
CLARKE, Lydia Catherine 80
CLARKSON, William 42
CLASTVER, M. 74
CLAUSSEN, J. C. 117,118,
145,146
CLAYBROOK, Mary 14,57
CLAYTON, Andrew 38
CLAYTON, Isham 38
CLAYTON, Jane 38
CLAYTON, Mary 57
CLEAPOR, Mrs. Ann W. 40
CLEAPOR, Charles 40
CLEMENTS, Catherine 80
CLEMENTS, Mary 107
CLEMENTS, Robert 80
CLEMMONS, Mary 107
CLENET, Margaret 36
CLENNAHAN, James B. 110
CLIFFEY, Raymond 34
CLOTHWORTHY, James 134
COASTE, Rev. Mr. 6
COBIA, Francis 40,49,72
COBIA, M. 122
COCHRAN, Margaret 19,35,52
CODY, Bridget 137
CODY, John 51
CODY, Sarah 137
COE, Anna 123
COFFIN, George M. 2
COGDELL, John S. 2
COGHLAN, Benjamin Franklin
57
COCHLAN, Elesnor 57
COCHLAN, Ellen 57
COCHLAN, Jackson 57
COHEN, Mordecai 2,40
COIT,___ 51
COLCOCK, Charles J. 2
COLE, Joseph 44
COLE, Richard 2
COLEMAN, Margaret 14
COLLINS, Catherine 57
COLLINS, Jane 137
COLLINS, Joanna 137
COLLINS, John 57
COLLINS, J. W. 127
COLLINS, Mary Catherine 137
COLLINS, Richard 137
COMMAULT, Ann 39
CONCHEY(see also CONOHET)
CONDON, Catharine 137
CONDON, David 137
CONDY, Jeremiah 67
CONKLIN, Harriet 80
CONLON, Catharine 133
CONLON, Maryann 11
CONLON, Peter 133
CONLON, Thomas 118
CONNELL, Ann 118
CONNELL, Ellen 118
CONNELLY, Henry 137
CONNELLY, James 80,137
CONNELLY, Melissa Ann 137
CONNELLY, Sarah 80
CONNELLY, Thomas 137
CONNER, Henry W. 81
CONNOR, John 76,91
CONNOR, Captain 109
CONNOLLY, John 24
CONNOLLY, Mary 22
CONNOLLY, Thomas 22
CONNOLY, Edward 57
CONNOLY, Eliza 57
CONNOLY, Frederick 57
CONNOLY, Maria 57
CONNOLY, Capt. Thomas 57
CONNOR, Hannah 39
CONNOR, John 22
CONOHET, Eugene 137
CONOLLY, John 118
CONOLY(see also CONOLLY)
CONOLOY(CONOLY), Susan 148

MC GUIRE, Barney 28
MC GUIRE, Elizabeth 28
MC GUIRE, Mary 45
MC GUIRE, Mary Ann 88
MC GUIRE, Roderick 45
MC INDOO, James 128
MC INDOO, Jane 12
MC INNES, Benjamin 152
MC INTOSH, James H. 105,112,
  119
MC INTYRE, Eliza 37
MC INTYRE, John 124
MC INTYRE, Julia 124
MC INTYRE, Louisa 124
MC INTYRE, Mary 124
MC IRIEL, John 67
MC IRIEL, John M. 67
MC KAIN, James 39
MC KAY(see also MACKAY)
MC KAY, Ann 88,89
MC KAY, Hugh 12,88
MC KAY, John 12,88
MC KAY, Robert 12,89,93,156
MC KAY, William 12,89
MC KEAN, Frances 12
MC KEE, James 45
MC KEE, John 20
MC KEEGAN, John 56
MC KELVEY(see also MCCALVEY)
MC KENZIE, James L. 124
MC KENZIE, Jane 89
MC KENZIE, John W. 124
MC KENZIE, Margaret 28
MC KENZIE, Sarah 28
MC KIE(see also MACKAY)
MC KIMMEY, John 28
MC KIMMEY, William 28
MC LANE(see also MC LEAN)
MC LANE, Ann Elizabeth 154
MC LANE, James 67
MC LANE, Susannah 67
MC LANE, William 67
MC LARTY, Janet 12
MC LARTY, Neal 26
MC LAUGHLIN, Elizabeth 151
MC LEAN, Elizabeth 28
MC LEAN, George 154
MC LEAN, Margaret 40
MC LEAN, Sarah 28
MC MILLAN, Charles 67
MC MILLAN, Daniel 35,68
MC MILLAN, James 67
MC MILLAN, Mary 67
MC MULLIN, John 28
MC MULLIN, Alexander 94
MC NAMARA, Anna 154
MC NAMARA, M. A. 154
MC NEAL, Ann 45
MC NEAL, Archibald 45
MC NEAL, Harriot 45
MC NEAL, Henry 45
MC NEAL, Mary 100,112
MC NEAL, Maria 45
MC NELLAGE, William 39,41
MC NICHOLAS, Bridget 124
MC NICHOLAS, Dominique 124
MC NINCH, John 44
MC PHERSON, Alexander 28
MC PHERSON, Eliza 12,89
MC PHERSON, John 12,89
MC PHERSON, Martha 12
MC PHERSON, Mary 12
MC PHERSON,Mrs. 111
MC PHERSON, Peter 89
MC PHERSON, Sarah 12,89
MC PHERSON, Susan/Susannah
  12,89
MC QUEEN, Donald 89
MC QUEEN, Jean 28
MC QUIEN(see MC QUEEN)
MC WRIGHT, William 20

MAC BETH, Charles 125

MACK, James 113
MACK, Mary 154
MACK, Michael 154
MAC KAY, Ann 12
MACKEY, James 45
MACKY, Mrs. 98
MADISON, Eunice E. 67
MAGILL, Mrs. James 150
MAGILL, Dr. William 101
MAGINNIS, James 125
MAGINNIS, Mary Dunn 125
MAGRATH, Edward 28
MAGRATH, Hannah 28
MAGRATH, John 4
MAGUIRE(see also MCGUIRE)
MAGWOOD, Simon 56
MAHAN, Elizabeth 22
MAHONEY, Anne 154
MAHONEY, Charles 154
MAHONEY, Cornelius 107
MAHONEY, John 28,107
MAHONEY, Mary 28
MAILLART(MAILLIART)
MAILLIART, Andrew 28
MAILLART,Francois 28
MAILLART, John 28
MAIN, James 49
MAIN, Lydia 61
MAIRS, Richard 28
MANGAN, Elizabeth 121
MANGAN, Peter 121
MANIGAULT, Edward 4
MANIGAULT, Gabriel 7
MANIGAULT, Joseph 4
MANNIHAN, Michael 154
MANNING, Elizabeth 125
MANNING, James 125
MANNING, Mr. 149
MANNING, Mrs. 149
MANNING, Nelly 12
MANNO, Mary 12,14,57,152
MANSON, Andrew 86
MANSON, Mrs. 86
MANSUET, Madame 39
MARCHANT, Peter Timothy 22,
  27
MARGART, George Marton 154
MARINER, ___ 58
MARINER, Frederick 89
MARINER, James 89
MARINER, Susan 89
MARINER, Susanna(h) 89
MARINER, William 89
MARIONER, Nathaniel M. 84
MARKEY, John 67
MARKLEY, Cecelia 149
MARKLEY, John 68
MARKLEY, Wade J. 149
MARLOW, George F. 127
MARLOW, James 127
MARMAJEAN, Eliza 67
MAROMET, Ann 12,28
MARSH, Catherine 28
MARSH, James 28,26,60
MARSH, Mr. 100
MARSH, William 29
MARSHALL, Alice 29
MARSHALL, Eliza 89
MARSHALL, John 33
MARSHALL, Margaret 12,29
MARSHALL, Sarah 29,89
MARSHALL, William 4
MARSO, Ann 112
MARTIN, Ann 67
MARTIN, Ann C. R. 63
MARTIN, Christina 27
MARTIN, Elizabeth 27,34
MARTIN, Eliza Jane 154
MARTIN, Frances Ann 154
MARTIN, John N. 20
MARTIN, John Valantine 67,
  89
MARTIN, L. 36,67

MASON, ___19,23
MASON, Mary 45
MASON, Samuel 45
MASSALON, Sarah 154
MASSALON, Thomas 154
MATHIESSON, William 140
MATTHEWS, David 55
MATTHEWS, Thomas 112
MATTHEWS, 58,62
MATTOX, Richard 118
MAULL, Ann 154
MAULL, Charles 67
MAULL, David M. 67
MAULL, Edwin H. 154
MAULL, James 25,154
MAULL, James David 67
MAULL, Martin 154
MAULL, Mary E. 67
MAURAY, Charlotte 21
MAURAY, Evereste 21,39
MAURY(see MAURAY)
MAXCEY, Ann 46,69
MAXEY, Elizabeth 46
MAXEY, Samuel T. 76
MAYER, Mrs. 63
MAYER, Rabbi 8
MAYER, Susan D. 60
MAYNARD, Dr. 41
MAYNARD, John 73
MAYS, Robert S. 148
MAZYCK, Nina 155
MEAD, James 71
MEADOWS(see also MEDERS)
MEARS, John 29
MEARS, Mary 29
MEARS, William 29
MEDERS, Sarah 67
MEEKER, Samuel 91
MEEKER, William 91
MELLAIN, Jean Baptiste Jo-
  seph Benjamin 29
MELLAIN, John Baptiste An-
  toine 29
MEMMINGER, C. G./Christopher
  Gustavus 4,15,17,46
MENDENHALL, M. T. 4
MENICKEN, Anthony 49
MERAY, Harriet 107
MERAY, John 107
MERAY, Margaret 107
MERAY, Mary 107
MERAY, William 107
MERCIER, Charles 155
MERCIER, Frederick William
  155
MERCIER, George 155
MERCIER, Josephine 155
MERCIER, Maria 29
MERCIER, Mary Ann 155
MERCIER, Samuel 46
MERKER, E. 131
MERLIN, Henry 29
MERLIN, Simon Francois 29
MERRALL, Benjamin 20
MERRATT, Ann 46
MERRATT, Catherine 46
MERRATT, George 46
MERRITT(see also MERRATT)
MERRITT, William 79
MESKER, George 89
MESKER, Samuel 90
MESSERVY, Sophia 82
MEYER, Corde 155
MEYER, Martin 155
MEYERS, Joseph 6
MICHEL, Benjamin 155
MICHEL, Edmund A. 155
MICHEL, John A. 141
MICHEL, Mary A. 12,155
MICHEL, Maximillian 155
MICHEL, Virginia 12,155
MICHELL, Eliza 82
MICHELL, Mary Ann 82

MICHELL, William 71
MIDDLETON, N. R. 4,110
MIDDLETON, Thomas 6
MIESENBERY, Susannah 67
MILES, Margaret 68
MILLAR, Ann 155
MILLAR, Louis 155
MILLARD, James H. 51
MILLER, Ann E. 140,141
MILLER, Archibald E. 8,166
MILLER, Chloe 111
MILLER, David 36
MILLER, Eliza 90
MILLER, Elizabeth 68,90
MILLER, H. 132
MILLER, Israel 79
MILLER, Jacob 46,49
MILLER, James 46
MILLER, Jessey 125
MILLER, John 29
MILLER, John Bradford 125
MILLER, John C. 80
MILLER, J. Claudius 123
MILLER, Mary 29,46,52,125
MILLER, Priscilla 125
MILLER, Sarah 40
MILLER, Sylvia 68
MILLER, Thomas 16
MILLER, Mr. 116
MILLER, Mrs. 116
MILLHOUSE, Charles 59
MILLIGAN, Alice 155
MILLIGAN, Edward 90,136
MILLIGAN, Elizabeth 29
MILLIGAN, Henry 155
MILLIGAN, Jacob 20
MILLIGAN, John 90
MILLIGAN, Joseph 18,29
MILLIGAN, Mrs. Martha 101
MILLIGAN, Mary E. 90
MILLIGAN, R. A. 155
MILLIGAN, William 29,90
MILLS, Caroline 155
MILLS, Elizabeth W. 155
MILLS, James Seabrook 155
MILLS, Mary Jane 155
MILLS, Mary Phelps 15
MILLS, Sarah Ann 156
MILLS, Rev. Thomas 69
MILLS, William 156
MILLS, Mrs. 155,156
MILNE, Andrew 114,122
MIMS, Amelia 51,61
MINER, Elizabeth 46
MINER, Henry Peregrine 46
MINNES, Calvin 45
MINOR(see also MINER)
MINOR, Elizabeth 40
MINSEY, Ann 41
MINUS, Ann 156
MINUS, Savage S. 156
MINUS, Susan 156
MIOT, Catharine 48
MIOT, Charles H. 74
MIOT, Harriet 68
MIOT, John 68
MISCALLY, Eliza 68
MISCALLY, Jane J. 117
MISCALLY, Martha 68
MISCALLY, Mary 68
MITCHELL, James 64
MITCHELL, John 5,29
MITCHELL, J. W. 92
MITCHELL, Mary 29
MITCHELL, Sarah 29
MODEREN, James 64
MOFFAT, George 97
MOFFETT, John 45
MOFFITT, David 37
MOLES, Ellen 43
MOLES, Margaret 40,47
MOLLER, A. E. 86
MONDAY(see also MUNDAY)

MONK, Rachel 34
MONTAG, Eliza 164
MONTGOMERY, James Henry 156
MOOD, John 101
MOOD, Margaret 125
MOORE, Ann 89
MOORE, Eliza 156
MOORE, George 64
MOORE, Henry H. 52
MOORE, James 108,156
MOORE, J. S. C. 122
MOORE, Malcolm 156
MOORE, Martha 19
MOORE, Philip 36
MOORE, Stephen 86
MOORE, Susannah 12,67
MOORE, Thomas 67,108
MOORER, James R. 106
MORAN(see also MORIEN)
MORAN, C. E. 156
MORAN, John 156
MORAN, Patrick 156
MORDECAI, Fanny 68
MORDECAI, Jane 68
MORECRAFT, William 16
MORGAN, Charles 30
MORGAN, J. E. 109,123
MORGAN, John Benjamin 122
MORGAN, Peter 90
MORIARTY, Jean Baptiste 29
MORIEN, Catharine 156
MORILLO, R. L. 137
MORK, James 43
MORRIS, Caroline 125
MORRIS, Dorcas 46
MORRISON, Charles 89,156
MORRISON, Henrietta Mon-
  umia 90
MORRISON, James 156
MORRISON, John 90
MORRISON, Maria 24
MORRISON, Sarah 90
MORRISON, Thomas 111
MORRISON, William 156
MORTIMER, Mrs. S. 161
MORTON, Ann 95
MORTON, Elizabeth 68
MORTON, John 68
MORTON, William 68
MOSELEY, ___ 144
MOSES, Charles B. 112
MOSES, G. B. 97
MOSES, Joseph 52
MOULTRIE, Dr. James 4
MOUSSEAU(also MARSO)
MOUSSEAU, Ann 112
MOWBRAY, Martha 40
MUCK, John Mitchell 68
MUIR, Jane 18
MUIR, Lydia 12
MUIR, William 18
MUIRHEAD, Eliza A. C. 81
MUIRHEAD, James 20
MULKAHY, James 156
MULLEN, Eliza 157
MULLEN, John 125
MULLEN, Matthew 125
MULLEN, Michael 125
MULLER, Rev. Albert A. 66
MULLER, F. M. 77
MULLINS, Eliza 157
MULLINS, Michael 157
MULRYNE, Ann Selina 12,68
MULRYNE, Jane 12,68
MULRYNE, Thomas Hill 12,68
MULVANY, J. M. 7
MUNCEY, John 48
MUNDAY, Jane 108
MUNDAY, John 108
MUNDAY, Mary 108
MUNRO, Martin E. 128
MUNROE, Martha 79
MURDEN, Eliza 71,92

MURPHY, Ann 68
MURPHY, David 100
MURPHY, Edward Hampton 90
MURPHY, Eliza 30
MURPHY, Elizabeth 13,14,58,
  68
MURPHY, Frances 122
MURPHY, Henrietta 90
MURPHY, Henry John 90
MURPHY, Isabella 90
MURPHY, John D. 68
MURPHY, Mary C. 108
MURPHY, M. 125
MURPHY, Robert Heyward 108
MURPHY, Mrs. Thomas 159
MURPHY, Thomas P. 68
MURPHY, William Henry 125
MURPHY, William Lewis 108
MURRAY, Andrew Buist 17,157
MURRAY, Ann Elizabeth 46
MURRAY, Charlotte 157
MURRAY, Elizabeth 143
MURRAY, Elizabeth Ann 157
MURRAY, Henry 125
MURRAY, James 46,157
MURRAY, Jane 64
MURRAY, John 157
MURRAY, Martha Eliza 157
MURRAY, Mary Ellen 157
MURRAY, Nancy 157
MURRAY, Robert 157
MURRAY, Sarah 157
MURRAY, Sarah S. 157
MURRAY, Susan 125
MURRAY, Terrence 157
MURRAY, William 46
MURRELL, John Robert 68
MURRELL, Mary Martha Le-
  Queux 68,69
MURRELL, Peter LeQueux 69
MURRILL, J. J. 104
MYATT, Catherine 108
MYATT, Edward 66,67,108
MYATT, Edward C. 108
MYATT, Lewis 108
MYATT, Mary Ann 108
MYERS, Charlotte Elizabeth
  157
MYERS, David 69
MYERS, Maachar 69
MYERS, Mary 157
MYLES, Jane 89

NAGEL, Elizabeth 39
NASH, William 107
NAUMAN, Catherine 29
NAUMAN, John 29
NAUMAN, Margaret 29
NEAL, John 9,14
NEAL, Rebecca 72
NEDDERMAN, Ann 29
NEDDERMAN, Maria Wilhelmina
  29
NEDDERMAN, Nancy 20
NEHLE, John 90
NEIL, Henry E. 108
NEIL, Jane 108,109
NEIL, Russell Alexander 108
NEIL, Thomas Benjamin 108
NEIL, William Boyd 109
NEILSON, Andrew 29
NEILSON, Charles 29
NEILSON, Esther 65
NELL, W. S. 86,88,95
NELLES, Philip David 109
NELSON, Eliza 109
NELSON, Eliza Ann 125
NELSON, Ellen 165
NELSON, Emily Christina 126
NELSON, George 109
NELSON, James 126
NELSON, Jane 30
NELSON, John 126

RIPLEY, Samuel 4
RIPLEY, S. P. 4
RITCHIE, Mary 31
RITFIELD, Frances 31
RITFIELD(RITIFIELD), Henry
31,38
RITFIELD, Sarah 18,19,31,48
RIVERS, David 13
RIVERS, David S. 111
RIVERS, E. F. 111
RIVERS, Eliza 13
RIVERS, Joseph 71
RIVERS, Mary G. 41
RIVERS, William 13,111
ROACH, John 128
ROACH, Maria 128
ROACH, Thomas 128
ROAN(see also RHONEY)
ROANEY(see also RHONEY)
ROBERTS, Mrs. Emily 144
ROBERTS, Francis 49
ROBERTS, James P. 125
ROBERTS, Louisa 160
ROBERTS, Mary 13
ROBERTS, Owen Philip 26
ROBERTS, Samuel Capers 160
ROBERTSON, George 22
ROBERTSON, John 1,4,48
ROBERTSON, Mary 16
ROBERTSON, Mary Ann 13
ROBERTSON, Samuel 50
ROBERTSON, Mrs. Samuel 143
ROBINSON, Ann 10
ROBINSON, James 30
ROBINSON, Martha Jane 160
ROBINSON, Stephen Clark 160
ROBINSON, T. 158
ROBINSON, Thomas 92
ROBINSON, Timothy Hampton
160
ROBINSON, William 68,77
ROBINSON, William Pinckney
160
ROGERS, Charles 68
ROGERS, Elias 111
ROGERS, John 42
ROGERS, Lewis 31
ROMA, Borriet 88
ROPER, Thomas 4,5,34
ROSANBOHN(see also ROZENBAUM)
ROSE(see also ROSS)
ROSENBOHN, Catherine 31
ROSENBOHN, John 31
ROSENBOHN, Mary 31
ROSENFELD, Jacob 105
ROSS, Ann Maria 128
ROSS, James 56
ROTHE(see also REETHY)
ROTUREAU, Peter 122
ROU, Andrew C. 72
ROU, Charles D. 72
ROU, George D. 72
ROUIER, Jean Baptiste Pierre
31
ROUIER, Marie 31
ROULAIN, A. 95
ROUSE, Christopher 110
ROUTH(see also RUTH)
ROWE, Dorothy 31
ROWE, Mary Magdalene 31
ROWE, Paul 31
ROWLY, Ann 27
ROYAS, Ann R. 57
ROYNEL, W. T. 93
ROZENBAUM, Francis 48
RUMPH, David 52
RUSSELL, John 121
RUSSELL, Maria F. 78
RUSSELL, Nathaniel 4
RUSSELL, Mrs. 5
RUTH, Ellen 160
RUTH, James 160
RUTH, John 160

RUTH, Thomas 160
RUTLAND, Joseph 128
RUTLAND, Lewis 128
RUTLAND, Mary 128
RUTLAND, William H. 128
RUTLEDGE, Andrew 31
RUTLEDGE, Rev. Edward 59
RUTLEDGE, Hugh R. 143
RUTLEDGE, John, Jr. 4
RUTLEDGE, Sarah 97
RYAN, Alice A. 160
RYAN, Ann 92
RYAN, Augustus K. 128
RYAN, Bridget 86
RYAN, Catharine Ann 110
RYAN, George K. 128
RYAN, Henry 160
RYAN, Henry J. 161
RYAN, James 160
RYAN, John 160
RYAN, Julia A. 128
RYAN, Julia K. 128
RYAN, Margaret 13,161
RYAN, Mary 118,160
RYAN, Patrick 161
RYAN, Theodore 128
RYAN, Thomas 161
RYAN, William H. Y. 161
RYBURN, Catharine 111
RYBURN, John 111
RYBURN, Mary 111
RYBURN, Peter 111
RYBURN, Matthew 111
RYBURN, William 111
RYCHBOSCH, Eliza 48
RYCHBOSCH, Francis 48
RYCHBOSCH, Joseph 48
RYCHBOSCH, Mary Ann 48

SALE, John 93
SAMS, John H. 165
SANFORD, Ann 48
SANFORD, Moses 14
SASS, Jacob 23,24,43
SAUNDERS, Roger Parker 28
SAWYER, Susannah 19
SCANLON, S. E. 140
SCHAFFER, Caroline 92
SCHAFFER, Catharine 92
SCHAFFER, Rosina 92
SCHAFFER, Sophia 92
SCHENFIELD(see also SHEN-
FIELD)
SCHENFIELD, Fredericke 72
SCHENFIELD, Mary Elizabeth
72
SCHENFIELD, William 72
SCHERER, Mary 92
SCHIERLE, John M. 61
SCHIRER, Mary 82
SCHMIDT, Andreas Maguire
161
SCHMIDT, Maria Henrietta
161
SCHMIDT, Sebastian 161
SCHOECOHLIN, Maria 92
SCHOECOHLIN, Roza 92
SCHOOLER, Thomas 48
SCHOUP(see also SMITH)
SCHULTZ, Eliza 93
SCHULTZ, Flizabeth 92
SCHULTZ, George Henry 92
SCHULTZ, Martha 93
SCOTT, Christiana 161
SCOTT, Isaac 72
SCOTT, James Stephen 128
SCOTT, Lewis 161
SCOTT, Margaret 161
SCOTT, N. C. 119,156
SCOTT, Rebecca 111,128
SCOTT, Rebecca S. 111
SCOTT, Robert 111
SCOTT, Ruth Ann 161

SCOTT, Thomas 29
SCOTT, William 31,43,61,111
SCRAM, John 111
SCURRY, John 93
SEALE, Catharine 32
SEALE, John 32
SEALE, Nancy 32
SEAMAN, Charlotte 72
SEAMAN, Sarah 72
SEBRING, C. C. 75
SEBRING, Edward 4,77
SEEBERT, Mary 41
SEELEY, William P. 105
SEIGNIOUS, Charles W. 154
SEIGNIOUS, F. P. 127
SEPECHEY, Catherine 72
SEPECHEY, Michel 72
SEPECHY, William Lewis 72
SERJEANT, Ann 13,15
SERJEANT, Mary Ann 64
SEREVEN, Amaranthia 34
SESSIONS, Ferdinand 161
SESSIONS, Julia 161
SESSIONS, Martha 161
SEWERS, Mary 46
SEWERS, Thomas 46
SEYLE, C. C. 142
SEYLE, R. E. 142
SEYMOUR, R. W. 105
SHAFER(see also SHAFFER)
SHAFFER(see also SCHAFFER)
SHAFFER, Catherine 32
SHAFFER, Charles G. 32
SHAFFER, Frederick 32
SHAFFER, Margaret 32
SHAFFER, Michael 32
SHAFTON, Catharine 48
SHANNON, Elizabeth 49,72
SHANNON, John 49,72
SHARP, James 41
SHAW, James 129,161,162
SHAW, Jane 161
SHAW, Jessie Ann 161
SHAW, Mary E. W. 161
SHAW, Melvina 161
SHAW, Susie Ann 162
SHAW, William 125
SHECUT, Francis 129
SHECUT, Mary 129
SHECUT, William 129
SHEIVENEL, Jeremiah Henry
111
SHEIVENEL, Mrs. 111
SHEKE, Eliza 81
SHEKE, Elizabeth 55
SHELBACK, Catherine 49
SHELBACK, Charles 49
SHELBACK, Eliza 49
SHELBACK, Sarah 49
SHENFIELD(also SCHENFIELD)
SHENFIELD, Fredericke 72
SHENFIELD, William 72
SHEPPERD, Ann 72
SHEPPERD, Eliza 72
SHEPPERD, Thomas 72
SHERE, Francis 93
SHERE, John 93
SHERER, John 93
SHERER, William John 93
SHERIDAN, John J. 74
SHETS, Chloe 72
SHETS, William Moultrie 72
SHEVING(see also SHWING)
SHEVLAND, Lawrence 162
SHEVLAND, Rosa 94
SHILBECK, Catharine 94
SHILLING, George 49
SHILLING, Robert 49
SHILLING, Samuel 49
SHIRER(see also SHERE/SHERER)
SHIRER, Eliza 50,64
SHIVERNALL, Almira Lucretia
Jane 111

WOOLCOCK, Elizabeth 115
WOOLCOCK, Jane 53,115
WOOLCOCK, John 53,115
WOOLCOCK, Mary Ann 115
WOOLF, Ann 35
WOOTEN(also WOOTON)
WOOTEN, Alfred 75
WOOTEN, Chloe 16,75
WOOTEN, Eliza 94
WOOTEN, Elizabeth 64
WRAGG, Mrs. Samuel 109
WRAGGE, I. H. F. 155
WRAINCH, ___ 14
WRAND(see also RAND)
WRAY, Ellen Eliza 96
WRAY, Henry 96
WRAY, James 96
WRAY, Sarah D. 96
WRIGHT, Christiana 75
WRIGHT, Daniel 75
WRIGHT, Mrs. H. 160
WRIGHT, Henry 75
WRIGHT, Hezekiah 75
WRIGHT, Littlebury John 75
WRIGHT, Margaret 53,75
WRIGHT, Norman 75
WRIGHT, Robert 9
WRIGHT, Susannah 75
WRIGHT, S. L. 75
WRIGHT, Rev. William 105
WRIGHT, W. H. 14
WRIGHT, Mrs. W. H. (see
Alice RIANS)
WYATT, Peter 5

YATES, Amelia 15,131
YATES, Eleanor 35
YATES, Elizabeth Ann 40
YATES, John 131
YATES, Joseph 57,58
YATES, Dr. Joseph 141
YATES, Samuel 37
YATES, Thomas H. 63
YATES, Rev. W. B. 146,147
YATES, William 35
YATES, William B. 137,159
YGLESIAS, Mrs. 143
YOUNG, Agnes Stewart 53
YOUNG, Andrew 45
YOUNG, Ann 47
YOUNG, James 65,165
YOUNG, Jane 50,53,165
YOUNG, William Mc. 80

ZACHARIAH, Amelia 99
ZACHMAN, Ann 53
ZACHMAN, Christina Eliza-
beth 53
ZACHMAN, Margaret 53
ZEMP, Francis 96
ZIEHEN, Lewis 75
ZOELLER, John Jacob 35
ZOELLER, Phillip 35
ZYLK, Anne 75
ZYLK, John 31,48
ZYLK, Margaret 75
ZYLK, Thomas 75

LIST OF OCCUPATIONS FOUND
IN THE TEXT:

Accountant
Apothecary
Assistant Teacher
Assistant Attorney
Baker
Bell Hanger
Blacksmith
Boatbuilder
Bookbinder
Bookseller
Brass Founder
Bricklayer/Plasterer
Broker
Butcher
Cabinetmaker
Carpenter
Chairmaker
Cigarmaker
Clerk
Coachmaker
Combmaker
Confectioner
Dentist
Doctor
Domestic
Drayman
Dryer
Enginemaker
Factor
Farmer
Gas Fitter
Gilder
Goldsmith
Gunsmith
Hatter
Inn Keeper
Jeweller
Locksmith
Lumber Merchant
Machinist
Mantuamaker
Mariner
Merchant
Metal Worker
Milliner
Millwright
Minister
Moulder
Navigator
Nurse
Organ and Pianomaker
Painter
Paperhanger
Photographer
Physician
Plumber
Porter/Gardner
Printer
Pump and Blockmaker
Purser
Railway Worker
Ropemaker
Saddler
Sailmaker
Schoolmaster
Schoolmistress
Seamstress
Sewing Mistress
Ship Chandler
Shoemaker
Slater
Spinner/Weaver
Steam Fitter
Steward
Stonecutter
Surveyor
Tanner and Currier
Tavern Keeper
Taylor(Tailor)
Teacher

Tinplate Worker
Turner
Umbrella maker
Upholsterer
Venetian Blind maker
Waggoner
Washer
Watchmaker
Wharfinger
Wheelwright

LIST OF PLACES MENTIONED IN
THE TEXT:

Abbeville County
Alabama
Albany, New York
Alsac
Americus, Georgia
Amsterdam
Anderson District
Anson County, N. C.
Argleshire, Scotland
Atkinson, Kansas
Augusta, Georgia
Bacon's Bridge, S. C.
Baden, Germany
Baltimore
Barnwell District
Beach Island, Georgia
Beaufort
Berkeley County
Black River
Boston
Bourdeaux
Bridgeport, Conn.
Buffalo, New York
California
Cannonsboro
Cape Francois
Charleston/Charleston Neck
Cheraw District
Chester District
Christ Church Parish
Claremont County
Colleton
Columbia
Connecticut
Conti
Covington, Louisiana
Cuba
Dalton, Georgia
Darlington District
Doll
Donaldsville
Dorcetshire
Dorchester
Due West
East Florida
Edgefield District
Edisto River District
England
Fairfield District
Farmville, Virginia
Florida
Four Holes
France
French Broad, N. C.
Gadsden, S. C.
Georgetown, S. C.
Georgia
Germany
Gladsden County, Florida
Goose Creek
Grahamville
Grand Riverre
Granitteville, S. C.
Green Pond
Greenville District
Gwinnet County, Georgia
Halifax
Halifax County, Virginia
Hamburg, S. C.

Hamburg, Germany
Hanover, Germany
Havanna, Cuba
Heimderdingen, Germany
Helena
Hilton Head, S. C.
Horry District
Indiana
Ireland
Jackson Creek
Jacksonborough
Jamaica
James Island, S. C.
Joppah(Copiah) County, Miss.
Kentucky
Kershaw District
Lancaster District
Laurens District
Laurenceville, Georgia
Lehe, Hanover
Lentenville, Anson Co., NC
Lexington District
Liverpool, England
Lodi
London
Louisville, Winston Co.,Miss.
Macon, Georgia
Maine
Maranjies
Marion District
Marietta, Georgia
Marlboro
Martinique
Massachusetts
Maysville
Mecklinburgh
Mexico
Mildorph, Holstein
Mineral Spring, Florida
Mississippi
Mount Pleasant
Mount Taber
Mt. Holly, New Jersey
Namby
Nassau
Netherlands
New Jersey
New Orleans
New York
Newark, New Jersey
Newberry District
Newburgh, New York
Newport, Rhode Island
Ninety-Six
Norfolk, Virginia
North Carolina
North Inlet
Norway
Nova Scotia
Orangeburgh District
Pendleton District
Pennsylvania
Philadelphia
Pocataligo
Portsmith, Virginia
Pourtsmouth
Prince Edward Co., Va.
Providence, Rhode Island
Prussia
Rantolls
Rhode Island
Richmond, Indiana
Ridgeville, S. C.
Ripley, Miss.
Roxbury, Mass.
Rutherford Co., N. C.
Sacket's Harbor, N. Y.
Salem County
Santee
Savannah
Saxe Weimar, Germany
Scotland
Selma, Alabama

Society Hill
South Carolina
Spartanburgh District
Statesboro
St. Augustine
St. Bartholomew's Parish
St. Domingo
St. George's Parish
St. James Parish
St. John's Parish
St. Luke's Parish
St. Mark's Parish
St. Matthew's Parish
St. Paul's Parish
St. Philip's Parish
St. Stephen's Parish
St. Thomas's Parish
Strasbourg
Sullivan's Island
Sumpter(Sumter) District
Surrey, England
Switzerland
Tennessee
Union District
Utica, New York
Virginia
Waccamaw
Walterborough District
Washington
Wassamasaw
Waynesborough, Georgia
West Indies
Whitfield County, Georgia
Williamsburg District
Willtown
Wilmington, N. C.
Winnsborough District
Winston County, Miss.
York District